The Commentarial Impulse

THE COMMENTARIAL IMPULSE

*Interpretation and Actualization
in the Pauline Tradition*

David Lincicum

WILLIAM B. EERDMANS PUBLISHING COMPANY
GRAND RAPIDS, MICHIGAN

Wm. B. Eerdmans Publishing Co.
2006 44th Street SE, Grand Rapids, MI 49508
www.eerdmans.com

© 2025 David Lincicum
All rights reserved
Published 2025
Printed in the United States of America

31 30 29 28 27 26 25   1 2 3 4 5 6 7

ISBN 978-0-8028-8420-6

Library of Congress Cataloging-in-Publication Data

A catalog record for this book is available from the Library of Congress.

For Beth and Leon Smart

CONTENTS

	Preface	ix
	List of Abbreviations	xi
	Introduction: The Commentarial Impulse	1
1.	How Did Paul Read Scripture?	10
2.	Paul and the *Testimonia*	23
3.	Intertextuality, Effective History, and Memory	38
4.	Genesis in Paul	52
5.	Paul's Engagement with Deuteronomy	71
6.	Transforming Stories and Permeable Selves	99
7.	Presentifying the Past	116
8.	Mirror-Reading a Pseudepigraphal Letter	130
9.	Elijah in Romans 11 and Justin's *Dialogue with Trypho*	157
10.	Learning Scripture in the School of Paul	169
	Afterword: Reading Scripture in the Messianic Community	189
	Acknowledgments	197
	Bibliography	199
	Index of Modern Authors	233
	Index of Subjects	240
	Index of Ancient Sources	243

PREFACE

The essays in this volume were written over the better part of two decades, and in that time I have incurred numerous debts, which are a humbling pleasure to recall and acknowledge here. To do so is a good reminder that any flourishing I've experienced in the strange calling that is the academic life has been due to the generosity, friendship, and hospitable critique of others. I have been fortunate to serve in two excellent departments of theology and religious studies, in Oxford and Notre Dame, and am grateful to my colleagues in New Testament (Oxford) and Christianity & Judaism in Antiquity (Notre Dame) for their kindness and collegiality. Several of these essays, in whole or in part, were presented to audiences whose feedback has spared the reader some of my worst mistakes. Part of the introduction was presented at the Notre Dame–Tel Aviv Collaborative Workshop on Interpretative Cultures in Late Antiquity. Chapter 3 was kindly presented in my absence by Ross Wagner at the International Society of Biblical Literature meeting in Vienna. Chapter 6 was discussed in the generous interdisciplinary meeting of the Center for the Philosophy of Religion at Notre Dame (my renewed thanks to Mike Rea and Laura Callahan). Chapters 7 and 9 were presented at different iterations of the Oxford-Leiden-Bonn colloquium. Audiences in St Andrews, Sheffield, Edinburgh, Windsor, and Notre Dame heard chapter 8 presented. Chapter 10 was presented in Oxford, and the afterword was delivered as the Macbride Sermon on messianic prophecy at Hertford College, Oxford. To all my hosts and audiences, I offer my sincere thanks. I also express my gratitude to the editors and publishers who gave permission for those previously published essays to be reprinted here. I have not attempted to systematically update the bibliography of these essays, though I have sometimes altered them where I now judge myself to have been mistaken, and I have occasionally added newer literature where it struck me as especially important.

I'm deeply grateful to the excellent Gabriel Parlin for his editorial help in gathering these untidy essays into coherence, and to the funds that made

Preface

his work possible by support from the Institute for Scholarship in the Liberal Arts, College of Arts and Letters, University of Notre Dame. Lilly Davis cheerfully undertook the work of producing the indexes with her customary attentiveness and care. At Eerdmans, Trevor Thompson has been a generous and incisive scholar-editor, and I am grateful to him and to James Ernest for taking this project on. Jenny Hoffman, Laurel Draper, and the rest of the team at Eerdmans added real value to this book through their editorial labors.

As ever, my deepest debts are to my family. Julia, Naomi, Edie, Margaret, and Theo: you have enriched me immeasurably, and offered me suitable distraction from the unwelcome task of revisiting my own writing. It is a pleasure to dedicate this volume, such as it is, to two of the most generous and supportive people I have ever known, my parents, Beth and Leon Smart.

Notre Dame, IN
Lent, 2024

Abbreviations

AB	Anchor Bible
AGJU	Arbeiten zur Geschichte des antiken Judentums und des Urchristentums
ANRW	*Aufstieg und Niedergang der römischen Welt: Geschichte und Kultur Roms im Spiegel der neueren Forschung*
BBR	*Bulletin of Biblical Research*
BETL	Bibliotheca Ephemeridum Theologicarum Lovaniensium
BHT	Beiträge zur historischen Theologie
Bib	*Biblica*
BibInt	*Biblical Interpretation*
BNP	*Brill's New Pauly: Encyclopaedia of the Ancient World*
BNTC	Black's New Testament Commentaries
BTB	*Biblical Theology Bulletin*
BTZ	*Berliner Theologische Zeitschrift*
BZ	*Biblische Zeitschrift*
BZNW	Beihefte zur Zeitschrift für die neutestamentliche Wissenschaft
CahRB	Cahiers de la Revue biblique
CBET	Contributions to Biblical Exegesis and Theology
CP	*Classical Philology*
CRINT	Compendia Rerum Iudaicarum ad Novum Testamentum
CurBR	*Currents in Biblical Research*
CurBS	*Currents in Research: Biblical Studies*
DBSup	*Dictionnaire de la Bible: Supplément*
DJD	Discoveries in the Judean Desert
EBib	Etudes bibliques
EDSS	*Encyclopedia of the Dead Sea Scrolls*
EvT	*Evangelische Theologie*
FAT	Forschungen zum Alten Testament
ForFasc	*Forum Fascicles*

Abbreviations

FRLANT	Forschungen zur Religion und Literatur des Alten und Neuen Testaments
HBS	History of Biblical Studies
HeyJ	*Heythrop Journal*
HTR	*Harvard Theological Review*
HUCA	*Hebrew Union College Annual*
HUT	Hermeneutische Untersuchungen zur Theologie
HvTSt	*Hervormde teologiese studies*
Int	*Interpretation*
JBL	*Journal of Biblical Literature*
JQR	*Jewish Quarterly Review*
JR	*Journal of Religion*
JRA	*Journal of Roman Archaeology*
JRH	*Journal of Religious History*
JSJ	*Journal for the Study of Judaism in the Persian, Hellenistic, and Roman Periods*
JSJSup	Journal for the Study of Judaism in the Persian, Hellenistic, and Roman Periods Supplement Series
JSNT	*Journal for the Study of the New Testament*
JSNTSup	Journal for the Study of the New Testament Supplement Series
JSOTSup	Journal for the Study of the Old Testament Supplement Series
JSP	*Journal for the Study of the Pseudepigrapha*
JSPSup	Journal for the Study of the Pseudepigrapha Supplement Series
JSS	*Journal of Semitic Studies*
JTS	*Journal of Theological Studies*
JTSA	*Journal of Theology for Southern Africa*
KD	*Kerygma und Dogma*
LCL	Loeb Classical Library
LEC	Library of Early Christianity
LHBOTS	The Library of Hebrew Bible/Old Testament Studies
LNTS	The Library of New Testament Studies
MTSR	*Method and Theory in the Study of Religion*
NA^{27}	*Novum Testamentum Graece,* Nestle-Aland, 27th ed.
NA^{28}	*Novum Testamentum Graece,* Nestle-Aland, 28th ed.
NIGTC	New International Greek Testament Commentary
NovT	*Novum Testamentum*
NovTSup	Supplements to Novum Testamentum
NTAbh	Neutestamentliche Abhandlungen
NTOA	Novum Testamentum et Orbis Antiquus

Abbreviations

NTS	*New Testament Studies*
NTSI	New Testament and the Scriptures of Israel
OECS	Oxford Early Christian Studies
OED	Oxford English Dictionary
PTMS	Pittsburgh Theological Monograph Series
PTS	Patristische Texte und Studien
ProEccl	*Pro Ecclesia*
RAC	*Reallexikon für Antike und Christentum*
RevQ	*Revue de Qumran*
RB	*Revue biblique*
RHR	*Revue de l'histoire des religions*
RTP	*Revue de théologie et de philosophie*
SBLDS	Society of Biblical Literature Dissertation Series
SBLSymS	Society of Biblical Literature Symposium Series
SCS	Septuagint and Cognate Studies
SC	Sources chrétiennes
Sem	*Semitica*
SFSHJ	South Florida Studies in the History of Judaism
SIJD	Schriften des Institutum Judaicum Delitzschianum
SJT	*Scottish Journal of Theology*
SNTSMS	Society for New Testament Studies Monograph Series
SSEJC	Studies in Scripture in Early Judaism and Christianity
STDJ	Studies on the Texts of the Desert of Judah
STRT	Studia Theologica Rheno-Traiectina
SUNT	Studien zur Umwelt des Neuen Testaments
TA	Theologische Arbeiten
TANZ	Texte und Arbeiten zum neutestamentlichen Zeitalter
ThH	Théologie historique
THKNT	Theologischer Handkommentar zum Neuen Testament
ThTo	*Theology Today*
TLZ	*Theologische Literaturzeitung*
TNTC	Tyndale New Testament Commentaries
TRu	*Theologische Rundschau*
TS	*Theological Studies*
TSAJ	Texte und Studien zum antiken Judentum
TU	Texte und Untersuchungen
VC	*Vigiliae Christianae*
VCSup	Supplements to Vigiliae Christianae
VTSup	Supplements to Vetus Testamentum

xiii

Abbreviations

WBC	Word Biblical Commentary
WMANT	Wissenschaftliche Monographien zum Alten und Neuen Testament
WUNT	Wissenschaftliche Untersuchungen zum Neuen Testament
ZNW	*Zeitschrift für die neutestamentliche Wissenschaft und die Kunde der älteren Kirch*

Introduction

The Commentarial Impulse

Commentary is born in difference: the difference between the lexical, historical, aesthetic, and intellectual assumptions of a culturally authoritative predecessor text, on the one hand, and those of a subsequent, posterior reading public on the other. To explain those points of difference is an attempt to bridge the gap, and so in some sense to actualize the past text from the perspective of the reader's present. But it is to do so with respect to the predecessor text as a significant original, a fixture whose alterity should be preserved. The original cannot simply be dissolved and washed diffusely into the present, or the spell of its authority will be broken. There is something in the form of the original that must be guarded, even as the attempt is made to understand it. How, then, should one mediate between an authoritative original, with all its concern for matters that do not pertain to the reader's present, and a reader or community that wishes to understand and so to draw on that authority? Commentary comes to mediate between the past text, in the face of the absence of the past that gave it sense, and the reader's present.[1]

In this introduction to a collection of essays on Pauline interpretation, I would like to think about the birth of the Christian commentary. To do so, I begin in a place that some of my colleagues might deem less than promising: the New Testament. Nothing is more obvious than the fact that the New Testament is not and does not contain a commentary. There is no book of the New Testament that refers to itself as an "exposition of the Law of Moses" or styles its approach as "Questions and Answers on Leviticus." Nevertheless, I suggest that it is in the New Testament, and in Paul in particular, that we find the first

---

1. Cf. Aaron Hughes, "Presenting the Past: The Genre of Commentary in Theoretical Perspective," *MTSR* 15, no. 2 (2003): 148–68. So also L. Fladerer and D. Börner-Klein "Kommentar," *RAC* 21:275: "Voraussetzung von K.[ommentar] ist die Existenz kanonischer oder klassischer Texte, die als abgeschlossene Grundtexte einer Religion, Philosophie oder Wissenschaft verbindlich die Identität einer Gruppe bestimmen (formative Funktion) sowie ihr Handeln u.[nd] Denken determinieren (normative Funktion)."

Introduction

stirrings of an early Jewish commentarial impulse that will come to fruition in the second and third centuries with the birth of the first proper Christian commentarial literature. This book is entitled *The Commentarial Impulse* as a way of signaling that we find in the New Testament the seed of a hermeneutical stance that will come to full fruition only in subsequent centuries, a fruition that is not inevitable and that might not have occurred without the grounding that the New Testament authors in general, and Paul in particular, provide.

COMMENTARY IN ANTIQUITY

But why do I imagine my colleagues will think the New Testament is an un-promising place to look for commentarial material? This suspicion stems largely from the ways in which we tend to think about the nature of commentary in antiquity. The grammatical or philological commentaries we associate with the Alexandrian Mouseion take as one of their primary aims the edition (ἔκδοσις) and elucidation of the Homeric epics and other "classics." Scholars like Aristonicus, Didymus, and especially Aristarchus developed a system of textual annotations to mark suspected interpolations, proposed emendations, and variant readings in Homer.[2] Some modern scholars, looking for genealogical pedigree in antiquity to their own critical labors in the present, have been only too happy to see their philological efforts standing in the tradition of the Alexandrian grammarians, and so to identify the sort of commentaries produced by the Mouseion as indicative of the genre as a whole. Arguably the types of concerns that animate this stream of the commentary tradition do not substantially affect the emerging Christian tradition before the late second century.

But of course the Alexandrian philological tradition had no monopoly on commentary. In the Hellenistic and early Roman periods onward, we see a turn toward the elucidation, actualization, and contestation of authoritative texts in a variety of textual communities around the Mediterranean. One might consider the Derveni papyrus and its allegoresis of the Orphic myths,[3] or the emerging tradition of philosophical commentary. Importantly, in these works

---

2. Francesca Schironi, *The Best of the Grammarians: Aristarchus of Samothrace on the Iliad* (Ann Arbor: University of Michigan Press, 2018).

3. Richard Janko, "The Derveni Papyrus ('Diagoras of Melos, Apopyrgizontes Logoi?'): A New Translation," *CP* 96.1 (2001): 1–32; Theokritos Kouremenos, George M. Parássoglou, and Kyriakos Tsantsanoglou, *The Derveni Papyrus*, Studi e testi per il Corpus dei Papiri Filosofici Greci e Latini 13 (Firenze: Leo S. Olschki, 2006); and André Laks and Glenn W. Most, *Early Greek Philosophy: Later Ionian and Athenian Thinkers, Part 1*, LCL 529 (Cambridge, MA: Harvard University Press, 2016), 373–435.

The Commentarial Impulse

we find a sort of substantive engagement with the original that does not lead to a slavish repetition of the former, but rather produces new knowledge. As Han Baltussen suggests,

> Whereas in most cases a modern commentary tends to be an end in itself, producing a set of disparate notes to a text and lacking a unifying principle of its own (a "plot"), the ancient philosophical commentaries emerging after the first century BCE tend to serve a higher purpose (philosophical understanding and truth) by way of interpreting the thoughts of a scholar.[4]

To take one particular form as an example, consider the tradition of philosophical and literary commentary that uses the question-and-answer or problem-and-solution format.[5] We already see this format adopted among the fragmentary Jewish Hellenistic authors. For example, Demetrius, in his exposition of the Joseph story, notes, "A crucial question arises as to why Joseph gave Benjamin a five-fold portion at the meal even though he would not be able to consume so much meat" (frag. 2; trans. Holladay), before going on to offer a solution based on the number of sons of Leah.[6] Or Aristobulus (frag. 2) takes up the conceit of a dialogue, and says,

> However, after we had said enough in reply to the questions set before us, you also called out, Your Majesty, (asking) why throughout our Law hands, arm, visage, feet, and ability to walk are used as signifiers for the divine power.[7]

He then goes on to offer a sustained exegetical (which is to say, an allegorical) explanation for the depictions of God's hands, arms, and so forth. The extent

---

4. Han Baltussen, "From Polemic to Exegesis: The Ancient Philosophical Commentary," *Poetics Today* 28.2 (2007): 247–81, here 249.

5. Cf. Hans Armin Gärtner, "Zetema," BNP Online, https://doi-org.proxy.library.nd.edu /10.1163/1574-9347_bnp_e12216680: "In general, however, the goal designated in the case of *aporía* and *próblēma* is called λύσις (*lýsis*, 'solution') (Aristot. An. 422b 28; Pol. 30,19,5), while 'finding' (εὕρεσις/*heúresis*) is first attributed to the more general *zēteîn* and its derivatives (cf. Pl. Tht. 202d; Pl. Ap. 24b.; this is still the case in Clem. Al. Strom. 6,14, p. 801: 'finding/ *heúresis* is the end and cessation of the search/*zétēsis*)'. Aristot. Eth. Nic. 1146b 7f. offers a combination of goals: 'for the solution (*lýsis*) of an *aporia* is finding (*heúresis*)' (cf. Aristot. Top. 163b 1)." See also Francesca Schironi, "Greek Commentaries," *Dead Sea Discoveries* 19 (2012): 399–441; and Maren R. Niehoff, *Jewish Exegesis and Homeric Scholarship in Alexandria* (Cambridge: Cambridge University Press, 2011).

6. Translation from Carl R. Holladay, *Fragments from Hellenistic Jewish Authors*, 4 vols. (Chico, CA: Scholars Press, 1983), 1:71.

7. Holladay, 3:135.

Introduction

to which the problem-and-solution genre permeated the Alexandrian Jewish tradition might be seen in the Letter of Aristeas (187–194), which employs the symposium as a setting for a long discourse in question-and-answer format in which the seventy-two translators of the Septuagint take turns answering the king's questions about ideal kingship. But it is especially in the *Questions and Answers on Genesis* and *Questions and Answers on Exodus* of Philo of Alexandria that we find the fullest record of this form of commentarial endeavor. Philo's other commentarial projects remind us of the variety of forms a commentarial treatment can take.

Outside of Alexandria, we can call to mind the pesharim from Qumran, which Markus Bockmuehl, followed by Reinhard Kratz and Pieter B. Hartog, among others, has argued participates in the broader Hellenistic turn toward commentary by preserving the lemmata of the biblical text in the initial quotation, followed by the contemporizing interpretation as a subsequent move.[8] This distinction between text and commentary is more important for conceptualizing the nature of the commentarial impulse, in my view, than is a requirement that the treatment be running or sustained or seriatim, which is a sustained repetition of the lemmatized action and so differs in intensity but not in kind from the basic commentarial impulse.

Finally, if we look ahead to the second and early third century CE to consider those texts that are usually heralded as the first Christian commentaries, we do not find there the sort of noncommittal philological commentarial work we associate with the level-headed modern commentary. Rather, we find rhetorically engaged, even agonistic treatments of scriptural texts. Heracleon's commentary on the Gospel of John is probably the first self-consciously Christian commentary of which we are aware, though it only survives fragmentarily in (mostly) Origen's refutation of it, and it might be described as an actualizing philosophical interpretation of the gospel that seeks to harmonize the lemmata with a mythic superstructure derived from elsewhere.[9] Something sim-

---

8. Markus Bockmuehl, "The Dead Sea Scrolls and the Origins of Biblical Commentary," in *Text, Thought, and Practice in Qumran and Early Christianity*, ed. Ruth Clements and Daniel R. Schwartz, STDJ 84 (Leiden: Brill, 2009), 3–29; Reinhard G. Kratz, "Text and Commentary: The Pesharim of Qumran in the Context of Hellenistic Scholarship," in *The Bible and Hellenism: Greek Influence on Jewish and Early Christian Literature*, ed. T. L. Thompson and P. Wajdenbaum (Durham: Acumen, 2014), 212–29; and Pieter B. Hartog, *Pesher and Hypomnema: A Comparison of Two Commentary Traditions from the Hellenistic-Roman Period*, STDJ 121 (Leiden: Brill, 2017).

9. See A. E. Brooke, *The Fragments of Heracleon* (Cambridge: Cambridge University Press, 1891); W. Foerster, *Gnosis: A Selection of Gnostic Texts*, trans. R. McL. Wilson, 2 vols.

4

The Commentarial Impulse

ilar could probably be said of Basilides's *Exegetica*, insofar as we can achieve a sense of what that work undertook.[10] The commentaries on Daniel and on the Song of Songs ascribed to Hippolytus are homiletical in nature, as are many of the early Christian texts that are designated by the term "commentary." It is not really until we reach, for example, Origen and Jerome that we can begin to find exceptions and a more self-consciously philological, seriatim treatment of the commented text, but even here the work is far from dispassionate.[11] All this is to make the point that there is a sort of graduated continuum of approaches to scriptural interpretation from the New Testament to Origen's great works in the third century and that, therefore, we may well be justified in questioning any attempt to seal off the New Testament from the broader commentarial turn in the surrounding Mediterranean world.

COMMENTARIAL STIRRINGS IN THE PAULINE TRADITION

If we disabuse ourselves of the assumption that commentary must be a sustained, sequential lemmatized treatment in a disinterested, objective, or historicist vein, then we can discover a commentarial impulse in the Pauline tradition. In this context, I do no more than mention two examples. First, we could point to the lemmatized quotation at Rom 10:5-9:

⁵Μωϋσῆς γὰρ γράφει τὴν δικαιοσύνην τὴν ἐκ τοῦ νόμου ὅτι ὁ ποιήσας αὐτὰ ἄνθρωπος ζήσεται ἐν αὐτοῖς. ⁶ἡ δὲ ἐκ πίστεως δικαιοσύνη οὕτως λέγει· μὴ

(Oxford: Clarendon, 1972–1974), 1:162–83; Harold W. Attridge, "Heracleon and John: Reassessment of an Early Christian Hermeneutical Debate," in *Essays on John and Hebrews*, WUNT 264 (Tübingen: Mohr Siebeck, 2010), 193–207; and Ansgar Wucherpfennig, *Heracleon Philologus: Gnostische Johannesexegese im zweiten Jahrhundert*, WUNT 142 (Tübingen: Mohr Siebeck, 2002). For Origen's commentary, see C. Blanc, *Origène: Commentaire sur Saint Jean*, 5 vols., SC 120, 157, 222, 290, 385 (Paris: Cerf, 1966–1992); and Ronald Heine, *Origen: Commentary on the Gospel according to John*, 2 vols. (Washington, DC: Catholic University of America Press, 1989–1993).

10. For Basilides and the difficulties of reconstructing his thought, see Birger A. Pearson, "Basilides the Gnostic," in *A Companion to Second-Century Christian 'Heretics'*, ed. Antti Marjanen and Petri Luomanen (Leiden: Brill, 2008), 1–31.

11. Bernhard Neuschäfer, *Origenes als Philologe*, Schweizerische Beiträge zur Altertumswissenschaft 18/1–18/2 (Basel: Friedrich Reinhardt, 1987); Peter W. Martens, *Origen and Scripture: The Contours of the Exegetical Life*, OECS (Oxford: Oxford University Press, 2012); and Adam Kamesar, *Jerome, Greek Scholarship, and the Hebrew Bible: A Study of the Quaestiones Hebraicae in Genesim* (Oxford: Clarendon, 1993).

Introduction

εἴπῃς ἐν τῇ καρδίᾳ σου· τίς ἀναβήσεται εἰς τὸν οὐρανόν; τοῦτ᾽ ἔστιν Χριστὸν καταγαγεῖν· [7]ἤ· τίς καταβήσεται εἰς τὴν ἄβυσσον; τοῦτ᾽ ἔστιν Χριστὸν ἐκ νεκρῶν ἀναγαγεῖν. [8]ἀλλὰ τί λέγει;
ἐγγύς σου τὸ ῥῆμά ἐστιν
ἐν τῷ στόματί σου καὶ ἐν τῇ καρδίᾳ σου,
τοῦτ᾽ ἔστιν τὸ ῥῆμα τῆς πίστεως ὅ κηρύσσομεν. [9]ὅτι ἐὰν ὁμολογήσῃς ἐν τῷ στόματί σου κύριον Ἰησοῦν καὶ πιστεύσῃς ἐν τῇ καρδίᾳ σου ὅτι ὁ θεὸς αὐτὸν ἤγειρεν ἐκ νεκρῶν, σωθήσῃ·

[5]Moses writes concerning the righteousness that comes from the law, that "the person who does these things will live by them." [6]But the righteousness that comes from faith says, "Do not say in your heart, 'Who will ascend into heaven?'" (that is, to bring Christ down) [7]or 'Who will descend into the abyss?'" (that is, to bring Christ up from the dead). [8]But what does it say?
"The word is near you,
on your lips and in your heart"
(that is, the word of faith that we proclaim); [9]because if you confess with your lips that Jesus is Lord and believe in your heart that God raised him from the dead, you will be saved. (NRSVUE)

The surprising content of Paul's interpretation apart—discussed at other points in this book—the form is precisely the citation of a lemma followed by interpretative comment. We could marshal further examples from elsewhere in Paul (e.g., Gal 3:16 or 4:21–31; cf. Heb 3:7–4:11). We also find, second, that Paul's diatribal style approximates the question-and-answer or problem-and-solution style of ancient commentaries as well. For example, at Rom 4:1, Paul asks:

Τί οὖν ἐροῦμεν εὑρηκέναι Ἀβραὰμ τὸν προπάτορα ἡμῶν κατὰ σάρκα;

What then are we to say was gained by Abraham, our ancestor according to the flesh?

Arguably we find in such examples, which could be multiplied, a basic hermeneutical stance that is largely shared across many New Testament authors and corpora: the Scriptures of Israel are the great authoritative original whose interpretation must authorize and attend the Christian message, the touchstone by which the novelty of recent events must be understood, and the collection of texts whose semantic world will enliven and give sense to the grasping for adequate language to describe God's action in the world. In other words, the

The Commentarial Impulse

way the New Testament authors relate to the Scriptures meets the basic condition for the production of commentary literature. In fact, if we trace out the impact of the New Testament's stance toward Scripture into the second and third century, we find that the New Testament sets the interpretative agenda for what comes next.

C. H. Dodd, in his famous little book, *According to the Scriptures*, argued that we find evidence of sustained textual work devoted to what he called "text plots." In Dodd's words,

> these sections were understood as *wholes*, and particular verses or sentences were quoted from them rather as pointers to the whole context than as constituting testimonies in and for themselves. At the same time, detached sentences from other parts of the Old Testament could be adduced to illustrate or elucidate the meaning of the main section under consideration. But in the fundamental passages it is the *total context* that is in view, and is the basis of the argument.[12]

For Dodd, these plots included especially the following:[13]

Joel 2–3; Zech. 9–14
Hosea; Isa. 6:1–9:7, 11:1–10, 28:16, 40:1–11; Jer. 31:10–34
Isa. 42:1–44:5, 49:1–13, 50:4–11, 52:13–53:12, 61
Ps. 69, 22, 31, 38, 78, 34, 118, 41, 42–43, 130
Ps. 2, 7, 110, Gen. 12:3, 22:18; Deut. 18:15, 19

One might—I would say, should—quibble with Dodd's concrete list (it is, for instance, striking that Deut 32 is missing), but the general suggestion that early Christian interpretation first centered its energies in discrete plots of Scripture seems cogent. As the New Testament authors expanded this functional canon by means of their citational work, the texts they produced set an interpretative agenda for second-century authors. In my essay "Learning Scripture in the School of Paul," included in this volume, I suggest that Paul's letters form a roadmap to the Scriptures of Israel that we can find being navigated in those who came after the apostle and wrote under inspiration from him. The same case could be made above all for the Gospel of Matthew, whose taking up and

12. C. H. Dodd, *According to the Scriptures: The Sub-Structure of New Testament Theology* (London: Nisbet, 1952), 126.

13. This is Dodd's thematic arrangement in *According to the Scriptures*, 107–8.

7

Introduction

intensifying of Mark's scriptural citations lent a rich field of interpretative inquiry to the developing Christian tradition.

So, when all is said and done, it is certainly true that the New Testament does not contain a commentary per se, but what it does contain is arguably the decisive commentarial impulse that came to such a rich fruition in the succeeding centuries. By binding self-consciously their message to the authoritative fixture of the scriptural tradition, the New Testament itself announced an unfinished task.

The Plan of This Book

This book represents my own attempt to grapple with the commentarial impulse in Paul's writings. In chapter 1, I offer a broad-strokes characterization of Paul as a *reader* of Scripture. The following two chapters take up the interrelated questions of how Paul accessed and thought with Scripture, one focusing on the material conditions of his access to Scripture, the other on the way in which modern scholars have conceptualized his intellectual work with sources. In both essays I attempt to avoid some of the potentially anachronistic assumptions that creep into the contemporary interpreter's mind unaware, and to think about how we might best approach the apostle's thought in his own time and embodied place. The next two essays take up Paul's engagement with discrete books of Scripture. A study of Paul's citations of and allusions to Genesis discloses that the book supplies Paul with a set of basic orientating narratives that structure and make sense of the world. Chapter 5, initially conceived as preparatory to my first monograph, *Paul and the Early Jewish Encounter with Deuteronomy*, charts the history of the investigation of Scripture's reception in the New Testament, and homes in on how Paul reads Deuteronomy in particular.

In chapter 6, "Transforming Stories and Permeable Selves: Conferring Identity in Romans 6," I argue that Paul is not only an interpreter of Scripture, but also an interpreter of the gentile past of his gentile audience. Borrowing from recent analytic philosophy on narrative selfhood, I argue that the apostle confers an identity on his gentile audience, an identity mediated to them by the technology of reading/hearing. Chapter 7 takes up the way that Paul treats the past as plastic, actualizing or "presentifying" it for the sake of his present concerns. We see this dynamic in his interpretation of Scripture, in his recollection of Jesus tradition, and in the early post-Pauline tradition that updates the apostle to deal with a new situation. Chapter 8 focuses on that

8

The Commentarial Impulse

pseudepigraphal practice more directly, and asks whether interpreters can apply their standard methods of "mirror-reading" an ancient text, even with all the cautions normally urged in orthonymous cases, to a letter deemed to be pseudepigraphal. I argue that the pseudepigraphal situation so troubles the author-recipient-situation triad that the attempt to mirror-read is highly problematized.

Chapters 9 and 10 attempt to demonstrate the early influence of Paul's selection and interpretation of Scripture. Chapter 9 offers a narrow study of a particular instance, Elijah in Rom 11 and Justin Martyr's reuse of Paul's exegesis, although silent about Paul himself, in the *Dialogue with Trypho*. Chapter 10 zooms out and argues that if we examine early texts where we already suspect literary dependence on Paul, we find there an overlap in the selection of scriptural passages that indicates Paul's letters have functioned as a sort of school for learning how to read the Jewish Scriptures and left traces of that education in subsequent writers. A brief afterword, originally delivered as the Macbride Sermon on the subject of messianic prophecy at Hertford College, Oxford, offers final reflections.

Together, these essays comprise an attempt to say something about Paul and the Pauline tradition's negotiation of an authoritative past and a demanding present. The pressures of correlation between the two, and the attempt to preserve the power of that past, whether in scriptural precedent or apostolic memory, while funding a contemporary vision inflected by an eschatological urgency, led to a profound and creative process of appropriation whose effects are still felt today.

1

How Did Paul Read Scripture?

Approaching Paul's letters for the first time, one might naturally be concerned with coming to grips with Paul as an author, a writer of pastoral and theological missives. But close attention to his activity as a writer inevitably leads to a distinct but related observation: that Paul is not simply an author creatively pulling his ideas out of thin air, or even from oral tradition, but rather that his letters give profound evidence of his activity as a *reader*. He constantly points back to predecessor texts, appealing to their authority to ground or illustrate his claims. And those texts are not drawn willy-nilly from a wide selection of ancient literature, from, say, Homer to Cicero, but rather come overwhelmingly, with only minor exceptions, from the ancient library of Jewish Scriptures.[1]

Why does the self-described apostle to the gentiles (Rom 11:13) make constant recourse to the sacred texts of Israel? If Paul is fairly described as a reader of Scripture, what kind of reader might he be? And why does he refrain from explicitly citing Scripture in some of his letters altogether? To answer those questions fully one would need to offer an account of virtually the entirety of Pauline thought. This essay does not attempt that grand synthesis, but rather offers an introductory account of Paul's reading of Scripture and of some of the questions his reading poses for our attempts to understand the apostle's corpus today.

Scriptural Sources and Citation Technique

By Paul's own testimony, he was "a Hebrew born of Hebrews" (Phil 3:5) who was "zealous for the traditions of [his] ancestors" (Gal 1:14). This zeal certainly contributed to his deep knowledge of the scriptural traditions of Israel. The precise

---

1. Exception: 1 Cor 15:33 (Menander, or possibly Euripides or a common maxim; cf. John Granger Cook, "1 Cor 15:33: The *Status Quaestionis*," *NovT* 62 [2020]: 375–91); cf. also Tit 1:12 (Epimenides) and the citation of Aratus in Paul's Areopagus speech in Acts 17:28.

How Did Paul Read Scripture?

contours of Paul's own education remain hazy at important points, but whether he undertook his primary education in Tarsus or in Jerusalem, he clearly developed an intimate acquaintance with Israel's Scriptures in their Greek form, habituated no doubt through long years of liturgical exposure and study.

It is important to guard against anachronism at this point. While scholars sometimes imprecisely speak of Paul's "Bible,"[2] there was no single book that contained all the authoritative scriptural traditions of Israel in Paul's day. Not only was such a feat technologically impossible before the invention and diffusion of the codex,[3] but it might also require a universal, or at least widespread, agreement as to which books counted as Scripture—that is, agreement regarding a closed canon. Such a fixed canon does not seem to have predominated in Paul's day (as the evidence of the Dead Sea Scrolls from Qumran suggests), even if there was broad agreement about the scriptural status of many texts. Rather than thinking of a closely bounded Bible or its virtual equivalent, it does better justice to the historical evidence to imagine Paul (like other Jews of his day) accessing a collection of scrolls containing authoritative scriptural texts. There was widespread agreement among Jews about the status and importance of the Pentateuch (Genesis through Deuteronomy), and only slightly less agreement about the prophets and some of the writings (in particular, the Psalms). We can detect no anxiety in Paul's letters about the extent of the canon, but the distributions and frequency of his citations of texts are fairly standard for Jewish practices of his day. Although the numbers vary slightly depending on the criteria by which one distinguishes a citation, Paul (like some of his Jewish contemporaries) seems to have favored Isaiah, Psalms, Genesis, and Deuteronomy.[4]

Close comparison of Paul's quotations with modern editions of the Hebrew Bible and the Septuagint (LXX, the Hebrew Bible in Greek translation) indicates that, on the whole, Paul draws his citations from Septuagintal texts

---

2. Note the classic study by Otto Michel, *Paulus und seine Bibel* (Darmstadt: Wissenschaftliche Buchgesellschaft, 1972 [1929]).

3. See, among others, Larry Hurtado and Chris Keith, "Writing and Book Production in the Hellenistic and Roman Periods," in *The New Cambridge History of the Bible, Volume 1: From the Beginnings to 600*, ed. James Carleton Paget and Joachim Schaper (Cambridge: Cambridge University Press, 2013), 63–80; and Harry Y. Gamble, *Books and Readers in the Early Church: A History of Early Christian Texts* (New Haven: Yale University Press, 1995), 42–81, 264–79.

4. George J. Brooke, "'The Canon within the Canon' at Qumran and in the New Testament," in *The Scrolls and the Scriptures: Qumran Fifty Years After*, ed. Stanley E. Porter and Craig A. Evans, JSPSup 26 (Sheffield: Sheffield Academic, 1997), 242–66.

Chapter 1

(though even those texts are often not identical to the initial text of the Old Greek as modern critical editions reconstruct it). What explains this variation? An answer to this puzzle must be sought in two places: first, in the state of the LXX's text in Paul's day, and second, in Paul's own citation technique.

We can deduce (from the apologetic Letter of Aristeas and other evidence) that after the Pentateuch was initially translated into Greek, certain detractors immediately began to criticize the translation and improve upon it. These alterations would eventually culminate in the three revisions to the LXX—posterity knows these as the work of Aquila, Symmachus, and Theodotion. The discoveries in the Judean Desert proved decisively that this process of revision was well under way by the first century BCE.[5] These revisions often involved "hebraizing" the translation—that is, attempting to ensure the Greek text adheres more closely to the Hebrew original.[6]

If we carefully analyze the textual form of Paul's quotations, we see that on the whole his citations are drawn from texts that are distinctively Septuagintal in nature. Several of Paul's citations seem to come from Septuagintal texts that show some degree of revision. For example, in 1 Cor 15:54 Paul cites Isa 25:8: "death has been swallowed up in victory." This citation deviates from both the Hebrew and the original Greek of Isaiah but agrees precisely with a rendering that the Theodotionic revision later adopts. Paul seems to have drawn on a contemporary tradition of revision that eventually became formalized in Theodotion. In other words, Paul often cited Greek texts as they circulated in his day.

The second major source of textual variation is Paul's own citation technique. We must remember that Paul is not writing studied philological treatises with an emphasis on precision and exactitude, with fully lemmatized citations that are only subsequently analyzed in detached commentary.[7] Rather, he is quoting Scripture *in scribendo*, on his way to making a point, and so he needs to contextualize his quotations to fit their epistolary context. This may at times appear to the modern reader as a certain freedom or looseness in

---

5. This is illustrated particularly well in texts like the Greek Minor Prophets scroll from Naḥal Ḥever (8ḤevXII gr). Note the classic study by Dominique Barthélemy, *Devanciers d'Aquila: Première publication intégrale du texte des fragments du Dodécaprophéton*, VT-Sup 10 (Leiden: Brill, 1963). For the edition of 8ḤevXII gr, see Emanuel Tov, Robert A. Kraft and P. J. Parsons, *The Greek Minor Prophets Scroll from Naḥal Ḥever (8ḤevXIIgr)*, DJD 8 (Oxford: Clarendon, 1990).

6. See the helpful treatment in Natalio Fernández Marcos, *The Septuagint in Context: Introduction to the Greek Versions of the Bible*, trans. Wilfred G. E. Watson (Leiden: Brill, 2001).

7. But for the commentarial nature of Paul's citations in a broader sense, see the introduction.

How Did Paul Read Scripture?

his citations, but this is only to be expected. At times he omits introductory particles, employs a limited selection from a verse, changes the word order, alters grammatical features, substitutes words or phrases, or adds to the text.[8] Moreover, it would be an anachronism to imagine Paul owning his own Bible, which would entail carting around the Mediterranean an unwieldy and expensive basket of scrolls from which to cite (although the author of 2 Timothy does imagine Paul requesting "the books, and above all the parchments," [4:13], which might refer to rolls of Scripture). Paul thus probably had recourse to citations from memory,[9] and may well also have kept a set of notes with choice scriptural quotations to employ in his argument, which may go some way toward understanding the types of variation we see in his citations.

Describing Paul's Scriptural Engagement

Paul's letters are replete with scriptural reminiscences, but not all of these can be accurately characterized as citations. Rather, Paul (like most authors who repay careful study) has used a variety of intertextual techniques to weave in references to predecessor texts. These range across a sliding scale of explicitness, and have been described with a bewildering array of terminology.[10] If we imagine these references laid out along a spectrum, at one end are verbatim quotations of Scripture that are marked for the reader by an introductory formula, such as "It is written" or "For Moses says."[11] At the other end are echoes of scriptural texts, and it is not always possible to decide whether Paul intended the echo or whether it simply slipped in as an unconscious reflection of one who had long soaked in Israel's scriptural traditions. Between these two poles

8. For a careful study that isolates such adaptations systematically, see Christopher D. Stanley, *Paul and the Language of Scripture: Citation Technique in the Pauline Epistles and Contemporary Literature*, SNTSMS 74 (Cambridge: Cambridge University Press, 1992).

9. See my argument in chapter 3.

10. Cf. Stanley E. Porter, "Pauline Techniques of Interweaving Scripture into His Letters," in *Paulinische Schriftrezeption: Grundlagen—Ausprägungen—Wirkungen—Wertungen*, ed. Florian Wilk and Markus Öhler, FRLANT 268 (Göttingen: Vandenhoeck & Ruprecht, 2017), 23–55; and Stanley E. Porter, "The Use of the Old Testament in the New: A Brief Comment on Method and Terminology," in *Early Christian Interpretation of the Scriptures of Israel: Investigations and Proposals*, ed. Craig A. Evans and James A. Sanders, JSNTSup 148/5 (Sheffield: Sheffield Academic, 1997), 79–96.

11. On citation formulae, see Dietrich-Alex Koch, *Die Schrift als Zeuge des Evangeliums: Untersuchungen zur Verwendung und zum Verständnis der Schrift bei Paulus*, BHT 69 (Tübingen: Mohr Siebeck, 1986), 25–32.

Chapter 1

we find unmarked citations and intentional allusions. The former are verbatim repetitions of substantial predecessor texts but without any quotation formula to signal to the reader that a predecessor text has been quoted. The latter are briefer but significant recollections of Scripture that bear some assertorial weight in context. We also find Paul referring to narratives or concepts derived from Scripture, even if not always in the form of an identifiable allusion to a particular text. Naturally it is not always possible or necessary to distinguish among these various categories, even if paying some attention to them helps us to grasp the range of Paul's scriptural engagements.[12]

In his groundbreaking book, *Echoes of Scripture in the Letters of Paul* (1989), Richard Hays roused Pauline scholars from their subliterary slumber and introduced them to the rich benefits of paying careful attention to the ways in which allusions can draw into the text something of the original context of the predecessor text.[13] As Hays put it (drawing on the sensibilities of John Hollander and others), echoes can activate the metaleptically suppressed original and resound in the cave of resonant signification, creating a complex poetics of intertextual significance for the reader who can appreciate the subtlety of "the hermeneutical event." For example, in Paul's letter to the Philippians, he urges them to "do all things without murmuring and arguing, so that you may be blameless and innocent, children of God without blemish in the midst of a crooked and perverse generation, in which you shine like stars in the world" (2:14–15). The descriptive phrase, "a crooked and perverse generation," echoes Deut 32:4–5:

> God—his works are genuine,
> And all his ways are justice.
> A faithful god, and there is no injustice,
> A righteous and holy Lord;
> Blemished children, not his, have sinned,
> A generation, crooked and perverse. (NETS)

Deuteronomy 32, which Paul cites numerous times throughout his letters, tells a story about God's people rebelling and growing faithless, before being

---

12. See further Matthias Henze and David Lincicum, introduction to *Israel's Scriptures in Early Christian Writings: The Use of the Old Testament in the New*, ed. Matthias Henze and David Lincicum (Grand Rapids: Eerdmans, 2023), 1–20.

13. Richard B. Hays, *Echoes of Scripture in the Letters of Paul* (New Haven: Yale University Press, 1989).

How Did Paul Read Scripture?

restored by God's showing of favor to a foreign people. In Romans, Paul seems to read this as a prophetic foretelling of God's intention to provoke Israel to jealousy by showing favor to the gentiles (more on this below). Does Paul's allusion here indicate that he wants the gentile Philippians to bear witness to an Israel that has become "crooked and perverse"? Or is it simply a turn of phrase that can be adroitly adapted to speak of the "pagan" world more broadly? In the nature of the case, it is difficult to make an argument with certainty, but the intertextual sensibilities Hays's book has inculcated in scholarship have sparked questions like this for a generation of readers, and sensitivity to such allusions heightens the reader's appreciation for Paul's literary achievements.

The invocation of a concept like "intertextuality" might, however, offer some readers pause. Initially stemming from the literary critic Julia Kristeva and post-structuralist literary circles in the 1960s, intertextuality was originally not a method of reading per se, but rather a theory about the nature of language as such.[14] The domestication of a theory into a method (a knack for which biblical scholarship has become well-known) might entail risks of distortion. In particular, for those with some concern to grasp Paul's meaning within the horizon of the first century, one might wonder whether a method that considers the interplay between two texts in a direct sense (Paul's letter and the scriptural text to which he cites or alludes) could lead to an unintentional collapsing of the distance between the original Scripture and Paul's own day. But of course, that distance between Paul and the scriptural text was peopled with other interpreters who also read, say, Genesis or Isaiah or Psalms, and so helped to fashion a trajectory of interpretation through which Paul approaches the text. Paul might accede to or resist this trajectory, but without some grasp of the long history of reading Scripture that the Second Temple literature preserves for us, do we risk the possibility of distorting what is either novel or commonplace in the apostle's interpretation of Scripture? Is Paul's way of reading Scripture comparable to other Jewish reading strategies in antiquity, or is he somehow unique?[15] Questions like these about the most productive sensibilities for understanding Paul's engagement with Scripture will no doubt continue to animate scholarship.

---

14. For a helpful introduction to these issues, see John Barton, "Déjà Lu: Intertextuality, Method or Theory?," in *Reading Job Intertextually*, ed. Katharine Dell and Will Kynes, LHBOTS 574 (London: Bloomsbury, 2013), 1–16.

15. For the argument that Paul does make good sense in the spectrum of Second Temple scriptural interpretation, see David Lincicum, *Paul and the Early Jewish Encounter with Deuteronomy*, WUNT 2/284 (Tübingen: Mohr Siebeck, 2010; repr., Grand Rapids: Baker Academic, 2013).

Chapter 1

Paul as a Reader of Scripture

If we turn now to consider Paul's letters as a record of his reading, what do we find? The apostle's letters do not intend to offer a disinterested commentary on Scripture that primarily attempts to respect the historical distance between the original text and Paul's contemporary situation. Rather, Paul operates under the profound conviction, commentarial in its own way, that "whatever was written in former days was written for our instruction" (Rom 15:4) and that the events in Scripture "were written down to instruct us, on whom the ends of the ages have come" (1 Cor 10:11).[16] This conviction imbues his scriptural interpretation with a tone of immediacy. Coupled with a deep certainty that whatever Scripture says God also says (cf. Rom 9:17; Gal 3:8), this sense of scriptural immediacy enables Paul to bring Scripture to bear on a broad array of theological, ethical, and practical questions in his foundling communities. In the givenness of the scriptural texts (expressed most tersely in Paul's invocation of what "is written," γέγραπται), Paul finds a pluripotent fund on which to draw for his varied purposes. We see this in play as Paul invokes the concept of "accordance": just as God has acted for Israel in her past and this action has been memorialized in her Scripture, so also in the history of Jesus we find a pattern of God's action that "accords" with Scripture. Paul surprisingly suggests, perhaps following early Christian tradition, that even the death of Christ for sin and his resurrection on the third day happened with such accordance (1 Cor 15:3–4).

All of this indicates that Paul operates with a contemporizing sense of Scripture as divine address to the present. As Paul says when he reflects on Deut 25:4: "Is it for oxen that God is concerned? Or does he not speak entirely for our sake?" (1 Cor 9:9–10; cf. Rom 4:23–24). In certain respects, Paul preaches a radical novelty—a message about a crucified Messiah that confounds the wisdom of the world. But even as he presents his gospel as being "apart from the law," in the same breath he alleges that it is "attested by the law and the prophets" (Rom 3:21). Thus, a certain productive tension exists in Paul's understanding of history. On the one hand, he can read the long history of Israel as a story of preparation for the Messiah's coming, full of foreshadowing, promise, and expectation. At other times, he can place stress on the unexpected nature of the proclamation, its character as a disruption or invasion of history-as-routine. Scripture can be marshalled to serve either end, and this suggests that for the apostle, Scripture and gospel are mutually interpretative.

16. Cf. Koch, *Die Schrift als Zeuge des Evangeliums*, 322–53.

How Did Paul Read Scripture?

Paul's letters, moreover, attest the fundamental importance of narratives in Paul's theological vision. Intriguingly, Paul does not pause to insert clarifying comments: "Adam, who, as you might not know, is the first-formed of all God's created people," or "Now David was an important king of Israel about whom you should know." Rather, he assumes the basic contours of the major structuring narratives of Israel's history: the creation account, the Abraham story, the exodus, the Sinai covenant. This may indicate that Paul took such knowledge for granted because he had taught these stories to those communities he had founded, or, in the case of the letter to the Romans, assumed that the early Christ-followers would have been catechized along such lines.[17] Scripture's narrative quality seeps into Paul's own vision, and he orients his basic thinking by means of Israel's founding stories.

But if the narratives are foundational for Paul's vision, it is to the prophets that he turns again and again (and above all to Isaiah) to make sense of the mission to the gentiles and his own vocation as an apostle.[18] In Isaiah's call to preach to a hardened Israel, Paul finds foreshadowed his own apostolic imperative to hold out the gospel to his contemporary coreligionists, many of whom did not receive it. In fact, much of Paul's explicit engagement with Scripture (above all in Romans and Galatians) could be subsumed under the rubric of reflection on and defense of the gentile mission.

Roughly twenty-five percent of all quotations in the *corpus Paulinum* are clustered in Rom 9–11, and accordingly it is worth examining this section in a bit more detail, since it allows us to see Paul's scriptural sensibilities in action. In light of tensions in the Roman churches between Jewish and gentile Christians, and in order to address a potentially defeating objection to faith in the fidelity of God, Paul offers an intensive engagement with the Scriptures of Israel as he advances his argument. In 9:1–5, Paul enumerates the advantages Israel has his-

---

17. For an attempt at a large-scale reconstruction of Paul's narrative sensibilities, see Francis Watson, *Paul and the Hermeneutics of Faith*, 2nd ed. (London: T&T Clark, 2015); and note the important essays in Bruce W. Longenecker, ed., *Narrative Dynamics in Paul: A Critical Assessment* (Louisville: Westminster John Knox, 2002).

18. For Paul's reading of Isaiah, see Shiu-Lun Shum, *Paul's Use of Isaiah in Romans: A Comparative Study of Paul's Letter to the Romans and the Sibylline and Qumran Sectarian Texts*, WUNT 2/156 (Tübingen: Mohr Siebeck, 2002); J. Ross Wagner, *Heralds of the Good News: Isaiah and Paul in Concert in the Letter to the Romans*, NovTSup 101 (Leiden: Brill, 2002); and Florian Wilk, *Die Bedeutung des Jesajabuches für Paulus*, FRLANT 179 (Göttingen: Vandenhoeck & Ruprecht, 1998). For the minor prophets, see Barbara Fuß, *"Dies ist die Zeit, von der geschrieben ist . . ." Die expliziten Zitate aus dem Buch Hosea in den Handschriften von Qumran und im Neuen Testament*, NTAbh 37 (Münster: Aschendorff, 2000), esp. 156–92.

Chapter 1

torically enjoyed and laments the lack of response among contemporary Jews to his message. This leads to the posing of a question about the fidelity of God to God's word: has God revoked Israel's election, and so made false promises in Scripture? No, Paul replies, "it is not as though the word of God had failed" (9:6). Paul then rereads the Pentateuchal narratives to discover a pattern of election by which only some from Israel are in fact Israel: Isaac is preferred over Ishmael, Jacob over Esau. The reversal of primogeniture authorizes Paul to make a generalizing deduction about God's electing activity, which he confirms by appealing to the example of God's raising up of Pharaoh to serve the purposes of God's own glory. Paul goes on to find in Hosea's rhetoric of reversal a precedent for including the gentiles in the bounds of the people of God: "those who were not my people I will call my people." At the same time, Paul sees in Isaiah a remnant theology that also helps to make sense of the weak response to his message. All this is the first major movement in his argument in 9:6–29.

A second major movement in Paul's argument turns from God's election to Israel's responsibility (9:30–10:21). Israel has stumbled on Isaiah's stone (9:33), since they sought to establish their own righteousness, according to Paul, rather than pursuing the righteousness from faith that comes by the Messiah. Rather than conceding that Israel has an excuse for not believing that Jesus is God's promised agent, Paul marshals a series of scriptural witnesses to accuse Israel of having clear access to the message of the gospel but failing to believe. The second movement, then, is accusation, supported by scriptural witnesses.

Third, Paul poses the logical question: "Has God rejected his people?" (11:1). The answer in reply is emphatic: "By no means!" Paul first appeals to the presence of a remnant, grounding his appeal in the example of the seven thousand righteous ones in Elijah's day. But then he goes beyond this to argue from especially Isaiah, Psalms, and Deuteronomy that God had partially hardened Israel in order to show favor to the gentiles, but this favor, in turn, was calculated to provoke Israel to jealousy and so ultimately to salvation—all Israel being saved once the full number of gentiles has come in. Arguably the language of provocation to jealousy is rooted in Deut 32:21 (cited in Rom 10:19) and the broader context of the Song of Moses, which Paul conceives of as a "mystery"—that is, a hidden truth that God's eschatological action has brought to light. This mystery ultimately pertains to the salvation of both Jew and gentile, and so to the fulfillment of Paul's apostolic vocation.

Thus, in these three dense, quotation-laden chapters, Paul evinces a deep and wide-ranging reading of Scripture in pursuit of a solution to the vexing problem of Jewish unbelief in Paul's christological message. The scriptural material is addressed to the specific situation of the Christ-following audience

How Did Paul Read Scripture?

in Rome by means of Paul's exhortation that gentiles should not boast over the stumbling of the Jews (cf. 11:20). But the response is much more than sufficient to answer a niggling problem in Rome, and indeed gives us our fullest picture of Paul's scriptural imagination at work. Throughout, Paul weaves quotation, allusion, and analysis with his own argumentation, offering eloquent testimony to the ways in which every word of Scripture can resource the urgent task of Paul's missionary endeavors.[19]

The engagement with Scripture is most intensive in Paul's letters to the Galatians and to the Romans—precisely where we might imagine it would be, as he wrestles with the terms of the gentile mission and the boundaries of the covenant. But paying careful attention to Paul's aims in citing Scripture also sheds some light on those places where he refrains from citing it. Calling attention to the relative paucity of Scripture in the Pauline letters beyond the *Hauptbriefe* (or "main letters" of Paul), Adolf von Harnack famously suggested that Paul himself turned to Scripture as a source of "edifying power," but that he "did not give the Old Testament to the young churches as the book of Christian sources for edification."[20] This striking judgment is usefully provocative, but most interpreters of Paul have rather preferred to see Paul's relative reticence to introduce quotations of Scripture in his shorter letters as due to the pressing questions he adjudicates and the epistolary constraints of brevity and focus. After all, even if these shorter letters do not contain the same density of quotation, they are full of allusion and scriptural turns of phrase, not to mention basic concepts that came to Paul by means of a reading of Scripture.

It would, moreover, be possible to point to a certain process of "scripturalization" in the deutero-Pauline tradition. If we were to compare Colossians and Ephesians in detail, and argue, with the majority of Pauline interpreters, for the use of Colossians as a literary source by the author of Ephesians, then one of the most significant changes that Ephesians has introduced to its Colossian *Vorlage* is the introduction of explicit scriptural citations and implicit allusions. Or again, the Pastoral Epistles do not feature citations of Scripture prominently,

---

19. Indeed, sometimes, it must be admitted, Paul's appeals to Scripture are downright alarming. For example, in the context of Rom 9–11, Paul seems to juxtapose Lev 18:5 with Deut 30:11–14, and to do so to Leviticus's detriment; see further Preston Sprinkle, *Law and Life: The Interpretation of Leviticus 18:5 in Early Judaism and Paul*, WUNT 2/241 (Tübingen: Mohr Siebeck, 2008).

20. Adolf von Harnack, "The Old Testament in the Pauline Letters and in the Pauline Churches," in *Understanding Paul's Ethics: Twentieth-Century Approaches*, ed. Brian Rosner (Grand Rapids: Eerdmans, 1995), 27–49, quotations from pp. 28, 44. (This essay originally appeared in 1928 in German.)

Chapter 1

but where Scripture is cited it seems to be largely "lifted" from the undisputed Pauline Epistles, even as the author reflects on the nature of Scripture more programmatically than Paul does in his own letters: "All scripture is inspired by God and is useful for teaching, for reproof, for correction, and for training in righteousness" (2 Tim 3:16).[21] This statement could be read without difficulty as a synthetic judgment about the nature of the Scriptures arrived at by careful reflection on how the apostle himself had put them to use in his letters.

How To Do Things with Scripture

Those interested in reconstructing Paul's own reading of Scripture from the evidence of his letters quickly come up against a complication: we do not have a raw, unprocessed record of the apostle's engagement with Scripture, but rather a highly rhetorical series of quotations and allusions designed to elicit some response from his audience. We see Paul citing his ancestral texts on the way toward some other point. He is attempting, for example, to dissuade the gentile Galatian churches from adopting Jewish ritual practices, while at the same time outmaneuvering rival teachers and their arguments for the necessity of adopting those very practices. Or again, he is constructing an account of the enduring election of Israel that is directed to the practical problem of gentile boasting in Rome. Precisely because the extant literary output that survives from Paul is a corpus of letters that are "situational" in nature, every engagement with Scripture bears the marks of specific rhetorical purposes occasioned by problems or concerns that arose in local communities.

This is not to say that Paul's reading of Scripture is *merely* rhetorical, as though he were somehow dishonestly representing his views or crassly attempting to associate his own advice with God's voice for the purpose of exercising power.[22] But it is the case that any adequate grasp of Paul's engagement with Scripture will have to pay careful attention to the ways in which he marshals it for effect.[23] Paul's own rhetorical purposes vary, and thus the interpreter will need to attend to the particular epistolary context into which

---

21. See Gerd Häfner, *'Nützlich zur Belehrung' (2 Tim 3,16): Die Rolle der Schrift in den Pastoralbriefen im Rahmen der Paulusrezeption*, HBS 25 (Freiburg: Herder, 2000); and chapter 10.

22. But cf. Christopher D. Stanley, *Arguing with Scripture: The Rhetoric of Quotations in the Letters of Paul* (London: T&T Clark, 2004).

23. See recently Katja Kujanpää, "From Eloquence to Evading Responsibility: The Rhetorical Functions of Quotations in Paul's Argumentation," *JBL* 136 (2017): 185–202; Katja Ku-

How Did Paul Read Scripture?

each quotation is placed, rather than focusing exclusively on the context of the cited original. Given that the Scriptures are charged with authority, to appeal to them is to draw on that authority, and so in some sense to join one's own discourse to the discourse of God.

We see this sensibility in action as Paul allows the words of Scripture to do the talking for him. For example, in Gal 4 Paul constructs an elaborate allegory about Abraham's two sons, Isaac and Ishmael. Isaac is the son of a free woman and stands, in Paul's reading, for the promise, while Ishmael is the son of a slave woman, Hagar, who corresponds to the Sinai covenant (4:21–31). At the end of Paul's subtle and complex set of identifications (which the Galatians themselves may or may not have been able to follow), Paul underscores the practical outcome of his exposition by asking: "what does the scripture say?" The answer allows Scripture to urge what Paul himself wants: "Drive out the slave woman and her child; for the child of the slave will not share the inheritance with the child of the free woman" (4:30). Paul wants the Galatians to expel the Judaizing agitators, and he employs Scripture rhetorically to make the point for him.

Paul makes a very similar move in 1 Cor 5. After detailing his concerns that the community in Corinth is harboring a man living with the wife of his father, Paul argues from multiple sources that such action should not be condoned. But his practical urging comes to a head with a citation of a line repeated in Deuteronomy: "Drive out the wicked person from among you" (1 Cor 5:13; cf. Deut 13:5; 17:7; 19:19, etc.). Rather than relying on his own authority, as he often does, Paul here invokes the command of Scripture to persuade the community in Corinth to act and so imbues his judgment with scriptural force.

Conclusion

In conclusion, it is instructive to step back and imagine Paul's letters denuded of their scriptural citations and allusions (as perhaps someone inspired by Marcion, a second-century interpreter of Paul, might wish to see them). What would be left of Romans, or Galatians, or even large swathes of the Corinthian correspondence? All that might remain would be mere tissue of phrases untouched by scriptural idiom, or perhaps some practical words of guidance drawn from the moral koine of the ancient world. The influence of Scripture is most in evidence when the argument of Paul's letters is most sustained, and

---

janpää, *The Rhetorical Functions of Scriptural Quotations in Romans*, NovTSup 172 (Leiden: Brill, 2019).

Chapter 1

this fact attests to the foundational importance of Scripture for Paul's own theology and missionary praxis.

Although we have not dwelled on it here, it would be equally possible to illustrate the significance of Scripture for Paul's ethical vision. While it is true that Paul does not always cite chapter and verse as motivating ground for his ethical teaching,[24] close examination of the paraenetic sections of his letters often discloses the deep scriptural roots of his teaching.[25] And of course Paul does sometimes cite Scripture explicitly as moral guidance for his gentile communities (e.g., Rom 7:7; 12:19; 13:8–10, etc.).

Above all, Paul reads the Scriptures of Israel as directed to the eschatological present, a gift of the God and Father of the Lord Jesus Christ to the communities of gentiles who seek to follow the Messiah. Paul walks a delicate line in balancing radical novelty and radical continuity, and he employs Scripture to explain each side of that balance. At the distance of almost two thousand years, we have to work hard to reconstruct the factors that gave shape to Paul's reading, and scholars will continue to debate the precise form of Paul's textual exemplar (*Vorlage*) and citation technique, as well as to seek the most adequate conceptual frame to grasp Paul's letters as "hermeneutical events." But to grapple with Paul's reading and use of Scripture is to come up against some of the deepest impulses in Paul's theology and practice, and so amply repays the reader for the effort.

---

24. Urging this point with particular force is Christopher M. Tuckett, "Paul, Scripture and Ethics: Some Reflections," *NTS* 46 (2000): 403–24.

25. Note, e.g., Peter J. Tomson, *Paul and the Jewish Law: Halakhah in the Letters of the Apostle to the Gentiles*, CRINT 3/1 (Minneapolis: Fortress, 1990); and Brian S. Rosner, *Paul, Scripture, and Ethics: A Study of 1 Corinthians 5–7*, AGJU 22 (Leiden: Brill, 1994; repr., Grand Rapids: Baker, 1999).

2

PAUL AND THE *TESTIMONIA*

For well over a century, various scholars have proposed that Paul and other New Testament authors may have made use of collections of excerpted quotations or topically arranged *testimonia* rather than having direct recourse to the scriptural texts. Though the theory has been set forth in varying forms, one proponent has suggested that "the core of all *testimonia* hypotheses is the claim that early Christians did not use the Jewish scriptures as an undifferentiated whole, but rather selected, shaped, and interpreted certain passages in support of emerging Christian beliefs."[1] Clearly such hypotheses might, though need not, form a *prima facie* challenge to any attempt to consider the New Testament authors as significantly engaged in holistic biblical interpretation. Some account of this nexus of theories is therefore germane to the question of Paul's engagement with Scripture. In this brief chapter, I offer a short review of the history of the question and set forth the *testimonia* hypothesis in its most promising form. Ultimately such approaches helpfully attune the interpreter to the realia of working with texts in antiquity, even if they are not able to provide a total context for Paul's scriptural engagements. A concluding attempt, therefore, is made to articulate an account of what alternative approaches must take into consideration in order to successfully supplement such theories.[2]

THE RISE AND FALL OF THE *TESTIMONY BOOK* HYPOTHESIS

The *testimonia* hypothesis received an early and sustained investigation at the hands of the industrious J. Rendel Harris.[3] Building on the work of his

---

1. Martin C. Albl, *"And Scripture Cannot Be Broken": The Form and Function of the Early Christian Testimonia Collections*, NovTSup 96 (Leiden: Brill, 1999).

2. For a fuller history of the discussion of the Testimonia hypothesis see Robert Hodgson, "The Testimony Hypothesis," *JBL* 98 (1979): 361–78; and Albl, *"And Scripture Cannot Be Broken"*, 7–69.

3. J. Rendel Harris, with Vacher Burch, *Testimonies*, 2 vols. (Cambridge: Cambridge

Chapter 2

predecessors,[4] Harris took as his point of departure the observation that a number of oddities appear in the scriptural citations of the New Testament and the early Christian period: shared variant readings ("peculiar texts"), recurrent sequences of quotations, erroneous ascriptions of authorship, editorial comments repeated by various authors, and polemical or "controversialist" themes.[5] For example, 1 Pet 2:6–8 presents a merged citation of Isa 28:16, Ps 118:22, and Isa 8:14, all connected by an emphasis on the word "stone"; in Rom 9:32–33 the conflation of Isa 8:14 and 28:16 again presents itself. Cyprian's *Testimonia* (2.16) contains Isa 28:16 with Ps 118:22, but not Isa 8:14; and the reference to Christ as the "stone" continues throughout early Christian literature.[6] The best way to account for this phenomenon and for others like it, according to Harris, is to posit the existence of a primitive *Testimony Book* from the hands of a versatile and creative theologian of the first century.[7] This book underwent various editorial adaptations and recensions, and Harris ultimately thought he could trace it all the way to a sixteenth-century manuscript in Mt. Athos.[8]

Despite the excesses of Harris's creative reconstruction of the afterlife of the *Testimony Book*,[9] his central contention had more to do with its existence and use in antiquity, even in the period of the formation of the New Testament. He concludes that "the *Testimony Book* is one of the earliest Christian documents, and . . . the earliest books of the New Testament must be interpreted in the light of such a document as we have shown, by so many considerations, to exist."[10] When Harris applied his *Testimony Book* to the Epistle to the Romans,

---

University Press, 1916–1920). While most of the work is from Harris, Burch wrote two short chapters in the first volume, and three more substantial chapters and an appendix in the second. On Harris's work, see especially the excellent and sympathetic treatment of Alessandro Falcetta, "The Testimony Research of James Rendel Harris," *NovT* 45 (2003): 280–99.

4. Harris and Burch, *Testimonies*, 1:1–4; 2:1–11. See further below.

5. Harris and Burch, *Testimonies*, 1:8; see 1:1–20 for a broad overview of his thesis.

6. Harris and Burch, *Testimonies*, 1:18–19.

7. According to Harris, this theologian was probably Matthew, and the *Testimony Book* should be identified with the logia ascribed to Matthew by Papias (see Harris and Burch, *Testimonies*, 1:118–23; 2:1–11). In this he follows a suggestion of F. C. Burkitt, who was not, however, as is sometimes stated, the first to speak of an early Christian (i.e., pre–New Testament) "collection of *Testimonia*" on analogy with that of Cyprian (*The Gospel History and Its Transmission* [Edinburgh: T&T Clark, 1906], 127–28). Rather, that distinction belongs, apparently, to Harris's earlier work (so Falcetta, "Testimony Research," 283–84).

8. Harris and Burch, *Testimonies*, 1:100–117; 2:109–21.

9. C. H. Dodd wrote, "This final stage of the argument, I fancy, no one, perhaps not even Harris himself, took very seriously." *According to the Scriptures: The Sub-Structure of New Testament Theology* (London: Nisbet, 1952), 25.

10. Harris and Burch, *Testimonies*, 1:25.

Paul and the Testimonia

he found that Paul had made extensive use of it: "It is surprising to find how little is left of scriptural quotation in the Epistle after this test is applied, and we may affirm, at all events for Romans, that St Paul was a traditionalist, operating with conventional and approved matter, to a degree far beyond what we should *a priori* have expected."[11]

Reaction to Harris's sweeping proposal, both appreciative and critical, was immediate.[12] Daniel Plooij fully endorsed and built upon the work of Harris:

> We find the Testimony Book quoted over and over again in the pages of the New Testament, and if duly studied, it spreads a flood of light on many passages otherwise only very imperfectly understood. The importance of the discovery is still greater when we realize, as I think we should, that the Testimony Book was extant and in use in the primitive Aramaic speaking Church of Palestine.[13]

Others reacted against Harris and his followers like Plooij.[14] But it was perhaps Dodd who offered the most widely accepted counterproposal to account for the evidence Harris adduced. While acknowledging Harris's "immense and curious learning,"[15] Dodd confessed, "I have come to think that his theory outruns the evidence, which is not sufficient to prove so formidable a literary

---

11. Harris and Burch, *Testimonies*, 2:29.

12. Contrast the positive review of T. Herbert Bindley (review of *Testimonies: Part II*, by J. Rendel Harris and Vacher Burch, *JTS* 22 [1921]: 279–82) with the more skeptical reviews of Charles Guignebert (review of *Testimonies*, by J. Rendel Harris and Vacher Burch, *RHR* 81 [1920]: 58–69) and M.-J. Lagrange (review of *Testimonies: Part II*, by J. Rendel Harris and Vacher Burch, *RB* 30 [1921]: 612–14). On reaction to Harris, see further Albl, *"And Scripture Cannot Be Broken"*, 23–25.

13. Daniel Plooij, *Studies in the Testimony Book*, Verhandelingen der Koninklijke Akademie van Wetenschappen te Amsterdam, Afdeeling letterkunde 32/2 (Amsterdam: Noord-Hollandsche Uitgevers-Maatschappij, 1932), 31.

14. See N. J. Hommes, *Het Testimoniaboek: Studiën over O.T. Citaten in het N.T. en bij de Patres, Met Critische Beschouwingen over de Theorieën van J. Rendel Harris en D. Plooy* (Amsterdam: Noord-Hollandsche Uitgevers-Maatschappij, 1935); for this reading I am indebted to Falcetta, "Testimony Research," 297–98. Of Paul, Hommes concluded: "With a Testimony Book, as it has been construed by Rendel Harris and Plooy [Plooij], he has not worked—just like the other NT writers" (*Het Testimoniaboek*, 370); cf. Otto Michel, *Paulus und seine Bibel* (Darmstadt: Wissenschaftliche Buchgesellschaft, 1972), 52. See further the literature referenced in Joseph A. Fitzmyer, "'4QTestimonia' and the New Testament," *TS* 18 (1957): 513–37; repr., in Joseph A. Fitzmyer, *Essays on the Semitic Background of the New Testament* (London: Geoffrey Chapman, 1971), 59–89, esp. 71n36.

15. Dodd, *According to the Scriptures*, 25.

Chapter 2

enterprise at so early a date."[16] The evidence, he argued, is not strong for shared variant readings and merged citations within the New Testament.[17] If such a book existed, it should have been preserved, possibly even in the canon, or at least explicitly mentioned before the third century.[18] Ultimately, "the composition of 'testimony-books' was the result, not the presupposition, of the work of early Christian biblical scholars."[19]

Rather than isolated quotations, Dodd thought that the New Testament authors "often quoted a single phrase or sentence not merely for its own sake, but as a pointer to a whole context."[20] Dodd then sought to identify contexts of Scripture from which repeated citations were drawn by various authors, and to group such contexts together as "the Bible of the Early Church" under four main headings: apocalyptic-eschatological Scriptures; Scriptures of the New Israel; Scriptures of the Servant of the Lord and the Righteous Sufferer; and a series of unclassified Scriptures that did not fit neatly in the other categories (e.g., Pss 2, 8, 110; Deut 18).[21] Though Dodd's own reconstruction of "the Bible of the Early Church" has rightly been criticized, his critique of Harris

---

16. Dodd, *According to the Scriptures*, 26.

17. Dodd, *According to the Scriptures*, 26. See further the remarks of Merrill P. Miller, "Targum, Midrash and the Use of the Old Testament in the New Testament," *JSJ* 2 (1971): 29–82, here 54–55.

18. Dodd, *According to the Scriptures*, 26. Dodd might also have mentioned that in almost every case the coincidence in citation between Paul and early Christian writers can be ascribed to their reliance on Paul and/or on revised Septuagintal texts. Note Harris's concessions (*Testimonies*, 2:38), although he did not follow through on these consistently. See further Krister Stendahl, *The School of St. Matthew and Its Use of the Old Testament*, 2nd ed. (Lund: Gleerup, 1968), 210–11. Cf. Stendahl's ultimate rejection of the *Testimony Book* hypothesis, at least for Matthew, on p. 217.

19. Dodd, *According to the Scriptures*, 126. See further E. Earle Ellis, *Paul's Use of the Old Testament* (Eugene, OR: Wipf & Stock, 2003; orig. Edinburgh: Oliver and Boyd, 1957), 98–107.

20. C. H. Dodd, *The Old Testament in the New* (Philadelphia: Fortress, 1963); repr. in *The Right Doctrine from the Wrong Texts? Essays on the Use of the Old Testament in the New*, ed. G. K. Beale (Grand Rapids: Baker, 1994), 167–81, here 176.

21. Dodd, *According to the Scriptures*, 61–110. As these headings serve to indicate, Dodd's study was perhaps too limited to the prophetic element of the New Testament appropriation of Scripture, without due concern for the abiding moral and more broadly theological authority of the latter. This is reflected in the space his study assigns to texts from Isaiah and Psalms, with a relative neglect of Genesis and Deuteronomy, even though these two books are also frequently cited in the New Testament.

Paul and the Testimonia

has endured.[22] The *Testimony Book* hypothesis, it seemed, had been dealt a resounding blow.[23]

THE *EXCERPTA* COLLECTION THEORY

Then, in 1956, with John Allegro's preliminary publication of two documents from Qumran, 4QFlorilegium (= 4Q174) and 4QTestimonia (= 4Q175),[24] the testimony hypothesis received new life. As Allegro himself predicted,[25] the

22. For further reactions against and for Dodd, see respectively, A. C. Sundberg, "On Testimonies," *NovT* 3 (1959): 268-81; and I. Howard Marshall, "An Assessment of Recent Developments," in *It Is Written: Scripture Citing Scripture; Essays in Honour of Barnabas Lindars, SSF*, ed. D. A. Carson and H. G. M. Williamson (Cambridge: Cambridge University Press, 1988), 1-21. Both of these are conveniently reprinted in Beale, *Right Doctrine*, 167-216. See further, contra Dodd, Dietrich-Alex Koch, *Die Schrift als Zeuge des Evangeliums: Untersuchungen zur Verwendung und zum Verständnis der Schrift bei Paulus*, BHT 69 (Tübingen: Mohr Siebeck, 1986), 253-55.

23. Other authors also distanced themselves in this period from Harris's hypothesis of a solitary *Testimony Book*. For example, Robert A. Kraft ("Barnabas' Isaiah-Text and the 'Testimony Book' Hypothesis," *JBL* 79 [1960]: 336-50), compared the Isaiah quotations in the Epistle of Barnabas with other extant instances of the same citations from Isaiah in early Christian literature. He notes a bewildering array of textual variants, such that reliance on a common source (e.g., a "Testimony Book") is improbable. Rather, he asserts, "Barnabas may represent one early stage in the adaptation and modification of late Jewish [*sic*] testimony literature by Christian authors, and in the transition of that literature toward its later, more developed anti-Judaic forms" (349). Jean Daniélou (*Études d'exégèse judéo-chrétienne [Les Testimonia]*) ThH 5 (Paris: Beauschesne, 1966) also distances himself from the "single testimony book" theory of Harris (9). Note T. W. Manson's modification to include oral traditions in "The Argument from Prophecy," *JTS* 46 (1945): 129-36, here 132: "The phenomena just considered seem to me to suggest that we should think of the 'Testimony Book', not as something that was turned out in written form in the earliest days of the Church, but rather as a collection of proof-texts assembled in the course of preaching, and forming part of the primitive kerygma." Plooij (*Studies in the Testimony Book*, 11) also allows for an oral form of the *Testimony Book*; cf. A. Lukyn Williams, *Adversus Judaeos: A Bird's-Eye View of Christian Apologiae until the Renaissance* (Cambridge: Cambridge University Press, 1935), 6-8, 12.

24. John M. Allegro, "Further Messianic References in Qumran Literature," *JBL* 75 (1956): 174-87; here, see, respectively, 176-77 and 182-87; cf. for 4Q174 John M. Allegro, "Fragments of a Qumran Scroll of Eschatological Midrashim," *JBL* 77 (1958): 350-54. See the edition of the two texts in John M. Allegro, *Qumrân Cave 4: I (4Q158-4Q186)*, DJD 5 (Oxford: Clarendon, 1968), 53-57 with pls. XIX-XX and 57-60 with pl. XXI, respectively. This should be read with the important remarks of John Strugnell, "Notes en marge du volume V des 'Discoveries in the Judaean Desert of Jordan,'" *RevQ* 7 (1970): 163-276, here 220-29.

25. Allegro, "Further Messianic References," 186n107.

27

Chapter 2

existence of apparently pre-Christian *testimonia* in Hebrew reopened the discussion of the viability of some form of the testimony hypothesis. In effect, this removed the objection from the chronological separation between the earliest extant *testimonia* collections (ca. 3rd century) and the time of New Testament formation,[26] thus making the supposition more historically plausible. While Harris's proposal was still regarded as outrunning the available evidence, new interest was shown in his predecessors' work, and in some suggestions of Edwin Hatch in particular.

In the course of lectures published in 1889, Hatch examined the composite quotations from the LXX in the New Testament and early Christian literature.[27] Speaking of non-Christian Judaism, he suggested,

> It may naturally be supposed that a race which laid stress on moral progress, whose religious services had variable elements of both prayer and praise, and which was carrying on an active propaganda, would have, among other books, manuals of morals, of devotion, and of controversy. It may also be supposed, if we take into consideration the contemporary habit of making collections of *excerpta*, and the special authority which the Jews attached to their sacred books, that some of these manuals would consist of extracts from the Old Testament.[28]

He went on to say, "The existence of composite quotations in the New Testament, and in some of the early Fathers suggests the hypothesis that we have in them relics of such manuals."[29] This more modest proposal of Hatch's seemed to acquire hard evidence in the Qumran finds.[30] What else were 4Q174

---

26. As voiced, e.g., by Michel, *Paulus*, 52.

27. Edwin Hatch, *Essays in Biblical Greek* (Oxford: Clarendon, 1889), esp. the essay "On Composite Quotations from the Septuagint," 203–14.

28. Hatch, *Essays in Biblical Greek*, 203.

29. Hatch, *Essays in Biblical Greek*, 203. Note Albl, *"And Scripture Cannot Be Broken"*, 9–10 for precursors to Hatch; contra Stendahl, *The School of St. Matthew*, 208, who suggests that Hatch was the first to propose such an idea. While Hatch did have some immediate successors (e.g., Hans Vollmer, *Die alttestamentlichen Citate bei Paulus textkritisch und biblisch-theologisch gewürdigt nebst einem Anhang Ueber das Verhältnis des Apostels zu Philo* [Leipzig: Mohr Siebeck, 1895], 43, took up Hatch's suggestion to account for LXX-deviant and composite quotations, though Vollmer conceived of the compilations as in Hebrew, deriving from rabbinic circles, rather than Hatch's Hellenistic Jewish Greek), the more grandiose theory of Harris overshadowed his suggestion.

30. Evidence which, in 1900, Henry St. John Thackeray had found lacking: "The existence of such an anthology is by no means improbable, but it must be said that no very

Paul and the Testimonia

and 4Q175 if not pre-Christian *excerpta* collections of Scripture? Time revealed that 4Q174 is probably better explained as a fragmentary eschatological midrash than as a florilegium or a witness to the genre of *testimonia* per se.[31] The second document, however, 4Q175, with its stand-alone character,[32] lack of

---

convincing proofs have yet been brought forward" (*The Relation of St. Paul to Contemporary Jewish Thought* [New York: Macmillan, 1900], 184).

31. As almost all acknowledge. See esp. Fitzmyer, "4QTestimonia and the New Testament," 81–82; and Koch, *Die Schrift als Zeuge des Evangeliums*, 247n6. As Fitzmyer notes, Allegro referred to 4Q174 as an "eschatological midrash," even though the poorly suited name the latter chose, "Florilegium," has remained attached to the text. George J. Brooke (*Exegesis at Qumran: 4QFlorilegium in Its Jewish Context*, JSOTSup 29 [Sheffield: JSOT Press, 1985], 82–83) notes the disagreements of scholars over the name and characterization of the fragmentary document, but retains the title "Florilegium" as "less restrictive a title than any other" (83). In the course of his study, however, it is clear that Brooke regards 4Q174 as a midrash rather than a mere collection of *excerpta* or *testimonia*. Annette Steudel prefers the name 4QMidrEschat[a] (*Der Midrasch zur Eschatologie aus der Qumrangemeinde [4QMidrEschat[a.b]]: Materielle Rekonstruktion, Textbestand, Gattung und traditionsgeschichtliche Einordnung des durch 4Q174 [„Florilegium"] und 4Q177 [„Catena A"] repräsentierten Werkes aus den Qumranfunden*, STDJ 13 [Leiden: Brill, 1994]). Timothy H. Lim (*Holy Scripture in the Qumran Commentaries and Pauline Letters* [Oxford: Clarendon, 1997], 157), however, regards 4Q174 as an example of an *excerpta* collection.

Admittedly, the distinction between midrash and *excerpta* may be a fine one, and the two should probably be thought of as on a sliding scale rather than as rigid opposites. Nevertheless, the volume of interpretative comments within the text is inversely proportionate to the heuristic usefulness of the term *excerpta*. See also Albl, *"And Scripture Cannot Be Broken"*, 38–42, for an attempt to distinguish the two, although his contention that midrash "takes scripture as its starting point and seeks to draw out further meaning" while the testimony genre "takes an extra-biblical subject as its starting point and refers to scripture as a witness to this subject" (40) has the simultaneous effect of implausibly restricting the definition of "midrash" (40n174 acknowledges the criticism, but Albl persists in the distinction) and defining the testimony genre too broadly (not distinguishing it from other approaches, e.g., typology or allegory, that also have starting points outside the text). As Renée Bloch ("Midrash," in *DBSup* 5:1263–81, repr., in *Approaches to Ancient Judaism: Theory and Practice*, ed. W. S. Green [Missoula, MT: Scholars Press, 1978], 29–50) points out, "When midrash consults the past, it is thinking of the present, and even, in a veiled manner, of the future" (46). Albl follows A. G. Wright ("The Genre Literary Midrash," *CBQ* 28 [1966]: 105–38, 417–57, reprinted as *The Literary Genre Midrash* [Staten Island, NY: Alba, 1967]), against whom see esp. Roger Le Déaut, "A propos d'une définition du midrash," *Bib* 50 (1969): 395–413 [ET in *Int* 25 (1971) 259–82]; note also the comments by E. Earle Ellis, "Midrash, Targum and New Testament Quotation," in *Neotestamentica et Semitica: Studies in Honour of Matthew Black*, ed. E. Earle Ellis and Max Wilcox (Edinburgh: T&T Clark, 1969), 61–69, here 64n21. On the diverse types and aims of midrash, see further the brief but informed account given by Jacob Neusner, *What Is Midrash?* (Philadelphia: Fortress, 1987).

32. Allegro says "it is clearly not part of a scroll, for there is none of the close stitching at the left-hand side one associates with a scroll page" ("Further Messianic References," 182).

29

Chapter 2

interpretative comments, and the potential of a central organizing theme, has a much stronger claim to represent such an *excerpta* collection.[33] As more of the Qumran finds were brought to light through publication, further excerpted text collections emerged.[34]

How, then, does the existence of such excerpted text collections play into a discussion of Paul's appropriation of Scripture? In short, the possibility is created to think less in terms of Paul's use of preformulated traditional *testimonia*, and more in terms of his adaptation of a conventional literary practice to suit his needs in the light of the practical exigencies brought about by the *realia* of books and reading in the ancient world. One of the most suggestive authors to examine Paul and Scripture in recent decades, Christopher Stan-

---

33. See esp. Fitzmyer, "4QTestimonia and the New Testament," 82–89. If this is to be characterized as an *excerpta* collection, it is striking that lines 21–30 apparently quote from a rewritten Joshua (formerly called 4QPsalms of Joshua but now 4QApocryphon of Joshua[a,b] [4Q378, 4Q379]).

34. Not all the excerpted texts are directly relevant to the discussion at hand, though they do provide a fascinating glimpse into the ways in which Scripture was encountered during this period. While some texts may have been excerpted for ideological or argumentative purposes, others were excerpted for devotional or liturgical or apotropaic reasons (among which should also be placed the phylacteries [i.e., *tefillin*] and *mezuzot* from Qumran; cf., e.g., J. T. Milik, "II. Tefillin, Mezuzot et Targums (4Q128–4Q157)," in Roland de Vaux and J. T. Milik, *Qumrân Grotte 4.II*, DJD 6 [Oxford: Clarendon, 1977], 33–89, esp. 48–85 and Plates VI–XXVII). See esp. Emanuel Tov, "Excerpted and Abbreviated Biblical Texts from Qumran," *RevQ* 16 (1995): 581–600; also note Sidnie White Crawford, "4QDtn: Biblical Manuscript or Excerpted Text?," in *Of Scribes and Scrolls: Studies on the Hebrew Bible, Intertestamental Judaism, and Christian Origins Presented to John Strugnell on the Occasion of His Sixtieth Birthday*, ed. H. W. Attridge, John J. Collins, and Thomas H. Tobin, College Theology Society Resources in Religion 5 (Lanham: University Press of America, 1990), 13–20; and Julie A. Duncan, "Excerpted Texts of *Deuteronomy* at Qumran," *RevQ* 18/69 (1997): 43–62. Julie A. Duncan ("Deuteronomy, Book of," *EDSS* 1:198–202, here 201) adds the important consideration: "In the phylacteries it was not considered necessary to write passages out in their entirety, whereas in the excerpted texts it is apparent, despite their fragmentary state, that the selections were written out fully and continuously. This difference probably reflects the more symbolic function of the phylacteries, as opposed to some more practical function of the excerpted scrolls as texts for study and/or for prayer services." Tov draws the further distinction between excerpted texts and rewritten Bible texts: "Excerpted texts should be regarded as biblical texts, excerpted for a special purpose, and presented without a commentary, while rewritten Bible texts, whose contents are often very close to what we are used to calling biblical manuscripts, do not pretend to present the text of the Bible," although Tov's final assertion is contestable. 4Q175 is the only "exegetical-ideological anthology" of strictly biblical passages listed by Tov, who suggests that most were for liturgical purposes or personal devotional reading ("Excerpted and Abbreviated Biblical Texts," 583; cf. 584–86, 598–99).

Paul and the Testimonia

ley,[35] elaborating a proposal by Dietrich-Alex Koch,[36] proposed that Paul, in the course of his personal reading of Scripture, would have taken notes and so formed a collection of *excerpta* for use in his mission and letter-writing. Stanley's description is worth quoting in full:

> This growing collection of biblical excerpts would then have become his primary resource for meditation and study in those times when he was traveling or staying in a private residence and had no immediate access to physical rolls of Scripture. When the time came to compose a letter to one of his churches, many of the points that he wishes to make would have been framed already around one of the excerpts contained in this by now well-worn and highly familiar anthology. While other verses not included in this collection may occasionally have found a place in one of his letters in the moment of composition, the great majority of Paul's quotations would have come directly from this Pauline anthology.[37]

In forming such a collection of notes, Paul would be conforming to a widespread practice in antiquity of making excerpts from one's reading[38]—a practice shared, the Qumran finds suggest, by other Jewish near-contemporaries.[39]

---

35. Christopher D. Stanley, *Paul and the Language of Scripture: Citation Technique in the Pauline Epistles and Contemporary Literature*, SNTSMS 74 (Cambridge: Cambridge University Press, 1992), 73–79.

36. "Paulus im Zuge seiner eigenen Schriftlektüre sich selbst geeignete Exzerpte von Schriftstellen angefertigt hat, auf die er dann bei der Abfassung der Briefe zurückgreifen konnte" (Koch, *Die Schrift als Zeuge des Evangeliums*, 253; cf. pp. 98–99).

37. Stanley, *Paul and the Language*, 74. Contra J. T. A. G. M. van Ruiten, review of *Paul and the Language of Scripture*, by Christopher D. Stanley, *JSJ* 25 (1994): 127, however, this is not to be construed as Stanley's "central thesis."

38. For analogues in the classical world, see H. Chadwick, "Florilegium," *RAC* 7:1131–60; Stanley, *Paul and the Language*, 73–78; Stanley, *Arguing with Scripture*, 43n15; Christopher D. Stanley, "The Importance of 4QTanhumim (4Q176)," *RevQ* 15 (1992): 569–82; Albl, "*And Scripture Cannot Be Broken*", 70–81. Stanley points especially to Xenophon, *Mem.* 1.6.14; Aristotle, *Top.* 1.14; Athenaeus, *Deipn.* 8.336d; Plutarch, *Mor.* 464F [in his *Paul and the Language*, this is given as *Peri Euthumias* 464F]; Cicero, *Inv.* 2.4; Pliny the Younger, *Ep.* 3.5, 6.20.5; Aulus Gellius, *Noct. att.* 17.21.1. For the continuation of the practice in the early Christian period, note esp. Robert Devreesse, "Chaînes exégétiques grecques," *DBSup* 1:1084–1233.

39. For an insightful overview of Jewish practice seen in light of the broader Greco-Roman environment, see Lutz Doering, "Excerpted Texts in Second Temple Judaism: A Survey of the Evidence," in *Selecta colligere, II: Beiträge zur Technik des Sammelns und Kompilierens griechischer Texte von der Antike bis zum Humanismus*, ed. Rosa Maria Piccione and

Chapter 2

Positing such a theory explains at least six types of difficulties, according to Stanley. (1) This would account for the evidence that Paul favored a written text.[40] (2) The physical availability of Scripture would have been limited in terms of both the prohibitive cost of scrolls and their large dimensions, so it is unlikely that Paul would have owned many such scrolls himself, if any at all.[41] It is no stretch of the imagination to think of Paul studying and taking notes during his visits to synagogues or fledgling churches that might have the benefit of a rich patron to provide them with a copy of (at least some of) the Scriptures.[42] (3) "The close integration of many of Paul's biblical citations into their present argumentative contexts becomes more comprehensible if the verses were selected from the start for their value in addressing a recurring problem than if they simply sprang to mind in the moment of composition."[43] (4) The diversity of text-types in his citations might be better explained if "Paul copied his excerpts from a variety of manuscripts housed at sites all around the eastern Mediterranean world, where he was a constant traveler."[44] (5) Moreover, "even the rather loose links between some of Paul's quotations and their original contexts might be due in part to his having copied them out of a personal anthology in which the only connection with the original passage is the one that appears in the mind of the compiler."[45] (6) Finally, perhaps even the intrusion of interpretative elements into the wording of his citations may have been a result of Paul's meditation on the verses contained in his anthology.[46]

PAUL AND THE *TESTIMONIA*: QUO VADAMUS?

A full adjudication of this theory is beyond the scope of this chapter. It is crucial to note, however, that the testimony hypothesis has been transformed into a significantly different excerpted text collection theory.[47] Both contain a

---

Matthias Perkams (Alessandria: Edizioni dell-Orso, 2005), 1–38; my thanks to the author for drawing this article to my attention.

40. Stanley, *Paul and the Language*, 69–71, 77.

41. Though Stanley does note the positions of Ellis and Michel (and, more hesitantly, Koch) that Paul may have owned scrolls (*Paul and the Language*, 73n27); cf. 2 Tim 4:13.

42. Stanley, *Paul and the Language*, 73n27.

43. Stanley, "The Importance of *4QTanḥumim*," 582; cf. Stanley, *Paul and the Language*, 73.

44. Stanley, *Paul and the Language*, 78. So also Lim, *Holy Scripture*, 149–60.

45. Stanley, "The Importance of *4QTanḥumim*," 582; cf. very similarly Stanley, *Paul and the Language*, 78.

46. Stanley, *Paul and the Language*, 78.

47. This is not to say that the testimony theory has been completely eradicated. For a

Paul and the Testimonia

common emphasis on texts isolated and removed from their original contexts, though, admittedly, more stress is placed on this in the former. Either form of the theory might—though strictly speaking need not—be seen to challenge the attempt to see Paul (or other authors) as engaged in some form of holistic scriptural exegesis or strategic reading. For if Paul primarily relied on either a traditional collection of excerpted citations or on his own anthology of notes culled from the Scriptures in lieu of direct engagement with the sacred text, perhaps to claim that Paul engaged with, say, Isaiah or with Deuteronomy as a book becomes less plausible.

Clearly, to deny that Paul incorporated traditional materials into his letters (e.g., 1 Cor 11:23–26; 15:3–5, etc.) can only have the effect of alienating and insulating Paul from the early Christian movement in a historically implausible manner. No doubt some of Paul's quotations of Scripture were traditional in nature (possibly Isa 28:16; 8:14 in Rom 9:33), but positing a primitive book or books of pre-Pauline *testimonia* insufficiently accounts for the manifold number and nature of Paul's scriptural engagements.[48] Likewise, in order to affirm Paul as a reader of Scripture it is not essential to deny that Paul used excerpt collections or notes of some kind; rather, it must simply be shown that Paul's engagement with Scripture in general, and any one book in particular, cannot be reduced to reliance upon such a collection, at least insofar as such reliance is correlated with an atomizing approach to textual interpretation.[49]

---

prime example applying the testimony theory to Paul, note Albl, *"And Scripture Cannot Be Broken"*, 159–79. Albl acknowledges Koch's and Stanley's theory but goes on in persisting with a more traditional notion of a loose collection of *testimonia* that Paul inherited and incorporated into his writings. To note only his conclusions most relevant to one book, Deuteronomy, he suggests (*"And Scripture Cannot Be Broken"*, 167–70) that Paul may have used *testimonia* for his citations of Deut 5:17–21 in Rom 13:8–10; Deut 19:15 in 2 Cor 13:1; and Deut 32 in both Rom 12:19 and 15:10. He says (*"And Scripture Cannot Be Broken"*, 178), "Jewish traditions have been incorporated into Paul's parenesis (Rom 12:19), his versions of the Decalogue (Rom 13:9–10), and his church orders (2 Cor 13:1)." Unfortunately, many of Albl's conclusions are simply asserted without any clear criteria to determine the presence of a testimony, so it is at times difficult to evaluate his judgments.

48. That the concept of traditional *testimonia* is useful in the study of the early Christian period is beyond doubt; here I simply claim that it is less helpful in studying the apostolic period that gave rise to the later *testimonia*.

49. Cf. the position of J. Ross Wagner, *Heralds of the Good News: Isaiah and Paul in Concert in the Letter to the Romans* (Leiden: Brill, 2002), 24: "I do not wish to deny that Paul may have had frequent recourse to written texts of scripture; neither do I dispute that the apostle may have compiled notebooks of scriptural excerpts, carried them along on his travels, and consulted them when composing his letters. However, the conclusion Stanley wishes to draw from all of this, that Paul knew Israel's scriptures *primarily* through

Chapter 2

Several factors suggest that such totalizing explanations (at least in the forms in which they are most often encountered)[50] for Paul's interpretative activity should be resisted and that Paul's encounter with Scripture would have been multifaceted. To proceed initially by way of engaging Stanley's six points enumerated above: First, it is unlikely that his numbers 3, 5, and 6 present issues that can be resolved exclusively by recourse to an *excerpta* collection theory; rather, each of these could also admit of various alternative explanations.[51] What is more, the diversity of text types in Paul's citations may well be less far-reaching than Stanley has asserted, as Ross Wagner has shown for Paul's reliance on Isaiah in an Alexandrian text type.[52] Further, the cost of papyrus rolls in antiquity, though certainly expensive to our typographic mindset, might not have been as prohibitive as is sometimes alleged—especially for a literate early Christian leader.[53] Finally, while some of the evidence for the use of written

---

the medium of written texts, simply does not follow." He goes on to argue: "Rather than posing the question in terms of mutually exclusive alternatives—*either* memorization *or* use of written texts and anthologies of excerpts—we should imagine Paul interacting with scripture in a variety of modes, including meditation on memorized passages, hearing of spoken texts, personal reading of written texts, and collection of and reflection on excerpts from larger texts. Such a multi-faceted approach . . . is absolutely necessary to capture the complex reality of books and readers in the first century" (25–26). This is precisely the position of the present chapter.

50. It is instructive to note the escalation inherent in the long quotation from Stanley adduced above: rather than Paul occasionally taking notes on his reading, the collection becomes the "primary resource" for meditation while traveling, and "the great majority" of Paul's quotations would have derived from this collection.

51. For example, his (3) presents something of a false dichotomy: either the texts were included beforehand in an *excerpta* collection *or* they "sprang to mind in the moment of composition." Rather, the texts may have been selected beforehand without thereby being completely removed from their original context or sequestered in a collection of notes. Stanley's (5) is certainly possible, but common experience suggests that one may disagree with an interpretation that someone offers of a text read in its context just as readily as one removed from its context. What is more, the degree to which Paul's citations are discordant with their original context is, of course, a matter of debate. Finally, his (6) is admittedly put forth with some hesitation, and it is unclear why such intrusions should necessitate an *excerpta* collection (though on the broader question of Paul's alterations to his quotations the rest of Stanley's book is the best treatment to date).

52. Wagner, *Heralds*, 24n86 and passim.

53. Cf. Naphtali Lewis, *Papyrus in Classical Antiquity* (Oxford: Clarendon, 1974), 133–34; Naphtali Lewis, *Papyrus in Classical Antiquity: A Supplement*, Papyrologica Bruxellensia 23 (Bruxelles: Fondation Égyptologique Reine Élisabeth, 1989), 40–41; T. C. Skeat, "Was Papyrus Regarded as 'Cheap' or 'Expensive' in the Ancient World?," in *The Collected Biblical Writings of T. C. Skeat*, ed. J. K. Elliott, NovTSup 113 (Leiden: Brill, 2004), 88–105. The evi-

Paul and the Testimonia

texts remains, in part this may be explained with an equal degree of satisfaction by consideration of quotation from memory—especially if this is allowed to do more work than serve as a convenient scapegoat for textual difficulties (the more appropriately named "memory-lapse" quotation theory).[54]

Indeed, this last point enables us to proceed beyond Stanley's formulations and indicate further some potential historical *loci* for Paul's scriptural encounters alternative to the *excerpta* or *testimonia* hypotheses, areas in which further research will be needed to carry the discussion forward. It seems to me that at least three types of consideration provide a way beyond the impasse: study of ancient memory capacity and practices, of the liturgical *Sitz im Leben* of encountering Scripture, and of broader literary indications of Paul's contextual reading strategies. The last of these points has been pursued more systematically in recent years, thanks in part to the influence of Richard Hays's seminal work *Echoes of Scripture in the Letters of Paul*,[55] so less space needs to be devoted to it here. The chief aspect of such work to note in connection with the issue at hand is that the more convincing such readings may be shown to be, the less likelihood there is that Paul was solely reliant on a collection of *excerpta*.[56]

---

dence from the Dead Sea Scrolls suggests that scriptural manuscripts were not yet confined to parchment, as later rabbinic halakah mandated (on which, see C. Sirat, "Le livre hébreu dans les premiers siècles de notres ère: Le témoignage des textes," in *Les débuts du codex*, ed. A. Blanchard, Bibliologia 9 [Brepols: Turnhout, 1989], 115–24). Further, Catherine Hezser suggests that in the Second Temple and the Tannaitic periods, "Rabbis and their students are the most likely candidates with regard to private ownership of Torah scrolls, since Torah study was essential for them" (*Jewish Literacy in Roman Palestine*, TSAJ 81 [Tübingen: Mohr Siebeck, 2001], 147). Although she cautions against assuming that all students of rabbis owned scrolls and may have an inflated view of the prohibitive cost of individual rolls, it is striking that her suggestion indicates the social space in which Paul may have come to ownership of at least some scrolls (even if the office of "rabbi" had not yet been formalized). Hezser also points to evidence in the Talmud Yerušalmi of a distinction between privately and publicly owned scrolls (y. Ned. 5.5–6, 39a).

54. Stanley in part acknowledges this, but neglects to take it into full consideration (*Paul and the Language*, 17, and 17n49 citing Ellis, *Paul's Use*, 14).

55. Richard B. Hays, *Echoes of Scripture in the Letters of Paul* (New Haven: Yale University Press, 1989). For some indication of the influence of Hays's work, see Kenneth D. Litwak, "Echoes of Scripture? A Critical Survey of Recent Works on Paul's Use of the Old Testament," *CurBS* 6 (1998): 260–88.

56. It is, of course, possible to construe such *excerpta* as simply providing the written records of Paul's own (sometimes) contextual reading of large sections of Scripture, but to construe them in this way effectively denies the force of at least some of the evidence from which they have been posited (e.g., the tenuous nature of a quotation's relation to its original context), and so renders the theory at once slightly more speculative and less objectionable.

Chapter 2

The other two areas, however, have received considerably less attention in recent scholarly discussion. Perhaps understandably, the appeal to memory has loomed larger in the study of the Gospels than in Paul.[57] Nevertheless, as indicated briefly above, there is a notable space within which memory could function in the study of Paul's recourse to Scripture. Given the fact that the "cognitive cultures" of antiquity were far more imbued with a sense of the interpenetration of the oral and the written than we are today,[58] to think of Paul committing long stretches of text to memory is not beyond the pale of the imagination. The evidence for surprising feats of memory among both Greco-Roman philosophers and *literati* and among Jewish rabbis has often been set forth, and we need not rehearse it here.[59] To consider the accounts of his upbringing found both in the Acts of the Apostles and in his own letters

---

57. E.g., Birger Gerhardsson, *Memory and Manuscript: Oral Tradition and Written Transmission in Rabbinic Judaism and Early Christianity with Tradition and Transmission in Early Christianity*, Biblical Resource Series (Grand Rapids: Eerdmans, 1998); Samuel Byrskog, *Story as History—History as Story: The Gospel Tradition in the Context of Ancient Oral History*, WUNT 123 (Tübingen: Mohr Siebeck, 2000); and James D. G. Dunn, *Christianity in the Making*, vol. 1, *Jesus Remembered* (Grand Rapids: Eerdmans, 2003), on whose use of the concept of memory, however, see Markus Bockmuehl, Review of *Jesus Remembered*, by James D. G. Dunn, *JTS* n.s. 56 (2005): 140–49; and Richard Bauckham, *Jesus and the Eyewitnesses: The Gospels as Eyewitness Testimony*, 2nd ed. (Grand Rapids: Eerdmans, 2017). While these studies are chiefly concerned with the role of memory and eyewitness testimony in the preservation and eventual recording of the oral tradition about Jesus, attention has also been drawn to the function of memory *of other texts* in the composition of ancient works, including the Synoptic Gospels; see esp. R. A. Derrenbacker Jr., *Ancient Compositional Practices and the Synoptic Problem*, BETL 186 (Leuven: Leuven University Press, 2005), 1–49; more broadly, see Jocelyn Penny Small, *Wax Tablets of the Mind: Cognitive Studies of Memory and Literacy in Classical Antiquity* (New York: Routledge, 1997) (on which, however, note the critical remarks of Nicholas Horsfall, "Methods of Writing, Memorisation, and Research," *JRA* 11 [1998]: 565–71).

58. Cf. Paul J. Achtemeier, "*Omne Verbum Sonat*: The New Testament and the Oral Environment of Late Western Antiquity," *JBL* 109 (1990): 3–27; Shemaryahu Talmon, "Oral Tradition and Written Transmission, or the Heard and the Seen Word in Judaism of the Second Temple Period," in *Jesus and the Oral Gospel Tradition*, ed. Henry Wansbrough, JSNTSup 64 (Sheffield: Sheffield Academic, 1991), 121–58; Alan K. Bowman, "Literacy in the Roman Empire: Mass and Mode," in *Literacy in the Roman World*, ed. J. H. Humphrey, Journal of Roman Archaeology Supplementary Series 3 (Ann Arbor: University of Michigan, 1991), 119–31; and Thomas E. Boomershine, "Jesus of Nazareth and the Watershed of Ancient Orality and Literacy," *Sem* 65 (1994): 7–36. This interpenetration of orality and literacy is arguably not sufficiently accounted for in Stanley, *Arguing with Scripture*; see esp. Brian J. Abasciano, "Diamonds in the Rough: A Reply to Christopher Stanley Concerning the Reader Competency of Paul's Original Audiences," *NovT* 49 (2007): 153–83, although Abasciano overstates his case in my view.

59. See, e.g., Small, *Wax Tablets*; and Gerhardsson, *Memory*, respectively.

Paul and the Testimonia

means that we must take seriously the possibility that Paul learned such texts as part of his education.[60]

The likelihood that Paul knew at least some parts of Scripture by heart is increased when we consider the third area, that of liturgy. Liturgical practice is surely anamnetic in its very essence, remembering the deeds of God by the mediation of the sacred text read aloud and received in hearing. The early synagogue, then, provides at least one more plausible *Sitz im Leben* for considering how Paul might have ingested large blocks of biblical text. Perhaps some have been wary of affirming this because of the excesses of overzealous attempts to link the Gospels to Jewish lectionaries in the previous generations. While it is true, however, that our knowledge of the lectionary cycle of first-century Palestine is hazy, the fact that at least the Torah was read in contiguous portions in sequential meetings seems beyond doubt. Greater acknowledgment of such practice could go some way toward explaining the widespread popularity texts like Genesis and Deuteronomy enjoyed in the Second Temple period.[61] The apostle Paul, after all, did not occupy an endowed chair of biblical studies in the proverbial academy of the ivory tower. Ultimately, of course, this historical evidence will need to be judged alongside the strength of the readings of Paul's citations of and engagements with Scripture that scholars offer: as the venerable axiom has it, the proof of the pudding is in the eating. This brief chapter has been able to do no more than to point out some of the possible ways forward. Nevertheless, that the apostle Paul's encounter with Scripture need not be seen primarily in terms of a written collection of pre-Pauline *testimonia* or his own set of excerpted notes has much to commend it; that there is more to grasp in Paul's reading of Scripture than we have yet accomplished is beyond doubt.

---

60. Cf. Joseph Bonsirven, *Exégèse rabbinique et exégèse paulinienne* (Paris: Beauchesne et ses Fils, 1939), 292: "Nous nous contenterons d'une remarque obvie: un juif, sachant par cœur de longs passages des Écritures, les redisant et les méditant, avait-il besoin de recourir à des recueils méthodiques?" Also, Wagner has suggested that Paul may have had the book of Isaiah memorized (*Heralds*, 22–27).

61. Sidnie White Crawford, "Reading Deuteronomy in the Second Temple Period," in *Reading the Present in the Qumran Library: The Perception of the Contemporary by Means of Scriptural Interpretations*, ed. Kristin de Troyer and Armin Lange, SBLSymS 30 (Atlanta: Society of Biblical Literature, 2005), 127–40; and Lincicum, *Paul and the Early Jewish Encounter with Deuteronomy*.

3

INTERTEXTUALITY, EFFECTIVE HISTORY, AND MEMORY

Conceptualizing Paul's Use of Scripture

In this chapter, I address ways of analyzing and evaluating Pauline scriptural references. The chapter proceeds by noting four major clusters of questions that have dominated scholarly attention—particularly, though not exclusively, in Anglophone scholarship. While acknowledging the major intellectual contributions by a distinguished series of scholars for each set of questions, under each heading I note some questions arising from current methodological discussions. In the end, studies of Pauline scriptural practices are arguably still overly textual in their orientation and should strive to incorporate insights from effective history and memory studies as a means of treating Paul's scriptural engagement more adequately.

We turn now to current approaches to Paul and Scripture.[1] While any typology of approaches will be of necessity reductive, it may be heuristically useful to consider in turn approaches that center on (1) quotations, (2) allusions or echoes, (3) narrative, and (4) rhetorical effects.[2] It is an artificial separation among these four approaches, and individual studies will often transgress from

---

1. For some account of approaches to the topic, see chapter 5, and the literature there cited. More recently, see J. Ross Wagner, "Paul and Scripture," in *The Blackwell Companion to Paul*, ed. Stephen Westerholm (Malden, MA: Blackwell, 2011), 154–71; Christopher D. Stanley, "What We Learned—and What We Didn't," in *Paul and Scripture: Extending the Conversation*, ed. Christopher D. Stanley (Atlanta: Society of Biblical Literature, 2012), 321–30; with Christopher D. Stanley, "Paul and Scripture: Charting the Course," in *As It Is Written: Studying Paul's Use of Scripture*, ed. Stanley E. Porter and Christopher D. Stanley, SBLSymS 50 (Atlanta: Society of Biblical Literature, 2008), 3–12.

2. I do not here intend to enter the debate concerning how Paul's textual engagements should be classified or characterized; for an orientation to this literature, see Stanley E. Porter, "Pauline Techniques of Interweaving Scripture into His Letters," in *Paulinische Schriftrezeption: Grundlagen—Ausprägungen—Wirkungen—Wertungen*, ed. Florian Wilk and Markus Öhler, FRLANT 268 (Göttingen: Vandenhoeck & Ruprecht, 2017), 23–55. Rather, this contribution attends to the questions posed to the Pauline texts and the methodological sensibilities such questions entail or produce.

Intertextuality, Effective History, and Memory

one to another or fall outside this design entirely,[3] but this way of dividing the field provides a heuristic that is useful for bringing divergent approaches into focus. The methodological focus here precludes, on the whole, sustained discussion of particular texts.

QUOTATIONS

Since the early years of critical biblical scholarship, when scholars first turned their attention to how the authors of the New Testament drew on Scripture, questions have arisen concerning the form of Paul's citations, his *Vorlage*, citation technique, accuracy, and the comparability of his practices with other authors of his day. These questions are necessarily bound up with studies of the apostle's education and background, and his means of accessing the scriptural text. Among our four poles of inquiry, the questions involved in the investigation of Paul's quotations have remained the most remarkably consistent over the past two centuries, consonant with the important role author-centered approaches have assumed in biblical studies more broadly, though the answers to these questions have been refined as each generation reappraises the issues for themselves. It is now four decades since the study of Paul and Scripture was put on entirely new footing with the publication of Dietrich-Alex Koch's groundbreaking monograph *Die Schrift als Zeuge des Evangeliums*.[4] This wide-ranging monograph took into account significant developments in the study of the LXX. By so doing, in addition to anticipating the currently flowering collaboration between LXX and New Testament scholars, he supplied an authoritative analysis of Paul's scriptural *Vorlagen*, his citation techniques and hermeneutical practices. While subsequent studies have occasionally corrected or supplemented Koch in matters of detail—one thinks particularly of Stanley's study of Paul's citation practices[5]—Koch's study remains one of the most significant attempts to grapple with Paul's practices with regard to his ancestral Scripture at the holistic level, and still repays close attention today. That Paul's citations for the most part evince a reliance on a Septuagintal text that has

3. Note the subtitle of Stanley, *Paul and Scripture: Extending the Conversation*.

4. See Dietrich-Alex Koch, *Die Schrift als Zeuge des Evangeliums: Untersuchungen zur Verwendung und zum Verständnis der Schrift bei Paulus*, BHT 69 (Tübingen: Mohr Siebeck, 1986).

5. See esp. Christopher D. Stanley, *Paul and the Language of Scripture: Citation Technique in the Pauline Epistles and Contemporary Literature*, SNTSMS 74 (Cambridge: Cambridge University Press, 1992).

Chapter 3

been partially revised toward the Hebrew and that Paul has exercised some limited freedom in his reproduction of his *Vorlage* are now well-established positions. Increasing attention is paid not simply to individual citations but to Paul's engagement with discrete books of Scripture—and in particular, Isaiah, Psalms, Genesis, and Deuteronomy.[6] This work tends to be taken for granted by subsequent approaches, as a basic datum.

While it may seem as though there is little new to say, in methodological terms, about such well-researched questions, further attention to the role of memory in mediating Paul's scriptural knowledge may be beneficial in considering his quotations. Those who work on the reception of Scripture in the New Testament have consigned memory to a curious fate when it comes to explicit quotations: on the one hand, the ancients are lauded for their prodigious feats of memory, and a supposed culture of memory is used to guarantee the accuracy of reproduction of textual *Vorlagen* in citing *memoriter*. On the other

---

6. Note the relevant chapters in Steve Moyise and Maarten J. J. Menken, eds., *Psalms in the New Testament*, NTSI (London: T&T Clark, 2004); Steve Moyise and Maarten J. J. Menken, eds., *Isaiah in the New Testament*, NTSI (London: T&T Clark, 2005); Steve Moyise and Maarten J. J. Menken, eds., *Deuteronomy in the New Testament*, LNTS 358 (London: T&T Clark, 2007); and Steve Moyise and Maarten J. J. Menken, eds., *Genesis in the New Testament*, LNTS 466 (London: T&T Clark, 2012). In addition, for Isaiah see esp. Florian Wilk, *Die Bedeutung des Jesajabuches für Paulus*, FRLANT 179 (Göttingen: Vandenhoeck & Ruprecht, 1998); Florian Wilk, "Paulus als Interpret der prophetischen Schriften," *KD* 45 (1999): 284–306; Florian Wilk, "Isaiah in 1 and 2 Corinthians," in Moyise and Menken, *Isaiah in the New Testament*, 133–158; Florian Wilk, "Between Scripture and History: Technique and Hermeneutics of Interpreting Biblical Prophets in the Septuagint of Isaiah and the Letters of Paul," in *The Old Greek of Isaiah: Issues and Perspectives*, ed. Arie van der Kooij and Michaël N. van der Meer, CBET 55 (Leuven: Peeters, 2010), 189–209; J. Ross Wagner, *Heralds of the Good News: Isaiah and Paul in Concert in the Letter to the Romans* (Leiden: Brill, 2002); J. Ross Wagner, "Isaiah in Romans and Galatians," in Moyise and Menken, *Isaiah in the New Testament*, 119–32; and J. Ross Wagner, "Moses and Isaiah in Concert: Paul's Reading of Isaiah and Deuteronomy in the Letter to the Romans," in *"As Those Who Are Taught": The Interpretation of Isaiah from the LXX to the SBL*, ed. Claire Matthews McGinnis and Patricia K. Tull (Atlanta: Society of Biblical Literature, 2006), 87–105. For Psalms, see Otfried Hofius, "Der Psalter als Zeuge des Evangeliums: Die Verwendung der Septuaginta-Psalmen in den ersten beiden Hauptteilen des Römerbriefes," in *Paulusstudien II*, WUNT 143 (Tübingen: Mohr Siebeck, 2002), 38–57; Moises Silva, "The Greek Psalter in Paul's Letters: A Textual Study," in *The Old Greek Psalter: Studies in Honour of Albert Pietersma*, ed. Robert J. V. Hiebert, Claude E. Cox, and Peter J. Gentry, JSOTSup 332 (Sheffield: Sheffield Academic, 2001), 277–88. For Deuteronomy, see Guy P. Waters, *The End of Deuteronomy in the Epistles of Paul*, WUNT 2/221 (Tübingen: Mohr Siebeck, 2006); and David Lincicum, *Paul and the Early Jewish Encounter with Deuteronomy*, WUNT 2/284 (Tübingen: Mohr Siebeck, 2010; repr. Grand Rapids: Baker Academic, 2013). For Genesis, see chapter 4.

Intertextuality, Effective History, and Memory

hand, we find an unwillingness to ascribe variation from textual predecessors to the role of memory. Although it is with reference to the Fourth Gospel, Maarten Menken would speak for many Pauline scholars when complaining about "unverifiable factors such as the freedom or the defective memory of the evangelist."[7] Similarly, Thorsten Moritz suggests that "the 'mnemonic apology' for textual deviations can be no more than a last resort."[8] On the other side, Geoffrey Turner suggests that a textual variation must be ascribed to "false memory" or a "faulty memory," rather than seeing such variations as simply characteristic indicators of memorial retrieval.[9]

In light of the broader turn to memory in the humanities, however, it may well be worth revisiting the question of the textual form of some of Paul's citations in light of the way in which recent work has focused on recollection and retrieval as active processes of the mind. Discussions of memory, bound up with questions of tradition as they are, have been much more at home in the study of the Hebrew Bible or the historical Jesus than in discussion of Paul, for obvious reasons. But there are insights from recent work on memory in both the Hebrew Bible and the Jesus tradition that would arguably benefit the discussion of Paul and Scripture.[10] At times one must translate this from the language of "oral variation" to "memory variation," since orality is only necessary when considering the intersubjective traditioning process (or the transmission of manuscripts at multiple stages of removal). At a more local and circumscribed level, the same types of memory variant may be at work in the move from Paul's *Vorlage* to his own compositions, a move facilitated (by necessity) through Paul's act of recollection and reproduction.

Thus, when Stanley comes, at the conclusion to his admirable study on *Paul and the Language of Scripture*,[11] to summarize the types of intentional grammatical adaptations Paul makes to his citations, he mentions changes in

---

7. Maarten J. J. Menken, *Old Testament Quotations in the Fourth Gospel: Studies in Textual Form*, CBET 15 (Leuven: Peeters, 1996), 13; cf. 14, 207. Also note the criticism of appeal to memory in Stanley, *Paul and the Language*, 16–17.

8. Thorsten Moritz, *A Profound Mystery: The Use of the Old Testament in Ephesians*, NovTSup 85 (Leiden: Brill, 1996), 7n23.

9. Geoffrey Turner, "The Righteousness of God in Psalms and Romans," *SJT* 63 (2010): 285–301, here 288 and 287 respectively.

10. In what follows, I call attention to work in the Hebrew Bible, but for memory in the Jesus tradition, important work has been done by scholars such as Dale Allison, Anthony Le Donne, Chris Keith, Rafael Rodriguez, Jens Schröter, and Tom Thatcher, inter alia.

11. Stanley, *Paul and the Language*, 260–61.

Chapter 3

word order,[12] alterations in grammar (person, number, gender, case, tense, mood),[13] omissions (words, phrases, clauses, etc.),[14] additions to the text,[15] substitutions (words, phrases, clauses, etc.),[16] and limited selection.[17] If we compare this with David Carr's summary of the types of changes characteristic of "memory variants" in the Hebrew Bible, the overlap is striking. Carr writes, "Though some variations in parallel lines or sayings may be the result of error or intertextual dialogue, we have seen a preponderance of exactly the sorts of variation that scholars in non-religious disciplines have explained as the result of recall of memorized texts: exchange of synonymous words, word order variation, presence and absence of conjunctions and minor modifiers, etc."[18]

The *comparanda* to which Carr and others have pointed should offer some control on what has often been perceived to be mere speculation in the appeal to memory.[19] To my knowledge we are still lacking a comprehensive evaluation of the effects of memory on Pauline citations, and this remains a desideratum. Such an undertaking would need to take its bearings from the work of memory theorists, including cognitive studies of memory,[20] and reconsider the variations analyzed to such good effect by Koch and Stanley in order to ascertain whether memorial interference might well be a more significant contributing factor than has hitherto been appreciated.

---

12. Citing Rom 2:24; 3:14 (bis), 15; 9:15, 25; 10:21; 11:3, 8; 14:11; 15:11; 1 Cor 1:31; 15:55; 2 Cor 6:17; 8:15; 10:17; Gal 3:6.

13. Cf. Rom 3:14, 18; 9:25 (bis); 10:5, 15, 19; 11:8; 1 Cor 14:21; 15:27; 2 Cor 6:16 (bis), 18 (bis); Gal 3:10, 12.

14. Cf. Rom 1:17; 3:10, 14, 15 (ter); 9:9, 13, 17, 25 (bis), 27, 33; 10:6–7, 15, 19; 11:3 (ter), 4, 8 (ter), 26; 13:9a; 15:3, 9, 12, 21; 1 Cor 1:19; 14:21; 15:45; 2 Cor 6:16 (ter); 10:17; Gal 3:6, 8 (bis), 10 (bis), 12, 13 (bis); 4:30.

15. Cf. Rom 3:11 (bis); 9:25 (bis); 10:11, 15; 11:8; 12:19; 1 Cor 14:21; 15:45; 2 Cor 6:18.

16. Cf. Rom 2:24; 3:10 (bis), 11; 9:9, 25, 27, 28; 10:7; 14:11; 1 Cor 1:19, 31; 3:20; 14:21; 15:27, 55 (bis); 2 Cor 6:16; 10:17; Gal 3:8, 13; 4:30.

17. Cf. Rom 3:4, 10, 11, 18; 4:8; 9:33; 10:6–8; 15:21; 2 Cor 8:15.

18. David M. Carr, *The Formation of the Hebrew Bible: A New Reconstruction* (Oxford: Oxford University Press, 2011), 33; cf. 13–36. I am grateful to Timothy Michael Law for suggesting Carr's book in this connection.

19. See also Leonard Greenspoon, "By the Letter? Word for Word? Scriptural Citation in Paul," in Stanley, *Paul and Scripture*, 9–24, who emphasizes a multifaceted approach to Paul's encounter with Scripture, including a robust knowledge of the text itself in memory and written *aides memoires*. But he stops short of suggesting that some of the basic patterns of deviation from known *Vorlagen* in the Pauline citations may be due to memory citation.

20. Compare the application of cognitive memory theory in Jocelyn Penny Small, *Wax Tablets of the Mind: Cognitive Studies of Memory and Literacy in Classical Antiquity* (London: Routledge, 1997).

Intertextuality, Effective History, and Memory

ALLUSIONS OR ECHOES

Just a few years after Koch's work, Hays published his justly famous *Echoes of Scripture in the Letters of Paul*.[21] If Koch had taken up traditional concerns in Pauline scholarship—*Vorlage*, citation technique, introductory formulae, contemporary analogues, and so forth—and treated them in a more exhaustive form than previously, Hays introduced an alternative set of sensibilities. Influenced particularly by John Hollander's work on the figure of echo, Hays treated Paul's citations and allusions to Scripture as "hermeneutical events" and so transposed some of the traditional questions about Paul and Scripture into a more literary-theological key. By paying attention to the way in which even subtle allusions to Scripture might trail with them soundings of their original scriptural context, Hays presented Paul as a sophisticated reader, and his letters as repaying the careful attention of the literary imagination.

Since the publication of *Echoes*, intertextuality has been one of the dominant modi operandi in the study of Paul's use of Scripture. At times, intertextuality has been conceived as merely a "sensibility"; this is how Hays himself seems to understand the term, and he later avows that "nothing is at stake for me in the use of the term."[22] Others, however, use the term to denote a method, one that takes as its focus a literary analysis of how two texts—usually, in Pauline studies, a predecessor scriptural text and a Pauline authorial text—interact.[23] Yet others point to the term's theoretical origins in the work of Julia Kristeva (or sometimes, Mikhail Bakhtin). As has often been discussed, the term intertextuality (*intertextualité*) was apparently first coined by Kristeva,[24]

---

21. See Richard B. Hays, *Echoes of Scripture in the Letters of Paul* (New Haven: Yale University Press, 1989).

22. Richard B. Hays, "On the Rebound: A Response to Critiques of *Echoes of Scripture in the Letters of Paul*," in *The Conversion of the Imagination: Paul as Interpreter of Israel's Scripture* (Grand Rapids: Eerdmans, 2005), 163–89, here 174.

23. Note the complaints about the "domesticating capacity" of the biblical studies guild, with particular reference to intertextuality, in Stephen D. Moore and Yvonne Sherwood, *The Invention of the Biblical Scholar: A Critical Manifesto* (Minneapolis: Fortress, 2011), 33–37.

24. See Julia Kristeva, "Le mot, le dialogue et le roman," in *Sēmeiōtikē: Recherches pour une Sémanalyse* (Paris: Éditions du Seuil, 1969), 143–73; ET in *Desire in Language: A Semiotic Approach to Literature and Art*, ed. Leon S. Roudiez (Oxford: Basil Blackwell, 1980), 64–91; and *The Kristeva Reader*, ed. Toril Moi (Oxford: Basil Blackwell, 1986), 34–61, cf. 90–136. Cf. also Julia Kristeva, *La révolution du langage poétique* (Paris: Éditions du Seuil, 1974), 57–61; and partial ET in *Revolution in Poetic Language*, trans. Margaret Waller (New York: Columbia University Press, 1984), 57–62, and (extracts) in Moi, *Kristeva Reader*, 90–136, here 109–12.

Chapter 3

before being developed by Roland Barthes and Harold Bloom, among many others. Intertextuality, at least in its most theorized versions, is not so much a theory of literary influence as it is a theory of the semiotic construction of all our perceptions of reality—and to claim that the genealogical pedigree of "intertextuality" has no bearing on its subsequent meaning is surely not without irony.[25] In this vein, Kristeva complains in her later writing that intertextuality "has often been understood in the banal sense of 'study of sources,'"[26] though it is equally ironic to see Kristeva attempt to control the use of a term like intertextuality. It is admittedly most often employed in Pauline studies in this latter, more "banal sense,"[27] but even in this under-theorized form it can tend toward an abstraction from history.

The use of the term "intertextuality" has been subjected to repeated critical scrutiny in biblical studies, and to do so again in this chapter is not my task.[28] It has come to function as a convenient shorthand for the analytic description of the

25. Note the remarks in Jonathan Culler, *The Pursuit of Signs: Semiotics, Literature, Deconstruction* (London: Routledge, 1981), 100–118, on the plasticity of the term. In further critique, note William Irwin, "Against Intertextuality," *Philosophy and Literature* 28 (2004): 227–42, and within biblical studies, Christopher M. Tuckett, "Scripture and Q," in *The Scriptures in the Gospels*, ed. Christopher M. Tuckett, BETL (Leuven: Leuven University Press, 1997), 3–26; Martin Rese, "Intertextualität: Ein Beispiel für Sinn und Unsinn 'neuer' Methoden," in Tuckett, *Scriptures in the Gospels*, 431–39 (though he arguably overstates the atomistic nature of early Christian exegesis); and Thomas R. Hatina, "Intertextuality and Historical Criticism in New Testament Studies: Is There a Relationship?," *BibInt* 7 (1999): 28–43.

26. Kristeva, "Revolution in Poetic Language," in Moi, *Kristeva Reader*, 111.

27. For example, Timothy W. Berkley, *From a Broken Covenant to Circumcision of the Heart: Pauline Intertextual Exegesis in Romans 2:17–29*, SBLDS 175 (Atlanta: Society of Biblical Literature, 2000), recognizes the tension in appealing to intertextuality in a historical study, but persists in adopting a position like that of Hays, which he calls a "minimalist intertextuality" (48–49).

28. In addition to the literature mentioned in note 25 above, cf. Steve Moyise, "Intertextuality and Historical Approaches to the Use of Scripture in the New Testament," in *Reading the Bible Intertextually*, ed. Stefan Alkier, Richard B. Hays, and Leroy A. Huizenga (Waco: Baylor University Press, 2009), 23–33; and John Barton, "Déjà Lu: Intertextuality, Method or Theory?," in *Reading Job Intertextually*, ed. Katharine Dell and Will Kynes, LHBOTS (London: T&T Clark, 2013), 1–16. The latter has argued that "intertextuality as a theory, along with other products of postmodernist thought, is highly challenging to any idea of the fixity, canonicity, and inspiration of the biblical text. In the biblical 'guild' we should face up to that, either accepting it or contesting it, rather than seeing it as one more handy tool to put in our exegetical kit" (16). Stefan Alkier, however, offers a reasoned argument for including intertextuality as a broader semiotic approach to textual meaning in his "Intertextuality and the Semiotics of Biblical Texts," in Alkier, Hays, and Huizenga, *Reading the Bible Intertextually*, 1–22.

Intertextuality, Effective History, and Memory

interplay of two texts, normally understood in diachronic terms.[29] Work done in this vein, following the lead of Hays, has been tremendously helpful, not least in sensitizing us to the subtle and productive lines of influence and interpretative possibilities that come to light when reading the Pauline letters closely with Israel's Scripture. Particularly when grounded in solid textual comparisons and sophisticated narrative sensibilities, as in J. Ross Wagner's magisterial work on Isaiah in Romans, such approaches have shed important light on Pauline theology.

Not all who appeal to intertextuality, however, are of the same intellectual or literary sophistication as Hays and Wagner, and one may sense a certain depreciation of the approach as it comes into lesser hands. By approaching Paul's encounter with Scripture as the interplay of two texts, one is sometimes presented with a Paul who bears a strange resemblance to his intertextual critics, engaged in a virginal act of interpretation apart from the pesky prejudices of corporeality and temporality as a first-century Jew. One may also sense a kind of interpretative exhaustion as the quest for fainter and fainter echoes of Scripture in Paul's letters is met with diminishing returns. Intertextual interpretation of Paul and Scripture has yielded unmeasured gains in our recovery of Paul as a thoughtful appropriator of Israel's sacred texts, but such an approach deserves to be supplemented by more historical considerations. In this context, approaching Paul from the horizon of Scripture's broader effective history[30] may go some way toward redressing the imbalance

---

29. Matthew W. Bates's term "diachronic intertextuality" is potentially confusing, since many scholars intend by using the term "diachronic" to indicate precisely that which he is critiquing, although his broader proposal is interesting; see Matthew W. Bates, "Beyond Hays's *Echoes of Scripture in the Letters of Paul*: A Proposed Diachronic Intertextuality with Romans 10:16 as a Test Case," in Stanley, *Paul and Scripture*, 263–92.

30. On "effective history" (*Wirkungsgeschichte*) note, e.g., Ulrich Luz, "Wirkungsgeschichtliche Exegese: Ein programmatischer Arbeitsbericht mit Beispielen aus der Bergpredigtexegese," *BTZ* 2 (1985): 18–32; Ulrich Luz, *Matthew in History: Interpretation, Influence, Effects* (Minneapolis: Fortress, 1994); Heikki Räisänen, "The 'Effective History' of the Bible: A Challenge to Biblical Scholarship," *SJT* 45 (1992): 303–24; Markus Bockmuehl, "A Commentator's Approach to the 'Effective History' of Philippians," *JSNT* 60 (1995): 57–88, esp. 57–63; Joachim Gnilka, "Zur Interpretation der Bibel: Die Wirkungsgeschichte," in *The Interpretation of the Bible: The International Symposium in Slovenia*, ed. Joze Krašovec, JSOTSup 289 (Sheffield: Sheffield Academic, 1998), 1589–1601; Rachel Nicholls, *Walking on Water: Reading Mt. 14:22–33 in the Light of Its Wirkungsgeschichte* (Leiden: Brill, 2008); and Robert Evans, *Reception History, Tradition and Biblical Interpretation: Gadamer and Jauss in Current Practice* (London: T&T Clark, 2014), etc. All of this work is ultimately indebted to Hans-Georg Gadamer; see, e.g., *Truth and Method*, 2nd ed., trans. Joel Weinsheimer and Donald G. Marshall (London: Continuum, 1989), 277–307; and Hans-Georg Gadamer, "Classical and Philosophical Hermeneutics," *Theory, Culture and Society* 23 (2006): 29–56.

Chapter 3

in intertextual presentations of the apostle and answering the question of how certain books or portions of Scripture as a whole are (or are not) perceived and (re)appropriated.[31]

We have witnessed the institutionalization of reception history in biblical studies, with the recent creation of a large encyclopedia, at least two journals, several monograph series and commentary series, and a chair in reception history at the University of Groningen. A reception-historical approach chiefly considers the afterlife of a text through time, beginning from the horizon of the source text and considering the hermeneutical force it gathers through the repeated processes of reception, interpretation, and reinterpretation, in formal and informal ways. There can be no question of an absolute or fundamental contrast between these approaches, but the differences in emphasis are significant. Where intertextuality tends to approach the issue from Paul's stance as an interpreter, an effective-historical approach may consider Paul as one instantiation of a scriptural text's broader effects, and so restore a sense of the productive temporal and historical distance between Paul and Scripture. For example, I have elsewhere argued that the phenomenon of the liturgical reading of, say, Deuteronomy must have created a hermeneutical space in which Pauline reception would have taken place.[32] Paul is certainly no *tabula rasa*, and by taking a broader view of the phenomenon of reception than intertextuality normally allows, we will be in a better position to assess both Paul's traditionalism and his novelty.

Narrative

Naturally, not all post-Hays work fits neatly beneath the banner of intertextuality. Indeed some recent work insists on the importance of narrative dynamics in Paul's engagement with Scripture, while other studies investigate the rhetorical function of quotations, including questions of audience competence.[33] The latter will be discussed below, but among the former approaches, one thinks

---

31. This paragraph and the preceding two are adapted, in part, from my remarks in *Paul and the Early Jewish Encounter*, 9–10.

32. See Lincicum, "The Liturgical Deuteronomy in the Second Temple Period," in *Paul and the Early Jewish Encounter*, chapter 2.

33. For the former, for all their differences, see N. T. Wright, *Paul and the Faithfulness of God* (London: SPCK, 2013), 1449–72 (summarizing his previous work); and Francis Watson, *Paul and the Hermeneutics of Faith*, 2nd ed. (London: T&T Clark, 2015); for the latter, see John P. Heil, *The Rhetorical Role of Scripture in 1 Corinthians*, Studies in Biblical Literature 14

Intertextuality, Effective History, and Memory

particularly of Francis Watson's large-scale attempt to see Paul as a narrative theologian, reading especially the Pentateuch in implicit conversation with his Jewish contemporaries, and finding there a striking hermeneutical priority of the promise over the command to obey. Similarly, though varying in important ways, N. T. Wright also contends that Paul's basic hermeneutical posture is narrative: "Paul's understanding of Israel's scriptures should have as its basic framework the *covenant narrative of Israel*. . . . Paul does a thousand different things with scripture, but the broad base from which one ought to start is his belief . . . that in Jesus and in the fresh work of the divine spirit Israel's God had brought to its climax the extraordinary, and often dark and disastrous, story of Abraham and his family."[34]

Insofar as these approaches consider Paul's citations and allusions the tip of an iceberg for Paul's understanding of Scripture and attempt to press beyond the charge of atomism with which Paul was so long painted, they are entirely welcome. Methodological difficulties arise, however, in light of the underdetermined nature of the evidence for Paul's narrative convictions. We have a handful of occasional letters from the apostle, and they offer us some sweeping judgments on the history of humanity and Israel but do not comment on large portions of Scripture. Paul is almost entirely silent about long stretches of Israel's history under the judges and the monarchy, with only very occasional citations drawn from the scriptural books that retell those stories. Particularly given Paul's hermeneutical flexibility in utilizing the same narrative or text for different purposes, albeit with some commonality,[35] to build with confidence an entire narrative construal of the history of Israel becomes difficult at any level of detail. In fact, if we ask about narrative elements in Paul, we will find that the vast majority of these come from Genesis, apart from a few significant exceptions (e.g., snippets from the exodus tradition in Rom 9 and 1 Cor 10, or the Elijah story in Rom 11).[36] Indeed, though there are some suggestive hints elsewhere, one is tempted to juxtapose the very different reconstructions of Watson and Wright and suggest that the differences between them point to a fundamental limitation in the possibility of the task, in that they show the many gaps in Paul's story that need to be filled in by his narrative critics. Nevertheless, even if these *grands projets* are not deemed equally successful at

---

(Leiden: Brill, 2005); and esp. Christopher D. Stanley, *Arguing with Scripture: The Rhetoric of Quotations in the Letters of Paul* (London: T&T Clark, 2004).

34. Wright, *Paul and the Faithfulness of God*, 1453.

35. Cf. particularly the repetition of Lev 18:5 in Gal 3:12 and Rom 10:5; Hab 2:4 in Gal 3:11 and Rom 1:17; and the use of the Abraham story in Gal 3 and Rom 4.

36. See chapter 4.

Chapter 3

every level, the basic sensibility is a useful one, and forces us to pause and ask important synthetic questions about Paul's individual scriptural engagements. It is likely that further large-scale comparisons between Paul and other important readers of Scripture in early Judaism and Christianity will continue to shed light on his narrative particularities.

RHETORICAL EFFECTS

Finally, we can point to recent attempts to approach Paul's quotations through their rhetorical function. John Paul Heil pays particular attention to Paul's rhetorical strategies in citing Scripture in 1 Corinthians,[37] and so his work remains a basically author-oriented investigation. Stanley, on the other hand, imagines a differentiated early audience for Paul's letters, with varying levels of scriptural knowledge, and attempts to imaginatively reconstruct their different responses to Paul's quotations.[38] In this way Stanley provides an audience-oriented approach, but one that intends ultimately to shed light on the historical Paul's argumentative motives in citing Scripture. The "Paul and Scripture" Society of Biblical Literature seminar revisited the question of Paul's audiences several times over the course of their years, and Stanley himself revisits the outcome in a retrospective piece. It is worth quoting him at length:

> Those who believed that Paul expected his audiences to follow and approve his interpretations of the biblical text tended to credit Paul with an active desire to shape his congregations through the content of his letters, including the expectation that they would continue to read and study his writings as a guide for Christian living under the direction of their more knowledgeable members. Those who argued that Paul framed his arguments so that the meaning of his biblical references could be understood with little or no resort to the original text tended to see Paul engaging in rhetorical fire-fights in which he appealed to the authority of Scripture to shore up his arguments and thus persuade his audiences to embrace or reject a particular course of action. The fact that his audiences might have

---

37. See Heil, *Rhetorical Role*.

38. See Stanley, *Arguing with Scripture*; cf. Brian J. Abasciano, "Diamonds in the Rough: A Reply to Christopher Stanley Concerning the Reader Competency of Paul's Original Audiences," *NovT* 49 (2007): 153–83, although some of this article is anachronistic in its assumptions.

Intertextuality, Effective History, and Memory

continued to study his letters after they had (hopefully) achieved their rhetorical purpose played little or no role in Paul's communicative purposes under this model.[39]

The discussion about the scriptural literacy of Paul's gentile communities is an interesting one and worth pursuing further, but caution should be urged in moving from early audience perception to authorial intention, particularly when that authorial intention is to be described in relatively strong terms. Stanley's own proposal about a multifaceted audience with varying scriptural competencies makes a good deal of sense, even if his application of the model can be criticized at various points. Scriptural competence cannot simply be reduced to questions of literacy as such, particularly if we have in mind a modern concept of literacy as the ability to read for oneself (much less to write for oneself). Rather, the oral and the written were much more permeable in antiquity, and an inability to read need not have precluded even profound engagements with recited texts like Scripture. Such texts at any rate needed to be read aloud for the vast majority of those who encountered them, in light of the generally prohibitive cost of owning books. Moreover, Paul's interaction with his audience by means of scriptural citations should not be reduced to punctiliar events of rhetorical force, since the Pauline communities were arguably sites of memory, whether one wishes to follow E. A. Judge in describing them as "scholastic communities" or not.[40] Finally, although there have been suggestive comments by scholars like Loveday Alexander,[41] we are still lacking in a thorough exploration of Greco-Roman sensibilities about scriptural citations and how this might have influenced the earliest reception of Paul's letters.

39. Stanley, "What We Learned," 327; cf. 325–27.

40. Edwin A. Judge, "The Early Christians as a Scholastic Community," *JRH* 1.1 (1960): 4–15; Edwin A. Judge, "The Early Christians as a Scholastic Community: Part II," *JRH* 1.3 (1961): 125–37; see the refinement of Judge's view in Claire S. Smith, *Pauline Communities as 'Scholastic Communities': A Study of the Vocabulary of 'Teaching' in 1 Corinthians, 1 and 2 Timothy, and Titus*, WUNT 2/335 (Tübingen: Mohr Siebeck, 2012), 377–93, who adopts the language of "learning communities." Note also Jeremy Punt, "Identity, Memory, and Scriptural Warrant: Arguing Paul's Case," in Stanley, *Paul and Scripture*, 25–53, who appeals to cultural memory, particularly in connection with the formation of identity in the Pauline groups: "It is clear that the apostle used texts from the Jewish tradition to foster, structure, maintain, and negotiate identity within his communities of Jesus-followers" (40).

41. Loveday Alexander, "*IPSE DIXIT*: Citation of Authority in Paul and in the Jewish and Hellenistic Schools," in *Paul Beyond the Judaism/Hellenism Divide*, ed. Troels Engberg-Pedersen (Louisville: Westminster John Knox, 2001), 103–27.

Chapter 3

CONCLUSION: AN EMBODIED ENCOUNTER

These remarks have been intended to supply a rough map of current methodological discussion concerning the analytic frameworks we employ in investigating the apostle Paul's engagement with Scripture and his rhetorical communication of the fruits of that engagement in his pastoral letters. In that light, the interlocutors discussed above have been selected for their exemplary function, rather than making an attempt to provide an exhaustive description of all recent methodological discussion of Pauline scriptural exegesis. The study of Paul and Scripture has benefited from enormous erudition over the past few decades. We have made substantial gains in understanding, benefiting from the fruits of previous generations' labors in order to push questions to new frontiers. Nevertheless, this chapter has suggested a few points at which further methodological refinement is in order. In contrast to purely textual means of ascertaining Paul's *Vorlage*, it would be worthwhile to reconsider the active role of the memory in retrieval and recollection, and the memory variants this may introduce into Paul's formal citations. Even as we understand more of the situation of textual plurality in the first century, we must resist the temptation to ascribe all variations to textual sources unless clear rhetorical pressures can demonstrate Pauline modification. Rather, our default position should consider the necessary mediation of memory between text and citation, and so the consideration of memory should take an equally prominent place alongside the consideration of textual *Vorlagen*.

By way of complementing the rich literary sensitivities of intertextual ways of reading Paul, effective-historical sensibilities should be employed as a way of ascertaining Paul's place in the broad force of Scripture's afterlife. To do so will go some way toward countering the atomistic temptation to which intertextual approaches sometimes succumb by enabling the interpreter to have some sense of the broader shape of a scriptural predecessor text's holistic reception. In the face of sweeping reconstructions of Paul's master story, caution should be urged, and proper narrative interest combined with chastened claims. Here again more focused comparative work should help to supply some controls as to the plausibility or otherwise of large narrative construals of Paul's exegetical activity. Finally, while acknowledging the complexity of asking about Paul's rhetorical aims through reconstruction of his earliest hearers, we should continue to explore the variegated ways in which Paul's quotations would have struck the ear of a gentile convert of minimal scriptural exposure.

In general terms, the study of Paul and Scripture evinces overly textual biases that have tended to predominate in studies of Paul's scriptural practices.

Intertextuality, Effective History, and Memory

We have witnessed in recent decades a turn, or perhaps return, to memory in the humanities, signaled by names like Jan Assmann, Maurice Halbwachs, Pierre Nora, or Paul Ricoeur.[42] These sensitivities to memorial practices should be brought to bear on our discussions here as well. As a faithful Jew, Paul's own encounter with Scripture would have been a profoundly embodied one, in both temporal and spatial dimensions. The liturgical exposure to the reading of Scripture in the synagogue, together with his years of study and daily ritual practices, would have exercised a habituating impulse binding the words and stories of Scripture to his very self. The internalization of this word by means of memory and in the presence of the community suggests that Paul's encounter with Scripture was deeply embodied, and that greater attention to the role of memory, both individually and in communities, is likely to shed further light on Paul's scriptural practice.

42. For introductory surveys, see, e.g., Anne Whitehead, *Memory*, The New Critical Idiom (London: Routledge, 2009); and Marie-Claire Lavabre, "Historiography and Memory," in *A Companion to the Philosophy of History and Historiography*, ed. Aviezer Tucker (Malden, MA: Wiley-Blackwell, 2009), 362–70.

4

Genesis in Paul

Genesis is a book of fundamental importance for the apostle Paul, in a manner that is not fully reflected in mere numerical tallies of his explicit citations. To be sure, Paul does often cite Genesis (15 times), but he also learns from it certain basic narratives, stories that order and make sense of his world: the creation of the cosmos, the formation of humanity, the sin of Adam, the covenant with Abraham, and the promises to the patriarchs. In fact, if we ask about narrative elements in Paul, we will find that the vast majority of these come from Genesis, apart from a few significant exceptions (e.g., snippets from the exodus tradition in Rom 9 and 1 Cor 10, or the Elijah story in Rom 11).

Paul's interest in the book of Genesis is not an idiosyncrasy of the apostle to the nations. Genesis, as the great beginning to the Pentateuch, was a profoundly catholic text, foundational to Second Temple Jewish authors of a variety of backgrounds and outlooks. Along with Psalms, Deuteronomy, and Isaiah, Genesis ranks high among the number of manuscripts attested in the Dead Sea Scrolls (19 or 20 manuscripts).[1] We also find Genesis paraphrased (e.g., 4Q158, 4Q364, etc.), rewritten (e.g., in Jubilees, the Genesis Apocryphon [1Q20], and Josephus, *Ant.* 1.27–2.200), and philosophically expounded (all of Philo's three great works, the *Allegorical Commentary*, the *Exposition of the Law*, and the *Quaestiones et solutiones in Genesin et Exodum*, devote sustained attention to Genesis).[2] The widespread influence of Genesis arguably reflects

---

1. See Emanuel Tov et al., *The Texts from the Judaean Desert: Indices and an Introduction to the Discoveries in the Judaean Desert Series*, DJD 39 (Oxford: Clarendon, 2002), 167–68. The fluctuation reflects uncertainty as to whether 4Q8 represents one manuscript or two.

2. For the Dead Sea Scrolls evidence, see, e.g., Katell Berthelot, Thierry Legrand, and André Paul, eds., *La Bibliothèque de Qumrân, 1: Torah—Genèse* (Paris: Editions du Cerf, 2008). One also finds, of course, various compositions spurred by individual figures or groups in Genesis, such as Adam (Apoc. Mos., LAE), the watchers (the Enochic literature), Noah (1Q19, 4Q534), Abraham (Apoc. Ab., T. Ab.), Melchizedek (11QMelch), and the patriarchs (T. 12 Patr.).

Genesis in Paul

the habituating impulses of liturgical reading in the synagogue, the context that supplies the most natural environment for Paul's own encounter with the book.[3] Given the popularity of the scroll of Genesis and the foundational nature of the themes it treats (the two phenomena are of course related), it will come as no surprise to find that Paul's citations and allusions range across the book and touch on some key elements in his theology. Together with Deuteronomy, Psalms, and Isaiah, the scroll of Genesis proved one of the most fruitful sources for Paul's theological reflection and pastoral guidance to his fledgling communities.

QUOTATIONS AND ALLUSIONS TO GENESIS

In line with Paul's general citation practices, his quotations of Genesis in the undisputed letters are confined to the *Hauptbriefe* (in the deutero-Pauline Epistles, note Gen 2:24 in Eph 5:31; cf. 1 Tim 2:13-15). Also reflecting his usual preferences, his citations seem to rely on a Greek version of Genesis, though he has occasionally modified his citations to suit their new epistolary context or followed Greek texts that deviate from our standard editions of the LXX.[4]

---

3. For the public reading of the Torah in the first century, see Philo, *Hypoth.* 7.12-13 (in Eusebius, *Praep. ev.* 8.7.12-13); Luke 4:16-20; Acts 13:15; 15:21; Josephus, *Ant.* 16.43-45; *C. Ap.* 2.175-178; 1QS 6:6-8; 4Q251 1:5; 4Q266 5 ii:1-3 = 4Q267 5 iii:3-5; T. Levi 13:2; and the so-called Theodotus inscription from Jerusalem. What is more, early Greek manuscripts of the Torah show evidence of being designed for public reading, and the importance of such an act of public reading is strengthened when approached via the more sociological concerns with low literacy rates and an interpenetration of oral and written media on the one hand, and from the more particularly archaeological and literary attestation to the synagogue and its activities on the other; cf. David Lincicum, "The Liturgical Deuteronomy in the Second Temple Period," in *Paul and the Early Jewish Encounter with Deuteronomy*, WUNT 2/284 (Tübingen: Mohr Siebeck, 2010), chapter 2; and Marguerite Harl, *La Genèse*, La Bible d'Alexandrie 1 (Paris: Éditions du Cerf, 1986), 33-45.

4. There is a broad, though not unanimous, consensus about this point in Pauline scholarship. Apart from the fact that such a high degree of coincidence in verbatim renderings of the Hebrew would be remarkable if Paul were independently translating his *Vorlage* (note here the astute comments of Philo, *Mos.* 2.38!), there are a number of features in Paul's Genesis citations that could not be derived from the Hebrew as we know it. To take but two examples: the reference to "two" (δύο) in Gen 2:24 is not in the Hebrew (but is in the Peshitta and Vulgate, and perhaps the Samaritan Pentateuch; cf. John William Wevers, *Notes on the Greek Text of Genesis*, SCS 35 [Atlanta: Scholars Press, 1993], 35); and the passive form of λογίζομαι in Gen 15:6 is likewise absent from the Hebrew. Many other such instances could be marshaled; for the textual character of Paul's Pentateuchal citations, see further Dietrich-

Chapter 4

The fact that Paul, even when writing to communities comprised of substantial numbers of gentiles, so often alludes to figures from Genesis without offering full explanations may suggest that he passed on its substance to his converts as part of their catechesis. As Christopher Stanley has aptly noted with regard to Galatians,

> From the many unexplained references to Abraham and his family, we can deduce that Paul expected the Galatians to know at least the broad outlines of two story-cycles from the Abraham narrative: (a) the stories of the inauguration (Gen 12:1-3) and confirmation (Gen 13:14-17, 15:1-6) of God's covenant with Abraham, including God's promises to Abraham (Gal 3:8, 16, 18, 29), Abraham's faith in these promises (3:6, 9), and God's proclamation of Abraham's righteousness (3:6); and (b) the stories of Sarah and Hagar and their respective sons, including Isaac's birth as the fulfillment of a divine promise (Gal 4:23, 28), Hagar's son 'persecuting' Isaac (4:29), and Hagar and her son being cast out into the desert (4:30).[5]

Paul likewise mentions Adam and the Patriarchs without pausing to explain them, also suggesting that Paul presupposed a knowledge of their stories among his converts. This, then, also provides some indication of the importance of Genesis for the apostle.

Given that Paul often engages with stories from Genesis rather than simply isolated verses, in what follows the investigation will proceed by examining the evidence under five broad headings: creation, Adam and Christ, Abraham in Galatians, Abraham in Romans, and finally other references to Genesis in Romans.[6]

Alex Koch, *Die Schrift als Zeuge des Evangeliums: Untersuchungen zur Verwendung und zum Verständnis der Schrift bei Paulus*, BHT 69 (Tübingen: Mohr Siebeck, 1986), 51-54 passim.

5. Christopher D. Stanley, *Arguing with Scripture: The Rhetoric of Quotations in the Letters of Paul* (London: T&T Clark, 2004), 117. Stanley also plausibly suggests that Paul assumes his readers in 1 Corinthians and Romans are familiar with the story of Adam (76, 139).

6. I have thus excluded from consideration some of the allusions suggested by NA[28]. For example, they suggest that Gen 6:12 may be alluded to in Rom 3:20, though the main allusion appears to be to Ps 142:2 LXX, and only the phrase "all flesh" (πᾶσα σάρξ) could be derived from Genesis. This phrase, however, is unlikely to recall Genesis specifically, as it is common in the Greek Scriptures. Other proposed allusions are likewise mere verbal similarities with little interpretative significance: e.g., Gen 8:21 in Phil 4:18 (sharing ὀσμὴν εὐωδίας); Gen 15:16 in 1 Thess 2:16 (sins being "filled up" using ἀναπληρόω); and Gen 32:31 in 1 Cor 13:12 ("seeing" God [though different verbs of sight are used] "face to face," πρόσωπον πρὸς πρόσωπον).

Genesis in Paul

CREATION

We find three major clusters of references to the creation account in Genesis, and a handful of other significant allusions. Paul's references to Adam as a type of Christ will be treated separately in the next section.

Quotation of Gen 2:24 in 1 Cor 6:16

In 1 Cor 6:16, Paul adduces Genesis's classic statement about marriage (2:24: "the two shall become one flesh") not to discuss that institution, which he will go on to do in 1 Cor 7, but to prohibit illicit sexual unions (πορνεία). The citation follows the LXX exactly, with an interspersed introductory word (φησίν).[7] Paul is arguing against a permissive Corinthian view of the body, which he counters in a series of staccato arguments against the possible sanction of fornication. The scriptural citation supplies grounds for Paul's assertion that the sexual act causes a union of persons—in this case, not the union of husband and wife, but the incongruous union of a Christian and a prostitute. Paul therefore takes Gen 2:24 not (merely) as a statement about procreation, but as a claim concerning a type of union between two people, a union that can be either beneficial or harmful.[8]

Allusions to Gen 1–2 in 1 Cor 11:2–12

In the course of his difficult argument about women being veiled in the assemblies in 1 Cor 11:2–12, Paul makes a number of allusions to Genesis. Most clearly, in 11:8–9, Paul argues from the manner of the creation account in Gen 2. In 11:8, Paul writes that "man was not made from woman, but woman from man (ἐξ ἀνδρός)," recalling Gen 2:22–23 in which God takes one of Adam's ribs to form Eve "from the man" (ἐκ τοῦ ἀνδρὸς). In 11:9, Paul writes that woman was created "for the sake of man" (διὰ τὸν ἄνδρα), recalling Gen 2:18 and the statement that God made the woman "for him as a helper corresponding to him" (αὐτῷ βοηθὸν κατ᾽αὐτόν). This reading of Gen 2 seems to control Paul's reading of Gen 1. In 1 Cor 11:7, Paul conceives of the man as the "image and glory of God" (εἰκὼν καὶ δόξα θεοῦ), while the woman

---

7. This occurs only here by Paul as an introduction to a scriptural citation; cf. Christopher D. Stanley, *Paul and the Language of Scripture: Citation Technique in the Pauline Epistles and Contemporary Literature*, SNTSMS 74 (Cambridge: Cambridge University Press, 1992), 195.

8. Note the different uses of the verse in Eph 5:31; Mark 10:7; and Matt 19:5.

Chapter 4

is the "glory of the man" (δόξα ἀνδρός). In Gen 1:27, it is "humanity" (τὸν ἄνθρωπον) that is made "male and female" (ἄρσεν καὶ θῆλυ) in the image of God (κατ᾽ εἰκόνα θεοῦ). Paul appears to have read this through Gen 2, which narrates the creation of the singular human (2:7, τὸν ἄνθρωπον), identified as Adam in 2:16, from whom woman is made at a subsequent point (2:18–24). This order of creation is taken by Paul to imply a corresponding social order that should be reflected in liturgical praxis (however difficult that may appear to his modern readers).[9]

Allusions to Gen 1 in 1 Cor 15:38–39

In the course of his argument about the reality of the resurrection in 1 Cor 15, Paul seeks to clarify the nature of the resurrected bodies by analogy to the different "bodies" in creation. In 1 Cor 15:38 ("God gives it a body as he wished, and to each of the seeds its own body"), Paul may be recalling the growth of plants that each had their "seed" in them, according to their kind, in Gen 1:11–12. In 1 Cor 15:39, Paul explicitly mentions the different kinds of flesh in reverse order of that found in the creation story of Gen 1:26 (cf. 1:20–27):

Gen 1:26 LXX	1 Cor 15:39
Ποιήσομεν <u>ἄνθρωπον</u> . . . καὶ ἀρχέτω-σαν τῶν <u>ἰχθύων</u> τῆς θαλάσσης καὶ τῶν <u>πετεινῶν</u> τοῦ οὐρανοῦ καὶ τῶν <u>κτηνῶν</u>	Οὐ πᾶσα σὰρξ ἡ αὐτὴ σὰρξ ἀλλὰ ἄλλη μὲν <u>ἀνθρώπων</u>, ἄλλη δὲ σὰρξ <u>κτηνῶν</u>, ἄλλη δὲ σὰρξ <u>πτηνῶν</u>, ἄλλη δὲ <u>ἰχθύων</u>

Paul here seems to achieve interpretative mileage out of the repeated prepositional phrase κατὰ γένος ("according to its kind"), which occurs in Gen 1:11, 12, 21, 24, and 25. Paul takes this to suggest that each category of creature has a different kind of flesh. Although σάρξ is not used in Gen 1, it is used in Gen 8:17 in connection with birds and beasts and reptiles, echoing Gen 1:26–27. But whether Paul derived the term from Genesis is of negligible significance. Paul uses the conceptuality of the creation account to suggest that it is not unreasonable to think of another kind of body entirely, a spiritual body.

---

9. NA[27] suggested an allusion to Gen 3:16 in 1 Cor 11:3, but to see the hierarchy as a result of the fall would seem to undercut Paul's subsequent argument from creation order in 11:7–9, and NA[28] has dropped the reference. Some have also seen a reference to the watcher tradition stemming from Gen 6:1–4 in Paul's cryptic statement that women should cover their heads "because of the angels"; this is possible, but by no means certain. Galatians 3:28 also probably alludes to the creation of man and woman in the LXX, since Paul there breaks the disjunction "neither (οὐκ) . . . nor (οὐδέ) . . ." pattern and speaks of "male and (καί) female"; I'm grateful to Gabriel Parlin for pointing this out to me.

Genesis in Paul

Other Allusions to Gen 1–3

We also find a handful of other allusions to the creation account in Paul's letters. In 2 Cor 4:6, Paul writes, "For it is the God who said, 'Let light shine out of darkness,' who has shone in our hearts to give the light of the knowledge of the glory of God in the face of Jesus Christ." Although there is "no specific grounding in either the Hebrew or Greek Scriptures,"[10] conceptually the connection is clear: God speaks, and light is created (Gen 1:3–4). This allusion thus recalls God's creative power and therefore stresses that "the God of redemption is none other than the God of creation."[11]

In 2 Cor 11:3, Paul writes, "But I am afraid that as the serpent deceived Eve by its cunning (πανουργίᾳ), your thoughts will be led astray from a sincere and pure devotion to Christ." Paul has just suggested that the church is betrothed to one husband (Christ), and so this may recall Paul's arguments (to be examined below) that consider the Messiah to be a new Adam. The allusion is to the deception of the woman by the serpent in Gen 3. Interestingly, while the Septuagint describes the serpent as "most wise" (φρονιμώτατος), Aquila and Theodotion both describe the serpent as "cunning" (πανοῦργος or in some manuscripts, πανουργότερος), using the same root word as Paul. It is possible that Paul had knowledge of a text that anticipated Aquila and Theodotion rather than the LXX at this point.[12]

Finally, Paul's oblique reference to the creation groaning under futility in Rom 8:20 seems to recall the curse of Gen 3:17–19, although the language of "futility" occurs in Ecclesiastes rather than Genesis. One also finds references to a "new creation" (Gal 6:15; 2 Cor 5:17) that ultimately hark back to Genesis, though perhaps through an Isaianic lens (cf. Isa 66:22–23).

ADAM AND CHRIST

In two places Paul explicitly pairs Adam and Christ: 1 Cor 15:21–22, 45–49 and Rom 5:12–21.

---

10. Stanley, *Paul and the Language*, 215.

11. Murray J. Harris, *The Second Epistle to the Corinthians: A Commentary on the Greek Text*, NIGTC (Grand Rapids: Eerdmans, 2005), 335.

12. Cf. also 1 Tim 2:14; compare Sir 25:24, which blames Eve for the "beginning of sin" (ἀρχὴ ἁμαρτίας) and the resultant death. Some have also suggested that a reference to God's judgment on Eve in Gen 3:16 may lie behind Paul's cryptic statement in 1 Cor 14:34 (cf. 1 Tim 2:12) that "the law also says" that women should be subordinate. This is impossible to prove, and at any rate, the originality of 1 Cor 14:33b–35 is disputable.

57

Chapter 4

Adam and Christ in 1 Cor 15

In the previous section it was noted that 1 Cor 15, Paul's great defense of the resurrection of the dead, contains several allusions to the creation account in Gen 1–2. He continues his focus on creation by arguing that the correspondences between the first human Adam and Christ reveal certain parallels that must be taken seriously by his Corinthian hearers. First in 15:21–22 Paul uses the common humanity of Adam and Christ to suggest a certain necessity of inversion: just as death came through a human being (δι᾽ ἀνθρώπου θάνατος), so the resurrection of the dead must come through a human being (15:21). Paul then repeats the same logic with explicit reference to Adam: "for just as all die in Adam, so also all will be made alive in the Messiah" (15:22). Paul alludes to Gen 3:17–19, in which Adam receives the punishment for eating the fruit. The prohibition in Gen 2:17 warned that "on the day that you eat of it, you shall die by death" (θανάτῳ ἀποθανεῖσθε),[13] and Paul sees Adam's disobedience as incurring the sanctions of this warning and so ushering death into the world.[14] Death entering the world through the actions of one human requires, according to Paul, an equal and opposite reaction, in which the dead are made alive again by the actions of one human, whom Paul here identifies as the Messiah.

This correspondence is developed further in 1 Cor 15:45–49. In arguing that a physical body requires also a spiritual body, Paul cites Gen 2:7. The citation differs slightly from the LXX:

Gen 2:7 LXX	**1 Cor 15:45**
καὶ ἐγένετο ὁ ἄνθρωπος εἰς ψυχὴν ζῶσαν	ἐγένετο ὁ <u>πρῶτος</u> ἄνθρωπος <u>Ἀδὰμ</u> εἰς ψυχὴν ζῶσαν

13. Following Robert J. V. Hiebert's translation in the *New English Translation of the Septuagint*, which captures well the jarring Greek rendition of the Hebrew infinitive absolute.

14. Although other streams of Jewish tradition looked to the events of Gen 6:1–4 as signaling the real decline of the human race (esp. Enochic literature), Paul may not be alone in reading Adam's actions as signaling the entrance of death into the world; note Wis 2:23–24: by the envy of the devil that resulted in his tempting Adam, "death entered the world" (θάνατος εἰσῆλθεν εἰς τὸν κόσμον). Jason M. Zurawski, however, has made a good case for identifying the *diabolos* in Wis 2:24 with Cain ("Separating the Devil from the *Diabolos*: A Fresh Reading of Wisdom of Solomon 2.24," *JSP* 21.4 [2012]: 366–99). Note also Philo, *Leg.* 1.105–107 for death as both physical and spiritual; cf. also 4 Ezra 3:7; 7:118–119. On the early reception of Gen 2–3 in Second Temple Judaism, see Konrad Schmid, "Loss of Immortality? Hermeneutical Aspects of Genesis 2–3 and Its Early Receptions," in *Beyond Eden: The Biblical Story of Paradise (Genesis 2–3) and Its Reception History*, ed. Konrad Schmid and Christoph Riedweg, FAT 2/34 (Tübingen: Mohr Siebeck, 2008), 58–78.

Genesis in Paul

In light of his argument, Paul has clarified that this is the "first" man, and also named him explicitly as Adam.[15] As Adam became "a living being/soul," so the Messiah, here identified as "the last Adam" (ὁ ἔσχατος Ἀδάμ), became a life-giving spirit (πνεῦμα ζῳοποιοῦν). The latter term appears to be modeled on the description of Adam in Gen 2:7, and that Paul used the verb ζῳοποιέω in his earlier reference to the Adam/Christ parallel in 15:22 may suggest that he already had this in view. Paul goes on to contrast Adam, the "man of dust" (χοϊκός), with Christ, the "man from heaven" (15:47). This alludes to the narration present in the first half of Gen 2:7, in which God forms "the human, dust from the earth" (τὸν ἄνθρωπον χοῦν ἀπὸ τῆς γῆς). Adam and Christ each represent one stage or type of humanity, and Paul argues that the progression from the first to the second comes via the resurrection. In 15:49 Paul expresses confidence that "just as we have borne the image of the man of dust, we shall also bear the image of the heavenly man." This may further recall Gen 5:3, in which Adam's son Seth is born "according to his image" (κατὰ τὴν εἰκόνα αὐτοῦ; cf. Gen 1:27).[16]

Adam and Christ in Rom 5:12-21

Similarly to his argument in 1 Cor 15:21-22, in Rom 5:12-21 Paul explores the similarities and points of contrast between Adam and the Messiah. His argument in Romans proceeds at greater length, affirming the assertion of 1 Cor 15:21-22 that the sin of Adam brought death, but also moves beyond that argument. In Rom 5:14, Paul suggests that Adam "is a type of the one who was to come." This conviction suggests that Paul sees Adam as prefiguring the Messiah in accordance with the divine plan that orders all of history. The argu-

15. Symmachus and Theodotion both also add Ἀδάμ to ἄνθρωπος (for the reading, see Wevers's Göttingen edition, ad loc.). Stanley (*Paul and the Language*, 207-9) suggests that Paul may be reliant on a variant Septuagintal text here, which is entirely possible, though it is just as likely that Paul supplies the name Adam as a clarification for the sake of his audience. On the question of whether 1 Cor 15:45b should be considered part of the citation, see Stanley, *Paul and the Language*, 209n99.

16. Many have noted the parallel to the idea of a heavenly and an earthly man in Philo, *Opif.* 134-135. While there are some striking similarities, unlike Philo, Paul nowhere clearly reads the two creation accounts as describing two different acts of creation. Against the position of Schmid ("Loss of Immortality," 72), who follows Martin Rösel in seeing a Platonic influence on the LXX translation of Gen 1-3 (which, it is suggested, encouraged Philo's reading), see Johann Cook, "The Septuagint of Genesis: Text and/or Interpretation?," in *Studies in the Book of Genesis: Literature, Redaction and History*, ed. André Wénin (Leuven: Peeters, 2001), 315-30.

Chapter 4

ment of Rom 5:12–21 is complicated and need not be fully expounded here.[17] But it is worth noting that Paul here conceives of Adam's act of disobedience to be not merely "sin" but "transgression" (παράπτωμα), the contravention of an explicit command or law. This is the difference between Adam and those who followed after him until Moses: Adam had a "law" (presumably, Gen 2:17), while those before the Torah was given at Sinai did not (Rom 5:13–14). While in 1 Corinthians Paul suggests that death comes to all because of Adam's sin, in Romans he goes beyond this by arguing that not only death, but also sin spread to all because of Adam's action.[18] But similarly to 1 Corinthians, here Paul casts Adam as a contrast to the Messiah, and Paul alludes to the tragedy of Gen 2–3 in order to celebrate the recovery now achieved in Christ.

Paul also subtly develops this representative status of Adam later in Romans. In Rom 7:7–11, Adam's transgression likely lies behind the brief narrative Paul supplies. While this is a matter of some debate and judgments here are informed by broader perspectives about the nature of the speaker in Rom 7, certain links between Rom 7:7–11 and Gen 2–3, however, make an Adamic (or at least, Edenic) background likely: the sequence of (a) being alive "apart from law," (b) commandment given, and (c) the concept of the serpent (Gen 3:13) or sin (Rom 7:11) "deceiving" with the result of death.[19]

The Story of Abraham in Galatians

Paul's engagement with Genesis in his letter to the Galatians is almost wholly centered on the story of Abraham. He conducts two sustained arguments about Abraham, first in 3:6–29 and then again in 4:21–31. He cites Gen 15:6 in Gal 3:6, Gen 12:3/18:18 in Gal 3:8, Gen 13:15 par. in Gal 3:16, and Gen 21:10 in Gal 4:30. In the course of his allegorical retelling of the story of Sarah and Hagar, he also alludes to Gen 16:15 in Gal 4:22, Gen 17:16 in Gal 4:23, Gen 21:2 in Gal 4:22, and Gen 21:9 in Gal 4:22, 29.

---

17. See further Otfried Hofius, "The Adam-Christ Antithesis and the Law: Reflections on Romans 5:12–21," in *Paul and the Mosaic Law*, ed. James D. G. Dunn (Grand Rapids: Eerdmans, 2001), 165–206.

18. See Joseph A. Fitzmyer, *First Corinthians*, AB 32 (New Haven: Yale University Press, 2008), 570.

19. See Hermann Lichtenberger, *Das Ich Adams und das Ich der Menschheit: Studien zum Menschenbild in Römer 7*, WUNT 164 (Tübingen: Mohr Siebeck, 2004).

Genesis in Paul

Abraham in Galatians 3

In Gal 3:6–14, as part of his larger argument that gentiles are children of Abraham through faith in Christ rather than by Torah observance (3:1–29), Paul seeks to advance a further stage in his argument, grounding in Scripture his assertion that the Galatian gentile believers received the Spirit through the hearing of faith and not by law observance, which he had previously established on the basis of the Galatians' experience (3:2). In 3:6–9 Paul argues from the example of Abraham that "those who are from faith are blessed together with Abraham, the man of faith" (οἱ ἐκ πίστεως εὐλογοῦνται σὺν τῷ Ἀβραάμ). In 3:6 Paul begins an argument from Scripture about two things: how Abraham was blessed, and who gets to be called a child of Abraham and so a partaker in that blessing. This will stretch until at least 3:29, with the climactic assertion that "you are Abraham's offspring," though Abraham remains "on stage" until 5:1. Many have suggested that Paul here responds to an alternative reading of Genesis previously proposed by his opponents, in which Abraham's circumcision is held up as a model of obedience for the Galatians to emulate.[20] It is not unlikely that Paul is responding to the legitimation strategy of his opponents, at least as it has been reported to him, but since we cannot know much of the details of the account, overly elaborate reconstructions should be avoided. In some Jewish literature of the day, Abraham is seen as the archetypal convert: a pagan worshiper of the moon in Mesopotamia, he is called by God and responds to that call, founding the people that comes to be known as Israel.[21] What Paul engages in, especially in 3:6–9 and 3:15–18, is an argument about relative chronology in the telling of the story of Abraham from Gen 12–22. It is possible that the agitators pointed to Gen 14 with Abram's good deed of tithing to Melchizedek and rescuing Lot, and especially to Abraham's circumcision in 17:4–14. Paul, in response, draws attention to 15:6 and 12:3/18:18, the first emphasizing faith, the second, the promise.

Galatians 3:6 closely follows the LXX of Gen 15:6, although Paul has brought the name Abraham forward[22] and substituted Ἀβραάμ for Ἀβράμ: "Abraham

---

20. For one influential reconstruction of the agitators' (or teachers', as Martyn prefers) reading of Genesis, see J. L. Martyn, *Galatians: A New Translation with Introduction and Commentary*, AB 33A (New Haven: Yale University Press, 1997), 302–6; and J. L. Martyn, *Theological Issues in the Letters of Paul* (Nashville: Abingdon, 1997), 7–24. But for cautions about our ability to reconstruct the situation in Galatia, see the classic article by John M. G. Barclay, "Mirror-Reading a Polemical Letter: Galatians as a Test Case," *JSNT* 31 (1987): 73–93.

21. Perhaps most fully in the Apoc. Ab. 1–8.

22. In fact, it is unclear whether "Abraham" should be considered as belonging to the

Chapter 4

believed God and it was credited to him as righteousness."[23] This is, in fact, the first occurrence of πιστεύω in the Pentateuch.[24] This is followed quickly by a citation of Gen 12:3/18:18 in Gal 3:8: Scripture "declared in advance the gospel to Abraham, saying, 'All the Gentiles shall be blessed in you' (ἐνευλογηθήσονται ἐν σοὶ πάντα τὰ ἔθνη)." This citation most likely bears the marks of Paul's shaping. Rather than speak of "all the tribes of the earth" (πᾶσαι αἱ φυλαὶ τῆς γῆς) as Gen 12:3 originally does, Paul imports "all the Gentiles/nations" (πάντα τὰ ἔθνη) from Gen 18:18 (cf. also 22:18) for the strategic importance of τὰ ἔθνη in his argument.[25] In the citations of both Gen 15:6 and Gen 12:3/18:18, Paul stresses not the obedience of Abraham that finds its due reward, but rather that Abraham believes and receives a promise before he has obeyed anything that might be construed as law (a reading in contrast to many of Paul's Jewish contemporaries). The language of "righteousness" in association with belief in Gen 15:6 has been anticipated in Paul's argument in Gal 2:15–21 and provides Paul with a lens by which to understand the promise to Abraham that he recalls from Gen 12:3/18:18 in Gal 3:8. The effect that Paul wants to draw from this is clearly stated in v. 9: "those who believe are blessed along with Abraham the believer." That is, Abraham's story, rather than pointing to the necessity of circumcision, displays how faith is the *sine qua non* of God's dealing with those who want to be like Abraham.

Paul's argument about the relative chronology of the Abraham story is expanded to a broader salvation-historical plane in 3:15–18. In arguing that the later imposition of the law cannot nullify the previously delivered promise, Paul writes, "Now the promises were spoken to Abraham and to his offspring" (Gal 3:16). He then goes on to indicate that he intends a citation by arguing that Scripture or God does not say "and to offsprings" (καὶ τοῖς σπέρμασιν) but "and

---

citation or to the introductory formula; for discussion, see Richard N. Longenecker, *Galatians*, WBC 41 (Waco: Word Books, 1990), 112.

23. In Genesis LXX, the shift in name comes in 17:5, after which Ἀβράμ does not occur again in the LXX or New Testament (the exception being a retelling of the change of name in 2 Esd 19:7 = Neh 9:7).

24. So Wevers, *Notes*, 205.

25. Genesis 18:18 reads ἐνευλογηθήσονται ἐν αὐτῷ πάντα τὰ ἔθνη τῆς γῆς, and 22:18 reads ἐνευλογηθήσονται ἐν τῷ σπέρματί σου πάντα τὰ ἔθνη τῆς γῆς; for other possible allusions to these texts, see Rom 4:13; Rev 1:7. Stanley convincingly argues that Paul has introduced the substitution himself, whether intentionally or due to a slip in memory (*Paul and the Language*, 237). For Paul following a preexistent LXX text with ἐνευλογηθήσονται see Koch, *Die Schrift als Zeuge des Evangeliums*, 52. More generally on Gen 12:3/18:18 in Gal 3:8, see Jeffrey R. Wisdom, *Blessing for the Nations and the Curse of the Law: Paul's Citations of Genesis and Deuteronomy in Gal 3:8–10*, WUNT 2/133 (Tübingen: Mohr Siebeck, 2001), 129–53.

Genesis in Paul

to your offspring" (καὶ τῷ σπέρματί σου), whom Paul then identifies as the Messiah (ὅς ἐστιν Χριστός). The precise wording καὶ τῷ σπέρματί σου occurs several times in Genesis (13:15; 17:8; 24:7).[26] Who is the original recipient of the promise? Abraham, Paul answers, and "his seed." Here Paul atomizes the word "offspring," and suggests that it refers to the Messiah, even though the singular noun had a collective sense, which Paul probably well knew. But this is an interpretative technique to imbue the Genesis narrative's forward horizon (the promise) with a focus. The point Paul draws is simply this: if the "inheritance" really came through the law (as Paul construes his opponents' argument to suggest), then God spoke falsely to Abraham. Clearly this is a *reductio ad absurdum* argument.

Sarah and Hagar in Gal 4:21–31

In the next chapter, Paul's argument takes a surprising turn toward an allegorical reading of the Sarah and Hagar narrative, once more returning to Genesis, this time to chapters 16–21. Some have even suggested that the section is misplaced or a mere afterthought on Paul's part. But when viewed in light of the argument Paul has been conducting since 3:1, this forms a sort of conclusion to Paul's argument, as he labors to cast his Galatian hearers in the roles that he believes will ultimately lead to them living faithfully in the new age under the Messiah. The fact that Paul here returns to the Abraham story has been taken by many as an indication that he is continuing his project of rereading Genesis in dispute with the agitators and the reading they had bequeathed to the Galatian congregations.[27] Given the tortured nature of the argument, such a state of affairs is not unlikely, though it should be treated with suitable caution.

Intriguingly, in 4:21b, the "law" is spoken of positively—in fact, for the first time in the letter. Paul writes, "Tell me, you who desire to be subject to the law, will you not listen to the law?" He then provides a summary of what he

---

26. Cf. also Gen 12:7 (τῷ σπέρματί σου, lacking καί). NA[28] suggests 13:15; 17:8; 24:7, while Steve Moyise suggests Gen 12:7 (*Paul and Scripture: Studying the New Testament Use of the Old Testament* [Grand Rapids: Baker Academic, 2010], 131). Stanley (*Paul and the Language*, 248n230) does not note the parallel in 17:8 but suggests that contextually Gen 13:15 makes most sense.

27. So, e.g., C. K. Barrett, "The Allegory of Abraham, Sarah, and Hagar in the Argument of Galatians," in *Rechtfertigung: Festschrift Ernst Käsemann*, ed. Johannes Friedrich, Wolfgang Pohlmann, and Peter Stuhlmacher (Tübingen: Mohr Siebeck, 1976), 1–16. On Gal 4:21–31 and contemporary Jewish exegesis see, e.g., Koch, *Die Schrift als Zeuge des Evangeliums*, 204–11; and Longenecker, *Galatians*, 200–206 (though he includes many much later Jewish sources).

Chapter 4

hopes to persuade the Galatians that the law does in fact say, though this is not unproblematic as a straightforward reading of Genesis. Key to Paul's presentation is the verb he mentions in 4:25, συστοιχέω, which originally referred to soldiers standing in the same line but came to denote the correspondence of categories in lists.[28] Thus, Paul reads the story with a binary hermeneutic and aligns the two columns roughly as follows:

Abraham had two sons (4:22)

one by a slave	and one by a free woman (4:22)
born according to the flesh	born through promise (4:23)

Allegorically, the women correspond to two covenants (4:24)

Mount Sinai for slavery (4:24)	free (4:26)
Hagar (4:24)	(Sarah, though not explicitly mentioned)
the present Jerusalem (4:25)	the Jerusalem above (4:26)
bearing children in slavery (4:25)	children of promise (4:28)
according to the flesh (4:29)	born according to the Spirit (4:29)

We should recall Paul's earlier contentions about his independence from the Jerusalem apostles. Here the polemic reaches perhaps its sharpest point: the present Jerusalem is in slavery and so are all those who want to align themselves with it (i.e., her children, and so the agitators). As James D. G. Dunn writes, "This is the language of polemic, an exegetical *tour de force*, a virtuoso performance, rather than sober theological argument."[29] Paul's reference to the contrast between the present Jerusalem and the Jerusalem that is above has its roots in apocalyptic thought. This seems to be based on the idea found in Exod 25:9, 40 (and the tradition stemming from it), where Moses is shown a pattern and told to construct a tabernacle according to that pattern, thus implying that the original is in heaven and awaiting revelation.

The main thrust of the section is an interpretation of the story of Sarah and Hagar from Gen 16–21 (the written text, γέγραπται), although with a contemporizing hermeneutic that sees the story as directed ultimately to the present

---

28. Cf. Henry George Liddell, Robert Scott, and Henry Stuart Jones, *A Greek-English Lexicon*, 9th ed. with revised supplement (Oxford: Claredon, 1996), s.v. συστοιχέω; so also, e.g., Martyn, *Galatians*, 431–66; and many others.

29. James D. G. Dunn, *The Theology of Paul's Letter to the Galatians* (Cambridge: Cambridge University Press, 1993), 97.

Genesis in Paul

(ἅτινα ἐστιν ἀλληγορούμενα). Galatians 4:22 does not introduce a direct citation but refers in broad strokes to the stories of sons borne by Hagar (Gen 16:15; 21:9) and Sarah (Gen 21:2). Both Hagar (Gen 16:10) and Sarah (Gen 17:16) were promised numerous descendants, and so to read them as symbolic figures is in itself not a novel interpretative move, especially after Paul has established a similar significance for Abraham in Gal 3. What is novel, however, is the inversion Paul attempts to achieve, regarding those who had historically viewed themselves as children of Sarah now to be children of Hagar. Paul does this in part by citing Isa 54:1 ("Rejoice, O barren one, you who bear no children, burst into song and shout, you who endure no birth pangs; for the children of the desolate woman are more numerous than the children of the one who is married"). As Paul identifies Sarah implicitly with this woman, we may see some of the path along which Paul traveled to arrive at this allegory.[30] Moreover, Paul follows a prominent stream of Jewish tradition in seeing Ishmael's "playing" with Isaac in Gen 21:9 as involving malicious behavior; Paul characterizes this as "persecution" (Gal 4:29), though the choice of word is likely determined by Paul's present circumstances more than the exegetical detail of the Genesis story itself.

But the practical point of his comparison is clear. In Gal 4:30 Paul writes, "But what does the scripture say? 'Drive out the slave woman and her child; for the child of the slave will not share the inheritance with the child of the free woman.'" Paul here cites Gen 21:10, having probably introduced a number of minor alterations to the citation that enhance his ability to contemporize it.[31] When Gen 21:10 here speaks, Paul claims, it tells the Galatian congregations exactly what they need to do. Once more, we see Genesis as a word directed to the present. But with the emphatic position of Gen 21:10, Paul promptly and forcefully brings to a climax the argument he has been developing since Gal 3:1.

To describe the function of the Abraham story in Galatians is to touch the central concerns of the letter: the Galatians must hold fast to the faith of Abraham and his promise, not allowing themselves to be circumcised and perhaps persuaded to keep calendrical observances. To keep the Torah in the present time as gentiles is to deny the reality of God's new action in the Messiah and to align oneself with the former things: the period of slavery, of adolescence, of

---

30. This may also align with Paul's tendency elsewhere to read negative epithets as references to the gentiles; cf. J. Ross Wagner, *Heralds of the Good News: Isaiah and Paul in Concert in the Letter to the Romans*, NovTSup 101 (Leiden: Brill, 2002), 83, 188.

31. He omits from Genesis two deictic words (ταύτην and ταύτης) and substitutes "the free one" (τῆς ἐλευθέρας) for "Isaac." By contrast, he probably followed a Greek text that included μή. See Koch, *Die Schrift als Zeuge des Evangeliums*, 52; Stanley, *Paul and the Language*, 248–51; and Wevers, *Notes*, 303.

Chapter 4

discipline, of restraint, of the earthly Jerusalem, of the elements of the world. But, as Paul will say in chapter 6, there has come about "a new creation" (a concept also indebted to a reading of Genesis and Isaiah together), and this, Paul is laboring to argue, changes everything. What is more, this new state of affairs is precisely that which was *promised*. Paul places a stress on *promise* as opposed to law—this is constitutive for the people of God, the promise that was given to Abraham, then to his seed, that is Christ, and those who believe in Christ through faith, and so realize the promise for themselves.

The Story of Abraham in Rom 4

The story of Abraham plays an equally significant role in the letter to the Romans. In what is one of the most sustained interpretative expositions in his epistles, Paul spends nearly twenty-five verses arguing from the story of Abraham. Following on from his rejection of boasting, Paul asks whether Abraham had reason to boast. In diatribe style, Paul asks, "What does the Scripture say?" (4:3a). He cites Gen 15:6, following the LXX with only minor changes, in response: "Abraham believed God, and it was credited to him as righteousness" (paraphrased again in 4:9, 22–23). As in Galatians, though with a more measured tone, Paul subsequently argues from the relative chronology of the Abraham story that he was reckoned as righteous "not after, but before he was circumcised" (4:10; cf. Gen 17:10–11). This supports first of all the conclusion that Abraham was reckoned righteous when he was ungodly, and so has no boast, in contrast to some contemporary Jewish portraits of the patriarch.[32] But second, that this occurred before he was circumcised means that Abraham is father of both the circumcised and uncircumcised (4:11–12)— expressed here in more conciliatory tones than in Galatians.

As in Gal 3, Paul pairs a concern with Abraham's justification by faith in Gen 15:6 with the promises given to the patriarch. In 4:13–15, Paul speaks of "the promise that he would inherit the world." Such a breadth of promise does not appear in the patriarchal narratives as such, but Paul seems to be generalizing from the promise for land and descendants that is repeated to Abraham several times (Gen 12:1–3; 18:18; 22:17–18). By dissociating the promise from the law, as in Galatians, "Paul's primary interest here is to overcome the ethnic prerogative with regard to the promise."[33]

---

32. See, e.g., the Testament of Abraham; Jub. 12:1–24; Tg. Ps.-J. Gen 15:1; Tg. Neof. Gen 15:1; cf. further Francis Watson, *Paul and the Hermeneutics of Faith* (London: T&T Clark, 2004), 167–269.

33. Robert Jewett, *Romans: A Commentary*, Hermeneia (Minneapolis: Fortress, 2007), 326.

Genesis in Paul

In Rom 4:16–25 Paul argues that the promise of Abraham, because it is based on faith, is guaranteed for all who share in Abraham's faith. Paul cites Genesis twice in these verses and alludes to the story of Isaac's miraculous conception. In Rom 4:17 Paul cites Gen 17:5: "I have made you the father of many nations," following the LXX exactly. This citation supports Paul's contention that both Jew and gentile comprise the heirs of Abraham, since otherwise God's statement that Abraham was the father of many nations would be void. Paul goes on to characterize the faith of Abraham: "hoping against hope" he believed the promise of God for an heir, the *sine qua non* of fathering many nations. In Rom 4:18, Paul cites Gen 15:5, again exactly following the LXX: "so numerous shall your descendants be." This brief phrase encapsulates the repeated promise in Genesis that God would multiply Abraham's descendants.[34] Although both he and Sarah were advanced in age (note Gen 17:17 in Rom 4:19), Abraham believed the promise fully, and this same faith is counted to him as righteousness. Here Paul has brought together once more the two important resources he takes from Abraham's story: justification by faith and the promise of many nations as Abraham's heritage. The two themes are, of course, closely related for Paul.

Other References to Genesis in Romans

Paul's letter to the Romans also includes three citations of the patriarchal narratives and one major allusion. All three of his citations occur in the argument of Rom 9:6–13, in which Paul seeks to support his contention that "the word of God has not failed" (9:6) by charting a revisionist history of election within Israel in anticipation of the current inflow of the gentiles into the church.

Quotation of Gen 21:12 in Rom 9:7

One important stage in this argument is Paul's strategy of redefining "Israel."[35] Paul makes a division within the history of Israel, contending that "not all Israel is Israel." He then adduces Gen 21:12 in Rom 9:7 to support this position. Paul's citation corresponds precisely to the LXX.[36] It is introduced somewhat

---

34. In Romans, some manuscripts (F G a) add "as the stars of the heaven and the sand of the sea" in apparent harmonization to Gen 22:17; cf. also 26:4 and, more loosely, 12:2.

35. Cf. Wagner, *Heralds*, 49–51.

36. This citation also occurs in Heb 11:18 (possibly dependent on Paul) though used to a slightly different end; cf. Clare K. Rothschild, *Hebrews as Pseudepigraphon: The History and Significance of the Pauline Attribution of Hebrews*, WUNT 235 (Tübingen: Mohr Siebeck, 2009), 95–96.

Chapter 4

abruptly, and an audience would probably only be aware that Paul is citing by the syntactical tension within its new epistolary context.[37] Recalling the story of Isaac and Ishmael that Paul allegorically expounded in Gal 4:21–31, Paul calls attention to the fact that not all of Abraham's sons were considered to be the line of Israel, but only those descended from Isaac ("in Isaac will seed be called for you"). Paul anticipates the citation by speaking of the "seed of Abraham" as the true Israel that does not correspond entirely with physical descent (9:7a).[38] In the following verse Paul offers an explanation (τοῦτ᾽ ἔστιν) in which he states what he takes Gen 21:12 to prove: "those who are children of the flesh, these are not children of God, but the children of the promise are reckoned as seed." The contrast between children of the flesh and children of the promise once more recalls Paul's exposition of the Sarah and Hagar story in Gal 4:21–31.

Quotation of Gen 18:10, 14 in Rom 9:9

Immediately after his brief exposition of Gen 21:12, Paul introduces the supporting witness of the promise itself. Paul has made alterations to the citation that enhance its contemporary ring. As the following table shows, Paul has introduced a prepositional phrase from Gen 18:10 into 18:14, substituted "I will come" for "I will return" (probably to avoid the distraction of his listeners wondering about the first visit), and abbreviated the whole. The changes should be laid at Paul's feet, though they do not substantially alter the meaning of the text.[39]

Gen 18:10, 14 LXX	**Rom 9:9**
18:10: ἐπαναστρέφων ἥξω πρὸς σὲ <u>κατὰ τὸν καιρὸν τοῦτον</u> εἰς ὥρας, καὶ ἕξει υἱὸν Σάρρα ἡ γυνή σου. 18:14: εἰς τὸν καιρὸν τοῦτον ἀναστρέψω πρὸς σὲ εἰς ὥρας, <u>καὶ ἔσται τῇ Σάρρᾳ υἱός.</u>	κατὰ τὸν καιρὸν τοῦτον ἐλεύσομαι καὶ ἔσται τῇ Σάρρᾳ υἱός.

Paul does not identify the speaker here and so probably sees the speaker (one of the three men who visited him by the oaks of Mamre) as "the Lord"

---

37. See Koch, *Die Schrift als Zeuge des Evangeliums*, 23.

38. The term σπέρμα Ἀβραάμ occurs in 2 Chr 20:7; Ps 104:6; Pss. Sol. 9:9; 18:3; Isa 41:8; cf. also 2 Cor 11:22; and Jewett, *Romans*, 575.

39. Stanley (*Paul and the Language*, 103–5) disputes the claim that this is the result of a conflation of vv. 10 and 14. But he rightly calls attention to the "dehistoricizing treatment accorded the Genesis passage" (104) and suggests that Paul introduced these changes to ensure that his point was duly emphasized.

Genesis in Paul

(cf. Gen 18:1, 13). Paul thus takes this to be the divine promise that guarantees that Isaac will be born and so indicates that Isaac is to be favored to Ishmael. This citation functions to support the assertion of 9:8 that election is a selective phenomenon in Israel's history and that the promise is what defines the lineage of true Israel (υἱός here being the concrete example of the τέκνα of 9:8).

Quotation of Gen 25:23 in Rom 9:12

The next stage in Paul's argument carries his point forward a generation, from Sarah to Rebekah. In contrast to Isaac and Ishmael, who shared the same father but had different mothers, Jacob and Esau were twins, conceived "by one husband" (Rom 9:10). Therefore, they serve to demonstrate that the choice between them did not depend on physical descent, which was identical in their case, but on divine initiative. In fact, to exclude any suggestion that divine favor was not an initiative but a response to the actions of Jacob and Esau (and here Paul seems to presuppose a knowledge of the divergent paths taken by the brothers in Genesis), he draws attention to the fact that God's decisive word is delivered *before* those actions had taken place—and in fact before they had even been born. This decisive word was spoken (ἐρρέθη) to Rebekah: "the elder shall serve the younger," a clear reversal of normal ancient Near Eastern family practice. In fact, a major theme in Genesis is reversal, and the younger son overtaking the elder recurs throughout the book.[40] Thus Paul's citation of Gen 25:23, which follows the LXX exactly, picks up a recurrent motif in the book expressed in pithy fashion. Paul finds this reading of Genesis confirmed with Mal 1:2-3 ("Jacob have I loved, but Esau have I hated"). This further confirms the significance of these figures as representing peoples. Although Paul does not extend his argument to gentiles explicitly at this point (contrast Barn. 13:1-6 in which Gen 25:23 is read in a fiercely supersessionist manner), Paul does find in Genesis a divine purpose that cannot be encompassed by physical lineage and so prepares for his argument that the gentiles have been grafted into the true Israel.

Allusion to Gen 22:12/22:16 in Rom 8:32

In the course of offering assurance of the love of God for believers, Paul marshals the handing over of God's own son to death as proof of his willingness to "give us all things." Paul's wording in Rom 8:32 (τοῦ ἰδίου υἱοῦ οὐκ ἐφείσατο

40. For the reception of this theme in early Christianity, see Harl, *Genèse*, 45–46.

Chapter 4

ἀλλὰ ὑπὲρ ἡμῶν πάντων παρέδωκεν αὐτόν, God "did not spare his own son but delivered him up for us all") recalls the description of God's commendation of Abraham when he displayed a willingness to kill Isaac, the child of promise, in response to the divine command (Gen 22:12/22:16: οὐκ ἐφείσω τοῦ υἱοῦ σου τοῦ ἀγαπητοῦ, "you did not spare your beloved son"). Given Paul's widespread use of the Abraham story elsewhere in his letters and the unique verbal correspondence (not sparing a son), it is likely that Paul here describes God's giving of his own son with echoes of Abraham's willingness to sacrifice Isaac. Within early Christianity, the *akedah*, or "binding" of Isaac (Gen 22), was often read as typologically anticipating God's giving of his son, and Paul seems to be an early (perhaps the earliest) example of that tendency.

Conclusion

In his reconstruction of Paul's theological reading of the Pentateuch, Francis Watson argues that Paul finds in Genesis above all the self-commitment of God to act for salvation, and so derives from Genesis "the hermeneutical priority of the promise."[41] This is an apt characterization of Paul's reading of the Abraham material in particular—in both Romans and Galatians, Paul wants to stress the inclusive and prevenient nature of the promises to Abraham and the subsequent community created in Christ. But Paul also derives ethical guidance from Genesis, which he applies to problems of sexual ethics or disunity in worship. Especially in Paul's correspondence with the Corinthians, Paul has repeated recourse to the opening chapters of Genesis, perhaps because he needs to stress the materiality of creation and new creation in his argument concerning the resurrection. And in both Romans and 1 Corinthians, the eschatological horizon of Paul's hermeneutic becomes clear, as he sees Adam pointing beyond himself to the coming Messiah. Above all, one sees that Paul has read and listened to Genesis intently, pondering not simply individual verses or pithy phrases, but its narrative elements in particular. These stories—of creation and ruination, of election and promise—order Paul's world of thought, and he attempts to pass on this storied world to his gentile audiences.

---

41. Watson, *Paul and the Hermeneutics of Faith*, 15n5 and passim; cf. pp. 167–269. For a brief response to Watson's larger construal of Paul's reading of the Pentateuch, see chapter 5.

5

PAUL'S ENGAGEMENT WITH DEUTERONOMY

Snapshots and Signposts

The apostle Paul was a consummate reader of Scripture. This sentiment, once controversial, has been endorsed by a substantial number of scholarly voices over the past few decades. Gone are the days when one could blithely dismiss Paul's scriptural quotations as mere flights of atomistic imagination: exit Paul the purveyor of pithy, free-floating axioms, enter Paul the reader.

In this chapter, I consider the discussion of one of Paul's favorite books, Deuteronomy, providing some snapshots of current work as well as indicating some signposts marking the way for future research. In light of the significance of the manuscript finds at Qumran and surrounding areas in the mid-twentieth century for the question, my remarks will in the first place examine works in the pre–Dead Sea Scrolls era before turning, second, to a more in-depth look at recent scholarship on the question of Paul's engagement with Israel's Scriptures generally, and Deuteronomy in particular. After a critical assessment of the current state of the question of Paul's engagement with Deuteronomy, I consider some possible directions forward.

This chapter was originally written as a history of research preparatory to my study, *Paul and the Early Jewish Encounter with Deuteronomy*, which first appeared in 2010, and the ground-clearing posture is evident. It surveys work published before 2008 or so. Although it would be possible to extend this survey to address the past fifteen years of scholarly work, that is a project for someone with fresher eyes who might make a novel contribution to the framing of research questions. I satisfied my intellectual curiosity about at least some of the larger lines of Paul's reading of Deuteronomy in that 2010 book, and I think this survey of research makes most sense as a product of its time. Therefore, those who wish to find analysis of work since 2010 will be best advised to supplement this chapter from elsewhere.[1]

---

1. One could do worse than to start with the numerous essays in Matthias Henze and David Lincicum, eds., *Israel's Scriptures in Early Christian Writings: The Use of the Old Testament in the New* (Grand Rapids: Eerdmans, 2023).

Chapter 5

Setting the Stage: Research Before the Mid-Twentieth Century

To inquire about Paul's reading of Deuteronomy is to step into a conversation that has been ongoing since at least the second century, with the strongly divergent reception paid to the Deuteronomy citations in Paul's letters by Justin Martyr on the one hand (*Dial.* 95, 96; where Deut 27:26 and 21:23 are quoted in a way that suggests dependence on Gal 3:10–13),[2] and Marcion on the other.[3] Nevertheless, focused study of the question in its current terms traces its roots to the second half of the sixteenth century. While the isolation of Deuteronomy for consideration must be judged a fairly recent phenomenon, clearly the question is related to Paul's broader engagement with Scripture, and, by extension, to the larger question of the reception of Jewish Scripture in the New Testament more generally. Thus, while a full history of scholarship on this question is beyond the limits of this chapter, to sketch briefly the broad lines of inquiry brings into focus the current questions.[4]

2. On which see, e.g., Charles H. Cosgrove, "Justin Martyr and the Emerging Christian Canon: Observations on the Purpose and Destination of the Dialogue with Trypho," *VC* 36 (1982): 209–32; Dietrich-Alex Koch, *Die Schrift als Zeuge des Evangeliums: Untersuchungen zur Verwendung und zum Verständnis der Schrift bei Paulus*, BHT 69 (Tübingen: Mohr Siebeck, 1986), 250–51; contra Philipp Vielhauer, "Paulus und das Alte Testament," in *Studien zur Geschichte und Theologie der Reformation: Festschrift für Ernst Bizer*, ed. Luise Abramowski and J. F. Gerhard Goeters (Neukirchen-Vluyn: Neukirchener Verlag, 1969), 33–62, here 39n28.

3. Adolf von Harnack, *Marcion: Das Evangelium von fremden Gott; Eine Monographie zur Geschichte der Grundlegung der katholischen Kirche*, TU 45 (Leipzig: J. C. Hinrichs, 1921), 125*; Edwin Cyril Blackman, *Marcion and His Influence* (London: SPCK, 1948), 44; and Harry Y. Gamble, "Marcion and the 'Canon,'" in *Origins to Constantine*, vol. 1, *The Cambridge History of Christianity*, ed. Margaret M. Mitchell and Frances M. Young (Cambridge: Cambridge University Press, 2006), 195–213.

4. See further Friedrich August Gottreu Tholuck, "The Use Made of the Old Testament in the New, and Especially in the Epistle to the Hebrews," in *A Commentary on the Epistle to the Hebrews*, 2 vols., trans. James Hamilton and J. E. Ryland (Edinburgh: Thomas Clark, 1842), 2:181–245, here 2:181–89; Eduard Böhl, *Die alttestamentlichen Citate im Neuen Testament* (Vienna: Braumüller, 1878), xix–xxviii; Crawford Howell Toy, *Quotations in the New Testament* (New York: Charles Scribner's Sons, 1884), xxxvii–xliii; Otto Michel, *Paulus und seine Bibel* (Darmstadt: Wissenschaftliche Buchgesellschaft, 1972 [1929]), 1–7; L. Venard, "Citations de l'Ancien Testament dans le Nouveau Testament," in *Supplément au Dictionnaire de la Bible*, ed. Louis Pirot (Paris: Letouzey et Ané, 1934), 2:23–51; E. Earle Ellis, *Paul's Use of the Old Testament* (Edinburgh: Oliver and Boyd, 1957), 2–5; Merrill P. Miller, "Targum, Midrash and the Use of the Old Testament in the New Testament," *JSJ* 2 (1971): 29–82; D. Moody Smith, "The Use of the Old Testament in the New," in *The Use of the Old Testament*

Paul's Engagement with Deuteronomy

In the wake of the Reformation, attention turned to the precise study of Paul's quotations and allusions to Scripture. In the late sixteenth century, both J. Drusius[5] and F. Junius[6] offered considerations of Paul's biblical quotations as part of larger projects on the reception of the Scripture in the New Testament. These early studies, setting the stage for much of the debate to come, focused on questions of text form and citation technique in an effort to defend the New Testament writers against their detractors. In the mid-seventeenth century, L. Cappellus examined the differences between New Testament quotations with reference to the LXX and the Hebrew,[7] and was apparently one of the first to argue that the New Testament writers generally followed the LXX.[8]

Perhaps the most impressive contribution of the eighteenth century was that of G. Surenhusius. Also responsible for a translation of the Mishnah, Surenhusius undertook an exhaustive comparison of the introductory formulae and exegetical methods in the New Testament with those found in rabbinic literature,[9] paving the way for later comparative work. More skeptically received was William Whiston's contention that the LXX (along with the Samaritan Pentateuch) represents the most original text, and that the Hebrew underlying the present MT was polemically altered at the beginning of the second century by Jewish opposition to the new Christian movement. In this way, he hoped to show that the New Testament citations that agree with the LXX against the MT preserve the original, uncorrupted text.[10] His thesis met with the

---

in the New and Other Essays: Studies in Honor of William Franklin Stinespring, ed. James M. Efird (Durham, NC: Duke University Press, 1972), 3–65; D. Moody Smith, "The Pauline Literature," in *It Is Written: Scripture Citing Scripture*, ed. D. A. Carson and Hugh Godfrey Maturin Williamson (Cambridge: Cambridge University Press, 1988), 265–91; E. Earle Ellis, *The Old Testament in Early Christianity: Canon and Interpretation in the Light of Modern Research*, WUNT 54 (Tübingen: Mohr Siebeck, 1991), 53–74; Christopher D. Stanley, *Paul and the Language of Scripture: Citation Technique in the Pauline Epistles and Contemporary Literature*, SNTSMS 74 (Cambridge: Cambridge University Press, 1992), 4–30; and Kenneth D. Litwak, "Echoes of Scripture? A Critical Survey of Recent Works on Paul's Use of the Old Testament," *CurBS* 6 (1998): 260–88.

5. Johannes Drusius, *Parallela Sacra: Hoc est, Locorum veteris Testamenti cum ijs, quae in novo citantur, coniuncta commemoratio, Ebraice et Graece* (Franeker: Aegidius Radaeud, 1588).

6. Franciscus Junius, *Sacrorum Parallelorum libri tres* (London: G. Bishop, 1591).

7. Louis Cappellus, *Critica Sacra, sive de variis quae in sacris veteris testamenti libris occurrunt lectionibus: Libri Sex* (Paris: Cramoisy, 1650), 53–67.

8. Louis Cappellus, *Critica Sacra*, 443–557.

9. Guilielmus Surenhusius, ספר המשוה *sive* ΒΙΒΛΟΣ ΚΑΤΑΛΛΑΓΗΣ *in quo secundum veterum theologorum Hebraeorum formulas allegandi, & modos interpretandi conciliantur loca ex V. in N. T. allegata* (Amsterdam: Johannes Boom, 1713).

10. William Whiston, *An Essay towards Restoring the True Text of the Old Testament*

Chapter 5

vigorous resistance of Anthony Collins[11] and J. G. Carpzov,[12] but nevertheless sheds light on the doctrinal pressure that was felt at the dawning, though by no means universal, consensus that the LXX was the favored text in the New Testament. In a sense these debates were a return to those occasioned by Augustine's and Jerome's differing stances toward the LXX (*Civ.* 18.42–44).[13] In fact, the arguments with which Collins sought to refute Whiston (i.e., that the New Testament authors practiced allegorical interpretation and this was perfectly legitimate) themselves implicitly acknowledge the force of the problem to which Whiston was responding.[14] Others later in the eighteenth century sought to excuse the New Testament authors from improper conduct[15] or to reaffirm the proximity of their quotations to the Hebrew.[16]

A number of studies in the nineteenth century investigated Paul's dependence on Israel's Scripture, usually in the context of broader studies of the reception of Scripture in the New Testament. Such studies most often focused on Paul's explicit quotations and clear allusions, some simply listing the quotations with brief comments.[17] Others offered more intensive discussion of

---

and for Vindicating the Citations Made Thence in the New Testament (London: Senex and Taylor, 1722).

11. Anthony Collins, *A Discourse on the Grounds and Reasons of the Christian Religion* (London: s.n., 1724).

12. Johann Gottlob Carpzov, *A Defence of the Hebrew Bible in Answer to the Charge of Corruption Brought against it by Mr. Whiston, in his* Essay towards restoring the true Text of the Old Testament, &c. *Wherein Mr. Whiston's Pretences are particularly Examined and Confuted*, trans. Moses Marcus (London: Bernard Lintot, 1729).

13. Martin Hengel with Roland Deines, *The Septuagint as Christian Scripture: Its Prehistory and the Problem of Its Canon*, trans. Mark E. Biddle (Edinburgh: T&T Clark, 2002), 47–54; note also Edward William Grinfield, *An Apology for the Septuagint in which its claims to biblical and canonical authority are briefly stated and vindicated* (London: Pickering, 1850).

14. Anthony Collins, *The Scheme of Literal Prophecy Considered: In a view of the Controversy, occasion'd by a late Book, Intitled*, A Discourse on the Grounds and Reasons of the Christian Religion, 2 vols. (London: London and Westminster, 1726).

15. E.g., Henry Owen, *The Modes of Quotation Used by the Evangelical Writers Explained and Vindicated* (London: J. Nichols, 1789).

16. E.g., Thomas Randolph, *The Prophecies and Other Texts, Cited in the New Testament, Compared with the Hebrew Original, and with the Septuagint Version, to which are added Notes* (Oxford: J. and J. Fletcher, [1782?]).

17. Edward William Grinfield, *Novum Testamentum Graecum, editio Hellenistica*, 2 vols. (London: Pickering, 1843), 2:1447–93; Edward William Grinfield, *Scholia Hellenistica in Novum Testamentum* (London: Pickering, 1848), 859–944; Henry Gough, *The New Testament quotations, collated with the Scriptures of the Old Testament, in the original Hebrew and the version of the LXX; and with the other writings, Apocryphal, Talmudic, and classical, cited or alleged so to be, with notes, and a complete index* (London: Walton and Maberly,

Paul's Engagement with Deuteronomy

Paul's *Vorlage*, introductory formulae, similarities with Jewish exegetical techniques, and the "use" for which the quotations were employed,[18] often with an apologetic slant.[19] In trying to account for the fact that many quotations evince a Septuagintal texture, while some depart from any known version or recension, E. Böhl put forth his novel *Volksbibel* thesis that an Aramaic Bible was in popular use that closely resembled the LXX in translation.[20] His thesis, while not well-received, provided a minority voice of protest against the majority that suggested the LXX as the dominant source text for New Testament quotations,[21] pointing to the ambiguity of some of the textual evidence for the biblical passages adduced in the New Testament.

1855); Thomas Hartwell Horne, *An Introduction to the Criticism of the Old Testament and to Biblical Interpretation, with an Analysis of the Books of the Old Testament and Apocrypha*, ed. John Ayr (London: Longman, Green, Longman, and Roberts, 1860), 113–208; August Clemen, *Der Gebrauch des Alten Testamentes in den Neutestamentlichen Schriften* (Gütersloh: Bertelsmann, 1895); Eugen Hühn, Die *alttestamentlichen Citate und Reminiscenzen im Neuen Testamente* (Tübingen: Mohr Siebeck, 1900); Wilhelm Dittmar, *Vetus Testamentum in Novo: Die alttestamentlichen Parallelen des Neuen Testaments im Wortlaut der Urtexte und der Septuaginta zusammengestellt*, 2 vols. (Göttingen: Vandenhoeck & Ruprecht, 1899–1903), which was created afresh in Hans Hübner, *Vetus Testamentum in Novo. Band 2: Corpus Paulinum* (Göttingen: Vandenhoeck & Ruprecht, 1997).

18. Johann Christian Carl Döpke, *Hermeneutik der neutestamentlichen Schriftsteller* (Leipzig: Friedrich Christian Wilhelm Vogel, 1829); Tholuck, "The Use Made of the Old Testament," 181–245; Friedrich August Gottreu Tholuck, "Citations of the Old Testament in the New," trans. Charles A. Aiken, *BSac* 11 (1854): 568–616, here 594–600; Samuel Davidson, *Sacred Hermeneutics: Developed and Applied* (Edinburgh: Thomas Clark, 1843), 334–515; David McCalman Turpie, *The Old Testament in the New: A Contribution to Biblical Criticism and Interpretation* (London; Edinburgh: Williams and Norgate, 1868); David McCalman Turpie, *The New Testament View of the Old: A Contribution to Biblical Introduction and Exegesis* (London: Hodder and Stoughton, 1872); Toy, *Quotations in the New Testament*; Franklin Johnson, *The Quotations of the New Testament from the Old Considered in the Light of General Literature* (Philadelphia: American Baptist Publication Society, 1896); and Henry St. John Thackeray, *The Relation of St. Paul to Contemporary Jewish Thought* (London: Macmillan, 1900), 180–222.

19. So, e.g., Davidson, *Sacred Hermeneutics*; Turpie, *The Old Testament in the New*; Turpie, *The New Testament View of the Old*; Helen MacLachlan, *Notes on References and Quotations in the New Testament Scriptures from the Old Testament* (Edinburgh: William Blackwood and Sons, 1872); contrast Döpke, *Hermeneutik der neutestamentlichen Schriftsteller*; and Toy, *Quotations in the New Testament*.

20. Böhl, *Die alttestamentlichen Citate im Neuen Testament*; see also Eduard Böhl, *Forschungen nach einer Volksbibel zur Zeit Jesu und deren Zusammenhang mit der Septuaginta-Übersetzung* (Vienna: Braumüller, 1873); and Ellis, *Paul's Use of the Old Testament*, 4–5.

21. Henry Barclay Swete, *An Introduction to the Old Testament in Greek*, rev. Richard Rusden Ottley, ed. Henry St. John Thackeray (Cambridge: Cambridge University Press, 1914), 404.

Chapter 5

In light of such ambiguity, two other scholars examined the textual evidence of Paul's scriptural citations and came to very different conclusions from those of Böhl. In a carefully executed dissertation, E. F. Kautzsch examined all of Paul's quotations against their possible sources, including individual manuscript traditions for the LXX, and concluded that in only two places, both quotations from Job, do Paul's citations more closely resemble the Hebrew than the Greek.[22] Hans Vollmer also examined Paul's quotations, concluding that Paul had recourse to the Greek manuscript tradition attested in the majuscules A and Q for most of the LXX (though more often F in the Pentateuch), but also to the predecessors of Aquila, Symmachus, and Theodotion.[23] He also suggested that for Paul, Scripture was a "pedagogical history book" (*ein pädagogisches Geschichtsbuch*), as well as a repository providing ethical direction, though its main significance to the apostle was as a "latent Gospel" (*ein latentes Evangelium*; also a *Verheissungskodex*).[24]

Perhaps two of the most significant contributions to study of Paul's engagement with Scripture in the early twentieth century were those by Otto Michel and Joseph Bonsirven. In his wide-ranging study (Bultmann once faulted Michel for trying to do too much),[25] Michel concluded that Paul used a canon coextensive with the modern Protestant canon, cited the Greek text, often from memory, shared some interpretive approaches of his rabbinic and Alexandrian near contemporaries (though he was closer to the former), and appealed to Scripture for a variety of purposes in his mission and letters. He also cast Paul as a "charismatic exegete" who found the true meaning of Scripture revealed only in Christ.[26] Bonsirven, on the other hand, focused more specifically on revisiting the concerns of Surenhusius, Döpke, and Thackeray, and compared rabbinic exegetical techniques[27] with Pauline exegesis.[28] He concluded that Paul evinced a significant methodological debt to his "rabbinic training," even while clearly differing in his conception of the ultimate meaning of Scripture:

22. Emil Friedrich Kautzsch, *De veteris testamenti locis a Paulo Apostolo allegatis* (Leipzig: Metzger & Wittig, 1869).

23. Hans Vollmer, *Die alttestamentlichen Citate bei Paulus textkritisch und biblisch-theologisch gewürdigt nebst einem Anhang Ueber das Verhältnis des Apostels zu Philo* (Leipzig: Mohr Siebeck, 1895), 21–35.

24. Vollmer, *Die alttestamentlichen Citate bei Paulus*, 77–78.

25. Rudolf Bultmann, review of *Paulus und seine Bibel*, by Otto Michel, *TLZ* 9 (1933): 157–59.

26. Michel, *Paulus*.

27. Joseph Bonsirven, *Exégèse rabbinique et exégèse paulinienne* (Paris: Beauchesne et ses Fils, 1939), 11–259.

28. Bonsirven, *Exégèse rabbinique et exégèse paulinienne*, 263–356.

Paul's Engagement with Deuteronomy

He uses the knowledge of the Bible and the exegetical methods which he owed, in large part, to the rabbinic schools, but the theses which he demonstrates by means of them come to him from elsewhere, and it is his Christian faith that opens to him an understanding of the Scriptures and causes him to recognize in its letters, until then veiled for him, the decisive texts which bear witness in favor of Christ and the Church.[29]

Bonsirven sums up his discussion by saying, "St. Paul is a Rabbi turned Christian evangelist."[30] Although it now appears that some of Bonsirven's comparisons are overdrawn or overly specific in light of both the intractable issues of dating rabbinic traditions and the late institution of the office of "Rabbi" itself, and dated in the light of the Qumran discoveries and other advances in the study of Second Temple Judaism, he rightly stressed the importance of comparative study for understanding Paul's exegesis.

At the risk of oversimplification, we may hazard the observation that questions before the mid-twentieth century tended to revolve around two or perhaps three main poles of inquiry: one centering around the issue of *accuracy* (including questions of *Vorlage* and the wording of his quotations); a second set around *legitimacy* (including discussion of Paul's "application" of the texts and the apologetic questions of whether Paul cited according to the original sense); and a third set, at times subsumed under the second, at other times pursued in its own right, concerning the *comparability* of Paul's citation technique to his Jewish or Greco-Roman contemporaries. All of these clusters of questions continue to the present time, and have been applied to Paul's appropriation of Deuteronomy, though they have been redefined in light of the Qumran manuscript finds, advances in our understanding of Second Temple Judaism as a culture with significant interest in scriptural interpretation, and more developed sensitivity to the literary function of quotations.

PAUL AND SCRIPTURE SINCE THE JUDAEAN DESERT DISCOVERIES

If Böhl could write in 1878 that the literature on the citations from Scripture in the New in his day was "scanty" (*dürftig*), the same can hardly be said today.[31] Nonetheless, the studies that impinge on the investigation of Paul's

---

29. Bonsirven, *Exégèse rabbinique et exégèse paulinienne*, 275.
30. Bonsirven, *Exégèse rabbinique et exégèse paulinienne*, 348.
31. Böhl, *Die alttestamentlichen Citate im Neuen Testament*, xix.

77

Chapter 5

recourse to Deuteronomy are of primarily three types: (1) considerations of the "mechanics" of Paul's citations of Scripture, including introductory formulae, citation technique and text form; (2) studies that examine the role of Scripture in Paul's theology more broadly; and (3) studies specifically concerned with the reception of Deuteronomy in Paul's theology and ethics. The first two of these concerns are drawn from studies of the use of scriptural traditions in Paul's letters more generally; thus, in this section, we will highlight the relevance of results gained in these two categories for the question at hand before turning in the next major section to studies specifically concerned with Paul's recourse to Deuteronomy itself.

Textual and Methodological Studies

From the preceding survey of research, one of the issues that has repeatedly surfaced concerns the original language and text form of Paul's *Vorlage*. The manuscript finds at Qumran and the surrounding areas in the late 1940s and early 1950s reopened such questions by bringing to light new evidence. Though many investigations of Paul and Deuteronomy are more concerned with matters of interpretation than text form per se, clearly the two are intertwined— and this has become even clearer in recent research. Three works in particular examined this question in the period under consideration.[32]

Dietrich-Alex Koch's work, *Die Schrift als Zeuge des Evangeliums*, remains unsurpassed as a penetrating study of the technical aspects of Paul's engagement with Scripture.[33] In the course of his discussion, he focuses on both Paul's *Verständnis* and *Verwendung* of Scripture. Koch argues that Paul has much in common with Hellenistic Diaspora Jews in his method of appropriating Scripture, although his Christian standpoint has introduced a new perspective from which he reads Scripture as a word to the present eschatological time and so as a "witness to the gospel." Koch further catalogues the numerous alterations evident in Paul's quotations, concluding that some of these are from Paul's own hand while other deviations from the standard Old Greek texts are the result of Paul's reliance on a hebraizing revision of the LXX.

---

32. On the earlier contribution of Ellis (*Paul's Use of the Old Testament*), note the comments of James Barr, "Paul and the LXX: A Note on Some Recent Work," *JTS*, n.s., 45 (1994): 593–601, here 593–97.

33. Koch, *Die Schrift als Zeuge des Evangeliums*; note also Hans Hübner, review of *Die Schrift als Zeuge des Evangeliums*, by Dietrich-Alex Koch, *TLZ* 113 (1988): 349–52; Richard B. Hays, review of *Die Schrift als Zeuge des Evangeliums*, by Dietrich-Alex Koch, *JBL* 107 (1988): 331–33.

Paul's Engagement with Deuteronomy

Christopher Stanley extended Koch's fundamental insights by focusing on one particular aspect of Paul's reliance on Scripture, namely, "the mechanics of the citation process itself."[34] Considering especially the freedom with which Paul seems to treat the wording of his *Vorlage*, Stanley argues two basic theses: first, that Paul adapted the wording of his biblical text at times to reflect his own understanding; and second, "that, in offering such 'interpretive renderings' of the biblical text, Paul was working consciously but unreflectively within the accepted literary conventions of his day."[35] Using rigid criteria to compile a set of "controlled" results,[36] Stanley's work laid the foundation for subsequent studies of the interpretative adaptations of Paul's quotations and provided some useful guidelines to distinguish between Paul's appropriation of divergent textual predecessors on one hand, and the intentional modification of his source text on the other.

Both Koch and Stanley draw on the significant advances in LXX studies over the preceding several decades in formulating their more refined theories of Paul's reliance on a Greek *Vorlage*.[37] Nevertheless, in view of the post-Qumran awareness of the textual plurality of the Second Temple period, Timothy H. Lim sought to challenge the assurance with which scholars identify modifications in Paul's quotations and the widespread agreement that Paul relied on a Septuagintal text.[38] Aligning himself especially with the "multiple-texts" theory of Emanuel Tov,[39] Lim argues that "the Qumran pesharim and Pauline letters are dated to a period when the textual situation is fluid and more than the three traditional textual traditions of the MT, LXX, and SP should be posited."[40] From this unobjectionable premise, Lim proceeds to question the prevalent opinion that Paul quoted from a Septuagintal text. While his insistence that one must consider the evidence of Hebrew texts and other versions is well-taken,[41] such evidence probably would have passed into Paul's hands via Greek texts. In the end, his study simply does not contain

---

34. Stanley, *Paul and the Language*, 3.

35. Stanley, *Paul and the Language*, 29; see also 348, 359.

36. Stanley, *Paul and the Language*, 31–61, 252–64.

37. Koch, *Die Schrift als Zeuge des Evangeliums*, 11–101 and passim; and Stanley, *Paul and the Language*, 37–51 and passim.

38. Timothy H. Lim, *Holy Scripture in the Qumran Commentaries and Pauline Letters* (Oxford: Clarendon, 1997).

39. Emanuel Tov, "A Modern Textual Outlook Based on the Qumran Scrolls," *HUCA* 53 (1982): 11–27.

40. Lim, *Holy Scripture*, 22.

41. Lim, *Holy Scripture*, 142.

Chapter 5

enough exegetical demonstration from the Pauline letters themselves to justify the overthrow of the relatively well-established hypothesis of Paul's reliance on a Greek text.[42] Lim has offered a salient warning against naive presumptions of textual stability but has not effectively demonstrated the impossibility of identifying at least some of Paul's own exegetical alterations to the generally Septuagintal text of his scriptural quotations.

These three studies together, then, suggest some of the possibilities and constraints within which study of Paul's engagement of Deuteronomy operates. The possibilities concern Paul's indebtedness to the Jewish exegetical milieu of the Second Temple period, his predilection for certain Greek parent texts, and his creative but not unbounded adaptation of the scriptural text to express his understanding of the source he quotes. The constraints center largely around the need to articulate a historically plausible account of Paul's encounter with the text in its pluriform diversity.

Two Important Studies on Scripture in Paul's Theology

Contemporary study of Paul's engagement with Scripture entered a new era with the publication of Richard Hays's *Echoes of Scripture in the Letters of Paul*.[43] While most scholarship until this time, as I have suggested above, had been devoted to issues centering on the accuracy, legitimacy, and comparability of Paul's citations, Hays transposed the question into a "literary-theological" key in order to focus on Paul's letters as "hermeneutical events," and this largely by drawing attention to the more subtle presence of Scripture in echoes and allusions in Paul.[44] Specifically, Hays appealed to what we might term a "weak" diachronic model of intertextuality: a study of "the imbedding of fragments of an earlier text within a later one"[45] rather than the poststructuralist synchronic model associated with Julia Kristeva, Roland Barthes,

42. Note also the criticism of Christopher D. Stanley, review of *Holy Scripture in the Qumran Commentaries and Pauline Letters*, by Timothy H. Lim, *JTS* 49 (1998): 781–84; J. Ross Wagner, review of *Holy Scripture in the Qumran Commentaries and Pauline Letters*, by Timothy H. Lim, *JBL* 120 (2001): 175–78; Dwight D. Swanson, review of *Holy Scripture in the Qumran Commentaries and Pauline Letters*, Timothy H. Lim, *JSS* 47 (2002): 153–56; and J. Ross Wagner, *Heralds of the Good News: Isaiah and Paul in Concert in the Letter to the Romans*, NovTSup 101 (Leiden: Brill, 2002), 7–8; all of whom fault Lim for his imbalanced presentation, focusing more on Qumran than on Paul.

43. Richard B. Hays, *Echoes of Scripture in the Letters of Paul* (New Haven: Yale University Press, 1989); see also Litwak, "Echoes of Scripture?"

44. Hays, *Echoes of Scripture*, 9–10.

45. Hays, *Echoes of Scripture*, 14.

Paul's Engagement with Deuteronomy

and Harold Bloom.[46] Particularly important for Hays's work is the concept of "metalepsis" or "transumption": "When a literary echo links the text in which it occurs to an earlier text, the figurative effect of the echo can lie in the unstated or suppressed (transumed) points of resonance between the two texts."[47]

Sensitized, then, to the presence of echo and allusion in Paul,[48] Hays proposed a series of influential tests by which to examine possible instances of intertextual echo and conducted a wide-ranging reading of Paul's subtle engagement with Scripture. The Paul that emerges from Hays's study operates with an "ecclesiocentric" hermeneutic, discerning in Scripture "a foreshadowing of the church."[49] He reads Scripture poetically, his appeals to Scripture often performing metaphorical transformations of the original text. His quotations and allusions are often only the tip of a sprawling narrative iceberg. In short, Hays brought forth a Paul who is neither slavishly bound by the written word of Scripture on the one hand, nor sovereignly free from its constraints on the other, but one who is a creative reader of Scripture in light of Christ, bringing "Scripture and gospel into a mutually interpretive relation."[50]

Hays's groundbreaking work inaugurated a fresh era in the study of Paul's relationship to what became the Christian Old Testament, and the number of new works in the area over the past thirty-five years testifies to the importance of his contribution. Nevertheless, at least two aspects of *Echoes* need to be supplemented. First, there is the question of how much Hays's dual dependence on literary criticism intended for poetic texts and on a certain model of intertextuality may have skewed his results. While it is certainly at least sometimes true that "Paul's citations of Scripture often function not as proofs but as tropes,"[51] Paul is still appealing to a sacred text viewed as having an authority by virtue of its divine origin, especially in the case of Deuteronomy. This is not to deny

---

46. See Hans Hübner, "Intertextualität—die hermeneutische Strategie des Paulus: Zu einem neuen Versuch der theologischen Rezeption des Alten Testaments im Neuen," *TLZ* 116 (1991): cols. 881–98, here 883–85; for cautionary remarks on the use of "intertextuality," see Christopher M. Tuckett, "Scripture and Q," in *The Scriptures in the Gospels*, ed. Christopher M. Tuckett, BETL 131 (Leuven: Leuven University Press, 1997), 3–26, here 3–6; Martin Rese, "Intertextualität: Ein Beispiel für Sinn und Unsinn 'neuer' Methoden," in *The Scriptures in the Gospels*, 431–39; Thomas R. Hatina, "Intertextuality and Historical Criticism in New Testament Studies: Is There a Relationship?," *BibInt* 7 (1999): 28–43; and William Irwin, "Against Intertextuality," *Philosophy and Literature* 28 (2004): 227–42.

47. Hays, *Echoes of Scripture*, 20, following John Hollander.

48. Hays, *Echoes of Scripture*, 21: "less a matter of method than of sensibility."

49. Hays, *Echoes of Scripture*, 86, 58; see 73 and passim.

50. Hays, *Echoes of Scripture*, 176.

51. Hays, *Echoes of Scripture*, 24.

Chapter 5

that Paul's readings sometimes have poetic character, but rather to wonder whether Hays's focus on texts with a strong potential of "resonant signification" has slighted Paul's more straightforward appeals to the authoritative Torah (the emphasis on the poetic is somewhat attenuated in his later essays).[52]

Second, some aspects of *Echoes* call for a firmer historical grounding. Paul at times appears as a solitary, creative, "strong misreader" of Israel's Scripture without enough attention given to his historical context in the Second Temple period.[53] Many of Paul's readings are odd to us, but some of his interpretative contemporaries display the same types of oddness in their readings of Scripture. This is not to claim that Paul can be explained without remainder by recourse to Qumran or to Philo or to other authors of the texts that came to make up the New Testament, but simply to note that Paul stands in a tradition of reflection and interpretation of Scripture—a dynamic captured well by Francis Watson's metaphor of a "three-way conversation" between Paul, his contemporaries, and Scripture.[54] Furthermore, as we have already seen, recent studies have pressed the need for responsible assumptions about the nature of the scriptural text in the Second Temple period. Nonetheless, with these adjustments to provide a more firm rooting in the historical soil of the Second Temple period, the debt of contemporary scholarship to Hays's work is evident.

Hays himself had highlighted the importance of Deuteronomy at key points for Paul, famously opining that "Deuteronomy 32 contains Romans *in nuce*,"[55] even while recognizing the programmatic role of Isaiah in Paul's mission and theology. Indeed, Paul's reliance on and engagement with the book of Isaiah has been the theme of much recent literature,[56] but it is Hays's student, J. Ross Wag-

---

52. See Richard B. Hays, *The Conversion of the Imagination: Paul as Interpreter of Israel's Scripture* (Grand Rapids: Eerdmans, 2005).

53. Craig A. Evans, "Listening for Echoes of Interpreted Scripture," in *Paul and the Scriptures of Israel*, ed. Craig A. Evans and James A. Sanders, JSNTSup 83, SSEJC 1 (Sheffield: Sheffield Academic, 1993), 47–51; James A. Sanders, "Paul and Theological History," in Evans and Sanders, *Paul and the Scriptures of Israel*, 52–57; James M. Scott, "'For as Many as Are of Works of the Law Are under a Curse' (Galatians 3.10)," in Evans and Sanders, *Paul and the Scriptures of Israel*, 187–221; in his response, Hays ("On the Rebound: A Response to Critiques of *Echoes of Scripture in the Letters of Paul*," in *The Conversion of the Imagination: Paul as Interpreter of Israel's Scripture* [Grand Rapids: Eerdmans, 2005], 163–89) more or less concedes the point.

54. Francis Watson, *Paul and the Hermeneutics of Faith* (London: T&T Clark, 2004). Given the chronological periodization in this essay, references to this book are to its first edition; a second edition was released in 2015.

55. Hays, *Echoes of Scripture*, 164.

56. C. J. A. Hickling, "Paul's Reading of Isaiah," in *Studia Biblica 1979: III. Papers on Paul*

Paul's Engagement with Deuteronomy

ner, who expanded and clarified his fundamental insights in a study on Paul's appropriation of Isaiah in Romans.[57] Because of both Paul's tendency to quote Deuteronomy in proximity to Isaiah, and because Wagner's study is a model of ascertaining the influence of a single book on Paul's thought, it is worthwhile briefly to consider Wagner's contribution here. Wagner attempts to ascertain the influence of Isaiah on Paul by posing three clusters of questions. First among these are questions concerning the manner in which Paul would have read Isaiah in the first century, bringing a welcome stress not simply on hermeneutical methods but also on questions of text-form and the *realia* of books and reading in the first century.[58] Second, Wagner inquires, "How did Paul's understanding of the gospel and of his own particular calling as an apostle shape his reading of Isaiah, and, conversely, how did Isaiah's oracles help to form Paul's conception of his own message and mission?"[59] Finally, Wagner asks how a focus on such questions materially enriches our understanding of Paul's letter to the Romans.

Wagner concludes that Paul's citations come from three major sections of Isaiah: chapters 1–11, 28–29, and 52–53 (the last of which can be extended to 40–51 by considering major allusions). He further notes the frequency with which Paul either conflates Isaiah with another scriptural source or places the prophet alongside another scriptural witness.[60] Specifically, Paul finds in Isaiah the fore-

---

and Other New Testament Authors, ed. Elizabeth A. Livingstone, JSNTSup 3 (Sheffield: JSOT Press, 1980), 215–23; Paul E. Dinter, "Paul and the Prophet Isaiah," *BTB* 13 (1983): 48–52; Craig A. Evans, *To See and Not Perceive: Isaiah 6.9–10 in Early Jewish and Christian Interpretation*, JSOTSup 64 (Sheffield: JSOT Press, 1989), 81–89; John F. A. Sawyer, *The Fifth Gospel: Isaiah in the History of Christianity* (Cambridge: Cambridge University Press, 1996), 21–41; Florian Wilk, *Die Bedeutung des Jesajabuches für Paulus*, FRLANT 179 (Göttingen: Vandenhoeck & Ruprecht, 1998); Florian Wilk, "Paulus als Interpret der prophetischen Schriften," *KD* 45 (1999): 284–306; Florian Wilk, "Isaiah in 1 and 2 Corinthians," in *Isaiah in the New Testament*, ed. Steve Moyise and Maarten J. J. Menken (London: T&T Clark, 2005), 133–58; H. H. Drake Williams III, *The Wisdom of the Wise: The Presence and Function of Scripture within 1 Cor. 1:18–3:23*, AGJU 44 (Leiden: Brill, 2001); Shiu-Lun Shum, *Paul's Use of Isaiah in Romans: A Comparative Study of Paul's Letter to the Romans and the Sibylline and Qumran Sectarian Texts*, WUNT 2/156 (Tübingen: Mohr Siebeck, 2002); Wagner, *Heralds*; Wagner, "Isaiah in Romans and Galatians," in Moyise and Menken, *Isaiah in the New Testament*, 119–32; Wagner, "Moses and Isaiah in Concert: Paul's Reading of Isaiah and Deuteronomy in the Letter to the Romans," in *"As Those Who Are Taught": The Interpretation of Isaiah from the LXX to the SBL*, ed. Claire Matthews McGinnis and Patricia K. Tull (Atlanta: Society of Biblical Literature, 2006), 87–105.

57. Wagner, *Heralds*.

58. Wagner, *Heralds*, 20–28, 33–39.

59. Wagner, *Heralds*, 3.

60. Wagner, *Heralds*, 352.

Chapter 5

telling of his own gospel and mission to the gentiles, the foreshadowing of Israel's unresponsiveness to the gospel and a narrative about the rebellion, punishment, and restoration of God's people.[61] This narrative substructure, Wagner points out, is also shared by Deut 29–32, which Paul links with Isaiah three times by way of quotation. Thus, Wagner concludes that as Paul read Isaiah, alongside a few other key texts, in light of his mission to the gentiles and the unresponsiveness of his kinsmen to the gospel, he found there a prophetic voice reshaping his own self-understanding, mission, and theology, giving him hope for the ultimate triumph of God over the nonreception of his message on the part of his fellow Jews.

Wagner must be regarded as having surpassed his mentor, Richard Hays, on at least two fronts. As he himself notes, he grants more attention to questions of the state of the text in the first century and to the variety of readings being offered in Second Temple Judaism.[62] On the former, Wagner's study has been the most well-informed to date, taking full notice of current LXX and Qumran studies. The latter emphasis, however, is often subsumed under text-critical discussions or relegated to footnotes. While perhaps this is an understandable omission in a study already large, one might wish for more sustained comparative engagement with other Second Temple interpretations of Isaiah, including other voices within the New Testament itself. Though Wagner has taken steps to counter the ahistorical tendencies of Hays, even more historical mooring in first-century interpretative practice would lend greater credence to the interpretations Wagner suggests. Furthermore, one might have wished for an extension of Wagner's conclusions to include both the influence of Isaiah on the other and some indication of Paul's construal of the book as a whole. Nevertheless, his study holds a dual significance in connection with the present analysis: he has produced a model study of Paul's reception of a single book of Scripture, and he has highlighted the significant role that Deuteronomy plays alongside Isaiah in the letter to the Romans. Several other recent studies, to which we now turn, further highlight the importance of Deuteronomy for Paul.

DEUTERONOMY IN PAUL'S THEOLOGY AND ETHICS

Turning, now, to examine the scholarly reception of Deuteronomy in Paul's letters, we proceed by first mentioning studies concerned with his theology, then considering those examining his ethics.

61. Wagner, *Heralds*, 351–54.
62. Wagner, *Heralds*, 15.

Paul's Engagement with Deuteronomy

Deuteronomy in Paul's Theology

Although a number of projects have concerned themselves with one or two central citations of Deuteronomy in Paul's letters, often in discussing Paul's stance toward the Jewish Law, four scholars in particular set about construing Paul's reading of Deuteronomy in a more holistic manner.[63]

Does Paul Employ a Deuteronomic Framework? Scott, Waters, and Wisdom

In a series of articles in the 1990s, James M. Scott argued that certain aspects of Paul's thought should be understood in the light of a widespread Deuteronomic framework, largely derived from Deut 27–32.[64] Such a framework, Scott argued, consists essentially of a "sin-exile-restoration" (SER) scheme as an interpretation of Israel's history and stresses the exile as protracted beyond the initial return to the land in the Persian period.[65] Alternatively, Scott sometimes follows Odil H. Steck's presentation of *das deuteronomistische Geschichtsbild*, consisting of six elements: (1) Israel's whole history has been one of disobedience; (2) God has constantly sent the prophets to urge his people to repent; (3) Nevertheless, Israel rejected the message of the prophets and treated them violently; (4) Therefore, God was angry with Israel and exiled them; (5) During the exile, Israel still has the opportunity to repent; (6) If Israel repents, God will restore them to the covenant blessings, including the possession of the land.[66]

---

63. Studies that show a more sustained attention to Deuteronomy include Dan O. Via, "A Structuralist Approach to Paul's Old Testament Hermeneutic," *Int* 28 (1974): 201–20; Dan O. Via, *Kerygma and Comedy in the New Testament: A Structuralist Approach to Hermeneutic* (Philadelphia: Fortress, 1975), 49–70; Frank Thielman, *From Plight to Solution: A Jewish Framework for Understanding Paul's View of the Law in Galatians and Romans*, NovTSup 6 (Leiden: Brill, 1989); Frank Thielman, *Paul and the Law: A Contextual Approach* (Downers Grove, IL: InterVarsity, 1994); Richard H. Bell, *Provoked to Jealousy: The Origin and Purpose of the Jealousy Motif in Romans 9–11*, WUNT 2/63 (Tübingen: Mohr Siebeck, 1994); Thomas L. Brodie, "The Systematic Use of the Pentateuch in 1 Corinthians," in *The Corinthian Correspondence*, ed. Reimund Bieringer, BETL 125 (Leuven: Leuven University Press, 1996), 441–57; C. Marvin Pate, *The Reverse of the Curse: Paul, Wisdom, and the Law*, WUNT 2/114 (Tübingen: Mohr Siebeck, 2000); and Moyise and Menken, *Deuteronomy in the New Testament*.

64. Scott, "'For as Many as Are of Works of the Law'"; James M. Scott, "Paul's Use of Deuteronomistic Tradition," *JBL* 112 (1993): 645–65; James M. Scott, "Restoration of Israel," in *Dictionary of Paul and His Letters*, ed. Gerald F. Hawthorne and Ralph P. Martin (Downers Grove, IL: InterVarsity, 1993), 796–805; James M. Scott, "The Use of Scripture in 2 Corinthians 6.16c–18 and Paul's Restoration Theology," *JSNT* 56 (1994): 73–99.

65. Scott, "'For as Many as Are of Works of the Law,'" 207–13; Scott, "Restoration of Israel."

66. Scott, "Paul's Use of Deuteronomistic Tradition," 647–50; Scott, "The Use of Scripture

Chapter 5

Bringing to the investigation a *traditionsgeschichtliche* approach (or what Steck sometimes calls a *theologiegeschichtliche* approach), Scott believes the pattern has been originally taken from the closing chapters of Deuteronomy but refracted and interpreted throughout Israel's history.[67] This interpretation is not only found in the so-called Deuteronomistic History (Joshua–2 Kings), but especially in the "penitential prayer tradition" reflected in Dan 9, Ezra 9, Neh 9, Bar 1:15–3:8, the Prayer of Azariah, and Sir 36:1–17 among other places.[68] This tradition of urging repentance looks forward to the ultimate restoration of Israel and the inflowing of the gentiles to God's covenant people.

Positing such a Deuteronomic framework helps elucidate Paul's thought, according to Scott, principally in three places. First, in light of this framework Paul's statement in 1 Thess 2:15–16 is understandable as an instance of prophetic critique-from-within rather than an anti-Semitic attack from without. Second, when Paul speaks of the "curse of the law" in Gal 3, he is speaking from an exilic perspective (much like Dan 9) in assuming that the curse spoken of in Deuteronomy has come upon Israel until its iniquity is atoned for. In this way, he expresses "the negative side of the traditional hope—already articulated in Deuteronomy 27–32—which looks forward to the inclusion of the Gentiles in the restoration of Israel (cf. Deut 32:43, cited in Rom 15:10)."[69] Finally, Paul's argument in Rom 9–11 that Israel has sinned but will ultimately be redeemed further stands in recognizable continuity with the Deuteronomic tradition.[70]

A number of recent studies have either drawn on the framework proposed by Steck and/or Scott directly or proposed strikingly similar readings of the pervasiveness of Deuteronomic tradition in the Second Temple period and the concomitant popular consciousness of a protracted exile.[71] Donald Gowan,

---

in 2 Corinthians 6.16c–18," 91; see Odil Hannes Steck, *Israel und das gewaltsame Geschick der Propheten: Untersuchungen zur Überlieferung des deuteronomistichen Geschichtsbildes im Alten Testament, Spätjudentum und Urchristentum*, WMANT 23 (Neukirchen-Vluyn: Neukirchener Verlag, 1967).

67. Odil Hannes Steck, "Das Problem theologischer Strömungen in nachexilischer Zeit," *EvT* 28 (1968): 445–58.

68. Scott, "'For as Many as Are of Works of the Law,'" 201–6.

69. Scott, "Restoration of Israel," 802; more fully, Scott, "'For as Many as Are of Works of the Law,'" 213–17.

70. Scott, "Paul's Use of Deuteronomistic Tradition," 659–65.

71. Michael A. Knibb, "The Exile in the Literature of the Intertestamental Period," *HeyJ* 17 (1976): 253–72; Michael A. Knibb, "Exile in the Damascus Document," *JSOT* 25 (1983): 99–117; Michael A. Knibb, *The Qumran Community*, Cambridge Commentaries on Writings of the Jewish and Christian World 200 BC to AD 200 (2) (Cambridge: Cambridge University Press, 1987), 19–21; Donald E. Gowan, "The Exile in Jewish Apocalyptic," in *Scripture in*

Paul's Engagement with Deuteronomy

in an essay published prior to Scott's work, expressed a representative conclusion from his study of laments and apocalyptic literature in the Second Temple period:

> The laments provide ample evidence for the existence in Judaism of a general conviction that the restoration experienced so far is by no means the fulfillment of God's intentions for Israel, so that the problems of the exile still remain unsolved. Against this background, apocalyptic may be seen as one type of effort to resolve a problem acknowledged by all.[72]

Most scholars, moreover, have understood such evidence for a protracted exile in terms of Deuteronomic themes or against a Deuteronomic background, especially when conceived in terms of an SER pattern. The Deuteronomic paradigm, however, has been challenged by two studies concerned with Paul's interpretation of Deuteronomy.

Jeffrey R. Wisdom has doubted whether it can be proven that there were "Jews living in Palestine [who] thought that they themselves were still under the curse."[73] Further, Wisdom argues, positing a Deuteronomic framework still does not help to explain why "Paul viewed the law as no longer necessary for believers in Christ (cf. Gal 3.23–29)."[74] Suggesting that the attempt to cast Paul in a Deuteronomic mold has "sought to soften the polemical edge" of Gal 3:10 by appealing to a supposedly widespread Jewish view,[75] Wisdom offers a different reading of Paul's Deuteronomy citation in Gal 3:10 while still appealing to a broad background in Deuteronomy.

History and Theology: Essays in Honor of J. Coert Rylaarsdam, ed. Arthur L. Merrill and Thomas W. Overholt, PTMS 17 (Pittsburgh: Pickwick, 1977), 205–23; Thielman, *From Plight to Solution*; N. T. Wright, "Curse and Covenant: Galatians 3.10–14," in *The Climax of the Covenant: Christ and the Law in Pauline Theology* (Minneapolis: Fortress, 1993), 137–56; N. T. Wright, *The New Testament and the People of God* (Minneapolis: Fortress, 1992), 268–72, 299–301; N. T. Wright, *Jesus and the Victory of God* (Minneapolis: Fortress, 1996), xvii–xviii, 126–27, 248–50; Craig A. Evans, "Jesus and the Continuing Exile of Israel," in *Jesus and the Restoration of Israel: A Critical Assessment of N. T. Wright's* Jesus and the Victory of God, ed. Carey C. Newman (Downers Grove, IL: InterVarsity, 1999), 77–100; Wagner, *Heralds*, 166n143, 254–57; and James M. Scott, ed., *Exile: Old Testament, Jewish, and Christian Conceptions*, JSJSup 56 (Leiden: Brill, 1997).

72. Gowan, "The Exile in Jewish Apocalyptic," 219–20.

73. Jeffrey R. Wisdom, *Blessing for the Nations and the Curse of the Law: Paul's Citations of Genesis and Deuteronomy in Gal 3:8–10*, WUNT 2/133 (Tübingen: Mohr Siebeck, 2001), 9.

74. Wisdom, *Blessing for the Nations*, 9.

75. Wisdom, *Blessing for the Nations*, 157–58.

Chapter 5

Instead of the traditional (sometimes: "Lutheran") assumption that obedience to the law is impossible, Wisdom looks to Deuteronomy to define what it might mean "to fail to live within all that the Lord had commanded Israel and thereby fail to remain faithful to the covenant,"[76] and spells out the answer in terms of apostasy and idolatry.[77] Paul's stress on the "curse of the law," then, is against "both Jewish Christians who compelled gentile believers to accept circumcision and other elements of the law which defined Israel's national existence and also gentile believers who accepted circumcision and these other elements of the law."[78] This is so because they have failed to demonstrate allegiance to the covenant by adhering to its original plan to secure blessing for the nations (note the tradition stemming from Gen 12:1–3) and have rather sought to impose a nationalistic exclusivism on the Galatian communities. The curse, however, is not primarily an instrument of punishment so much as an instrument of exclusion to prevent "polluting influences" from damaging the community.[79]

In response to Wisdom's interesting thesis, the following points may be here noted: (1) Even if it were impossible to find other Jews who thought of themselves or the nation as living under the curse of the law (itself a debatable point, as even his ch. 5 suggests), this would not militate against Paul's imaginative construal of them to be so living. In other words, one need not accept Steck and Scott's *traditionsgeschichtliche* approach in its entirety to agree that Paul is applying the curses of Deut 27–30 to people in his current day, for a lack of precedent does not render inherently impossible such an interpretative move on Paul's part. (2) Paul's statement in Gal 3:13a that "Christ redeemed *us* from the curse of the law" renders unlikely a limited reference of the curse to the Galatian agitators and their adherents. (3) Such a proposal labors under the unexpressed premise that the "curse of the law" is not really the curse of the Sinaitic law, but the curse of the law as taken up in Christ. For if, for Paul, the cursed ones are chiefly those who show themselves to be apostate by not believing in Christ and in hindering gentiles from receiving blessing *qua* gentiles, the curse of the law could not have existed before the blessing of Abraham had been initiated by Christ's crucifixion. But clearly, Gal 3:13 suggests that the "curse of the law" is something under which "we" functioned before Christ's death. What is more, Wisdom's own research in Second Temple Jewish understandings of the "curse" suggests more plausible options within which Paul's understanding of the curse might operate.

---

76. Wisdom, *Blessing for the Nations*, 18.
77. Wisdom, *Blessing for the Nations*, 167.
78. Wisdom, *Blessing for the Nations*, 155; see passim.
79. Wisdom, *Blessing for the Nations*, 18, 165, and passim.

Paul's Engagement with Deuteronomy

Guy P. Waters also challenged this Deuteronomistic framework from within the context of his own substantive proposal about Paul's engagement with Deuteronomy. Waters undertakes an examination of Deut 27–30, 32 in Paul's letters (because Deut 31 is not explicitly cited in Paul, Waters prefers not to speak of "Deut 27–32" as a unit read by Paul), chapters that he believes Paul read as two distinct, though ultimately related units of Scripture. Before proceeding to examine these chapters in Second Temple Judaism and to trace Paul's reading of these chapters through Paul's letters in a chronological fashion (first Galatians, then 1 Corinthians, Philippians, and finally, Romans), Waters challenges the theses of Steck, Scott, et al.[80] The problems that Waters notes are the following: (1) Such a reading of Deut 27–32 "admits of little room for development in Pauline thought."[81] Waters hopes to demonstrate that Paul first read Deut 27–30 separately from Deut 32, and it was only in Romans that he began to view Deut 27–30 through the lens of chapter 32. Essentially, Waters argues that "there are patterns of reading that are peculiar to Deut 27–30, and patterns of reading that are peculiar to Deut 32."[82] (2) Second, this framework "assumes, frequently without demonstration, that Paul regarded these chapters of Deuteronomy as a single narrative moving from 'sin' through 'exile' to 'restoration.'"[83] Waters concedes that the movement may be within Deuteronomy itself, but that Paul himself saw such a narrative in these chapters must be proven: "The absence of engagements of Deut 31 from Paul; Paul's reading of Deut 27–30 as a 'unit'; and the independence, outside Romans, of Deut 27–30 and Deut 32 are *prima facie* indications that Paul's reading of these chapters admits of more nuance than these proposals admit."[84] (3) Finally, Waters urges that if one wants to sustain such a reading, "one must demonstrate that Paul drew 'restoration' teaching specifically, for example, from Deut 27–32 at Gal 3:10–14."[85]

Waters's examination of Steck's and Scott's theses provides a helpful corrective in stressing the complexity of the evidence and demonstrating that the SER conception of Israel's history has become more definite in recent scholarly literature than in the literature of early Judaism itself.[86] Nevertheless, Waters may have overstated his case, and to respond briefly to these three points

80. Guy P. Waters, *The End of Deuteronomy in the Epistles of Paul*, WUNT 2/221 (Tübingen: Mohr Siebeck, 2006), 26–42.

81. Waters, *The End of Deuteronomy*, 27.

82. Waters, *The End of Deuteronomy*, 237; see also 237–41.

83. Waters, *The End of Deuteronomy*, 27.

84. Waters, *The End of Deuteronomy*, 27.

85. Waters, *The End of Deuteronomy*, 27.

86. Waters, *The End of Deuteronomy*, 32n35, and 27–42 more generally.

Chapter 5

provides a manner of entering into his study of Deuteronomy in Paul and observing both its strengths and its limitations.

First, then, Waters's contention that such a paradigm "admits of little room for development in Pauline thought" presumes without adequate argument that Paul's thought about Deut 27–30, 32 did undergo development. To demonstrate such development is, however, notoriously difficult, and it appears that Waters has only succeeded in doing so at the cost of a somewhat atomistic approach to Paul's engagement with these chapters. For example, although Waters is very strongly against the suggestion that Paul read Deut 27–32 as a sequential unit, at least before Romans, it is unclear how one would arrive at an eschatological reading of Deut 32 apart from Deut 31. In other words, even if Deut 31 is not explicitly cited in Paul's work, it is quite possible that, as Wagner has argued, Deut 31 provides the hermeneutical framework for the eschatological reading of Deut 32 that Paul certainly does evince (note Deut 31:29 LXX).[87] Furthermore, by Waters's own logic, not only should we speak of no more than Deut 27–30 in Galatians (as Waters argues), we should only speak of Deut 29, 30, and 32 in Romans. While Waters's restraint is perhaps understandable in view of his focus on explicit verbal references, it should be admitted that the evidence that Paul read Deut 27–30 as a unit is no stronger than the evidence that he read Deut 27–32 as a unit. Historically speaking, since Waters rejects the various forms of the testimony hypothesis to explain the source of Paul's citations, it makes more sense to understand Paul's reading of these sequential chapters in Deuteronomy as continuous unless one has good grounds to do otherwise; in other words, Waters fails to provide a plausible *Sitz im Leben* for the type of reading that he ascribes to Paul. That Paul did not quote Deut 32 in concert with Deut 27–30 before Romans is clear; that he refrained from doing so out of an underdeveloped reading strategy is an argument *e silentio*.[88]

Waters's second and third contentions may be handled in tandem. His work provides a trenchant warning for those who would naively import all the surrounding context of a cited verse of Scripture into its new Pauline epistolary context. Is it really true, though, that Paul's reading of Deut 27–30 did not suggest the theme of restoration, even if it is not cited explicitly to such an end? Further, can Paul's reading of Deuteronomy in Galatians be termed "eschatological"[89] if this is divorced from Deut 32 or any of the overtures toward

87. Wagner, *Heralds*, 192.

88. "Although he had ample opportunity to do so, he purposely refrained from engaging any text within Deut 27–30 in order to give expression to 'blessing' at Gal 3:14." Waters, *The End of Deuteronomy*, 131.

89. Waters, *The End of Deuteronomy*, 113.

Paul's Engagement with Deuteronomy

restoration in chapter 30 as well? To borrow the terminology of Waters's supervisor Richard Hays, is there any hint of transumption of the metaleptically suppressed blessing? Our comments on Waters's first point apply equally to his second and third as well. In short, Waters has voiced a healthy challenge to a paradigm that is sometimes more assumed than argued. Further work on the reception of Deuteronomy in the Second Temple Period is needed to provide an independent overview of the evidence.

Finally, however, whether one agrees with Waters's conclusion that "the data from Romans evidence an advance in Paul's reading of these texts,"[90] his careful examination of the evidence provides both a solid foundation and a dialogue partner for further investigation. Waters's suggestion that Paul appeals to Deut 32 in 1 Cor 10:20–22 and Phil 2:15 to help the church members "to conceive their own identity as members of the people of God" by means of a "typological and eschatological" reading of Israel in Deut 32 is persuasively argued.[91] Equally plausible is his contention that in the Epistle to the Romans Paul reads Deut 27–30 and 32 together in order to answer the questions: "(1) What has warranted Gentile entry into the people of God? (2) Is there a future for Israel? If so, what is it?"[92] Although the book was published at the end of 2006, Waters's bibliography only covers works published until 2001, so several important recent studies do not receive interaction, notable among which are those by Wisdom, Stanley, and especially Watson.[93]

Waters's thesis, especially in what I have argued are its shortcomings, thus raises the need to explore at least two further questions: (1) Does the picture of Paul and his contemporaries as readers of Deuteronomy change when one considers the broader reception of Deuteronomy as a whole in their work? Asking this sort of question will help substantiate claims about whether the final chapters of Deuteronomy held a place of special importance in other writers of the time, or if interest was more broadly distributed among its thirty-four chapters. In this way, the risk of distorting contemporary positions is reduced, and Paul's reading of these final chapters can be related to his equally numerous engagements with the rest of the book. (2) Is Paul's reception of Deuteronomy distinctive in early Christianity, or does it find analogues in other books of the New Testament? More generally, the range of disagreement between the positions of Scott, Steck, et al. and of Wisdom and Waters, not to

---

90. Waters, *The End of Deuteronomy*, 240.

91. Waters, *The End of Deuteronomy*, 131–32.

92. Waters, *The End of Deuteronomy*, 240; see also 198.

93. See Wisdom, *Blessing for the Nations*; Stanley, *Arguing with Scripture: The Rhetoric of Quotations in the Letters of Paul* (London: T&T Clark, 2004); Watson, *Paul and the Hermeneutics of Faith*.

Chapter 5

mention others we could name,[94] suggests that the question of Paul's recourse to some sort of Deuteronomic frame, especially in his appeal to the "curse of the law" in Galatians, may yet be susceptible to further investigation.

Ending the Pentateuch, Ending the Law? Francis Watson's Approach

The fourth major recent contribution to discussion of the reception of Deuteronomy in Paul, that by Watson, presses questions about a synthetic approach to Deuteronomy even further than the previous three contributors.[95] His discussion of Deuteronomy is found in the final chapters of his study of Paul's engagement with Scripture. Paul, Watson argues, as an exegetical theologian, had a comprehensive scriptural hermeneutic by which he read the Pentateuch as a complex narrative unity—a narrative unity that both discloses and resolves major tensions in its own self-presentation as law and promise. The metaphor of a three-way conversation is key to Watson's presentation: Paul engages with Scripture, but also engages with his fellow Jews who likewise read the sacred text—even when that engagement must be characterized as tacit.[96] In a series of fascinating juxtaposed readings, Watson presents Paul as an exegete who reads Scripture in light of God's action in Christ and God's action in Christ in light of Scripture, and so definitively stresses "the hermeneutical priority of the promise."[97] Watson labors to demonstrate that "Paul cites individual texts not in an *ad hoc* manner but on the basis of a radical construal of the narrative shape of the Pentateuch as a whole, highlighting and exploiting tensions between Genesis and Exodus, Leviticus and Deuteronomy."[98]

---

94. E.g., Kelli S. O'Brien, "The Curse of the Law (Galatians 3.13): Crucifixion, Persecution, and Deuteronomy 21.22–23," *JSNT* 29 (2006): 55–76; Timothy G. Gombis, "The 'Transgressor' and the 'Curse of the Law': The Logic of Paul's Argument in Galatians 2–3," *NTS* 53 (2007): 81–93; and Todd A. Wilson, *The Curse of the Law and the Crisis in Galatia: Reassessing the Purpose of Galatians*, WUNT 2/225 (Tübingen: Mohr Siebeck, 2007).

95. Watson, *Paul and the Hermeneutics of Faith*; note also J. L. Martyn, "Francis Watson, *Paul and the Hermeneutics of Faith*," *SJT* 59 (2006): 427–38; Troels Engberg-Pedersen, "Once more a Lutheran Paul?," *SJT* 59 (2006): 439–60; Douglas A. Campbell, "An Evangelical Paul: A Response to Francis Watson's *Paul and the Hermeneutics of Faith*," *JSNT* 28 (2006): 337–51; Christopher D. Stanley, "A Decontextualized Paul? A Response to Francis Watson's *Paul and the Hermeneutics of Faith*," *JSNT* 28 (2006): 353–62; Francis Watson, "A Response from Francis Watson," *SJT* 59 (2006): 461–68; Francis Watson, "Paul and the Reader: An Authorial Apologia," *JSNT* 28 (2006): 363–73; Francis Watson, "Response to Richard Hays," *ProEccl* 16 (2007): 134–40; and Richard B. Hays, "Paul's Hermeneutics and the Question of Truth," *ProEccl* 16 (2007): 126–33.

96. Watson, *Paul and the Hermeneutics of Faith*, 78–79.

97. Watson, *Paul and the Hermeneutics of Faith*, 15n5 and passim.

98. Watson, *Paul and the Hermeneutics of Faith*, 3.

Paul's Engagement with Deuteronomy

Having argued that Paul's doctrine of justification functions as a hermeneutical key to Scripture, and that his doctrine, in turn, is derived from a reading of Hab 2:4 in its context and in light of Christ, Watson turns to construe the shape of Paul's narrative reading of the Pentateuch. In the end, from Paul's perspective, so Watson argues, readings of the law fall on either side of the fault line of human agency: does the Torah ultimately teach the way to live righteously before God in faithful fulfillment of the covenant commandments, or does it rather (as Watson's Paul believes), in a complex narrative, ultimately subvert human agency to suggest that only divine action in fulfillment of the promise can bring life?

Deuteronomy, Watson proceeds to argue, bears for Paul a dual function in this complex narrative: on the one hand, he can cite its commandments as precepts for the Christian community to follow; on the other hand, he reads the book as both disclosing and resolving the second great tension in the Pentateuch. Watson devotes a mere ten pages to the former category before dismissing the problem of Paul's appeal to the law he is criticizing:

> There is a striking discrepancy between this parenetic use of texts from Deuteronomy and the motif of "the curse of the law," which likewise appeals to Deuteronomy. How can it be that laws which continue to guide individual and communal conduct are at the same time the bearers of a curse? This is one of the more obvious examples of a real "contradiction" within Paul's understanding of the law.[99]

Paul's main theological appeal to Deuteronomy, Watson suggests, is twofold: in chapters 27–30, the curse of the law is set forth—not simply as a contingent possibility, but in the fusion of horizons as a historical actuality realized within Israel's history (as told in the Deuteronomistic History) and in Christ's death. This historical actuality effectively eviscerates an appeal like that of the author of Baruch for a return to the law with renewed zeal. Second, then, Paul reads the Song of Moses (Deut 32) as foretelling the failure of the law, the future inclusion of the gentiles, and the ultimate salvation of Israel by divine action—thus foreshadowing the victory over the curse of the law. In questioning the adequacy of the law, Paul in this respect demonstrates an affinity to the author of 4 Ezra. With this, Watson has completed his creative reconstruction of Paul's reading of Torah.

The scope and penetration of Watson's reading of Deuteronomy are exemplary. The overall thesis of his work blends creativity, boldness, and theological

---

99. Watson, *Paul and the Hermeneutics of Faith*, 425; note Watson's explicit agreement with Heikki Räisänen's position (426n24).

Chapter 5

concern—unfortunately less common than it should be in Pauline exegesis. On the whole, his contention that "Paul engages with these texts by way of representative narratives and individual texts which are supposed to articulate the fundamental dynamics of the Torah as a whole" must be regarded as having received solid substantiation.[100]

At times, however, one wonders whether Watson oversteps the evidence. Occasionally he appears to present Paul almost as a proto-deconstructionist reader, subverting the dominant interpretation of the Torah by looking for the *aporiai*, reading at the margins of the Pentateuch, finding and exploiting the loopholes like Gen 15:6 in the Abraham narrative, or the death associated with the giving of the law in Exodus. This is fine insofar as it goes—we know that Paul's readings were forged in controversy. Watson's construal, however, focuses almost exclusively on the theological instances in Paul's citations, but marginalizes Paul's *ethical* appeals to the law as a source of ongoing moral formation for the community of Christ-believers.[101] While it is a crucial corrective for Watson to argue that "Paul's 'view of the law' is his reading of a text," the text that Paul reads in turn makes demands.[102] These demands are not reducible to moral suggestions under the loose guidance of the Spirit, but still perceived as, in some sense, commands reflecting the will of God, and so sharing something in common with ethical appeals to the law by other Jews of the period. I noted above, for example, Watson's quick dismissal of Paul's ethical appeals to Deuteronomy and his recourse to the category of "contradiction" to explain these.[103] Watson's approach deserves to be supplemented by approaches that focus on the use of Scripture in ethical contexts and the presence of halakah in Paul's letters (on which see below). We might ask whether Paul has a "second" reading of the law, a law beyond the curse, given back to the community through the matrix of Christ's death and resurrection and the presence of the Spirit, so that Christians now "fulfill" the law (e.g., Rom 8:1–4).

Clearly one of the strongest points of Watson's presentation, and one of the most promising for future investigation, is his attempt to produce a big picture, holistic reading of Paul's reception of Deuteronomy. While his reading is less integrated and so less comprehensive than is ideal,[104] he has demonstrated the value of examining the presence of Deuteronomy in Paul, even as others have

100. Watson, *Paul and the Hermeneutics of Faith*, 275.

101. Susan Eastman, review of *Paul and the Hermeneutics of Faith*, by Francis Watson, *JBL* 125 (2006): 610–14.

102. Watson, *Paul and the Hermeneutics of Faith*, 514 and passim.

103. Watson, *Paul and the Hermeneutics of Faith*, 416–26.

104. Hays, "Paul's Hermeneutics," 130.

Paul's Engagement with Deuteronomy

done for Isaiah in Paul. Incidentally, it is striking to note Watson's complete silence with regard to Isaiah in Paul,[105] as well as a number of other specific texts that do not fit within Watson's proposed schema.[106] While omissions will be a problem in any account purporting to give the shape of Paul's overall hermeneutic, this is especially true of such a strong reading as Watson's (see, e.g., Hos 1–2 in Rom 9; the Adam-Christ parallels in Rom 5 and 1 Cor 15; the catena at 2 Cor 6:16–18; Ps 112:9 in 2 Cor 9:9; Exod 16:18 in 2 Cor 8:15; Prov 25:21–22 in Rom 12:20; and all of the Major Prophets and the Writings). The fundamentally antithetical nature of the reading of the Pentateuch he posits, moreover, may not do justice to the texture of the apostle's thought. Though this claim must be borne out in the course of subsequent study, we may here note that where Watson may be correct that Paul discovers two major tensions in the Torah, namely, "between the unconditional promise and the Sinai legislation" and "between the law's offer of life and its curse,"[107] these tensions are arguably resolved *diachronically* for the apostle—in the unfolding story of the covenant and the gospel.[108] At times Watson transposes this into starkly synchronic categories to posit an absolute dichotomy between law and promise. This may also partially explain why Watson never explores precisely *why* the law failed in Paul's view, beyond stating the law's claim to be operative at the level of human agency.[109]

Deuteronomy in Paul's Ethics

In contrast to the rather dense interpretative activity surrounding the final chapters of Deuteronomy in Paul's theology, the end of the Pentateuch in his ethics has received comparatively little attention. While the roots of this neglect are complex, probably at least partially attributable to the common notion that Paul preached a "law-free" gospel, it is also true that Paul's ethical engagements with Scripture are by no means as entirely straightforward as we might expect from a first-century Jew. As long ago as 1928, Adolf von Harnack, noting that Scripture seems to play little formative role in Paul's instruction outside of the *Hauptbriefe*, concluded, "From this it follows that from the beginning Paul did not give the Old Testament to the young churches

---

105. Hays, "Paul's Hermeneutics"; but see Watson, "Response to Richard Hays," 136.

106. See also Stanley, "A Decontextualized Paul?," 359.

107. Watson, *Paul and the Hermeneutics of Faith*, 23.

108. Watson, *Paul and the Hermeneutics of Faith*, 24.

109. Though note Watson, *Paul and the Hermeneutics of Faith*, 518.

Chapter 5

as the book of Christian sources for edification. Rather, he based his mission and teaching wholly and completely on the gospel and expects edification to come exclusively from it and from the Spirit accompanying the gospel."[110]

Harnack did not deny the importance of Jewish Scripture for the formation of Paul's own thought but argued that Paul had recourse to Scripture in his letters only when he needed to extricate the gospel from Judaizing influence, and did not intend to pass on his own estimation of his Scriptures to his young churches.[111] Nowhere, perhaps, is this lack of substantiation and dependence upon Scripture more noticeable than in the ethics Paul prescribes—even within the *Hauptbriefe*. Until quite recently this position was relatively unchallenged.[112]

By contrast, however, a number of recent substantive studies have sought to challenge this widespread view by demonstrating Paul's indebtedness to Scripture and to Jewish tradition based on Scripture for the formation of his ethics.[113] Such studies have shown that, while Paul's engagement with scriptural ethical material is by no means entirely straightforward,[114] he remained firmly rooted within the Jewish milieu of his day. Without denying the importance of contemporary Greco-Roman philosophical ideas and dominical

---

110. Adolf von Harnack, "The Old Testament in the Pauline Letters and in the Pauline Churches," in *Understanding Paul's Ethics: Twentieth-Century Approaches*, ed. Brian Rosner (Grand Rapids: Eerdmans, 1995), 27–49, here 44.

111. Harnack, "The Old Testament in the Pauline Letters," 27–28.

112. Note the impressive list of scholars who hold this position in Rosner, *Understanding Paul's Ethics*, 3–4; see also, e.g., Christopher M. Tuckett, "Paul, Scripture and Ethics: Some Reflections," *NTS* 46 (2000): 403–24.

113. Michel, *Paulus*, 158–59, 212; Bonsirven, *Exégèse rabbinique et exégèse paulinienne*, 295–97; Traugott Holtz, "Zur Frage der inhaltlichen Weisungen bei Paulus," *TLZ* 106 (1981): 385–400, repr. as "The Question of the Content of Paul's Instructions," in Rosner, *Understanding Paul's Ethics*, 51–71; Eckart Reinmuth, *Geist und Gesetz: Studien zu Voraussetzungen und Inhalt der paulinischen Paränese*, TA 44 (Berlin: Evangelische Verlagsanstalt, 1985); Peter J. Tomson, *Paul and the Jewish Law: Halakhah in the Letters of the Apostle to the Gentiles*, CRINT 3/1 (Minneapolis: Fortress, 1990); Karin Finsterbusch, *Die Thora als Lebensweisung für Heidenchristen: Studien zur Bedeutung der Thora für die paulinische Ethik*, SUNT 20 (Göttingen: Vandenhoeck & Ruprecht, 1996); Richard B. Hays, "The Role of Scripture in Paul's Ethics," in *The Conversion of the Imagination*, 143–62; more generally note Karl-Wilhelm Niebuhr, *Gesetz und Paränese: Katechismusartige Weisungsreihen in der frühjüdischen Literatur*, WUNT 28 (Tübingen: Mohr Siebeck, 1987); and Markus Bockmuehl, *Jewish Law in Gentile Churches: Halakhah and the Beginning of Christian Public Ethics* (London: T&T Clark, 2000).

114. Hays, "The Role of Scripture in Paul's Ethics."

Paul's Engagement with Deuteronomy

traditions for the behavior Paul promotes, Scripture and the interpretative tradition issuing from it are increasingly recognized as exerting pressure on the ethical direction Paul provides.

The role of Deuteronomy in Paul's ethics has recently been highlighted by two studies, both focusing on 1 Corinthians. In a study of 1 Cor 5–7, Brian Rosner concludes, "when Paul regulates conduct in the churches, he is dependent on the Scriptures in general and on Deuteronomy, it appears, in particular."[115] His results have been further corroborated by the doctoral dissertation of Edwin G. Perona on "The Presence and Function of Deuteronomy in the Paraenesis of Paul in 1 Corinthians 5:1–11:1."[116] Although not focusing solely on the ethical appropriation of Deuteronomy, Perona repeatedly stresses that "Paul makes use of Deuteronomy mainly as normative warrant," which most often includes prescriptions for behavior.[117] While in other respects Perona's study suffers from some methodological weaknesses, both he and Rosner stress that normative texts shape ethics in ways that go beyond direct quotation. Allusions and echoes often provide clues to the rich texture of Paul's thought and his striking identification of the situation of his assemblies with that of Israel in Scripture.

Such studies have provided an important starting point for further investigation of Paul's reliance on Scripture in general, and on Deuteronomy in particular, for his ethical norms and prescriptions. Nevertheless, it is striking that no systematic investigation of the role of Deuteronomy in Paul's ethics has yet been undertaken. Indeed, as we have seen in the previous section, even those who carry out more systematic investigations of Paul's reliance on Deuteronomy rarely relate their findings to Paul's ethical appeals.

Conclusion

From this overview of some of the major contributors to the discussion about Paul's reception of Deuteronomy, the following conclusions may be drawn for scholarship before around 2008. As suggested above, research before the Qumran discoveries tended to focus on issues of *accuracy, legitimacy*, and *comparability*; the first and third of these concerns have been taken up, though

---

115. Rosner, *Understanding Paul's Ethics*, 178, see also 188–89.

116. Edwin Perona, "The Presence and Function of Deuteronomy in the Paraenesis of Paul in 1 Corinthians 5:1–11:1" (PhD diss., Trinity Evangelical Divinity School, 2006).

117. Perona, "The Presence and Function of Deuteronomy," 3, see also 317–19 and passim.

Chapter 5

with admittedly varying emphases and much less apologetic interest, in recent research. Strikingly, however, the second concern, that of the legitimacy of Paul's readings, has been transposed into a substantially different "literary-theological" key, often with the desire to understand Paul himself as, in some sense, a narrative theologian with his own "per se" voice. In addition, we may note the following desiderata for further research:

1. Compared to the relatively high number of studies concerned with the reception of Isaiah in Paul, Deuteronomy has received little attention. While some of this can surely be attributed to the greater frequency of Isaiah citations in Paul, Deuteronomy also functions as an important theological and ethical resource for the apostle and should be examined accordingly.

2. Recent studies on the *Vorlage* of Paul have set the stage for a more intensive investigation of the types of engagement Paul makes with individual books and sections of Scripture.

3. Many contributors have suggested that Paul's understanding of the "curse of the law" is explicable by recourse to Deuteronomy, but there is as yet no agreement as to either how much of Deuteronomy provides the context for the assertion or what theological import recourse to Deuteronomy has for one's construal of the "curse of the law."

4. Most major studies have been concerned *either* with Paul's ethical appeals to Deuteronomy (e.g., Rosner, Perona) *or* with his theological readings (e.g., Scott, Waters). The only study to have examined all of Deuteronomy in Paul, that by Watson, has concluded that the two aspects are fundamentally incompatible.

5. Systematic study of Paul's ethical engagement with Deuteronomy has not been carried out beyond 1 Cor 5–11.

In light of these five considerations, future study of Paul's reception of Deuteronomy seems both justified and desirable, and may help contribute in some way to the resolution of these problems and to an understanding of the texture of Paul's theology as a whole.

6

TRANSFORMING STORIES AND PERMEABLE SELVES

Conferring Identity in Romans 6

> We might dare say, then, that the Gospels are the firstfruits of all
> Scriptures, but that the firstfruits of the Gospels is that accord-
> ing to John, whose meaning no one can understand who has
> not leaned on Jesus' breast nor received Mary from Jesus to be
> his mother also. But he who would be another John must also
> become such as John, to be shown to be Jesus, so to speak. For
> if Mary had no son except Jesus, in accordance with those who
> hold a sound opinion of her, and Jesus says to his mother, "Behold
> your son" and not, "Behold, this man also is your son," he has
> said equally, "Behold, this is Jesus whom you bore." For indeed
> everyone who has been perfected "no longer lives, but Christ lives
> in him" and since "Christ lives" in him, it is said of him to Mary,
> "Behold your son" the Christ.
>
> Origen, *Comm. Jo.* 1.23[1]

> In our experience the life history of each of us is caught up in the
> histories of others.
>
> Paul Ricoeur[2]

In a remarkable passage from the introduction to Origen's *Commentary on
John*, he suggests that the one who wishes to understand the gospel must
undergo a transformation of self. The reader or hearer must in some sense
become the author, experience Jesus as John did, and receive Mary with fil-

1. Trans. Heine.
2. Paul Ricoeur, *Oneself as Another*, trans. K. Blamey (Chicago: University of Chicago
Press, 1992), 161.

99

Chapter 6

ial devotion. This involves a kind of double transformation—first, becoming John who received Mary from Jesus, and then becoming Jesus himself, the proper son of Mary. An elision of the self, achieved by means of inhabiting the narrative world, enables one in turn to understand that narrative. Lest the reader think of this as a mere flight of the rhetorical imagination, the claim is grounded, startlingly, in a paraphrase of Gal 2:20: "everyone who has been perfected 'no longer lives, but Christ lives in him.'" The grounding move is startling because it is clear that Origen reads Paul's participationist language in a realist manner, as when he elsewhere cites Gal 2:20, and asks, "Since, then, he [that is, Christ] was in Paul, who will doubt that he was in a similar manner in Peter and in John and in each of the saints, and not only those who are on earth, but also those who are in heaven?" (*Princ.* 4.4.2, Behr). Even if we make allowances for Origen's rhetoric—presumably he does not think that we are "in John" in any strong sense—the passage attests a kind of fluidity or plasticity in the selfhood of Origen's would-be understander of the Fourth Gospel, a selfhood open to modification by intersection with another. If that is so, Origen has not invented the concept of a permeable self. Rather, it goes at least as far back, as his citation of Galatians would suggest, to the apostle Paul and his striking interpretation of the story of the life, death, and resurrection of the Messiah.

One of the most salient facets of the New Testament is the extent to which a series of such stories about the death of Jesus and its implications occupy center stage. Where a Roman official might have registered simply another routine crucifixion outside a troublesome provincial capital, early Christian proclamation found a bundle of entailments that extended to many other people, remote in time and distance from that solitary execution. In the inchoate theological reflections of the first apostles, stories about the death and resurrection of Jesus came to structure claims about the nature of the self and about the nature of the communities in which that selfhood was shaped.

This chapter takes up one narrow slice of the broader interpretative project within early Christianity and asks how Paul employs narratives to shape the conceptions of selfhood in the communities to which he writes. How do accounts about the Messiah cease to be simply stories about the past and become performative interventions in the reader's or hearer's present? I consider particularly Paul's views on gentile Christ-believers in Rom 6. As I hope to show, attending to the narrative elements in Rom 6 with an eye on the formation of early Christian selfhood, tutored with sensibilities derived from contemporary philosophical discussion, discloses the transformative role of

Transforming Stories and Permeable Selves

story in structuring how the earliest followers of Jesus thought of themselves and their role in the world.

Narrative and Selfhood in Pauline Scholarship

For the past several decades, narrative and its connection to identity or selfhood has risen to prominence as a focus of analysis in fields as diverse as evolutionary biology,[3] psychology,[4] and the humanities,[5] most notably for my interests, in theology.[6] Identities and identity formation have been heavily investigated in recent scholarship on the New Testament and Early Christianity, identity being most often understood as a function of group belonging.[7] Given the prominent role of identity politics in contemporary society, it has been natural to investigate the ways in which early Christians similarly (or

3. E.g., Brian Boyd, *On the Origin of Stories: Evolution, Cognition, and Fiction* (Cambridge, MA: Belknap, 2009).

4. E.g., Dan P. McAdams, "The Psychology of Life Stories," *Review of General Psychology* 5.2 (2001): 100–122; Katherine Nelson, "Self and Social Functions: Individual Autobiographical Memory and Collective Narrative," *Memory* 11.2 (2003): 125–36; Dan P. McAdams, Ruthellen Josselson, and Amia Lieblich, eds., *Identity and Story: Creating Self in Narrative* (Washington, DC: American Psychological Association, 2006); and J. B. Hirsh, R. A. Mar, and J. B. Peterson, "Personal Narratives as the Highest Level of Cognitive Integration," *Behavioral and Brain Sciences* 36.3 (2013): 216–17.

5. E.g., Lewis P. Hinchman and Sandra K. Hinchman, eds., *Memory, Identity, Community: The Idea of Narrative in the Human Sciences* (Albany: SUNY Press, 1997).

6. E.g., Stanley Hauerwas and L. Gregory Jones, *Why Narrative? Readings in Narrative Theology* (Grand Rapids: Eerdmans, 1989); Gerhard Sauter and John Barton, eds., *Revelation and Story: Narrative Theology and the Centrality of Story* (Aldershot: Ashgate, 2000); R. Ruard Ganzevoort, Maaike de Haardt, and Michael Scherer-Rath, eds., *Religious Stories We Live By: Narrative Approaches in Theology and Religious Studies*, Studies in Theology and Religion 19 (Leiden: Brill, 2014); Kate Finley and Joshua Seachris, "Narrative, Theology, and Philosophy of Religion," in *The Encyclopedia of Philosophy of Religion*, ed. S. Goetz and C. Taliaferro (Hoboken, NJ: Wiley-Blackwell, 2022), 3:1688–94.

7. See the influential, sophisticated studies of Judith Lieu, *Image and Reality: The Jews in the World of the Christians in the Second Century* (Edinburgh: T&T Clark, 1996); Judith Lieu, *Neither Jew nor Greek? Constructing Early Christianity* (Edinburgh: T&T Clark, 2002); Judith Lieu, *Christian Identity in the Jewish and Graeco-Roman World* (Oxford: Oxford University Press, 2004); though many others could be mentioned, e.g., Daniel Boyarin, *A Radical Jew: Paul and the Politics of Identity* (Berkeley: University of California Press, 1994); William S. Campbell, *Paul and the Creation of Christian Identity* (London: T&T Clark, 2006); and James D. G. Dunn, *Neither Jew nor Greek: A Contested Identity*, vol. 3 of *Christianity in the Making* (Grand Rapids: Eerdmans, 2015).

Chapter 6

dissimilarly) negotiated problems of boundary-marking, hybridity, ethnicity, and emerging religious difference. At the same time, the emphasis on the social construction of identity has not attended as directly to the ways in which narrative also contributes to a form of self-identity that makes meaning for the individual as well as the group of which they are part. No doubt this is due in part to reservations, sometimes overstated, about the extent to which, for Paul's letters at least, the individual comes into focus. These reservations have been fueled by social-scientific approaches that have stressed group-belonging as a fundamental dynamic of ancient life, and also by historical correctives issued against a reading of Paul that took him to be offering in a narrow sense a sort of *ordo salutis* for the individual believer. Over the past several decades, Pauline scholarship has learned to emphasize again the importance of covenant, ethnicity, group boundaries, and belonging as fundamental concepts. This salutary correction should not, however, obfuscate the role of individual response for which Paul's letters call.[8]

Studies that attend more explicitly to the theological locus of "Pauline anthropology" and its concern to understand the person have sometimes tended to focus on a concern with the "whatness" of the human that leads to partitive or aspectual accounts of the person as, say, soul, body, and spirit (or some comparable variation).[9] This is certainly a defensible approach, but it is susceptible to the risk of distortion as the interpreter abstracts from the accounts (or embedded narrative fragments within letters) toward some more fundamental fixed essence and is problematized by the variation in terminology even within the *corpus Paulinum*. But if, as theologians such as Hans Frei and David Kelsey have argued, narrative, like metaphor, is in some sense irreducible or *un*substitutable, then to attempt to abstract from narrative is to invite deformation.[10]

Some recent scholarship—Susan Eastman's remarkable *Paul and the Person* comes most readily to mind—has demonstrated the promise of approaching

---

8. See Gary W. Burnett, *Paul and the Salvation of the Individual*, BibInt 57 (Leiden: Brill, 2001).

9. Probably most famously in Rudolf Bultmann's *Theology of the New Testament*, but for an example of a more recent good work in this vein, see Lorenzo Scornaienchi, Sarx *und* Soma *bei Paulus: Der Mensch zwischen Destruktivität und Konstruktivität*, NTOA/SUNT 67 (Göttingen: Vandenhoeck & Ruprecht, 2008).

10. David H. Kelsey, *Proving Doctrine: The Uses of Scripture in Modern Theology* (Harrisburg, PA: Trinity Press International, 1999); Hans W. Frei, *The Eclipse of Biblical Narrative: A Study in Eighteenth and Nineteenth Century Hermeneutics* (New Haven: Yale University Press, 1974); and Hans W. Frei, *The Identity of Jesus Christ* (Philadelphia: Fortress, 1975).

Transforming Stories and Permeable Selves

questions about personhood in an interdisciplinary manner.[11] Similarly, I hope that thematizing identity and narrative will lend some analytic precision to an attempt to tease out Paul's complicated discourse in Rom 6 and the entanglement we find there of several selves and stories.

Narrative Selves

In employing the language of "narrative selves" I am relying on a series of arguments by analytic philosophers, especially Marya Schechtman and Michael Rea. In her 1996 book, *The Constitution of Selves*, Schechtman contends that "individuals constitute themselves as persons by coming to think of themselves as persisting subjects who have had experience in the past and will continue to have experience in the future, taking certain experiences as theirs."[12] This consideration of experiences in the past and future, insofar as they are integrated into an overall story that structures and interprets them, can be characterized as a "narrative self-conception."[13] For such a view, "we constitute ourselves as selves by understanding our lives as narrative in form and living accordingly."[14] This is a stronger claim than merely suggesting that our lives have a narrative quality by virtue of the fact that we live in time and therefore experience the world sequentially. It also requires that "an identity-constituting narrative be capable of local articulation," which Schechtman calls the "articulation constraint."[15] She also suggests that one cannot invent wild fantasies and appropriate them as self-constituting narratives, but rather that the view is subject to a "reality constraint" that involves answerability to external environmental conditions and the stories of others around us, thereby avoiding significant errors of both fact and interpretation.[16]

---

11. Susan Grove Eastman, *Paul and the Person: Reframing Paul's Anthropology* (Grand Rapids: Eerdmans, 2017). In certain ways, Eastman's study is the closest analogue to the approach I take in this chapter, though in her dialogue with contemporary philosophy and neuroscience, she is not particularly concerned with narrative.

12. Marya Schechtman, *The Constitution of Selves* (Ithaca, NY: Cornell University Press, 1996), 94.

13. Schechtman, *Constitution of Selves*, 97.

14. Schechtman, "The Narrative Self," in *The Oxford Handbook of the Self*, ed. Shaun Gallagher (Oxford: Oxford University Press, 2011), 398.

15. Schechtman, *Constitution of Selves*, 114–19, quotation from 114.

16. Schechtman, *Constitution of Selves*, 119–30.

Chapter 6

This basic sensibility has received further precision and explication in the work of Michael Rea.[17] Interrogating the sense in which selves might relate to persons and identities, Rea argues selves are like characters in a narrative, and that "a person's true self is, in effect, the character at the center of their autobiographical identity *as that character would be understood by a perceptive reader of the narrative* who wants to stick to the text in forming their understanding of the character, but who is willing to suspect the character of being unreliable in their own self-understanding."[18] This autobiographical identity is related to but distinct from other identities "which are collectively hosted, biographical in form, and comprise our various social identities."[19]

In both Schechtman and Rea, the individual person occupies an important role in the determination or elucidation of their own selfhood, but both accounts also allow for an answerability with reference to external conditions and other people that can function to correct self-deception or simple disassociation from reality. The emphasis on the role of the individual in achieving the narrative perspective also resonates with what the psychologist Dan McAdams describes as "life stories": "Life stories are based on biographical facts, but they go considerably beyond the facts as people selectively appropriate aspects of their experience and imaginatively construe both past and future to construct stories that make sense to them and to their audiences, that vivify and integrate life and make it more or less meaningful."[20]

Following these theorists, in this chapter, by the use of the term "self," I have in mind the sense in which, in ordinary language, the term sometimes refers to the subject or person, but also sometimes refers to something more abstract—roughly, a conception of "who the person is" that is captured not by a set of claims about *what* they are, but rather by claims about their distinctive *role* and *purpose* in history, or about what attributes are central to them and salient for that role, or both ("her true self"). For these purposes, I will take

---

17. I'm also indebted to Allison Krile Thornton, "Narrating Narrative" (draft paper presented to the Center for Philosophy of Religion, University of Notre Dame, 25 March 2022).

18. Michael Rea, "The Metaphysics of the Narrative Self," *Journal of the American Philosophical Association* 8.4 (2022): 586–603, here 602, italics original. Note that he relatedly argues, "An autobiographical identity is a proposition that includes and integrates information about a person's most central first- and second-order self-centered and others-centered preferences, values, and goals; their various social identities and their significance to them; the events and experiences that have contributed most to defining their own sense of self (and why they have so contributed); and so on" (596).

19. Rea, "The Metaphysics of the Narrative Self," 602.

20. McAdams, "The Psychology of Life Stories," 101.

Transforming Stories and Permeable Selves

narrative to be, following Finley and Seachris, a "diachronically-extended story which presents a sequential account of events unified around a character or set of characters,"[21] although the type of "sequence" involved may differ according to the story in question.

PAUL AND THE GENTILE SELF

The apostle Paul's letters are discursive interventions in particular situations of pastoral concern that arose in his missionary work across the Mediterranean world. And yet, in spite of their argumentative and epistolary structure, they are also shot through with fragments of narrative.[22] Why does Paul constantly allude to stories in his letters, and how do those stories serve his constructive ends? I suggest that pagan converts to the early Christ movement are tutored in a retrospective revaluation of their past selves, now learning to see themselves as gentiles who had been alienated from God and from Israel, strangers to divine promise, and complicit in open rebellion against the creator. They are taught to conceive of their identity in a novelly flexible manner, extended through time backward in genealogy and forward in eschatology.

Informed by some of the categories employed in more recent discussions of the nature of the self and the role of narrative in its constitution, we turn now to the apostle Paul's letter to the Romans.[23] In this, the longest and most

21. Finley and Seachris, "Narrative, Theology and Philosophy of Religion," 1689. Note also Rea: "A narrative, for the purposes of this paper, is a narratively structured representation of a state of affairs or a sequence of events. A narratively structured representation is a representation whose content is unified by an interpretation (tacit or explicit) that orders the various components of the representation in such a way as to highlight their significance in relation to some particular collection of interests (often but not always the interests of the storyteller, the protagonist, or the expected audience), or to identify causal or explanatory relations among those components that are salient in relation to some collection of interests, or both" ("The Metaphysics of the Narrative Self," 587).

22. For substantial discussions of narrative approaches to Paul, see, inter alia, R. B. Hays, *The Faith of Jesus Christ: The Narrative Substructure of Galatians 3:1–4:11*, 2nd ed. (Grand Rapids: Eerdmans, 2002); Bruce Longenecker, ed., *Narrative Dynamics in Paul: A Critical Assessment* (Louisville: Westminster John Knox, 2002); John L. Meech, *Paul in Israel's Story: Self and Community at the Cross* (Oxford: Oxford University Press, 2006); and Christoph Heilig, *Paulus als Erzähler? Eine narratologische Perspektive auf die Paulusbriefe*, BZNW 237 (Berlin: de Gruyter, 2020). I am grateful to Heilig for also sharing with me portions of his then forthcoming English-language work on Paul and narrative, now published as *Paul the Storyteller: A Narratological Approach* (Grand Rapids: Eerdmans, 2024).

23. Note also the differing but helpful approach of Valérie Nicolet-Anderson, *Con-*

105

Chapter 6

complex of Paul's letters, we have the special advantage of seeing the apostle's theology in action as he writes to an assembly or assemblies he did not found,[24] and so may spell out certain foundational teachings at greater length than if he were writing to one of his own assemblies. In particular, this essay employs Rom 6 as a laboratory in which we can observe the Pauline rendering of the narrative self in action.

Paul has already identified his audience as gentiles (Rom 1:5; cf. 11:13). No one in antiquity thinks of themselves as a gentile, at least not until they are taught to do so.[25] The designation "gentile" (ἔθνος, גוי) is simply the privative binary of the term "Jew," and so to think of oneself as a gentile is to adopt a position relative to the Jewish people—whether of opposition or simple alterity. This designation then functions at least in part analogously to the terms "Jew" or "Judean" and becomes a kind of meta-ethnic conglomerating label that bundles together Greeks and Gauls, Baltics and British. As Ishay Rosen-Zvi and Adi Ophir argue, for Paul, "Greeks cannot join the *ekklesia* as 'Greeks,' a category which has no meaning in the sacred history of salvation. Neither can they join as 'universal humans,' which is a concept that Paul, who relies on the biblical narrative, can hardly grasp. They also cannot join as Jews since they were neither born Jewish nor circumcised. . . . The result is that Greeks can join the *ekklesia* only as *goyim*."[26] In fact, Paul seems to be the ancient author who first elevates the concept of "gentileness" to theoretical prominence and so marks it indelibly. Using the term to describe his addressees is not simply a neutral description; it is rather, as Rosen-Zvi and Ophir have suggested, something like an interpellation in the Althusserian sense.[27]

---

structing the Self: Thinking with Paul and Michel Foucault, WUNT 2/324 (Tübingen: Mohr Siebeck, 2012).

24. Puzzlingly, Paul does not describe the Romans as an (or several) ἐκκλησία, which has given rise to various speculations that need not detain us.

25. Cf. S. Fowl, "Learning to Be a Gentile," in *Christology and Scripture: Interdisciplinary Perspectives*, ed. A. T. Lincoln and A. Pattison, LNTS 348 (London: T&T Clark, 2007), 22–40.

26. Adi Ophir and Ishay Rosen-Zvi, *Goy: Israel's Multiple Others and the Birth of the Gentile* (Oxford: Oxford University Press, 2018), 154–55.

27. Ishay Rosen-Zvi and Adi Ophir, "Paul and the Invention of the Gentiles," *JQR* 105.1 (2015): 1–41, with reference to Louis Althusser, "On Ideology," in *On the Reproduction of Capitalism* (London: Verso, 2014), 171–207, esp. 188–99. Christine Hayes has raised some salient objections to elements of Rosen-Zvi and Ophir's thesis, but her criticisms do not materially affect this point; see Christine Hayes, "The Goy: A Synchronic Proposal," *Ancient Jew Review*, 27 February 2019, https://www.ancientjewreview.com/read/2019/2/13/the-goy-a-synchronic-proposal; see also Christine Hayes, "The Complicated Goy in Classical Rabbinic Sources," in *Perceiving the Other in Ancient Judaism and Early Christianity*, ed. Michal

Transforming Stories and Permeable Selves

Paul invites his gentile hearers to take a twofold stance toward their past. On the one hand, he asks them to re-remember their personal pasts as stories of an attenuated self, in which their agency was limited and they lacked self-mastery. At the same time, he encourages them to adopt as their own an unremembered past, that is, a series of events in prior time that he characterizes as nontrivially self-involving for them. Let's take each of these in turn and attempt to unpack the movements of Paul's story.

First, Paul offers a retrospective reinterpretation of his readers' collective past. Their history is bifurcated into a before and an after. In a striking combination of singular and collective expressions, he refers to the fact that "our old person" (ὁ παλαιὸς ἡμῶν ἄνθρωπος; NRSV: "our old self") was crucified with the Messiah. The dividing line between old (Rom 6:6, παλαιός) and new (v. 4, ἐν καινότητι) is thus located in an event some decades previous to Paul's writing: the execution of Jesus. We will need to return to the surprising entanglement of biographical life stories.

The former self was one that lived in sin (v. 2), and in fact was simply a "body of sin" (τὸ σῶμα τῆς ἁμαρτίας). The old self used the body as an implement or a weapon of unrighteousness, was a slave to sin and to impurity and to lawlessness, and anticipated only death as payment for its servitude to sin. Strikingly, Paul does not know the gentiles to whom he writes this letter but generalizes about them from his experience. We find, therefore, a number of significant echoes or correspondences between his description of the universal wickedness of gentiles in 1:18–32 and his depiction of the old self in 6:1–23.[28] Paul charges the gentiles with wickedness (ἀδικία) in 1:18, 29 and 6:13; with impurity (ἀκαθαρσία) in 1:24 and 6:19; with shamefulness (ἀσχημοσύνη, ἐπαισχύνεσθαι) in 1:27 and 6:21; and with disordered lusts or desires (ἐπιθυμίαι) in 1:24 and 6:12. Paul doesn't need to know the Roman gentiles personally to understand their former life; he knows what gentiles are like and pivots easily from the third person descriptions in ch. 1 to the second person statements in ch. 6. We can imagine the righteous protests of some gentile hearers who hadn't lived in debauchery, but these negative descriptions of the "before time" function in the construction of an attenuated retrospective self.[29] That self is

---

Bar-Asher Siegal, Wolfgang Grünstaudl, and Matthew Thiessen, WUNT 394 (Tübingen: Mohr Siebeck, 2017), 147–67.

28. See Stanley Stowers, *A Rereading of Romans: Justice, Jews, & Gentiles* (New Haven: Yale University Press, 1994), 255–56.

29. The phrase "retrospective self" is taken from Paula Fredriksen, "Paul and Augustine: Conversion Narratives, Orthodox Traditions, and the Retrospective Self," *JTS* 37.1 (1986): 3–34.

Chapter 6

forged in contrast, as Paul sketches a story of darkness that prepares for the dawning of light.[30] The past is prologue.

But in a second movement, he depicts at least two other moments in their collective past. In 6:1–4, as part of his argument that grace should not enable or encourage sinning, Paul reminds or instructs[31] the gentiles about the meaning of their baptismal rite: the water bath of baptism was a point of intersection between their individual life narratives and the narrative of the Messiah. In baptism, they were plunged into the death of Jesus and buried with him. On the other side of death comes a resurrection of sorts, to a new or renewed life. This is the process by which the old self was executed, and the body of sin cast off. This way of framing the point of transition from past to present focalizes the act of baptism as the fulcrum on which the gentiles' story pivots. By appealing to a common ritual act, Paul can express both collective and individuated participation; we have to assume that the members of the Roman Christ-assemblies would have been baptized at different times as they joined the association, but since they have all been baptized (at least the text addresses them as the baptized), the act of baptism becomes a common intervention in their past lives.

But Paul does not remain at the temporal horizon of the Romans' baptismal entrance. Rather, he presses back to the crucifixion itself, a historical event that could be pinpointed roughly twenty-five or thirty years prior to Paul's letter.[32] In a remarkable interpretation of that event, Paul urges that the crucifixion of Jesus somehow also entailed the death of the Roman gentiles: they have been co-crucified with him (συνεσταυρώθη), and so can be considered as having died. Union with the death of Jesus in his body also ensures that the gentiles will be resurrected. Here Paul steps back from his assertion in v. 4. It might have been possible to understand Paul's statement that the baptismal burial guaranteed that "just as the Messiah was raised from among the dead by the Father's glory, so also we might walk in newness of life" as indicating that the gentiles had already received the full effects of the resurrection. Paul walks this argument back in v. 5 by orienting the gentiles toward the future in hope of resurrection.

This all amounts to a messy fusion, or at least an interlinking, of five temporal horizons. The Roman gentile, Paul asserts, (1) lived as a former self in wickedness,

---

30. Note how Paul uses the language of "darkness" in Rom 1:21; 2:19; 13:12; cf. 11:10, citing Ps 68:23–24.

31. The force of the rhetorical question is not entirely clear: see the analysis of similar questions in 1 Corinthians by Benjamin A. Edsall, "Paul's Rhetoric of Knowledge: The OYK OIΔATE Question in 1 Corinthians," *NovT* 55 (2013): 252–71.

32. Most scholars date Romans in the 50s, with a notable cluster opting for 57/58 CE. The precise date is immaterial for my purposes.

Transforming Stories and Permeable Selves

but (2) by baptism that self was killed by means of (3) a participation in the event of crucifixion, which means that they (4) will one day experience full resurrection in union with the Messiah but (5) now live as those who are "dead to sin and alive to God in Jesus the Messiah." The complexity of the temporal movements arises from Paul's attempt to align two different narratives: that of the Messiah and that of his Roman gentile followers. Jesus's story, insofar as it is reflected in Rom 6, involves crucifixion, death, burial, and resurrection to immortality. The gentiles' story goes from wickedness to baptism, to renewed life marked by slavery to righteousness, to the hope of the life of the age to come in resurrection. Aligning and intertwining the two narratives is complicated but enables Paul to offer his gentile hearers a new kind of self, one that takes its bearing from the Messiah's story. He encourages them to adopt, as it were, autobiographies in which the *bios* of the *autos* is shared with Christ by union achieved through baptism. Or perhaps we should say that he confers on them an "allobiographical" account of their selfhood, an account they can assume or resist.

The entanglement of the biographies is also facilitated by Paul's utilization of an apocalyptic temporal framework that bifurcates history into two ages: the present evil age and the age that is to come. The traditional dividing line between the two had been the judgment of humanity, the resurrection of the righteous, and the condemnation of the wicked at the end of normal human time. Paul offers us our first glimpse of the developing early Christian conviction that in the death and resurrection of the Messiah there is an architectonic shifting of the ages, in which the age that is to come intrudes into the present evil age without entirely displacing it, such that Paul can locate himself and his gentile converts as those on whom "the ends of the ages have come" (1 Cor 10:11; note the double plural: τὰ τέλη τῶν αἰώνων). The present evil age is characterized by Paul as the age of Adam, of the flesh, of the law's dominion, while the age that is to come is the age of the Messiah, of the Spirit, and of the freedom and maturity of the adopted children of God.

Paul's remarkable interpretative move is to overlay the story of salvation history onto the lives of his gentile converts and to offer them a conception of their own lives as a history of salvation writ small.[33] Their past becomes their own participation in the present evil age, and they are taught to look with expectation to the full arrival of the age that is to come and the conformity of their bodies to that of the immortal Messiah. In the tensive overlap of their

---

33. For reflections on the ultimate congruity of apocalyptic and salvation-historical approaches to Paul, see Grant Macaskill, "History, Providence and the Apocalyptic Paul," *SJT* 70.4 (2017): 409–26.

Chapter 6

past and future, they experience the ongoing weakness of the flesh (cf. Rom 6:19) and the temptation to orient themselves toward sin's dominion, but they are liberated subjects whom Paul characterizes as liberated precisely to consider themselves dead to sin and alive to God, by virtue of their participation in Jesus the Messiah (v. 11).

READING AS A TECHNOLOGY OF THE SELF IN EARLY CHRISTIANITY

Paul's narrative characterization of his gentile hearers is complex and subtle, and certainly not easily graspable on an initial hearing of the letter. Nevertheless, Paul's characterization achieves a performative quality precisely through its status as a written text, and so capable of being read and reread. In this sense, Paul's role in the formation of new gentile selves is facilitated by the employment of reading as a "technology of the self."

One theorist has argued that technologies of the self "permit individuals to effect by their own means or with the help of others a certain number of operations on their own bodies and souls, thoughts, conduct, and way of being, so as to transform themselves in order to attain a certain state of happiness, purity, wisdom, perfection, or immortality."[34] Reading—with which I include also aurally listening to written texts—fits this description nicely and resonates with a broader set of what Pierre Hadot has described as spiritual practices.[35]

Hadot has in mind specifically the practices that arise within ancient philosophy, understood as actions designed to internalize one's philosophy, to transform one's self, and ultimately to prepare for death, as in Socrates's famous dictum: "Those who go about philosophizing correctly are in training for death" (*Phaed.* 67e). At two places in his corpus, Philo of Alexandria lists techniques of *askēsis* designed to train one in philosophy: "inquiry, examination, reading (ἡ ἀνάγνωσις), listening to instruction, concentration (ἡ προσοχή),

---

34. M. Foucault, "Technologies of the Self," in *Technologies of the Self: A Seminar with Michel Foucault*, ed. L. H. Martin, H. Gutman, and P. H. Hutton (Amherst: University of Massachusetts Press, 1988), 16–49, here 18. I acknowledge here the moral complexity of citing Foucault after the plausible allegations surfaced of his sexual abuse of Tunisian boys (see Matthew Campbell, "French Philosopher Michel Foucault 'Abused Boys in Tunisia,'" *The Times*, 28 March 2021, https://www.thetimes.com/world/europe/article/french-philosopher-michel-foucault-abused-boys-in-tunisia-6t5sj7jvw). Since Foucault is dead and will not benefit from the citation, and since intellectual honesty requires me to acknowledge my debt, I cite him, though not without reluctance.

35. Pierre Hadot, *Philosophy as a Way of Life: Spiritual Exercises from Socrates to Foucault*, ed. Arnold I. Davidson, trans. Michael Chase (Oxford: Blackwell, 1995), esp. 81–144.

Transforming Stories and Permeable Selves

self-mastery, and the power to treat things indifferent as indeed indifferent" (*Her.* 253, LCL); and "readings (ἀναγνώσεις), meditations (μελέται), acts of worship, and of remembrance of noble souls, self-control, discharge of daily duties" (*Leg.* 3.18, LCL, slightly modified).[36] The lists are not identical to one another, nor are they to other sets of practices we find among other authors—the Stoics in particular—but they share a stress on the necessity of reading, reflection, and self-examination as crucial practices in forging changed viewpoints, attitudes, convictions, and ultimately a sense of self. Reading becomes a practice that does not terminate in knowledge but rather leads to practice. As the Stoic Epictetus says: "What do you lack? Books? . . . What, is not the reading of books a kind of preparation for the act of living?" (*Diatr.* 4.4.14, LCL; cf. 14–18).

It is clear that such reading—which, again, might be an act of hearing or remembering rather than, say, a visual decoding of symbols on a sheet of parchment—will not be superficial. It will be, in Paul Griffiths's terms, a "religious reading" rather than a consumerist one. Religious reading "has to do primarily with the establishment of certain relations between readers and the things they read, relations that are at once attitudinal, cognitive, and moral."[37] The religious reader relates deferentially to the text and sees in it a pluripotentiary fund of meaning. Such a reader will revisit an authoritative text in slow, meditative engagements that might include memorization as an aid to internalization. Acts of reading designed to transform the self are necessarily iterative. Training for death, or perhaps training for death and the life beyond death, requires an attentive *askēsis* to achieve a perspective on one's own life and history *sub specie aeternitatis*, or perhaps better, *sub specie crucis*.

We know much less about early Christian reading practices than we might like, nor do we possess the evidence we would prefer to have in order to assess the earliest reception and engagement with Paul's letters.[38] Judging the empirical success of Paul's performative attempts to reform his hearers' identity will therefore be

36. Hadot calls attention to both these texts.

37. Paul J. Griffiths, *Religious Reading: The Place of Reading in the Practice of Religion* (Oxford: Oxford University Press, 1999), 41. He also suggests: "The first and most basic element in these relations is that the work read is understood as a stable and vastly rich resource, one that yields meaning, suggestions (or imperatives) for action, matter for aesthetic wonder, and much else" (41).

38. For recent studies of ancient reading practices, see William A. Johnson, *Readers and Reading Culture in the High Roman Empire: A Study of Elite Communities*, Classical Culture and Society (Oxford: Oxford University Press, 2010); Jonas Leipziger, *Lesepraktiken im antiken Judentum: Rezeptionsakte, Materialität und Schriftgebrauch*, Materiale Textkulturen 34 (Berlin: de Gruyter, 2021); Jan Heilmann, *Lesen in Antike und frühem Christentum: Kulturgeschichtliche, philologische sowie kognitionswissenschaftliche Perspektiven und deren Bedeutung für die neutestamentliche Exegese*, TANZ 66 (Tübingen: Francke, 2021); and Jan Heilmann,

Chapter 6

difficult; but armed with some sense of the possibilities of reading as a technology of the self, one might well imagine a pliant ideal hearer of Rom 6 repeatedly and deeply engaging the passage until their very self is shaped by the Pauline vision for a new kind of selfhood, perhaps reinforced by local teaching and community consensus.[39] In that case, reading becomes the site of mediation between two biographies: the individual gentile (although presented in aggregate form and the subject of second-person plural imperatives) and the Jewish Messiah.

Some scholars have referred to early Christian gatherings as "textual communities" or even "scholastic communities,"[40] but given the significance of orality and liturgy, it is more precise to describe them as sites of memorial recollection, traditioning, and anamnetic performance—perhaps simply as "narrative communities," that is, communities shaped by a set of stories and claims arising from those stories, together with their attendant practices. The fact that Paul's letters were preserved at all testifies to their ongoing usefulness to the assemblies that kept and copied them, and the ritual performance of rites like baptism would have offered regular opportunities for Paul's interpretations of these rituals to have been brought before the gathered participants.[41]

Conferring a Narrative Identity

To this point, I have argued that Paul has offered to the Roman gentiles a story he hopes they will adopt as their own. The story concerns them personally

---

"Ancient Literary Culture and Meals in the Greco-Roman World: The Role of Reading during Ancient Symposia and Its Relevance for the New Testament," *JTS* 73.1 (2022): 104–25.

39. Of course, nonpliant hearers of Romans or other Pauline texts will have been disinclined to accept the conferral of gentile identity in the robust form in which Paul presents it. Their presence in the listening assembly already suggests they are in some sense committed to the messianic project of the early Jesus-communities, but opposition to Paul and his message for gentiles was not rare in the first century, as Romans already suggests (cf. 15:30–32). Cf., e.g., Gerd Lüdemann, *Opposition to Paul in Early Christianity*, trans. E. Boring (Philadelphia: Fortress, 1989); and Patrick Gray, *Paul as a Problem in History and Culture: The Apostle and His Critics through the Centuries* (Grand Rapids: Baker Academic, 2016).

40. E.g., Claire S. Smith, *Pauline Communities as 'Scholastic Communities': A Study of the Vocabulary of 'Teaching' in 1 Corinthians, 1 and 2 Timothy, and Titus*, WUNT 2/335 (Tübingen: Mohr Siebeck, 2012); and E. A. Judge, "The Early Christians as a Scholastic Community: Parts I and II," in *The First Christians in the Roman World: Augustan and New Testament Essays*, ed. J. R. Harrison, WUNT 2/229 (Tübingen: Mohr Siebeck, 2010).

41. There are obviously alternative interpretations of baptism in antiquity, but for communities shaped by Paul it stands to reason that his interpretation would be at least one viable take among others.

Transforming Stories and Permeable Selves

and is thus presented by means of a second-person address, but it is also a public story—the second-person address is in the plural, and the same story is repeated with variation across Paul's letters to other communities. Can we characterize the kind of speech act that we see operative in Paul's letter to the Romans?

It is clear that Paul's expressed judgment is presented as simply "constative" in nature, that is, as statements about what simply is the case.[42] It is equally clear, however, that many of Paul's grammatically indicative statements bear a performative quality. Paul's statements cannot neatly be considered under Austin's typology of performative utterances (as, e.g., verdictives or exercitives). But here we are helped by Ásta's category of conferrals. For Ásta, the act of conferral creates or bestows a property, and so this is "a way to articulate the idea that we have a social property because of something about other people by saying that a social property is conferred upon us by other people."[43] Ásta refers especially to categories like sex, gender, and race as the result of conferral, but we can arguably apply the category to Paul's discourse about Roman gentiles: he confers on them a social property consisting of a particular past, a union with the Messiah, and a determinate future. These are social properties rather than merely individual ones, since the gentiles as such belong to a class of actors in salvation history, and Paul invites them to agree with and take on his conferral. From Paul's perspective, the set of properties he mentions may perhaps simply have been a statement of objective fact, but whatever one might say about the reality of such judgments, for them to become effective and functional properties, the Romans need to internalize and accept them.[44] In other words, there must be a passage from conferred social identity to an accepted autobiographical identity "focused on the attributes that play a central, unifying role in their own total self-conception."[45] Part of what it means to belong to a Pauline assembly is to accede, in broad outline at least, to the apostolic conferral of gentile, Christ-believing identity.

42. I take the language of "constative" and "performative" from the classic presentation in J. L. Austin, *How to Do Things with Words*, 2nd ed. (Cambridge, MA: Harvard University Press, 1962).

43. Ásta, *Categories We Live By: The Construction of Sex, Gender, Race, and Other Social Categories* (Oxford: Oxford University Press, 2018), 23.

44. Though in a somewhat different vein, note the insightful reflections of Grace Hibshman, "Narrative, Second-Person Experience, and Self-Perception: A Reason It Is Good to Conceive of One's Life Narratively," *Philosophical Quarterly* 73.3 (2022): 615–27: "The narratives we internalize shape what kind of narrative arcs we can envision for our lives" (626).

45. Michael Rea, "Gender as a Self-Conferred Identity," *Feminist Philosophy Quarterly* 8.2 (2022), doi.org/10.5206/fpq/2022.2.13959. I'm indebted to Rea's discussion of social and autobiographical identity more broadly.

Chapter 6

Such a conferral must, if it is to have lasting power, be accepted, echoed, repeated, and affirmed in a community. In this light, the early Christian habit of referring to themselves by means of fictive kinship language as members of a family is particularly notable, since families are key to the formation of identity, and perform an act, to use Hilde Lindemann's phrase, of holding a family member in their identity. As she writes, "Just as families are primarily responsible for initially constructing the child's identity, so, too, are they primarily responsible for holding the child in it. They do this by treating him in accordance with their narrative sense of him, and in so doing, they reinforce those stories. But identity maintenance also involves letting go: weeding out the stories that no longer fit and constructing new ones that do. It's in endorsing, testing, refining, discarding, and adding stories, and then acting on the basis of that ongoing narrative work, that families do their part to maintain the child's identity."[46] The work of identity maintenance will necessarily involve negotiating among competing conferrals, and Paul's letters attest to his competitive attempts to out-confer other rival apostles and teachers, striving to ensure that his own particular construal of gentiles is embraced against other options.

CONCLUSION

In this essay, I have sought to understand the function of the narrative fragments in Rom 6 and specifically the way in which they bear on the formation of a particular kind of self. Paul emplots the Roman gentiles in the middle of an ongoing story that lends both meaning and direction to their moral lives. His letter wants not simply to inform but to transform the hearing audience.

46. Hilde Lindemann, *Holding and Letting Go: The Social Practice of Personal Identities* (Oxford: Oxford University Press, 2014), 85. Cf. further 203: "To be *held* in personhood is to interact with other persons who recognize us as persons and respond accordingly. Much of this holding therefore has to do with the narratives we create or borrow from the common stock to make depictions of who a particular person is. These depictions are our personal identities; what they depict is the self, understood as the embodied locus of idiosyncratic causation and experience. Identities are the personae we perform in our dealings with others; they indicate how we are supposed to act and how we wish or expect to be treated. All persons have personal identities, even if they are incapable of contributing their own, first-person stories to the narrative tissue that represents them. But those who are capable of full participation in personhood act on the basis of the stories by which they understand who they are, the stories others use to make sense of who they are, and the stories they themselves contribute to others' identities."

Transforming Stories and Permeable Selves

The story Paul tells is therefore a nontrivial and self-involving one that invites his hearers to live within and from it.

Narratives, perhaps especially biographical narratives, always involve selection, abridgement, interpretation, and arrangement, and to this extent history and fiction proceed identically. This is why fiction can tutor us in forming life stories. As Ricoeur writes, "It is precisely because of the elusive character of real life that we need the help of fiction to organize life retrospectively, after the fact, prepared to take as provisional and open to revision any figure of emplotment borrowed from fiction or from history."[47] Or as Umberto Eco puts it, "Since fiction seems a more comfortable environment than life, we try to read life as if it were a piece of fiction."[48] If we take "fiction" in its etymological sense from the Latin *fingere*, meaning "to fashion or form" (OED s.v.), then we can appreciate that both history and fiction are formed stories, each with a range of possible stances toward the referential world. Paul's narrative in Rom 6 is not obviously "historical" in a positivist sense of the term, but nevertheless does claim to be describing reality. We might say of Paul what James H. Cone writes of the role of story in Black theology: "The story was both the medium through which truth was communicated and also a constituent of the truth itself."[49]

In the end, Paul might have suggested, as Origen after him was to do about the Fourth Gospel, that the one who wishes to understand his message must undergo a transformation of selfhood, indeed to die and rise to new life in order to know herself anew.

---

47. Ricoeur, *Oneself as Another*, 162.

48. Umberto Eco, *Six Walks in the Fictional Woods* (Cambridge, MA: Harvard University Press, 1994), 118.

49. James H. Cone, "The Story Context of Black Theology," *ThTo* 32.2 (1975): 144–50, here 147. Further on Cone and narrative, see Jonathan C. Rutledge, "Narrative and Atonement: The Ministry of Reconciliation in the Work of James H. Cone," *Religions* 13 (2022): 985.

7

PRESENTIFYING THE PAST

Actualization in the Pauline Tradition

The apostle Paul operates with distinctive ways of conceptualizing the past, the present, and the future. His terminology and ideas evince a certain fluidity and their expression is often determined by the rhetorical setting of his epistolary communications, but it is still possible to sketch some of the definite lines of the temporal dimensions of his thought.[1] His angle of vision shifts depending on the situation he addresses and may widen to consider the primal past in the creation of Adam and the history of Israel or narrow to consider the crucifixion of the Messiah or his own conduct as a missionary to his fledgling churches. Likewise, the present, as with the future, may be conceived as an age or a moment.

But how do past, present, and future relate for Paul? Undoubtedly the question has been most often discussed not in terms of Paul's conception of time in an abstract sense but under the specific angle of his apocalyptic thought and soteriology.[2] Signaled above all by Christ's resurrection, for Paul the expected future age, the time of the new creation, has arrived, in part at least, in the present, and so determines the lives of his converts. At the same time, they are not yet removed from the present evil age, and so they become those on whom "the ends of the ages have come" (1 Cor 10:11). The plural of both substantives

1. R. Reuter, "Paul's Terminology Describing Time, Periods of Time and History," in *Lux Humana, Lux Aeterna: Essays on Biblical and Related Themes in Honour of Lars Aejmelaeus*, ed. A. Mustakallio, Publications of the Finnish Exegetical Society 89 (Göttingen: Vandenhoeck & Ruprecht, 2005), 247–67. The Pastoral Epistles develop these concepts in their own manner; see Wilfried Eisele, "Chronos und Kairos: Zum soteriologischen Verhältnis von Zeit und Ewigkeit in den Pastoralbriefen," *Early Christianity* 3 (2012): 468–89. See now L. Ann Jervis, *Paul and Time: Life in the Temporality of Christ* (Grand Rapids: Baker Academic, 2023).

2. Consider the rousing description in J. L. Martyn, *Galatians*, AB 33A (New York: Doubleday, 1997), 97–104; cf. Volker Rabens, "'Schon jetzt' und 'noch mehr': Gegenwart und Zukunft des Heils bei Paulus und in seinen Gemeinden," *Jahrbuch für biblische Theologie* 28 (2013): 103–27.

Presentifying the Past

should be given full force here: the ends of both ages, the end of the present age and the beginning of the age that is to come, have overlapped one another.[3] Paul thus characteristically speaks with reference to the "eschatological now."[4] In this way, as Udo Schnelle aptly observes, "A past event determines the present and anticipates the future as the paradigm of what is to come."[5]

It would be unfair to press Schnelle unduly on the linearity of this schema, but it is true that most Pauline scholarship has been content to examine the movement from the past to the present and future, from the present to the future, or from the future to the present, but relatively little consideration has been given to the influence of the present on the past. This might seem straightforwardly justifiable: if the past is anything, it is complete—done, finished, expired. But as I turn now to argue, Paul, together with the authors of the deutero-Pauline letters, operates with a notion of the permeable past, or at least a past that can be brought into the present in an actualized form or, we might say, "presentified."

By "presentification," unseemly term that it is, I have in mind the process of making some aspect of past history, or some written account of that past, forcefully present in an updated form, to address an author's or speaker's current concerns. The term "actualization" is sometimes used synonymously (as in my subtitle) but is potentially misleading if one merely thinks of the move from potentiality to actuality without the temporal horizon in view. Lurking behind both these terms is the German *Vergegenwärtigung*, made famous especially by Gerhard von Rad in the mid-twentieth century, but used by many others since, though it should be noted that my application of the term differs in certain ways from von Rad's tradition-historical approach.[6]

---

3. This point seems to be missed in Reuter's otherwise rich study of Paul's temporal thought.

4. See, e.g., Rom 3:26; 6:22; 7:6; 11:30; 1 Cor 15:20; 2 Cor 5:16; cf. Eph 2:13; Col 1:22, 26; 3:8; 2 Tim 1:10; on which, cf. J. D. G. Dunn, *The Theology of Paul the Apostle* (Grand Rapids: Eerdmans, 1998), 178–81. But Paul can also use such adverbial markers in rhetorical rather than temporal manner: Johannes Woyke, "'Einst' und 'Jetzt' in Röm 1–3? Zur Bedeutung von νυνὶ δέ in Röm 3,21," *ZNW* 92 (2011): 185–206.

5. Udo Schnelle, *Apostle Paul: His Life and Theology*, trans. M. Eugene Boring (Grand Rapids: Baker Academic, 2005), 593; cf. 592–97. More broadly, note J. van der Watt, ed., *The Eschatology of the New Testament and Some Related Documents*, WUNT 2/315 (Tübingen: Mohr Siebeck, 2011).

6. Gerhard von Rad, *The Theology of Israel's Prophetic Traditions*, vol. 2 of *Old Testament Theology* (New York: Harper & Row, 1965), 319–35. For some indication of the influence of von Rad's concept in Old Testament theology, see G. F. Hasel, *Old Testament Theology: Basic Issues in the Current Debate*, rev. ed. (Grand Rapids: Eerdmans, 1972), 57–75; Frederick C. Prussner, *Old Testament Theology: Its History and Development* (London: SCM, 1985), 233–39; J. W. Groves, *Actualization and Interpretation in the Old Testament* (Atlanta: Scholars

Chapter 7

ACTUALIZATION

It is worth pausing to home in on the concept of actualization as I will use it. Drawing an insight from modern historiography may help. Every engagement with the past begins from the speaker's or author's present, and in this sense, every attempt to say something about what has happened previously is approached via the present. Since the early twentieth century, we have observed a debate between advocates of "presentism" on the one hand, and advocates of "contextualism" on the other.[7] While the former suggest the validity of writing history directed in a teleological fashion toward the present and self-consciously composing accounts in light of the contemporary situation, the latter place emphasis on providing broad coverage of the past in categories and with judgments that would have been available in some sense to those of that era. This constitutes an appeal to the so-called "availability (or accessibility) principle": "The availability principle disallows the use of knowledge, descriptive terms or classification schemes in interpretations which were unavailable or inaccessible to the contemporaries of the object of interpretation."[8]

Modern historical-critical interpretation of the *corpus Paulinum* received its determinative shape at the same time that much of modern European thought was undergoing a profound historicist revision.[9] Central to this historicist

---

Press, 1987); and D. Driver, *Brevard Childs, Biblical Theologian* (Grand Rapids: Baker Academic, 2012), 130–33. See also Martin Noth, "Die Vergegenwärtigung des Alten Testaments in der Verkündigung," *EvT* 12 (1952): 6–17, translated as "The 'Re-Presentation' of the Old Testament in Proclamation," in *Essays on Old Testament Interpretation*, ed. C. Westermann, trans. J. L. Mays (London: SCM, 1963), 76–88: "'Re-presentation' is founded on this—that God and his action are always present, while man in his inevitable temporality cannot grasp this present-ness except by 're-presenting' the action of God over and over again in his worship" (85). The theme of "actualization" is also addressed in the 1993 Pontifical Biblical Commission's document, "The Interpretation of the Bible in the Church," on which see Roland E. Murphy, "Reflections on 'Actualization' of the Bible," *BTB* 26 (1996): 79–81.

7. On presentism, see Elizabeth Clark, *History, Theory, Text: Historians and the Linguistic Turn* (Cambridge, MA: Harvard University Press, 2004), 19–20; D. L. Hull, "In Defense of Presentism," *History and Theory* 18 (1979): 1–15; D. L. Hull, "In Defense of Anti-Presentism," *Scientia Poetica* 8 (2004): 251–54; and Adrian Wilson and T. G. Ashplant, "Whig History and Present-Centred History," *The Historical Journal* 31 (1988): 1–16.

8. Carlos Spoerhase, "Presentism and Precursorship in Intellectual History," *Culture, Theory & Critique* 49 (2008): 49–72, here 49. He goes on: "The procedure of describing and judging a precursor's achievements only with regard to what they have contributed to the formation and development of the current *state of the art* seems particularly problematic when the retrospectively constructed and plotted development lines are backdated offhand as teleologies, and so interpreted as anticipations" (53).

9. On the rise of historicism more broadly, as well as the term's polyvalence, see Frederick C.

Presentifying the Past

impulse, when expressed in historiographical terms, is the contextualist observation of this availability principle. It has often carried over into discussions especially of Pauline interpretation of Scripture, in which some interpreters have attempted to vindicate the apostle from any impugning charge of reading Scripture "out of context."[10] In contrast to these exegetes, I wish to stress Paul's presentist interpretative strategies. Paul does not merely allow the past to "speak for itself," but contends that it should "speak for us" (cf. 1 Cor 10). And it is arguably the case that Paul has presentist impulses also in his depiction of the past as past, as for example, in his teleological retelling of the Abraham story in Gal 3. By "actualization" I have in view then, not simply his presentist retelling of the past, but a stronger form of mediation in which the past event is not simply retold or recounted from the standpoint of the present and for the author's contemporary concerns, but updated and mediated more robustly to the present. We could, therefore, plot many of Paul's uses of the past on a sliding scale of present-centeredness. In this sense, one may perhaps compare actualization to a "virtuous anachronism," save that the determinative temporal horizon lies now in the present rather than the past.[11]

What this might mean will become clearer in the following. The rest of this chapter takes up three clusters of topics in the Pauline tradition, centered on three respective events or persons in the past that are mediated to the author's present: Scripture, Jesus, and Paul's own presence.

PAUL AND SCRIPTURE

One could say that there is something in Paul's epigrammatic γέγραπται that already presupposes Scripture's ability to transcend time and historical circum-

---

Beiser, *The German Historicist Tradition* (Oxford: Oxford University Press, 2011); Robert D'Amico, "Historicism," in *A Companion to the Philosophy of History and Historiography*, ed. Aviezer Tucker (Oxford: Wiley-Blackwell, 2009), 243–52; G. C. Iggers, "Historicism: The History and Meaning of the Term," *Journal of the History of Ideas* 56 (1995): 129–52; G. C. Iggers, "The Intellectual Foundations of Nineteenth-Century 'Scientific' History: The German Model," in *1800–1945*, vol. 4 of The *Oxford History of Historical Writing*, ed. Stuart Macintyre, Juan Maiguashca, and Attila Pók (Oxford: Oxford University Press, 2011), 41–58; G. Scholtz, "The Notion of Historicism and 19th Century Theology," in *Biblical Studies and the Shifting of Paradigms, 1850–1914*, ed. W. R. Farmer and H. G. Reventlow, JSOTSup 192 (Sheffield: Sheffield Academic, 1995), 149–67.

10. See some of the essays in G. K. Beale and D. A. Carson, eds., *Commentary on the New Testament Use of the Old Testament* (Grand Rapids: Baker Academic, 2007).

11. For the term "virtuous anachronism" see A. Barnes and J. Barnes, "Time Out of Joint: Some Reflections on Anachronism," *The Journal of Aesthetics and Art Criticism* 47 (1989): 253–61, here 253.

Chapter 7

stance to address the present. At times this comes to be explicitly expressed. Perhaps most well-known are the statements in which Paul writes that "whatever was written in former days was written for our instruction, so that by steadfastness and by the encouragement of the scriptures we might have hope" (Rom 15:4). Or again, "These things happened to them to serve as an example, and they were written down to instruct us, on whom the ends of the ages have come" (1 Cor 10:11).

But by "actualization," again, something more specific is meant, though clearly it operates on the basis of Paul's conviction about the eschatological-directedness of Scripture. Let us examine a few instances in which Paul "updates" or "presentifies" the voice of Scripture itself, participating in the broad Second Temple Jewish phenomenon of rewriting Scripture to address the present. For example, the Temple Scroll expresses its halakic judgments by placing them in the mouth of God, Philo finds Hellenistic virtues expressed already in Genesis, and Josephus rewrites the biblical ceremonies of blessing and cursing to exclude a Samaritan interpretation. Many other instances could be adduced.

We see Paul rewriting with intention to actualize perhaps most clearly in his citation of Deut 30:11–14 in Rom 10:6–8.[12] As I have argued elsewhere, Paul engages in what we might call transformative deixis by interspersing comments in his citation of the text that specify Christ as the object of the actions (as opposed to "the commandment"): "Do not say in your heart, 'Who will ascend into heaven?'—that is, to bring Christ down, or 'Who will descend into the abyss?'—that is, to bring Christ up from the dead. But what does it say? 'The word is near you, in your mouth and in your heart'—that is, the word of faith that we proclaim." Here can also be observed the characteristically Pauline "slippage" as Deuteronomy's commandment is replaced with Christ who, in turn, is metonymically elided into the message about him, the "word of faith" (ῥῆμα τῆς πίστεως). This word of faith, however, itself carries the force of a commandment to be met with ἡ ὑπακοὴ πίστεως (1:6; 16:26).

Paul's formal method can be paralleled in part from both the Qumran pesharim and from Philo's writings, and progress in understanding the nature of biblical interpretation in Second Temple Judaism over the past fifty years or so has put an end to at least some of the scandal that Paul's use of Deuteronomy in these verses once caused. It is also clear, however, that such formal parallels cannot *materially* explain Paul's interpretation here. Paul normally operates

---

12. In more detail, see David Lincicum, *Paul and the Early Jewish Encounter with Deuteronomy* (Grand Rapids: Baker Academic, 2013), 153–58, from which I have drawn some material in the following two paragraphs.

Presentifying the Past

with a certain christological reticence in his reading of Scripture (though see also 1 Cor 8:4-6); what prompts him to the transformation of the text we see here? Part of the answer may in fact lie in a global construal of Deuteronomy. If one asks, What is Deuteronomy fundamentally about? one could do worse than to answer: the Torah. But already within the horizon of Deuteronomy itself we find a certain identification of God with Torah (e.g., Deut 4:7-8). So for Paul to identify the "word" of Deuteronomy with Christ simply extends (and to a certain extent radicalizes) a trajectory already begun within Deuteronomy itself. Arguably then, Paul infuses Deut 30:12-14 with a christological *pro nobis*. Within Deut 30, these verses function as an exhortation to the obedience requisite to restoration, but Paul suggests that God has fulfilled the condition for restoration in Christ. Paul is convinced that his updating or actualizing of Deut 30 addresses the present in a true manner.

Other, similar instances of Paul contemporizing Scripture might be mentioned. For example, in Rom 10:16 Paul offers one of his only citations of Isa 53: "But not all have obeyed the good news; for Isaiah says, 'Lord, who has believed our message?'" Here Paul musters Isa 53:1 in a manner that fuses the apostle's proclamation with that of Isaiah's. It is striking here that Isa 53 is not used in a strictly christological manner but is rather employed in reference to Paul's apostolic vocation. This coheres with Paul's broader strategy of bringing Isaiah into the present to serve as a prosecuting witness (cf. Rom 10:19-21) and to affirm that Paul's proclamation is in line with his own.[13] To take another example: in 2 Cor 6:2, Paul buttresses his urging of the Corinthians not to receive the grace of God in vain by citing Isa 49:8, "For he says, 'At an acceptable time I have listened to you, and on a day of salvation I have helped you.'" Paul goes on to add the interpretative gloss: "See, now is the acceptable time; see, now is the day of salvation!" Paul once more fuses the horizons of Isaiah's day with his own by means of leaving the direct address (σου, σοι) of the quotation ambiguous. The audience is thus enabled to find themselves addressed by the Isaianic divine speech, and conversely the speech is brought forcefully into the present in both promise and warning.[14]

Since we are interested in the broader *corpus Paulinum*, it is worth noting that in 1 Timothy, we find that two of Paul's references to Deuteronomic precepts elsewhere are translated into straightforward regulations for church practice. In

---

13. On which see esp. J. Ross Wagner, *Heralds of the Good News: Isaiah and Paul in Concert in the Letter to the Romans*, NovTSup 101 (Leiden: Brill, 2002), 170-79 and passim.

14. Cf. M. Thrall, *The Second Epistle to the Corinthians*, ICC (London: T&T Clark, 1994), 1:452-53.

Chapter 7

1 Cor 9:9–10, Paul offers an innovative exegetical transformation of Deut 25:4— and his explanatory comments there may implicitly acknowledge the novelty of the interpretation he advances.[15] In 1 Tim 5:18, however, the interpretative comments are lacking and we find the same citation introduced, not as "the Law," but as "Scripture" (ἡ γραφή)—perhaps indicating a change in stance toward the law, reflected also in the Pastor's comments in 1 Tim 1:8–11.[16] Now it appears that γραφή functions as a broad category to encompass the apparently dominical tradition with which this Deuteronomy citation is coupled.[17] This is followed immediately by appeal to Deuteronomy's "law of witnesses," cited by Paul in 2 Cor 13:1 but also widespread in the early church, for example, in Matt 18:16 in an analogous context. Whether the presence of the "law of witnesses" should be ascribed to Pauline tradition or not,[18] the nonchalant use of Paul's potentially scandalous interpretation of Deut 25:4 as a rule to govern the remuneration of elders offers eloquent testimony to the routinization of Paul's exegetical charisma. In this case, the prominence of the scriptural texts in Paul has served to draw them to the Pastor's attention but not necessarily precluded further interpretative developments to address the needs of the Pastor's community. While Paul wrote with an eschatologically determined sense that the remuneration of apostles was at stake, the author of the Pastoral Epistles writes with an application to the remuneration of church officials—so we have here a double actualization, an actualization of Paul's initial actualization, as it were.

But we also see the actualizing tendency at work in broader narrative terms. Rather than simply appeal to a scriptural story as supplying necessary background information, or as belonging to a realm of memory now past, in 1 Cor 10:1–4, Paul evokes the story of the exodus and wilderness wanderings with clearly contemporizing impulses. He offers a retrospective rereading of the wilderness tradition that sees the Israelites being led by the cloud and passing through the sea as typifying baptism, and the miraculous provision of manna typifying the Lord's Supper. In other words, he approaches the past with a

---

15. "For it is written in the law of Moses, 'You shall not muzzle an ox while it is treating out the grain.' Is it for oxen that God is concerned? Or does he not speak entirely (πάντως) for our sake? It was indeed written for our sake" (1 Cor 9:9–10a).

16. Cf. L. Donelson, *Pseudepigraphy and Ethical Argument in the Pastoral Epistles*, HUT 22 (Tübingen: Mohr Siebeck, 1986), 191.

17. G. Holtz, *Die Pastoralbriefe*, THKNT 13 (Berlin: Evangelische Verlagsanstalt, 1965), 126–27.

18. See the broad survey of traditions in H. van Vliet, *No Single Testimony: A Study in the Adoption of the Law of Deut 19:15 par. into the New Testament*, STRT 4 (Utrecht: Kemink & Zoon, 1958).

Presentifying the Past

strategy of recovery, an updating stance that makes the past usable for his gentile converts in Corinth. In this way, he attempts to instruct them in their own means of appropriating the scriptural tradition as well.

PAUL AND JESUS

Intriguingly, Paul does not show much concern, on the whole, to actualize or update the words of Jesus (though an exception is noted below). This stands, of course, in contrast to the sorts of moves we find in the canonical Gospels, in which explicit statements guarantee the relevance of Jesus's words to their new audiences. For example, Mark places the statement on Jesus's lips: "What I say to you I say to all" (Mark 13:37). Or consider the saying in Luke 10:16 par.: "Whoever listens to you listens to me." Or the way in which the Johannine Paraclete reminds the community of Jesus and everything he taught them (John 14:26; 15:26; 16:13-15). But when it comes to the words of Jesus, Paul seems to resist actualizing them by drawing a distinction between his own words or opinion and the word of the Lord, as he does in his comments on marriage in 1 Cor 7:10-12, 25. We do find other strategies of actualizing the past actions of Jesus in the Pauline tradition, but these often function as much on an experiential, enacted level as a literary one. The two most striking examples are the rituals of the Lord's Supper and baptism.

In 1 Cor 11:17-34, Paul offers guidance about the Lord's Supper to the divided Corinthian church. While acknowledging the process of *traditio*, Paul does not merely recite a formula but actualizes it to engage the Corinthians. At first blush, it seems as though by citing the words of institution in 11:23-26,[19] Paul simply recollects for the Corinthians the past event of a meal that Jesus shared with his disciples:

> [23] For I received from the Lord what I also handed on to you, that the Lord Jesus on the night when he was betrayed took a loaf of bread, [24] and when he had given thanks, he broke it and said, "This is my body that is for you. Do this in remembrance of me." [25] In the same way he took the cup also, after supper, saying, "This cup is the new covenant in my blood. Do this,

---

19. On which see Jens Schröter, "Die Funktion der Herrenmahlsüberlieferungen im 1. Korintherbrief: Zugleich ein Beitrag zur Rolle der 'Einsetzungsworte' in frühchristlichen Mahltexten," *ZNW* 100 (2009): 78-100.

Chapter 7

as often as you drink it, in remembrance of me." [26] For as often as you eat this bread and drink the cup, you proclaim the Lord's death until he comes.

[23] Ἐγὼ γὰρ παρέλαβον ἀπὸ τοῦ κυρίου, ὃ καὶ παρέδωκα ὑμῖν, ὅτι ὁ κύριος Ἰησοῦς ἐν τῇ νυκτὶ ᾗ παρεδίδετο ἔλαβεν ἄρτον [24] καὶ εὐχαριστήσας ἔκλασεν καὶ εἶπεν· τοῦτό μού ἐστιν τὸ σῶμα τὸ ὑπὲρ ὑμῶν· τοῦτο ποιεῖτε εἰς τὴν ἐμὴν ἀνάμνησιν. [25] ὡσαύτως καὶ τὸ ποτήριον μετὰ τὸ δειπνῆσαι λέγων· τοῦτο τὸ ποτήριον ἡ καινὴ διαθήκη ἐστὶν ἐν τῷ ἐμῷ αἵματι· τοῦτο ποιεῖτε, ὁσάκις ἐὰν πίνητε, εἰς τὴν ἐμὴν ἀνάμνησιν. [26] ὁσάκις γὰρ ἐὰν ἐσθίητε τὸν ἄρτον τοῦτον καὶ τὸ ποτήριον πίνητε, τὸν θάνατον τοῦ κυρίου καταγγέλλετε ἄχρι οὗ ἔλθῃ.

Paul does not offer explicit appropriative guidance to the Corinthian church, as for example if he were to say, "In the same way that Jesus shared this meal with his first followers, so you also should share it with one another." Rather, in what amounts to a contemporizing presentation of this scene, Jesus himself is allowed to address the Corinthians: "This is my body that is for *you*. You do this in remembrance of me." By transposing Jesus's words to this new context, Paul has effectively actualized them as the directive of Jesus to the Corinthians. The distance between past and present is collapsed, or transcended, though it is couched in the language of the transmission of tradition in v. 23. Liturgical action characteristically functions as a means of mediating the past to the present and the present to the past, of collapsing horizons and uniting an event and its memorial appropriation.

Similarly, especially in Rom 6:1–11, Paul portrays the baptized as having been crucified with Christ (v. 6), baptized into the death of Jesus (v. 3), and buried with him by baptism into death (v. 4), also sharing in some sense in his resurrection (vv. 4–5). Here Paul is more precisely presenting a fusion of two events that belong equally to the past—namely the death of Jesus and the baptism of Roman Christians, though of course from the perspective of one about to be baptized this would appear as an actualization of the death of Christ, a fusion of horizons as it were. Paul's words here go beyond a mere rhetorical strategy to express the reality of his participationist soteriology, but this arguably demonstrates the permeability of the boundary between past and present for Paul, as the ritual of baptism in some sense re-presents the death, burial, and resurrection of Jesus in the sacramental act.[20]

---

20. More fully on this theme, see the previous chapter, "Transforming Stories and Permeable Selves: Conferring Identity in Romans 6," in this volume.

Presentifying the Past

It is perhaps a broader sense of actualization, but the theme of participation in the suffering and death of Christ occurs elsewhere beyond baptismal contexts in Paul's letters as well. We find repeated references to the realization and repetition of Christ's own sufferings in Paul's life and ministry, for example, 2 Cor 4:10–11, "always carrying in the body the death of Jesus, so that the life of Jesus may also be made visible in our bodies. For while we live, we are always being given up to death for Jesus's sake, so that the life of Jesus may be made visible in our mortal flesh." One might note here Paul's use of verbs formulated with the συν prefix: συσταυρόω (Gal 2:19; Rom 6:6); συνθάπτω (Rom 6:4; cf. Col 2:12); συμπάσχω (Rom 8:17; 1 Cor 12:26); συναποθνήσκω (2 Cor 7:3; cf. 2 Tim 2:11); συζάω (Rom 6:8; 2 Cor 7:3; cf. 2 Tim 2:11); συνωδίνω (Rom 8:22) (and in the deutero-Pauline letters, raised with Christ: συνεγείρω in Col 2:12; 3:1; Eph 2:6). This implies a particular fusion of past and present in which the past comes to make sense of the present by addressing it directly, or by binding the believer to a past event in an act of appropriative repetition. In the early deutero-Pauline tradition, this is expressed most clearly in Col 1:24—Paul fills up what is lacking with regard to the sufferings of Christ for the sake of the church. The suffering of Christ is read against the present, and Paul's imprisonment and affliction are given meaning by being related in a contemporizing manner to the sufferings of Christ, with which they become not quite identical, but synonymous. One might say that the *imitatio Christi* is an embodied form of actualization, even if here the term begins to stretch.

PAUL AND HIS OWN PRESENCE

Third, we turn to examine one final context in which we encounter actualization in the Pauline tradition—in discussions of Paul's own presence. Paul writes letters, of course, because he is unable to be physically present with the assemblies he wishes to exhort. In this sense, his literary deposit is precisely the result of his absence, an absence the letter seeks to overcome. The letter therefore functions as a sort of "parousia," a substitute presence for the geographically distant apostle (e.g., 2 Cor 10:11; cf. Col 2:5).[21] We find Paul reminding his readers of his own presence as a model for imitation in letters to the communities from which he is now absent: 1 Cor 4:17, "For this reason I sent

---

21. Classically argued in R. W. Funk, "The Apostolic *Parousia*: Form and Significance," in *Christian History and Interpretation: Studies Presented to John Knox*, ed. W. R. Farmer, C. F. D. Moule, and R. R. Niebuhr (Cambridge: Cambridge University Press, 1967), 249–68.

Chapter 7

you Timothy, who is my beloved and faithful child in the Lord, to remind you of my ways in Christ Jesus, as I teach them everywhere in every church."[22]

It is this aspect of the letter—its substitution for the writer's presence—that comes to be most useful to the pseudepigrapher. The absence of the writer can be exploited to interpose an alternative voice that competes with that of the living but absent writer (i.e., a malicious forgery), or it can be used to fictionalize the author's voice to overcome not geographical distance but temporal separation and carry on an author's message after his or her death. Both postures arguably involve some measure of deception but for entirely different ends. Early Christians are aware of Paul as a writer of letters. Second Peter refers to Paul's letters (3:15–16), Clement of Rome refers to a letter to the Corinthians (1 Clem. 47.1–3), Ignatius says that Paul remembers the Ephesians "in every letter" (Ignatius, *Eph.* 12.2), and Polycarp mentions to the Philippians that Paul wrote them "letters" that they should study (Polycarp, *Phil.* 3.2).

In the later Pauline pseudepigrapha, we see clear attempts to actualize or update Paul and his message to address later conditions. In 3 Corinthians Paul explicitly says, "I delivered to you in the beginning what I received from the apostles who were before me"—something he explicitly denies in Galatians (though cf. 1 Cor 11:23)—as a means of guaranteeing the continuity of his message there with the primitive apostolic church. He then goes on to defend an emerging doctrinal orthodoxy—particularly with regard to the resurrection. We can also recognize in its phraseology a number of Pauline fragments, which again suggests that its author has proceeded by way of imitation, in order to bring Paul's message authentically to bear on a later controversy in an actualizing manner. Indeed, a similar strategy is undertaken in the so-called Epistle to the Laodiceans, which apparently fills the lacuna reflected in Col 4:16 ("And when this letter has been read among you, have it read also in the church of the Laodiceans, and have the one from Laodicea come to you that you may read it also"). This brief document, even more than 3 Corinthians, is comprised of a tissue of Pauline phrases, taken especially from Philippians. The purpose of the epistle is, however, far from clear, since it does not appear to clearly address a certain theological issue or practical need.[23]

In pseudepigraphal compositions, Paul's recollection of his own example in his absence can be used to authorize and add weight to pastoral advice

22. Cf., e.g., 1 Thess 2:9–12; 4:1–2; 1 Cor 11:1; and also Paul's autobiographical statements in Gal 1–2; 2 Cor 11–12, on which see George Lyons, *Pauline Autobiography: Toward a New Understanding* (Atlanta: Scholars Press, 1985).

23. The attempt of Bart Ehrman to read this as a polemic against Marcionism fails to convince (*Forgery and Counterforgery: The Use of Literary Deceit in Early Christian Polemics* [Oxford: Oxford University Press, 2012], 439–45).

Presentifying the Past

that may be "Pauline" in a certain sense but appears now as an extension or updating of Paul's message. Paul's own absence can open a space in which the audience can find their own problems addressed, even if the pseudepigraphal letters are of necessity not addressed to them directly. This is because, as Richard Bauckham has insightfully written:

> The problem for the author . . . is that he wants his pseudepigraphal letter to perform for him and his readers something like the function which an authentic real letter from him to his readers would perform. He wants, under cover of his pseudonym, to address his real readers, but his genre allows his letter to be addressed only to supposed addressees contemporary with the supposed author. Thus, he needs to find some way in which material that is ostensibly addressed to supposed addressees in the past can be taken by his real readers as actually or also addressed to them.[24]

We arguably find such devices several times in the deutero-Pauline letters. For example, in Col 2:1, 5a, we read, "For I want you to know how much I am struggling for you, and for those in Laodicea, and for all who have not seen me face to face. . . . For though I am absent in body, yet I am with you in spirit." Or, if 2 Thessalonians is taken to be pseudepigraphal, then 2:5 would make good sense along these lines: "Do you not remember that I told you these things when I was still with you?" (although here this is said by way of introducing new information).[25] Or again, in 1 Tim 3:14–15, we find the statement, "I hope to come to you soon, but I am writing these instructions to you so that, if I am delayed, you may know how one ought to behave in the household of God, which is the church of the living God, the pillar and bulwark of the truth." Taking 1 Timothy to be pseudonymous, the real author knows that Paul will be interminably delayed, since he had died years earlier, and so he makes use of the fictive author's absence to authorize the message he thinks the community now needs to hear.

If these letters are pseudepigraphal, we observe Paul's assertion that he wishes to be present with an audience, even though in reality death has drawn a veil across any possibility of Paul's presence. In this situation, the letter itself supplies an actualization of Pauline teaching, supplying in his absence what Paul might have said. In the space opened up by Paul's absence, we see the

---

24. Richard Bauckham, "Pseudo-Apostolic Letters," *JBL* 107 (1988): 469–94, here 476. See the fuller discussion in the next chapter, "Mirror-Reading a Pseudepigraphal Letter," in this volume.

25. Although if 2 Thessalonians is taken to be genuine, then this simply provides a specimen of the original of which the pseudepigraphic statements are imitations.

Chapter 7

autobiographical descriptions of Paul shift subtly: from "the violent persecutor of the church" in Gal 1:13–14 to one who "lived among the disobedient in the passions of [my] flesh, following the desires of flesh and senses" in Eph 2:3 to the "chief of sinners" in 1 Tim 1:12–16—changes that arguably make Paul's call more and more into a conversion of the type one might expect of a pagan and so provide a model for the growing gentile faction of the church.

Similarly, in a way that begins to point to the justification of the pseudepigraphal letters themselves, especially in 1 and 2 Timothy we find in Paul's absence the occasion for letters that provide reflection on what is future from Paul's perspective, but what is in reality contemporaneous with the author and his target audience. So Paul sees by the Spirit what will take place "in later times" and denounces it (1 Tim 4:1–5). Similarly in 2 Tim 3:1, Paul writes, in testamentary fashion, "You must understand this, that in the last days distressing times will come," followed by a list of vices that presumably would have been recognizable to the recipients of the letter (cf. 4:3–4).[26]

These well-known features of the pseudonymous epistolary strategy of the deutero-Pauline letters can be seen as in some sense extending strategies of updating and actualizing already found in the genuine Pauline letters themselves. In the same way that Paul offers an epistolary re-presentation of his own presence for communities from which he is absent, the pseudonymous authors employ the same vehicle to cross an even wider gap, and so bring the past authority of the apostle to bear on their present problems in a presentifying rhetorical strategy.

CONCLUSION

In conclusion, even this rather brief treatment of three *topoi* in the *corpus Paulinum* is sufficient to suggest that Paul and the Pauline tradition are interested in mediating not simply between present and future, but also between past and present. In the areas of scriptural interpretation, the death of Jesus, and Paul's own presence, we see evidence of actualization in the Pauline tradition. In this way, the "virtuous anachronism" of his present-directed pastoral strategies serves to overcome the "highly particularized quality of contingency"[27]

---

26. The Pastorals frequently instruct Timothy and Titus to pass on their teaching to others (1 Tim 4:6, 11; 6:2; 2 Tim 2:2, 14; Tit 2:2, 6, 9, 15; 3:1); cf. Bauckham, "Pseudo-Apostolic Letters."

27. Brevard Childs speaks of the "highly particularized quality of contingency" of the Pauline letters (*The Church's Guide to Reading Paul: The Canonical Shaping of the Pauline Corpus* [Grand Rapids: Eerdmans, 2008]).

Presentifying the Past

of some elements of the past and to bring his hearers to an encounter with the present reality of the crucified and risen Lord.

Paul clearly belongs to a time before the historicist imperative of contextual historiography had taken hold. That much is obvious, but it is striking how regularly he and his heirs render the past usable for their communities by refusing to see it as simply unalterably completed. Rather, they approach it as a living resource that can be brought into the present by interpretative or liturgical strategies, a fact that also probably attests to a more flexible view of the nature of reality in Christ than is customary to the modern student of Paul. By constantly mediating the past into the present, Paul's letters both attest and create a deeply memorial culture in which the anamnetic recollection of the past in performative ways served as an ongoing source of identity formation and theological reflection. In this way, Paul—and the deutero-Pauline authors after him—helped his converts to inhabit the scriptural tradition, climaxing in the Messiah, and so to think of themselves as residents of a new creation.[28]

28. Compare the suggestive reflections on Ephesians in Stephen Fowl, "Learning to Be a Gentile: Christ's Transformation and Redemption of Our Past," in *Christology and Scripture: Interdisciplinary Perspectives*, ed. Andrew Lincoln and Angus Paddison (London: T&T Clark, 2007), 22-40.

8

Mirror-Reading
a Pseudepigraphal Letter

Can we treat a letter judged to be pseudepigraphal just like any other and apply our process of mirror-reading in order to reconstruct the situation addressed? Or are the complications introduced by pseudonymity so severe that any attempt so to do risks being, in John Barclay's words, "a tissue of wild guesses"?[1] In what follows, I use the letter to the Colossians as a laboratory in which to explore this question. Many have assumed that their success in proposing plausible parallels for, to take but one significant example, the Colossian error in itself serves as evidence for the correctness of the identification of the opponents, the false teaching, or the situation of the letter (though plausibility is in the eye of the beholder, as the number of scenarios proposed would suggest). But when pseudepigraphy is taken into consideration, arguably any appeal to the ostensive reference of text to world is complicated. The communicative triad of author, addressee, and situation becomes opaque. As I hope to show, on the assumption of pseudonymity, a pseudepigrapher poses as the apostle Paul in order to write a letter to the Colossians, who, in turn, are fictional addressees masking an unknown actual group of recipients, about a situation that may well prove to be as much a construct as the author (Paul) and the recipients (the Colossians). Pseudepigraphy is usually taken as troubling the first point of the triad (the author, *per definitionem*), sometimes the second (the addressees) but rarely the third (the situation). But arguably the complications introduced by pseudepigraphy have not penetrated study of the New Testament as they might have done. This is all the more true the more successful a pseudepigrapher has been. In particular, we need to take into account the pseudepigraphal attempt to achieve a "reality effect" by employing tropes and concerns from authentic Pauline letters to lend the forged writing an air of verisimilitude. But in this way our ability, if we judge a text pseudepi-

---

1. John M. G. Barclay, "Mirror-Reading a Polemical Letter: Galatians as a Test Case," *JSNT* 31 (1987): 73–93, here 83.

Mirror-Reading a Pseudepigraphal Letter

graphal, to discern reality from appearance is severely problematized, and we should therefore consider the possibility that pseudepigraphal letters should be treated more as rhetorical compositions[2] than as epistolary literature, since all the ostensive elements of epistolarity are fictionalized in a pseudepigraphal letter (or at least the burden of proof falls to the interpreter who wants to suggest that one element of the triad of author-recipient-situation is not fictionalized while the others are).

In short, we should expect commentators' interpretations of texts like Colossians to look very different depending on whether they judge the letter to be orthonymous or pseudonymous,[3] but this is often not the case. It is all too easy to find examples of scholars who discuss the question of authorship, only to sideline it as not having any relevance to broader interpretative issues. To take but one example of dozens that could be marshaled, in his study identifying the Colossian opponents as adherents of a Cynic philosophy, Troy Martin sidelines the question of Pauline authorship, but then goes on to suggest, "The problems encountered in identifying the opponents at Colossae are very similar to the problems involved in the identification of the opponents in other New Testament letters."[4] As I now turn to argue, the problems are in fact quite different.

The arguments about whether Paul wrote Colossians are finely balanced, even if a noticeable majority of scholars favors non-Pauline authorship.[5] But while I will mention some of the principal arguments for non-Pauline authorship of the letter in passing, the question at hand is about the implications

---

2. Of course, epistles can also be highly "rhetorical," but the contrast I have in mind is between discretely situational epistolary interventions on the one hand, and texts that employ epistolary form as a fictional choice in order to convey a message to a broader set of readers who will not stand in a direct relationship to the ostensive addressees of the letter; see further discussion below.

3. For some discussion of these terms, see Bart Ehrman, *Forgery and Counterforgery: The Use of Literary Deceit in Early Christian Polemics* (Oxford: Oxford University Press, 2013), 29–67.

4. Troy W. Martin, *By Philosophy and Empty Deceit: Colossians as Response to a Cynic Critique*, JSNTSup 118 (Sheffield: Sheffield Academic, 1996), 16–17n4; 20. The assumption that the question of authorship is not substantially related to determining the false teaching envisaged by the letter is widespread; see further Richard E. DeMaris, *The Colossian Controversy: Wisdom in Dispute at Colossae*, JSNTSup 96 (Sheffield: Sheffield Academic, 1994), 11–12.

5. See the helpful survey of opinion in Nijay Gupta, "What Is in a Name? The Hermeneutics of Authorship Analysis Concerning Colossians," *CurBR* 11 (2013): 196–217, although some of his assumptions about the nature of pseudepigraphy remain, in my judgment, unproven; see further below.

Chapter 8

of such a judgment rather than about the judgment itself. In what follows I hope to call into question some of the certainty with which some interpretative judgments are rendered, with a view to Colossians in particular. I further hope that my argument may shed light on other cases in which a judgment of pseudonymity is returned, though space precludes discussing other examples of pseudepigraphal compositions explicitly.

The Problem of Mirror-Reading in General

First, we turn to the problem of mirror-reading in general. The difficulties inherent in mirror-reading are well known. In his 1987 article, "Mirror-Reading a Polemical Letter: Galatians as a Test Case"[6] (to which my title is an allusion), John Barclay famously cautioned interpreters of Galatians not to assume they can reconstruct the situation in Galatia from the text of Paul's letters without stringent methodological constraints. He suggests that in the process of mirror-reading, "we must use the text which answers the opponents as a mirror in which we can see reflected the people and the arguments under attack."[7] Here I use the term to speak, not simply of constructing the opponents' views, but also to speak of reconstructing the situation more broadly. Barclay offers several complicating factors that plague attempts at such mirror-reading in Galatians: (1) Paul is not talking directly to the opponents but talking to the Galatians about the opponents; (2) Galatians is full of rhetorical polemic rather than calm discussion; (3) Since we only hear one partner in a two-way conversation, we are unable to interpret statements in their proper historical and linguistic contexts. He then offers a devastating criticism of several major interpretations of Galatians, mentioning the dangers of (1) undue selectivity; (2) overinterpretation (believing that every statement of Paul's must be correcting a problem or accusation by the agitators); (3) mishandling polemics;[8] (4) latching onto particular words and phrases as echoes of the opponents' vocabulary; and some other significant interpretative errors.

If Colossians is a genuine letter by Paul, we must grapple with both the indirection of Paul's address—writing to the Colossians about the opponents

---

6. Barclay, "Mirror-Reading."

7. Barclay, "Mirror-Reading," 73–74.

8. Polemical language is often highly stereotyped, making inferences about the reality to which it points tenuous; cf. also R. J. Karris, "The Background and Significance of the Polemic of the Pastoral Epistles," *JBL* 92 (1973): 549–63.

132

Mirror-Reading a Pseudepigraphal Letter

rather than addressing the opponents directly—and the highly rhetorical character of the letter. For example, it is difficult to imagine the opponents willingly describing themselves as "taking the Colossians captive" (2:6) or as "being puffed up without cause by a human way of thinking" (2:18). So all of Barclay's cautions for mirror-reading a polemical letter would hold were Colossians judged to be an orthonymous letter of the historical Paul.[9]

Even taking Barclay's cautions seriously, the difficulty in offering a persuasive reconstruction of the Colossian "error" or "heresy" or "false teaching" or "philosophy" persists. The nature of the opponents' teaching seems to be one of those Pauline problems, like the baptism for the dead or the meaning of Gal 3:20, for which commentators delight in claiming impressive numbers of proffered solutions: forty-four interpretations by the 1970s, dozens more since.[10] The alleged culprits behind the trouble range from syncretistic, gnosticizing groups to those influenced by Jewish mysticism, from Pythagorean, Middle Platonic or Cynic philosophy to Essenism, Christian apocalypticism or simply the Jewish synagogue.[11] Morna Hooker, in a refreshingly bold es-

9. Note also Nijay Gupta, "Mirror-Reading Moral Issues in Paul's Letters," *JSNT* 34 (2012): 361–81, which extends and adapts Barclay's work to address ethical teaching in Paul, especially in 1 Thessalonians and Romans. But this does not get us far in Colossians, given the very general nature of the ethical commands.

10. For the tally of forty-four interpretations, see J. J. Gunther, *St. Paul's Opponents and Their Background: A Study of Apocalyptic and Jewish Sectarian Teachings*, NovTSup 35 (Leiden: Brill, 1973), 3–4.

11. Of the almost endless literature that could be cited, for discussion of the Colossian "error" or "heresy" or "false teaching" or "philosophy," with references to other literature, see Fred O. Francis and Wayne A. Meeks, eds., *Conflict at Colossae: A Problem in the Interpretation of Early Christianity Illustrated by Selected Modern Studies*, rev. ed. (Missoula, MT: Scholars Press, 1975); Eduard Schweizer, *The Letter to the Colossians*, trans. Andrew Chester (London: SPCK, 1982), 125–34; Christopher Rowland, "Apocalyptic Visions and the Exaltation of Christ in the Letter to the Colossians," *JSNT* 19 (1983): 73–83; F. F. Bruce, "The Colossian Heresy," *BSac* 141 (1984): 195–208; Ambrose M. Moyo, "The Colossian Heresy in the Light of Some Gnostic Documents from Nag Hammadi," *JTSA* 48 (1984): 30–44; Roy Yates, "Colossians and Gnosis," *JSNT* 27 (1986): 49–68; Thomas J. Sappington, *Revelation and Redemption at Colossae*, JSNTSup 53 (Sheffield: Sheffield Academic, 1991); DeMaris, *The Colossian Controversy*; Clinton E. Arnold, *The Colossian Syncretism: The Interface between Christianity and Folk Belief at Colossae*, WUNT 77 (Tübingen: Mohr Siebeck, 1995); Martin, *By Philosophy and Empty Deceit*; Robert M. Royalty, "Dwelling on Visions: On the Nature of the So-Called 'Colossians Heresy,'" *Bib* 83 (2002): 329–57; Hans Hübner, "Der Diskussion um die deuteropaulinischen Briefe seit 1970: Der Kolosserbrief (I)," *TRu* 68 (2003): 263–85, 395–440; R. McL. Wilson, *Colossians and Philemon*, ICC (London: T&T Clark, 2005), 35–58; Jerry L. Sumney, "Studying Paul's Opponents: Advances and Challenges," in *Paul and His Opponents*, ed. Stanley E. Porter, Pauline Studies 2 (Leiden: Brill, 2005), 7–58, esp. 29–33,

133

Chapter 8

say that seems to have convinced few commentators, goes so far as to suggest that there was no real problem of "false teaching" in Colossae at all, but that Paul is simply addressing the potential pressures to conform to Jewish or pagan neighbors.[12]

In the course of his own methodological proposal for reconstructing the opponents in Colossians using a perspectival reading strategy, Peter Müller suggests that "the question is . . . not how we can avoid a mirror-reading. We cannot avoid it (at least not as long as we do not give up on the question of the determination of the opponents altogether)."[13] For Müller, as for many other exegetes, giving up on the reconstruction of the Colossian philosophy is a kind of *reductio ad absurdum*, something that New Testament scholarship should not countenance. But arguably one's judgments about the genuineness of the Pauline authorial ascription have an effect on our ability to pursue the quest for the Colossian error. Indeed, two of the most widely discussed problems in Colossians are the authorship of the epistle, on the one hand, and the nature of the teaching being opposed, on the other.[14] There is, however, curiously

---

50–58, with references to previous literature; Christian Stettler, "The Opponents at Colossae," in Porter, *Paul and His Opponents*, 169–200; Ian K. Smith, *Heavenly Perspective: A Study of the Apostle Paul's Response to a Jewish Mystical Movement at Colossae*, LNTS 326 (London: T&T Clark, 2006), 19–38; and Kobus Kok, "Die Irrglaube in Kolosse: Aanbidding van of met engele in Kolossense," *HvTSt* 66 (2010).

12. M. D. Hooker, "Were There False Teachers in Colossae?," in *Christ and Spirit in the New Testament: Essays in Honour of C. F. D. Moule*, ed. Barnabas Lindars and Stephen S. Smalley (Cambridge: Cambridge University Press, 1973); repr. in M. D. Hooker, *From Adam to Christ: Essays on Paul* (Cambridge: Cambridge University Press, 1990), 121–36. She writes, "Paul's teaching in Colossians, then, seems to us to be quite as appropriate to a situation in which young Christians are under pressure to conform to the beliefs and practices of their pagan and Jewish neighbours, as to a situation in which their faith is endangered by the deliberate attacks of false teachers; in view of the absence from Colossians of any clear reference to the supposed error, or hint of distress on Paul's part, this explanation seems far more probable" (134); see also N. T. Wright, *The Epistles of Paul to the Colossians and to Philemon*, TNTC (Grand Rapids: Eerdmans, 1986), 23–30.

13. Peter Müller, "Gegner im Kolosserbrief: Methodische Überlegungen zu einem schwierigen Kapitel," in *Beiträge zur urchristlichen Theologiegeschichte*, ed. Wolfgang Kraus (Berlin: de Gruyter, 2009), 365–94: "Die Frage ist also nicht, wie wir ein mirror-reading vermeiden können. Wir können es nicht vermeiden (jedenfalls nicht so lange wir die Frage nach einer Bestimmung der Gegner nicht generell aufgeben)" (373). The article offers a perspectival reading in that Müller attempts to take into account the varying perspective of the authors and the opponents.

14. Indeed, the survey of Colossians research by Wolfgang Schenk restricts itself to basically these two points in particular: "Der Kolosserbrief in der neueren Forschung (1945–1985)," *ANRW* II.25.4 (1987): 3327–64.

Mirror-Reading a Pseudepigraphal Letter

little reflection about how these two major topics of discussion might relate to one another. Mirror-reading an orthonymous letter is perilously difficult; mirror-reading a pseudepigraphal one is even more complex, for reasons to which we will shortly turn.

THE NARRATIVE WORLD OF COLOSSIANS

First it is worth reiterating one of the points that Norman Petersen made several decades ago in his important study, *Rediscovering Paul: Philemon and the Sociology of Paul's Narrative World*.[15] In that book, among other things, Petersen contended that letters have a narrative world embedded in them, an interpretation that is not a transparent reflection of the world but an active rendering of it in sequential form. At its most basic level, we might suggest that this story consists of an interaction between (a) the author and (b) the addressees concerning (c) a particular situation. In the case of Philemon, clearly this story can be told in different ways but concerns Paul, Philemon, and a runaway named Onesimus.

In Colossians, we might suggest that the story goes something like this: The apostle Paul has heard from Epaphras (1:8) about the faith of the Colossians (1:2). These Colossians (and in close connection, Laodiceans and Hierapolitans) are Christ-believers with a gentile past (1:21, 27; 3:7) who do not know Paul personally (2:1, 5) but learned the gospel from Epaphras (1:7; cf. 4:12–13). Paul writes to them to encourage them in their faith and to warn them against a threatening danger. Insert reconstruction of false teaching here.

No doubt we could nuance this story considerably and tell it from different perspectives, but most of that short retelling should be unobjectionable. The complications set in as we attempt to move from the world of the narrative within the letter to the ostensive referential world, the world "behind the text."[16] The normal practice within New Testament scholarship is to attempt to interpret texts by situating them in their circumstances of origin. This is one of the reasons why *Einleitungsfragen* have typically been so heatedly debated. The attempt to fix the circumstances of origin in view, as a means of gaining a

---

15. Norman Petersen, *Rediscovering Paul: Philemon and the Sociology of Paul's Narrative World* (Minneapolis: Fortress, 1985).

16. These categories are indebted to Hans Frei's classic work, *The Eclipse of Biblical Narrative: A Study in Eighteenth and Nineteenth Century Hermeneutics* (New Haven: Yale University Press, 1974).

135

Chapter 8

purchase for interpretation, involves moving from the narrative world to the referential world. That is, this involves the process of moving from the statements within the letter to the historical world behind the letter. At the heart of this attempt is the identification of a triad of elements: author, addressee, situation. In the case of orthonymous letters, some tentative reconstruction of these three is often possible, though even here interpreters differ (to recall the debates concerning the addressees and situation of Paul's letter to the Galatians is sufficient proof of this point).

But this normal process of interpretation is arguably highly complexified by the judgment of pseudonymity, in a way that has not always been appreciated in scholarship on Colossians, although there have been some notable exceptions to which I will return. In what follows, we turn to examine each of these three elements of the triad of author, addressees, and situation and ask about the implications of pseudonymity for our process of interpretation. Can we trouble one element without disturbing the other two?

Authorial Fictions and Strategies of Legitimation: The Death of the Author

The authorial element of this triad has of course received the most sustained attention in scholarship on Colossians. Ever since Ernst Mayerhoff in 1838 (and before him, though seldom noted, the English clergyman Edward Evanson in 1792), Colossians has been seen by many to have been written by an author other than the historical Paul.[17] The reasons for this judgment are accessible in most introductions to the New Testament or commentaries on Colossians and need not be repeated *in extenso*, but include several lines of argument: (1) stylistic differences between Colossians and the undisputed Pauline letters. These have been set forth in massive detail by Walter Bujard.[18] As one scholar summarizes this line of argument, Colossians's "syntax is characterized by a relative lack of qualifying conjunctions and articular infinitives, accompanied

17. Ernst T. Mayerhoff, *Der Brief an die Colosser, mit vornehmlicher Berücksichtigung der drei Pastoralbriefe* (Berlin: Hermann Schultze, 1838); and Edward Evanson, *The Dissonance of the Four Generally Received Evangelists, and the Evidence of their Respective Authenticity Examined* (Ipswich: G. Jermyn, 1792), 263. Mayerhoff himself seems ignorant of Evanson's work ("Da nun der Brief an die Colosser bisher noch gar nicht angezweifelt ist," 5).

18. Walter Bujard, *Stilanalytische Untersuchungen zum Kolosserbrief als Beitrag zur Methodik von Sprachvergleichen* (Göttingen: Vandenhoeck & Ruprecht, 1973); cf. also Eduard Lohse, *Colossians and Philemon*, Hermeneia (Philadelphia: Fortress, 1971), 84–88.

Mirror-Reading a Pseudepigraphal Letter

by a relative predominance of participles and relative clauses. The resultant thought structure is loose. The rhetorical profile of the letter is marked by a certain 'fullness', all in contrast to Paul."[19] (2) More significant is the role that has been played by the more developed theology attested in Colossians. Scholars have pointed to the more universal horizon of Colossians, the use of the body of Christ to express a cosmic understanding, differences in the portrayal of Paul and the identity of believers, the role of slavery, realized vs. future eschatology, and the translation of temporal eschatology into spatial terms.[20] Finally, (3) there are some parallels with the undisputed Pauline letters that might suggest dependence (cf., e.g., Col 1:26-27 with 1 Cor 2:7; Rom 16:25-26; Rom 9:23-24), though the question of literary dependence in Colossians is a controverted one. Some suggestions, such as Kiley's contention that the lack of mention of the financial transactions characteristic of the genuine Pauline letters in his collection for the poor tells against the authenticity of Colossians, seem to assume what they wish to prove.[21]

None of these differences is significant enough in itself to force the conclusion of inauthenticity, but their cumulative weight has led many to consider Colossians to be a post-Pauline writing. This type of argument is necessarily circular, since an authentic Paul constructed by excluding Colossians is then used as a heuristic lens to exclude Colossians, but this is our only means of proceeding in such cases, and the circular nature of the argument is not as such a reason to discount it.

There are, though, not simply two binary positions in play on the question of authorship: genuine vs. false, authentic vs. forgery. Some scholars, perhaps especially those writing in English, have sought to make use of mediating positions to account for some of the perceived differences between the undisputed Pauline letters and Colossians, without relinquishing the claim to a genuine Pauline stamp on the letter.[22] So perhaps Paul simply offers general guidance for the letter to an amanuensis and adds a greeting at the end,[23] or

---

19. Mark Kiley, *Colossians as Pseudepigraphy* (Sheffield: JSOT Press, 1986), 73.

20. For a recent discussion, with references to earlier literature, see Ehrman, *Forgery and Counterforgery*, 171-82.

21. Kiley, *Colossians as Pseudepigraphy*, 46-51; so rightly John M. G. Barclay, *Colossians and Philemon* (Sheffield: Sheffield Academic, 1997).

22. For a typology of the variety of authorial models proposed, see the appendix to this chapter.

23. Compare the personal greeting (1 Cor 16:21; Gal 6:11; Col 4:18; 2 Thess 3:17; Phlm 19) or note from the secretary (Rom 16:22); for examples of other letters that follow this convention of adding a personal greeting in the author's own hand, see Stanley K. Stowers,

Chapter 8

perhaps Colossians was written by an associate or student of Paul within his own lifetime on his behalf in a nondeceptive manner but with enough substantial differences from his thought for us to detect the fact.[24] These various halfway houses are attractive to some, because they allow the interpreter to do justice to the significance of the differences between Colossians and the undisputed Paulines without having to relegate Colossians to the theological scrap heap labeled "forgery."[25]

But there are a number of problems with such attempts to see Colossians as non-Pauline but not substantially pseudepigraphal, or as only openly so in a transparent fiction that the audience clearly recognizes—what we might call the exercise of an accepted literary convention (as, for example, James D. G. Dunn's student David Meade famously suggested in his book, *Pseudonymity and Canon*).[26] Recent trends in pseudepigraphy research tell against such attempts to mitigate the affront of deception.[27] There are virtually no analogues to such suggestions as that Colossians was written by an associate of Paul on his behalf in a nondeceptive manner but with some substantial differences from his thought.[28] Scholars such as Jeremy Duff, Terry Wilder, Armin Baum,

---

Letter Writing in Greco-Roman Antiquity, LEC (Philadelphia: Westminster, 1989), 60–61; and Thomas J. Bauer, *Paulus und die kaiserzeitliche Epistolographie: Kontextualisierung und Analyse der Briefe an Philemon und an die Galater*, WUNT 276 (Tübingen: Mohr Siebeck, 2011), 24–25, 241–45.

24. Note, influentially, the position of James D. G. Dunn, *The Epistles to the Colossians and to Philemon: A Commentary on the Greek Text*, NIGTC (Grand Rapids: Eerdmans, 1996).

25. Whether, of course, pseudonymity should have such theological entailments is another question entirely and one that is well worth asking in another context.

26. David G. Meade, *Pseudonymity and Canon*, WUNT 39 (Tübingen: Mohr Siebeck, 1986; repr., Grand Rapids: Eerdmans, 1987).

27. For surveys of research, see Martina Janssen, *Unter falschem Namen: Eine kritische Forschungsbilanz frühchristlicher Pseudepigraphie* (Frankfurt: Lang, 2003); Meade, *Pseudonymity and Canon*; Norbert Brox, ed., *Pseudepigraphie in der heidnischen und jüdisch-christlichen Antike* (Darmstadt: Wissenschaftliche Buchgesellschaft, 1977).

28. Dunn, *Colossians*, represents an admirable attempt not to smooth over unevenness in the text, but this in the end simply transfers the unevenness to his own commentary. So he suggests that the letter may have been written by Timothy under Paul's instructions but "with a fair degree of license," though Paul is still seen to have signed off on the content and added his signature (4:18) (*Colossians*, 35–39). This creates interpretative difficulties: on the one hand, Dunn uses the undisputed Pauline corpus as a guide to normal lexical usage but then finds recourse in the amanuensis when these data are irregular. In particular, Dunn's interpretation of 4:7–18 suffers from a somewhat convoluted attempt to navigate the personal notices (and their attendant historical difficulties) as sometimes Pauline and sometimes betraying another hand, when arguably seeing them as involved in a strategy of verisimilitude provides a more economical solution.

Mirror-Reading a Pseudepigraphal Letter

and others have made this case convincingly.[29] If, for example, Paul merely added his signature (4:18) to a letter with substantial differences from his own thought, it is difficult to account for this oversight, unparalleled in his other correspondence. The problem becomes more pronounced when one notes that Colossians has a relatively robust authorial presence, one that cannot be easily effaced. So, for example, Paul does not simply figure in 1:1 as a cosender, but also in 1:23–25, 29; 2:1, 5; 4:3–4, 7–8, 18. The choice seems to be between substantially orthonymous authorship (even with the use of a secretary or amanuensis) and substantially pseudonymous authorship. How interpreters judge the significance of the stylistic, theological, and literary problems mentioned above determines on which side of that line they fall.

This leads now to the point, perhaps deadeningly obvious, that a judgment of pseudonymity entails a construction of the author, and so as well entails a destabilization of the first member of the triad of author, addressees, and situation. If Colossians is seen to be pseudonymous, then various elements of the letter that appear to be personal statements on an orthonymous reading now take on the status of legitimizing fictions, part of a broader attempt to lend verisimilitude to the letter as a means of helping it succeed in its aims. As several have suggested with regard to the personal notices in the Pastoral Epistles, the personal information about Paul in Colossians can be seen to pick up on and exploit known elements of Paul's reputation as part of this process of lending verisimilitude to the letter. Arguably the most significant form of this practice in Colossians is the emphasis on Paul's suffering. Paul's suffering, even within his own lifetime and in his own interpretation, provides a certain legitimacy to his apostolic vocation. It is a point on which others did not hesitate to press the apostle, but Paul sees suffering as a fundamental element of the union with Christ that runs through the heart of his soteriological vision. One might follow James Kelhoffer's appropriation of Pierre Bourdieu to suggest that Paul's suffering accrued cultural, social, and spiritual capital.[30]

---

29. Jeremy Duff, "A Reconsideration of Pseudepigraphy in Early Christianity" (DPhil thesis, University of Oxford, 1998); Armin Baum, *Pseudepigraphie und literarische Fälschung im frühen Christentum*, WUNT 2/138 (Tübingen: Mohr Siebeck, 2001); Terry L. Wilder, *Pseudonymity, the New Testament, and Deception* (Lanham, MD: University Press of America, 2004); cf. also Annette Merz, "The Fictitious Self-Exposition of Paul: How Might Intertextual Theory Suggest a Reformulation of the Hermeneutics of Pseudepigraphy?," in *The Intertextuality of the Epistles: Explorations of Theory and Practice*, ed. Thomas L. Brodie, Dennis R. MacDonald, and Stanley E. Porter (Sheffield: Sheffield Phoenix, 2006), 113–32.

30. For this general application of Bourdieu to suffering in the New Testament, I am indebted to the fine book by James A. Kelhoffer, *Persecution, Persuasion and Power:*

Chapter 8

One of the most striking conceptions of the apostle's suffering is found in 1:24, in which Paul speaks of suffering "for the sake of" the Colossians, even "filling up what is lacking in the Messiah's afflictions for the sake of his body, the church." The precise connotations of these phrases are debated, but arguably the martyrological tradition of vicarious suffering has informed this presentation. If the letter is written by someone other than Paul, it is not difficult to see here an implicit reflection on the apostle's own death, understood to be that of a righteous martyr. Colossians 2:1 and 5 may also have the death of the apostle in the background. After Paul's death, the recipients of the letter could identify with the Colossians and Laodiceans and "all who have not seen me face to face" (2:1). Similarly, the letter's use of a Pauline epistolary *topos* takes on new meaning when viewed through the prism of Paul's death: "For though I am absent in body, yet I am with you in spirit" (2:5). Hans Dieter Betz might have pressed this too far when he described Colossians as a "heavenly letter" sent from the departed Paul back to the congregation on earth,[31] but if Colossians is taken to be pseudepigraphal, then one can see the connection between the themes of suffering and absence, which together serve to justify, in some sense, the writing of the letter. This seems to be a legitimizing presentation of Paul's sufferings, heightened from Paul's own letters, in which, to use again Bourdieu's terms, Paul's cultural, social, and spiritual capital, accrued through suffering and persistent beyond his death, are spent posthumously and pseudonymously on behalf of gentiles. His life cut short by martyrdom, Paul's blood still speaks from the ground, and the message he would have addressed to these Christ-believers is now offered in his absence but with a tacit claim to his authorization.

There are other more minor ways in which the presentation of Paul serves to add a "reality effect" to the letter. We will come to the greetings shortly, but one can see how the closing in Paul's own hand in 4:18, on the assumption of pseudepigraphy, imitates the similar closing in 1 Cor 16:21–24; Gal 6:11–18; 2 Thess 3:17–18 (if genuine); Phlm 19. Once the non-Pauline authorship of Colossians is granted, then details in the text that seem to be authentic no-

---

Readiness to Withstand Hardship as a Corroboration of Legitimacy in the New Testament, WUNT 270 (Tübingen: Mohr Siebeck, 2010), although he does not draw these conclusions about pseudepigraphy. For a basic introduction to Bourdieu, see Craig Calhoun, "Pierre Bourdieu," *The Blackwell Companion to Major Contemporary Social Theorists*, ed. George Ritzer (Oxford: Blackwell, 2003), 274–309.

31. Hans Dieter Betz, "Paul's 'Second Presence' in Colossians," in *Texts and Contexts: Biblical Texts in Their Textual and Situational Contexts; Essays in Honor of Lars Hartman*, ed. Tord Fornberg and David Hellholm (Oslo: Scandinavian University Press, 1995), 507–18.

Mirror-Reading a Pseudepigraphal Letter

tices now become part of the persuasive (if deceptive) strategy of lending an aura of authenticity to the letter, and so attempting to prepare a space for the reception of its message.

It is tautologous to suggest, then, that the first pole of the triad, that of the author, is the one most obviously troubled by a judgment of pseudonymity. But once pseudonymity is granted, we are also then alerted to a compositional strategy of the author—the quest for legitimacy through the creation of what might be called a reality effect. This insight should not be left aside, as it often is, in evaluating the other two poles of inquiry, the addressees and the situation. We turn now to the second member of the triad.

Is Colossians a Letter? To the Colossians?

In his admirable commentary on the letter to the Colossians, after noting the difficulties attending the question of authorship, Dunn suggests, perhaps incautiously, "There is no dispute regarding where and to whom the letter was addressed: 'to the saints in Colossae' (1:2)."[32] At the basic level of the words of the text, of course, Dunn is correct: the letter presents itself as addressing a group of Christ-followers in Colossae whom Paul has not met personally. For Dunn himself, who attempts to see Colossians (unpersuasively in my view), as written by a close associate of Paul within his own lifetime, the move from the world of the text to the ostensive world is less problematic than it is for those who deny Pauline authorship more consistently.

It is not difficult to find many examples of exegetes who deny Pauline authorship of Colossians but go on to treat it as a letter with many close similarities to the genuine Pauline Epistles. For example, in a recent essay, Harry O. Maier suggests that someone other than Paul wrote Colossians, but then proceeds to attempt an analysis of Colossians as an epistolary response to imperial propaganda by utilizing archaeological evidence from Colossae and nearby Aphrodisias as a way of reconstructing an imperial situation to which Colossians may be seen to reply. He even goes so far as to suggest "an intriguing iconographic parallel for interpreting the realized eschatology of Colossians" in the Gemma Augustea.[33] The plausibility or otherwise of this interpretation

---

32. Dunn, *Colossians*, 20.

33. Harry O. Maier, "Reading Colossians in the Ruins: Roman Imperial Iconography, Moral Transformation, and the Construction of Christian Identity in the Lycus Valley," in *Colossae in Space and Time: Linking to an Ancient City*, ed. Alan H. Cadwallader and Mi-

Chapter 8

aside, does the basic presupposition that the letter was sent to Christians in Colossae hold up?

It is perfectly reasonable and defensible for a scholar like Paul Trebilco, who thinks Paul wrote Colossians, to use it, together with Philemon, as a witness for the presence of Christ-believers in the Lycus Valley.[34] But for those who do not count Colossians as genuinely Pauline, can we know that *either* Colossians *or* Philemon was genuinely addressed to Christians in the Lycus Valley?[35] It is clear that the "narrative world" of Colossians has in view not only Colossae (1:2), but also Laodicea (2:1; 4:13, 15, 16) and Hierapolis (4:13). But do we have any resources at our disposal to ascertain whether this claim in the narrative world has an ostensive referent in the historical world?

Philemon is often placed in Colossae or the Lycus Valley because of the impressive overlap in names in the greetings in both letters. If we assume, for the moment, that at least the name of Archippus, addressed in both Philemon and Colossians, is an accurate reflection of a historical individual in Colossae, but that Colossians is pseudonymous, it is difficult to imagine how the ruse would have been successful. How would Archippus, addressed by the historical Paul in Philemon, have reacted to hearing his own name in a Pauline letter some years after Paul's death (of which, as an associate of Paul, he presumably would have known)? It is possible that, as pseudepigraphers sometimes do, appeal could be made to the rediscovery of a lost letter or book. But we have no hint of this in Colossians. At any rate, we can here simply note the awkwardness of reusing a name from an authentic letter in a letter composed pseudepigraphally years later and the potential difficulties this might pose if both Colossians and Philemon are seen as sent to Colossae.[36]

---

chael Trainor (Göttingen: Vandenhoeck & Ruprecht, 2011), 212–31, here 222; the concrete identification in the Lycus Valley is also found, for example, in Michael Trainor, "Excavating Epaphras of Colossae," in Cadwallader and Trainor, *Colossae in Space and Time: Linking to an Ancient City*, 232–46; so also Royalty, "Dwelling on Visions," 336.

34. Paul Trebilco, "Christians in the Lycus Valley: The View from Ephesus and from Western Asia Minor," in Cadwallader and Trainor, *Colossae in Space and Time*, 180–211.

35. See, rightly, Outi Leppä, *The Making of Colossians: A Study on the Formation and Purpose of a Deutero-Pauline Letter*, Publications of the Finnish Exegetical Society 86 (Helsinki: Finnish Exegetical Society, 2003), 12–14. See also now, independently, Vicky Balabanski, "Where Is Philemon? The Case for a Logical Fallacy in the Correlation of the Data in Philemon and Colossians 1.1–2; 4.7–18," *JSNT* 38 (2015): 131–50.

36. Andreas Dettwiler has recently suggested that a thorough-going fictionalization would be risky: "Une tell stratégie de triple dissimulatio—en particulier celle des destinataires et des collaborateurs—serait, selon toute probabilité historique, vouée à l'échec ou du moins hautement risqué" ("La lettre aux Colossiens: Une théologie de la mémoire," *NTS* 59

Mirror-Reading a Pseudepigraphal Letter

But here we should observe a further strategy of legitimation employed in Colossians. Not only Archippus, but also Epaphras, Mark, Aristarchus, Demas, and Luke (companions of Paul) offer their greetings to the Colossians. All these names, in fact, also appear in Philemon, though with some slight differences between the two lists (e.g., Epaphras is the fellow prisoner in Philemon, while Aristarchus is the fellow prisoner in Colossians).[37] On the assumption of pseudepigraphy, it is even possible that Colossians has read "Jesus" as an independent proper name in Phlm 23 and transformed this into "Jesus who is called Justus."[38] Table 1 presents this evidence.

Table 1: Named coworkers in Philemon and Colossians

Philemon	**Colossians**
(a) Archippus (2)	(e) Aristarchus (4:10)
(b) Epaphras (23)	(d) Mark (4:10)
(c) [Jesus] (23)	(c) Jesus Justus (4:11)
(d) Mark (24)	(b) Epaphras (4:12-13)
(e) Aristarchus (24)	(g) Luke (4:14)
(f) Demas (24)	(f) Demas (4:14)
(g) Luke (24)	(a) Archippus (4:17)

[2013]: 109–28, here 111). But is it not the case that a partial fabrication would in certain ways be even more risky?

37. For this comparison, see Angela Standhartinger, "Colossians and the Pauline School," *NTS* 50 (2004): 571–93, here 574; cf. also Lohse, *Colossians and Philemon*; E. P. Sanders, "Literary Dependence in Colossians," *JBL* 85 (1966): 28–45; and many others. But there may be, as Standhartinger has suggested (*Studien zur Entstehungsgeschichte und Intention des Kolosserbriefs*, NovTSup 94 [Leiden: Brill, 1999]), more interplay between literary and oral modes of retrieval than is customarily allowed. For a perceptive analysis of the ways in which "Paul's" coworkers are portrayed in Colossians, see Günter Röhser, "Der Schluss als Schlüssel: Zu den Epistolaria des Kolosserbriefes," in *Kolosser-Studien*, ed. Peter Müller, Biblisch-Theologische Studien 103 (Neukirchen-Vluyn: Neukirchener Verlag, 2009), 129–50 (my thanks to Prof. Röhser for kindly sending his essay to me).

38. As Standhartinger notes ("Pauline School," 574), one may follow Ernst Amling and Theodor Zahn in reading Jesus as a proper name in front of Mark—or indeed, only suggest that the author of Colossians may have done so. See Ernst Amling, "Eine Konjektur im Philemonbrief," *ZNW* 10 (1909): 261–62; Theodor Zahn, *Einleitung in das Neue Testament*, vol. 1 (Leipzig: Deichert, 1906), 321. Standhartinger here cites the third German edition of Zahn's work, to which I have not had access. In the first edition (1897), the reference is to page 319; cf. the English translation of the third edition, *Introduction to the New Testament* (Edinburgh: T&T Clark, 1909), 451.

Chapter 8

If Colossians is pseudepigraphal, then there seems to be a relatively good case for literary dependence on at least this one Pauline letter, to Philemon. But unless we are able to assume that the author of Colossians has direct historical knowledge that Philemon was in fact sent to Colossae, we lose the ability to place Philemon securely with reference to Colossae. It seems that one of two scenarios is likely: either that the author knows that Philemon has been sent to Colossae and so addresses his letter there but does not have it sent there as a letter (because of the risks of discovery), or that Colossians exploits the lack of geographical precision in Philemon to transfer its destination to Colossae, to which the author may or may not have sent his letter (on the latter supposition, Colossae is chosen simply because it can function as a typical gentile location in Asia Minor). Or as a third possibility, perhaps somewhat less likely, Colossians could have been sent to Colossae, to which Philemon was also sent, and its author simply took the risk.[39] It is very difficult to move beyond these options to something more concrete.

I have already noted that Colossians has in view not only Colossae (1:2), but also Laodicea (2:1; 4:13, 15, 16) and Hierapolis (4:13). Some have seen the emphasis on the Lycus Valley, and Colossae in particular, as significant for the placement of Colossians because of the earthquake that many, following J. B. Lightfoot and William Ramsay, have suggested destroyed much of the valley in the early 60s. On the assumption of authenticity, this is sometimes appealed to in order to suggest that any letter sent to Colossae must have been before the earthquake, and so written by Paul or within his lifetime. This proceeds on the assumption, of course, that the letter was actually sent to Colossae. Alternatively, those who suggest that Colossians is pseudepigraphal have equally attempted to achieve interpretative mileage from its putative destruction. Vacant cities tell no tales, and so a city that was destroyed within Paul's lifetime would have made a nice candidate to choose as the geographical recipient, since its receipt of the letter would be unverifiable. As Wolfgang Schenk suggests, "A dead Paul and a destroyed place were clearly the given presuppositions for this oldest pseudepigraphy."[40] But was the city really destroyed by the earthquake? While some, including James Dunn and Angela Standhartinger,

---

39. So Röhser, "Schluss als Schlüssel."

40. "Ein toter Paulus und ein zerstörter Ort waren offenbar die gegebenen Voraussetzungen für diese älteste Pseudepigraphie," cited in Nicole Frank, "Der Kolosserbrief und die 'Philosophia': Pseudepigraphie als Spiegel frühchristlicher Auseinandersetzungen um die Auslegung des paulinischen Erbes," in *Pseudepigraphie und Verfasserfiktion in frühchristlichen Briefen*, ed. Jörg Frey et al., WUNT 246 (Tübingen: Mohr Siebeck, 2009), 411–32, here 414.

Mirror-Reading a Pseudepigraphal Letter

have expressed tentative doubts about the destruction hypothesis, recently Alan Cadwallader has offered a persuasively comprehensive rereading of the archaeological and literary evidence to suggest that the claim that Colossae was destroyed in the first century is tenuous at best.[41] The earthquake, it seems, offers us no help.

If we are able to say little with certainty about the specific addressees envisaged by Colossians, can we make any progress on the question of whether Colossians is an actual letter, and if so, in what sense? What might we be able to say about the implications of authorial fiction for the epistolarity of pseudepigraphal letters?

In an insightful article first published in 1988, Richard Bauckham explores the mechanics of "Pseudo-Apostolic Letters" in a way that sheds light on our problem.[42] Since this is one of the clearest statements of the problem available, I will quote it at some length. As he rightly notes, "Not only does the 'I' in a pseudepigraphal letter not refer to the real author, but 'you' does not refer to the real readers."[43] He then argues,

> The pseudepigraphal letter, by its very nature, requires a distinction between the supposed addressee(s) and the real readers. . . . In no indubitably pseudepigraphal letter known to me are the supposed addressees and the real readers identical. This means that a pseudepigraphal letter cannot, as scholars sometimes too readily assume, perform the same function as an authentic real letter. The authentic real letter . . . is a form of direct address to specific addressee(s). The pseudepigraphal letter, it seems, can be this only fictionally. The real author of a pseudepigraphal letter can only address real readers indirectly, under cover of direct address to other people. This is what distinguishes the pseudepigraphal letter from most other types of pseudepigraphal literature, which do not need to have addressees at all.[44]

41. Alan H. Cadwallader, "Refuting an Axiom of Scholarship on Colossae: Fresh Insights from New and Old Inscriptions," in Cadwallader and Trainor, *Colossae in Space and Time*, 151–79. He offers a rousing critique of the majority line in New Testament scholarship, stemming from Lightfoot and Ramsay.

42. Richard J. Bauckham, "Pseudo-Apostolic Letters," *JBL* 107 (1988): 469–94; reprinted in Richard J. Bauckham, *The Jewish World around the New Testament: Collected Essays I*, WUNT 233 (Tübingen: Mohr Siebeck, 2008), 123–49. All page numbers refer to the original publication.

43. Bauckham, "Pseudo-Apostolic Letters," 475.

44. Bauckham, "Pseudo-Apostolic Letters," 475.

Chapter 8

He goes on to suggest,

> The problem for the author in this case is that he wants his pseudepigraphal letter to perform for him and his readers something like the function which an authentic real letter from him to his readers would perform. He wants, under cover of his pseudonym, to address his real readers, but his genre allows his letter to be addressed only to supposed addressees contemporary with the supposed author. Thus, he needs to find some way in which material that is ostensibly addressed to supposed addressees in the past can be taken by his real readers as actually or also addressed to them.[45]

Bauckham suggests that Colossians (as well as 1 Peter and Jude) do not describe the troublesome situation they address, as pseudepigraphal letters do, but merely presuppose it,[46] and so sees his study as offering a vindication of Colossians as authentic. But arguably Colossians can be seen as a subtle form of what he terms a typological pseudepigraphal letter.[47] Faced with the problems Bauckham describes, he argues that a pseudepigraphal author has open to him three main options: (1) Set fictional addressees in a genealogically related situation—a historical situation that continues up to the present day. (2) Set fictional addressees in an analogous situation to the real addressees, and so create a situation that is typological for the real addressees. (3) Write a farewell speech in the form of a letter, or a testamentary letter.

While clearly Colossians is not a farewell speech in the form of a letter, it does contain warnings that are open-ended and future-oriented ("See to it that no one takes you captive," 2:8), or warnings about what "someone" (τις) might do in 2:16–19. Bauckham is correct that the "heresy" is not described in detail (a point to which we will return shortly), but the lack of precision can arguably be seen as due to intentional flexibility and open-endedness.[48] If the lack of

---

45. Bauckham, "Pseudo-Apostolic Letters," 476.

46. Bauckham, "Pseudo-Apostolic Letters," 490. In the typological pseudepigraphal letter, Bauckham suggests that an author might "depict the historical situation of the supposed addressees as a kind of type of the similar present situation of the real readers, so that what is said to the supposed addressees applies typologically to the real readers" (477).

47. Cf. Bauckham, "Pseudo-Apostolic Letters," 470.

48. Kiley suggests that 2:6–23 "almost look[s] like a warning geared toward the future against possible developments which may distract the community from Christ" (*Colossians as Pseudepigraphy*, 64); cf. also Tor Vegge, "Polemic in the Epistle to the Colossians," in *Polemik in der frühchristlichen Literatur: Texte und Kontexte*, ed. Oda Wischmeyer and Lorenzo Scornaienchi, BZNW 170 (Berlin: de Gruyter, 2010), 254–93.

Mirror-Reading a Pseudepigraphal Letter

detail is intentional, then Colossians can be understood as another example of Bauckham's typological pseudepigraphal letter.

Moreover, one can without difficulty see Epaphras as a figure symbolizing continuity between Paul, whom the Colossians have not seen in person, and the addressees. Not unlike, in structural terms, the way the Johannine Paraclete substitutes for and mediates, in some sense, the presence of Christ to the early community after Jesus's ascension, so Epaphras stands as a genealogical link between the apostolic authority of Paul and the Christian gentile communities that come to flourish after the apostle's death. If Paul is "absent in body," there are still leaders who knew Paul and can offer guidance for the church. So in fact it is possible to see Epaphras and his role in the narrative world of the letter performing a type of bridge function for the actual audience to make their act of identification with the addressees.

But it appears that, on the whole, the move from narrative world to ostensive referent is once more fraught. The judgment of pseudepigraphy introduces a number of complications for the question of the addressees as well the author. Several different reconstructions are possible, but the false authorial claim erects a wall of fiction that is difficult to penetrate. So the second member of our triad of author, addressees, and situation is not unperturbed.

SHOULD WE BE HUNTING FOR A COLOSSIAN HERESY?

Finally, then, we turn to the last member of the triad: the situation. As in other areas of New Testament study, so also here it was Ferdinand Christian Baur who pioneered the search for what one might term the pseudepigraphal situation. Although he was not the first to question their authenticity, in his 1835 book on the Pastoral Epistles, published as an outgrowth of his work on Christian Gnosticism, Baur self-consciously went beyond previous interpreters by not contenting himself with a denial of the authenticity of the letters, but suggesting a second-century setting for them as a response to the growing phenomenon of Gnosticism.[49] Baur's broader bequest to New Testament scholarship was to contribute decisively to seeing the circumstances of origin, critically perceived, as determining the crucial hermeneutical lens through which the documents should be interpreted. Holders of both orthonymous

---

49. Ferdinand Christian Baur, *Die sogenannten Pastoralbriefe des Apostel Paulus aufs neue kritisch untersucht* (Stuttgart: Cotta, 1835).

Chapter 8

and pseudonymous positions with regard to Colossians have been attempting to follow Baur ever since, in offering plausible settings for the letter.

With regard to Colossians, I have already noted in passing the sharply divergent scholarly reconstructions of the error to which the letter addresses itself. But the same type of "referential interference" we have observed with the authorial claims and the identity of the addressees may be at work in the situation as well.[50] Above all, the compositional strategy of attempting to achieve verisimilitude by appeal to reality-like elements problematizes our ability to mirror-read the Colossian problem with any certainty. It is extremely difficult to say whether the Colossian error looks like other phenomena in antiquity because it was happening on the ground in the community, on the one hand, or because the author drew from his or her own knowledge of religious traditions directly, on the other. One might call this the problem of the successful pseudepigraphon. So when Christian Stettler quotes Daniel Harrington to the effect that "the situation presupposed by the letter seems real, not fictive" even though he thinks of Colossians as written by "an admirer or student of Paul," one might reply that the seeming reality of the situation can be ascribed equally to an efficacious pseudepigraphal strategy as to a correspondence between text and world.[51]

For those who see Colossians as pseudepigraphal, there are roughly three broad ways in which the relationship between the error described in the text of Colossians can be laid over the referential world. First, that there is a more or less transparent fit, or at least as transparent as our process of mirror-reading (with Barclay's cautions in mind) will allow. This seems to be the default position of most commentators who go to great lengths to identify the nature of the false teaching in view, even when non-Pauline authorship is conceded. For example, Bart Ehrman thinks that Colossians is pseudonymous, further that Colossians may not have been sent to Colossae, but still treats it as a pseudepigraphal letter addressing a concrete situation: "Colossians . . . may be considered a counterforgery in the weaker sense, in that it attacks a distinct—if hard to localize and identify—set of opponents representing an aberrant view."[52]

---

50. Even more problematic, then, is the attempt to ascertain the social standing of the various parties in the debate, on the supposition of pseudonymity, that one finds in Harold Van Broekhoven, "The Social Profiles in the Colossian Debate," *JSNT* 66 (1997): 73–90.

51. See Stettler, "The Opponents at Colossae," 170n4, citing D. J. Harrington, "Christians and Jews in Colossians," in *Diaspora Jews and Judaism: Essays in Honor of and in Dialogue with A. T. Kraabel*, ed. Andrew J. Overman and Robert S. MacLennan, SFSHJ 41 (Atlanta: Scholars Press, 1992), 153–61, here 154.

52. Ehrman, *Forgery and Counterforgery*, 182.

Mirror-Reading a Pseudepigraphal Letter

But arguably, in Ehrman's case at least, he has made a gratuitous assumption based on the supposition that polemical concerns are the animating force of pseudepigraphal compositions—a point that should be proven for each text rather than assumed to be universal.[53] In assuming that Colossians is directed polemically against an actual, localized set of errant teachings, however, Ehrman simply represents the position of the vast majority of commentators. Second, that there is an analogous situation in view, and so the author has described, in broad strokes, a false teaching that is recognizable to the actual addressees as analogous to challenges they now face, leaving them to imaginatively fill in the gap by an act of identification with the putative Colossian addressees. Or third, that the description is intentionally vague and open-ended, an "empty signifier" by which the author can put forth his message of perseverance in hope in the face of broadly conceived challenges from Jewish and pagan neighbors alike. Angela Standhartinger and Nicole Frank might be seen as representatives of this third position, although occasionally their statements tend toward the second.[54] Standhartinger suggests that "the opposition against which Col. 2:4–23 cautions is the uncertainty caused by doubt, internal criticism which endangers the strength, steadfastness, and internal unity of the church. Condemnation from external sources (2:18) is another cause of concern."[55] In a somewhat different vein, Frank argues that "Col 2:16–23 is to be received as a general help for the handling of divergent teachings and practices, and so certainly exhibits no specific referential profile in looking back to a concrete group."[56] In this sense, Colossians may borrow some technical language from the mysteries or from Jewish apocalyptic groups because it had some currency at the time, but the overall rhetorical push of the letter is to use such language as a foil to encourage fidelity to the tradition its recipients had already received.

These three types of solutions to account for the situation reflected in Col 2 are very difficult to weigh against one another. Within each frame of reference one can judge one solution to be preferable or less persuasive against others

---

53. This problem plagues his otherwise rich study; see Ehrman, *Forgery and Counterforgery*.

54. Standhartinger, *Studien zur Entstehungsgeschichte*; Nicole Frank, *Der Kolosserbrief im Kontext des paulinischen Erbes: Eine intertextuelle Studie zur Auslegung und Fortschreibung der Paulustradition*, WUNT 2/271 (Tübingen: Mohr Siebeck, 2009).

55. Standhartinger, "Pauline School," 588; in more detail, Standhartinger, *Studien zur Entstehungsgeschichte*.

56. "Kol 2,16–23 will also allgemeine Handrechnung für den Umgang mit abweichenden Lehren und Praktiken rezipiert werden und weist daher bewusst kein spezifisches Referenzprofil im Hinblick auf eine konkrete Gruppierung auf" (Frank, "Kolosserbrief," 415).

Chapter 8

within that frame. But between the frames of reference we arguably come up against our ignorance, made severe by means of the compositional strategies of an author writing pseudonymously. This, in turn, suggests that we should be much less sanguine about our ability to arrive at a concrete situation addressed by the letter and then to use, in turn once more, this hypothetical situation as the heuristic lens through which to assess the author's response to it. One thinks of some clear instances in which this has been done in Colossians—as in the common strategy of reading the hymn or exalted prose section of 1:15–20 as already a response to the opponents, for example.[57] But the pile of hypotheses is growing very high indeed by this point. Thus, it seems that the third member of the triad, the situation, is also problematized by a judgment of pseudonymity.[58]

Conclusion

In conclusion, my purpose in this essay is to pose a question about the implications of pseudonymity: can we treat a pseudepigraphal letter just like any other and apply our process of mirror-reading in order to reconstruct the situation addressed? A highly successful pseudepigraphon achieves its success precisely by the reality effect it is able to achieve. Verisimilitude is the entry card to acceptance. And the success of Colossians, if it is pseudonymous, is attested not least by its place as Scripture in the Christian canons. Once the authorship of a text is called into question, those who embrace the verdict of pseudepigraphy should be consistent in treating the text as pseudonymous. In particular, this requires a more thorough process of thinking through the implications of pseudonymity. This is not to say that there was definitively no Colossian philosophy, nor that the letter was certainly not sent to Colossae, but simply to call into question the certainty with which these questions are

---

57. Smith goes so far as to attempt to read "the letter as one integrated piece of writing concerned with one issue: the Colossian error" (*Heavenly Perspective*, 205).

58. One might compare the ways in which the polemic in 1 John has recently been read as, in some ways, a text-immanent phenomenon; see, e.g., Daniel R. Streett, *They Went Out from Us: The Identity of the Opponents in First John*, BZNW 177 (Berlin: de Gruyter, 2011), 112–31; and Hansjörg Schmid, "How to Read the First Epistle of John Non-Polemically," *Bib* 85 (2004): 24–41. Schmid writes, "It may be concluded that the main function of the opponents interacting with the reader is to operate as a counter-concept to the community. The opponents are what the reader should never become, but what he or she will become if he or she does not follow the basic commandments and lines of the Johannine system" (38–39).

Mirror-Reading a Pseudepigraphal Letter

often treated. We would expect substantial divergences between studies that assume orthonymity and those that assume pseudepigraphy, but we find such divergences rather less often than we should.

Arguably this inability to identify the author, addressees, or situation with confidence suggests that we should be especially cautious about using our reconstructed triadic interpretation to interpret Colossians (or other pseudonymous letters) in the same way we would interpret, say, the undisputed Pauline letters. While this may appear as loss to those who are trained in reading the Pauline letters for their historical particularity, arguably the requisite focus on the text itself is better suited to constructive appropriation of the letter for theological and ecclesial ends—a purpose the pseudonymous author knew only too well. As Martin Hengel once wrote, "We must learn to recognize our limits at the point at which we can no longer establish probability, but can only guess. We should not therefore be ashamed to speak candidly of our great uncertainty."[59]

Appendix: Twelve Ways of Looking at a Pauline Author

Judging a work to be pseudonymous involves denying the facticity of its authorial claim or self-presentation. This process therefore clearly involves a sense of the original of which the forgery is an imitation, the genuine by which the nongenuine can be measured and discerned lacking. Before one can speak meaningfully of "pseudo-Pauline authorship," then, one must be able to specify what Pauline authorship itself entails. While this may seem to be an obvious or trivial observation, in practice what precisely passes for Pauline authorship has often lacked systematic clarity.

In what follows I stop short of offering a characterization of authentic Pauline authorship but rather offer the preparatory work of sketching a spectrum of approaches to Pauline authorship of the epistles in the *corpus Paulinum* (including Hebrews). One might conceive of this as a variety of approaches ranging from strict orthonymity to strict pseudonymity, though each of those terms has been understood in varying ways. This brief typology seeks simply to describe the possible understandings of Pauline authorship in the critical discourse of New Testament studies, without posing the next logical question of where one might draw the line (and whether its position is important) between Pauline and non-Pauline authorship. While there is naturally already

59. Martin Hengel, "Tasks of New Testament Scholarship," *BBR* 6 (1996): 67–86, here 76.

Chapter 8

some good understanding of the complexities of Pauline authorship in current discussion, this contribution is meant to provide an analytic overview of the options, in hopes of lending further precision to the question.[60]

At the risk of transposing the discussion of authorship into a faux-scientific key by employing algebraic symbolism, I hazard a shorthand for identifying models of Pauline authorship at play in contemporary Pauline studies. Using the following abbreviations, one can discern (at least) a dozen models of Pauline authorship.

<u>Key:</u>
IA: implied author
HA: historical author
W: writer
E: editor
D: disciple/student
A: anonymous
AA: attributed author
n: to the nth power

1. IA = HA: Paul writes his own letters, using his own material entirely (1a) or incorporating some pre-formed (e.g., hymnic) material (1b). This might be termed the naive or intuitive understanding of authorship, projected backward from our contemporary experience of authoring texts. Modernity has often privileged the singular author, ranging from Rembrandt's depictions of the lone apostle pondering his compositions in prison through the Romantic ideals of the solitary genius to twentieth-century *auteurism*.[61] While virtually all scholars acknowledge in theory that Pauline authorship is more complex than Paul simply putting pen to paper (or reed-pen to papyrus), it is difficult to sustain this acknowledgment and refrain from lapsing into anachronistic projections.[62] One could open virtually any volume on Pauline theology and adduce dozens of references to Paul "writing" or to a "slip

60. The secondary literature cited is therefore purely illustrative of larger trends.

61. Among many studies one could cite, for a brief but engaging study of the changing fate of the "author," see Andrew Bennett, *The Author*, The New Critical Idiom (London: Routledge, 2005); note also the collection of important primary texts in Fotis Jannidis et al., eds., *Texte zur Theorie der Autorschaft* (Stuttgart: Reclam, 2000).

62. An application, *mutatis mutandis*, of the observation in Morna Hooker, "In His Own Image?," in *What about the New Testament? Essays in Honour of Christopher Evans*, ed. Morna Hooker and Colin Hickling (London: SCM, 1975), 28–44.

Mirror-Reading a Pseudepigraphal Letter

of the pen" or other turns of phrase that betray a modern conception of authorship. This may be perfectly permissible for many settings; after all, who wants to read an inevitably tortuous circumlocution repeated *ad nauseam* simply for the sake of precision? But when the question of authorship per se comes into view, the usual conveniences of writing should be set aside for the sake of precision. It is notable, moreover, that even were one to conceive of Paul as solitary author, there are numerous places in which one would still need to reckon with "foreign bodies" in the corpus: as many as a hundred citations of Scripture together with numerous allusions,[63] as well as the possibility of other pre-Pauline material of a hymnic,[64] confessional, or catechetical[65] variety.

2. IA = HA via W: Paul dictates his own letters to an amanuensis. Close attention to the Pauline letters indicates the clear presence of the voice of a secretary in a number of places, either by means of a personal greeting (1 Cor 16:21; Gal 6:11; Col 4:18; 2 Thess 3:17; Phlm 19) or a note from the secretary (Rom 16:22).[66]

---

63. The precise number varies depending upon criteria used for determining citations; for two representative attempts, see the margin of the NA[28] (or the appendix IV, "Loci citati vel allegati") and H. Hübner, *Vetus Testamentum in Novo: Band 2; Corpus Paulinum* (Göttingen: Vandenhoeck & Ruprecht, 1997).

64. Most famously, Phil 2:5–11; Col 1:15–20; but occasionally also 1 Tim 3:16. Neither hymnic nor catechetical materials are as easily identified today as they were in the heyday of the influence of form criticism. For hymnic material, see the critical survey of previous attempts in Michael Peppard, "'Poetry', 'Hymns' and 'Traditional Material' in New Testament Epistles or How to Do Things with Indentations," *JSNT* 30 (2008): 319–42; and Benjamin Edsall and Jennifer Strawbridge, "The Songs We Used to Sing: Hymn 'Traditions' and Reception in Pauline Letters," *JSNT* 37 (2015): 290–311.

65. For one, not unproblematic, attempt to assess 1 Timothy for catechetical material (*inter alia*) see Mark Yarbrough, *Paul's Utilization of Preformed Traditions in 1 Timothy: An Evaluation of Paul's Literary, Rhetorical, and Theological Tactics*, LNTS 417 (London: Continuum, 2009), whose work especially follows E. Earle Ellis, *The Making of the New Testament Documents* (Leiden: Brill, 1999). For a survey and critique of attempts to discern preformulated tradition behind the New Testament, see Benjamin Edsall, "*Kerygma*, Catechesis and Other Things We Used to Find: Twentieth-Century Research on Early Christian Teaching since Alfred Seeberg (1903)," *CurBR* 10 (2012): 410–41.

66. For examples of other letters that follow this convention, see Stowers, *Letter Writing in Greco-Roman Antiquity*, 60–61; Bauer, *Paulus und die kaiserzeitliche Epistolographie*, 24–25, 241–45. See also Hans-Josef Klauck, *Ancient Letters and the New Testament: A Guide to Context and Exegesis*, trans. and ed. D. P. Bailey (Waco, TX: Baylor University Press, 2006), 55–60; E. Randolph Richards, *Paul and First-Century Letter Writing: Secretaries, Composition and Collection* (Downers Grove, IL: InterVarsity, 2004), 59–93; E. Randolph Richards, *The Secretary in the Letters of Paul*, WUNT 2/42 (Tübingen: Mohr Siebeck, 1991); and M. Luther Stirewalt Jr., *Paul the Letter Writer* (Grand Rapids: Eerdmans, 2003), 9–11.

Chapter 8

3. IA = HA + W: Paul offers general direction to an amanuensis, who then composes the letter.

4. IA = HA^n: Paul and coauthor(s) contribute to the letter (as in 1–3).[67]

5. IA = HA + E (±W): Paul writes or dictates (as in 1–3), while a secondary editor rearranges (5a) or interpolates with non-Pauline material (5b) the original. It has been fairly common in Pauline scholarship to see certain Pauline letters as composite in their canonical form, most often 2 Corinthians or Philippians, but scholars have also sometimes made a case for seeing other letters such as 1 Thessalonians as the product of editorial rearrangement.[68] One might follow William O. Walker in drawing a distinction between interpolation (intentional insertion into the text) and gloss (marginal or interlinear annotation that was subsequently incorporated into the text by later scribes), but either action would result in the presence of post-Pauline elements in the text.[69]

67. Jerome Murphy-O'Connor, "Co-Authorship in the Corinthian Correspondence," *RB* 100 (1993): 562–79; more cautious is Samuel Byrskog, "Co-Senders, Co-Authors and Paul's Use of the First Person Plural," *ZNW* 87 (1996): 230–50.

68. To take two illustrative examples: for 2 Corinthians, see Margaret M. Mitchell, *Paul, the Corinthians and the Birth of Christian Hermeneutics* (Cambridge: Cambridge University Press, 2010); and for Philippians, see John Reumann, *Philippians*, AB 33B (New Haven: Yale University Press, 2008). For an example of the hypothesis, more unconventional in contemporary scholarship though drawing on a long exegetical tradition, of a rearrangement of 1 Thessalonians that includes the use of a short missive in a longer original Pauline letter, see Earl Richard, "Early Pauline Thought: An Analysis of 1 Thessalonians," in *Pauline Theology, Volume 1: Thessalonians, Philippians, Galatians, Philemon*, ed. Jouette M. Bassler (Minneapolis: Fortress, 1991), 39–51; Earl Richard, *Jesus, One and Many: The Christological Concept of New Testament Authors* (Wilmington, DE: Glazier, 1988), 248–52, who sees 2:13–4:2 as an earlier missive concerning the initial response of the community to the message and 1:1–2:12 + 4:3–5:28 as a later letter to a maturing community.

69. Generally contemporary Pauline scholarship has been averse to finding interpolations, though some famous suggestions have been much discussed (e.g., 1 Thess 2:14–16; Rom 16:25–27; or 1 Cor 14:33b–36). For some further suggestions, see J. C. O'Neill, "Paul Wrote Some of All, but Not All of Any," in *The Pauline Canon*, ed. Stanley E. Porter (Leiden: Brill, 2004), 169–88; William O. Walker, *Interpolations in the Pauline Letters*, JSNTSup 213 (Sheffield: Sheffield Academic, 2001) and a series of subsequent articles; Winsome Munro, *Authority in Paul and Peter: The Identification of a Pastoral Stratum in the Pauline Corpus and 1 Peter*, SNTSMS 45 (Cambridge: Cambridge University Press, 1983); and Winsome Munro, "Interpolation in the Epistles: Weighing Probability," *NTS* 36 (1990): 431–43. For a critique of interpolation hypotheses, with attention to Walker's views in particular, see Frederik W. Wisse, "Textual Limits to Redactional Theory in the Pauline Corpus," in *Gospel Origins & Christian Beginnings in Honor of James M. Robinson*, ed. James E. Goehring et al., *ForFasc* 1 (Sonoma, CA: Polebridge, 1990), 167–78, esp. 172–78.

Mirror-Reading a Pseudepigraphal Letter

6. IA = E + ~HA (±W): An editor expands upon a genuine letter (6a) or fragments of letters (6b) to create a new composition, with the balance of compositional weight now in the editor's favor.[70]

7. IA = D as W for HA: Paul commissions a disciple to write in his name, though with considerably more freedom than in (3).[71]

8. IA = D actualizing HA: A historical disciple writes after the death of Paul as a means of updating Paul's message to a new situation.[72]

9. IA ≠ HA ≠ D: An unknown writer with no historical connection to Paul writes in Paul's name, with some access to (genuine and/or nongenuine) Pauline letters.[73]

10. A long and complex process involving multiple stages in 1–9 (e.g., 6+9), analogous to what Robert Kraft once described as "evolved literature."[74]

11. ~IA ≠ HA: An unknown author implicitly suggests that he or she is writing as Paul.[75]

---

70. For such a suggestion with reference to Colossians, see Marie-Émile Boismard, *La lettre de Saint Paul aux Laodicéens*, CahRB 42 (Paris: Gabalda, 1999); Marie-Émile Boismard, "Paul's Letter to the Laodiceans," in Porter, *The Pauline Canon*, 45–57, who argues that one can extract the genuine Pauline Laodiceans out of Colossians. For Ephesians, note Marie-Émile Boismard, *L'énigme de la letter aux Éphésiens*, EBib 39 (Paris: Gabalda, 1999), who suggests that there is an authentic Ephesian letter that has been filled out by a later editor, while Colossians itself is a combination of a letter originally written to the Laodiceans with that written to the Colossians. For an analogous suggestion about Ephesians, see John Muddiman, *The Epistle to the Ephesians*, BNTC (London: Continuum, 2001), 2–54. And for the Pastoral Epistles, see James D. Miller, *The Pastoral Letters as Composite Documents*, SNTSMS 93 (Cambridge: Cambridge University Press, 1997); P. N. Harrison, *The Problem of the Pastoral Epistles* (London: Oxford University, 1921); and P. N. Harrison, *Paulines and Pastorals* (London: Villiers, 1964).

71. One might point on Colossians to James D. G. Dunn, *The Epistles to the Colossians and to Philemon*, 35–39; or on 2 Thessalonians to Karl P. Donfried, *Paul, Thessalonica, and Early Christianity* (Grand Rapids: Eerdmans, 2002), 51–56.

72. Note Peter Müller's concept of "deuteronymity" in *Anfänge der Paulusschule: Dargestellt am zweiten Thessalonicherbrief und am Kolosserbrief* (Zürich: TVZ, 1988), 318–20.

73. This is how most treat the Pastoral Epistles, though note that some have argued that 2 Timothy should be distinguished from 1 Timothy and Titus (so J. Murphy-O'Connor, "2 Timothy Contrasted with 1 Timothy and Titus," *RB* 98 [1991]: 403–18; J. Murphy-O'Connor, *Paul: A Critical Life* [Oxford: Oxford University Press, 1996], esp. 356–59; and Michael Prior, *Paul the Letter-Writer and the Second Letter to Timothy*, JSNTSup 23 [Sheffield: Sheffield Academic, 1989]).

74. Kraft was speaking of the Apostolic Fathers; see Robert A. Kraft, *The Apostolic Fathers: A Translation and Commentary; vol. III: The Didache and Barnabas* (New York: Nelson, 1965), 1–3.

75. Hebrews is taken in this way by Clare K. Rothschild, *Hebrews as Pseudepigraphon:*

Chapter 8

12.   A → AA: An originally anonymous composition is later ascribed an authorial claim, whether correct (12a) or incorrect (12b).[76]

Given this spectrum of approaches to authorship, at what stage should one
judge the authorship of a letter to be non-Pauline? Arguably there are many
varieties of non-Pauline authorship, and a simple judgment of "pseudonymous" has not yet clarified for the reader how the Pauline attribution came to
be arrived at. The phenomenon of authorship, both genuine and nongenuine,
is more complex than has often been acknowledged: there are varieties of both
orthonymity and pseudonymity.

The History and Significance of the Pauline Attribution of Hebrews, WUNT 235 (Tübingen:
Mohr Siebeck, 2009). Contrast K. Backhaus, "Der Hebräerbrief und die Paulus-Schule,"
BZ 37 (1993): 183–208; repr. in *Der sprechende Gott: Gesammelte Studien zum Hebräerbrief*,
WUNT 240 (Tübingen: Mohr Siebeck, 2009), 21–48. See the discussion by Warren Camp-
bell, *The Pauline History of Hebrews* (Oxford: Oxford University Press, 2025).

76. Hebrews is taken this way by most interpreters; e.g., Walter Schmithals, "Der
Hebräerbrief als Paulusbrief: Beobachtungen zur Kanonbildung," in *Die Weltlichkeit des
Glaubens in der Alten Kirche: Festschrift für Ulrich Wilckert zum siebzigsten Geburtstag*, ed.
Dietmar Wyrwa, BZNW 85 (Berlin: de Gruyter, 1997), 319–37; cf. David Trobisch, *Paul's
Letter Collection: Tracing the Origins* (Minneapolis: Fortress, 1994), 25–26.

9

Elijah in Romans 11 and Justin's *Dialogue with Trypho*

This chapter examines the figure of Elijah portrayed in 3 Kgdms 19 as he is received in the eleventh chapter of Paul's letter to the Romans and in Justin's *Dialogue with Trypho* a hundred years or so later. Justin's *Dialogue*, in fact, provides the earliest reading of Elijah *through* Rom 11, and so attests a double reception: the reception of Paul's reception of Elijah. To read both Paul and Justin side by side on the question of Elijah brings to light not only shared traditions but also intriguing differences that shed further illumination on their respective purposes in writing.

Elijah in Rom 11

Paul's citations of 3 Kgdms 19 in Rom 11 offer a number of distinctive features. The book of Kingdoms is not among those frequently cited by Paul. Outside the citations of 3 Kingdoms in Rom 11, one might mention several places where Kingdoms preserves a text that is also attested elsewhere, complicating a judgment about source. So, for example, in Rom 15:9 we find a similar text in Ps 17:50 and 2 Kgdms 22:50; in 1 Cor 1:31 and 2 Cor 10:17 there is an apparent citation of either Jer 9:22–23 or 1 Kgdms 2:10; and in the immediate context of Rom 11, Rom 11:2a alludes to either Ps 93:14a (LXX) or 1 Kgdms 12:22a. Romans 11:3–4 is the only unambiguous place where Kingdoms is cited in Paul.[1]

Furthermore, Paul here follows his customary practice of assuming, whether erroneously or not, some level of prior understanding of the scriptural narrative on behalf of the recipients of his letter. He does not introduce Elijah as a prophet, though this might be garnered from the substance of his citations.

---

1. Though one should note the interesting but somewhat speculative suggestion that Paul modeled his persecution of Christians and subsequent sojourn in Arabia on the Elijah cycles; see N. T. Wright, "Paul, Arabia, and Elijah (Galatians 1:17)," *JBL* 115 (1996): 683–92.

Chapter 9

Nor does he provide the outlines of Elijah's conflicts with Ahab and Jezebel in a way that would provide the hearer with context for the cited words. He simply assumes both knowledge of and shared conviction about the relevance of the Elijah story, providing selective citations and interpretive comments that, in turn, shape the way he expects the story to be heard.[2]

Within the progression of Rom 9–11, verses 11:1–6 occupy an important transitional role. In the course of his attempt in Rom 9–11 to address theologically the problem of Jewish unbelief in the gospel and the concomitant gentile boasting, Paul first heightens the stakes by juxtaposing the various blessings Israel has enjoyed with his own sorrow at their unbelief (9:1–5). Immediately, however, he affirms that "it is not as though the word of God has fallen" (9:6a)—the thesis that he labors to establish in the ensuing chapters. He first argues that "not all from Israel are Israel," and seeks to demonstrate that God's "purpose according to election" has always been at work in Israel's history, choosing some and rejecting others (9:6b–29). Indeed, the Lord's creative calling has even constituted his people "not from the Jews only but also from the Gentiles" (9:24). The inclusion of gentiles in the righteousness of the covenant community is closely (and paradoxically) bound up with the failure of most Jews to recognize the τέλος of the law in the Messiah (9:30–10:4). The "righteousness" that Israel unsuccessfully sought and the gentiles unintentionally found is available to all indiscriminately on the basis of faith in the Messiah (10:5–21).[3] In Rom 11, however, Paul goes beyond the solution of election within history expressed as a remnant in order to express a hope, grounded in his apocalyptic sensibilities, that ultimately "all Israel will be saved." A temporal distinction between these movements in the historical drama with Israel keeps Paul's argument from collapsing into contradiction.[4]

One of the most noticeable facets of Paul's argument in Rom 9–11 is his desire to establish a continuity of God's action in Christ with Israel's history—a concern that admittedly runs throughout Romans (cf. Rom 4) but is especially focused in these chapters on the question of the people of God. In this process, we observe the apostle engaged in the "creation" of salvation

---

2. See Christopher D. Stanley, *Arguing with Scripture: The Rhetoric of Quotations in the Letters of Paul* (London: T&T Clark, 2004), 2. Stanley points to further instances in which Paul's citations appear to depend upon at least some background knowledge of the scriptural text: Gal 3:6–9, 16–18; 4:21–31; 1 Cor 9:13; 10:1–10; 15:45–49; 2 Cor 3:7–18; 11:3; Rom 1:3; 3:25; 4:1–22; 5:12–21; 9:4–17, 25–29; 10:16–21; 11:1–4.

3. Notice the extensive use of πᾶς in this section.

4. Cf. Bruce W. Longenecker, "Different Answers to Different Issues: Israel, the Gentiles and Salvation History in Romans 9–11," *JSNT* 36 (1989): 95–123.

Elijah in Romans 11 and Justin's Dialogue with Trypho

history: by forging an "as once . . . so also now" structure that correlates the circumstances of the present with God's action in the past, Paul includes his present missionary endeavors within the scheme of God's covenantal dealing with Israel, and so offers to his Roman hearers a means of including themselves within that larger framework in a way that underlines the fidelity and trustworthiness of God on the one hand, and excludes gentile boasting over Jews on the other.

In 11:1 Paul asks the question that could be inferred from his previous argument in 10:18–21: "has God rejected his people?" The question is already phrased by means of an allusion to Ps 93:14a (LXX)/1 Kgdms 12:22 and so anticipates the answer that Paul supplies in verse 2. But he first offers a preliminary ground to support his emphatic μὴ γένοιτο: Paul himself is an Israelite and so attests the fidelity of God in his very person. But this is not simply an instance of Israel, c'est moi. Rather, Paul's own existence as an apostolic envoy to gentiles on behalf of Israel attests to God's persistent intention not to reject his people. This prophetic self-consciousness of Paul is further emphasized in the two citations of the Elijah episode that immediately follow.

Paul goes beyond his preliminary answer to the question of whether God has rejected his people by now supplying an important argument from the history of Israel that recapitulates his statements in Rom 9 but also prepares for his fuller discussion in Rom 11:11–32.[5] In 11:3–4 Paul supplies two citations from 3 Kgdms 19 to encapsulate the Elijah story and provide a historical precedent to his present situation. Paul first cites 3 Kgdms 19:10 (or the parallel 19:14) in a unique form, which probably owes to a combination of Pauline adaptation and reliance on an early Greek text of 3 Kingdoms:[6] "Lord, your prophets they have killed, your altars they have torn down, and I am left alone and they are

---

5. That is, his further argument supports verse 2a rather than 1b; so rightly James D. G. Dunn, *Romans 9–16*, WBC 38B (Dallas: Word, 1988), 637.

6. See esp. Christopher D. Stanley, "The Significance of Romans 11:3–4 for the Text History of the LXX Book of Kingdoms," *JBL* 112 (1993): 43–54, who suggests that Paul's citation may preserve the earliest form of the Greek text of 3 Kgdms 19, an essentially proto-Lucianic version. Note also Christopher D. Stanley, *Paul and the Language of Scripture: Citation Technique in the Pauline Epistles and Contemporary Literature*, SNTSMS 74 (Cambridge: Cambridge University Press, 1992), 147–58; and Dietrich-Alex Koch, *Die Schrift als Zeuge des Evangeliums: Untersuchungen zur Verwendung und zum Verständnis der Schrift bei Paulus*, BHT 69 (Tübingen: Mohr Siebeck, 1986), 73–77. Stanley is more convincing than Koch's contention that the differences are to be ascribed to Paul's reliance on a text that has undergone stylistic improvements.

159

Chapter 9

seeking my life" (11:3).[7] Paul has brought forward the Deuteronomistic accusation of killing the prophets,[8] perhaps because of the more immediate relevance than the destruction of altars, which has less contemporary resonance.[9] Counterpoised against this, Paul sets the answer of the oracular divine speech (χρηματισμός) from 3 Kgdms 19:18: "I have kept for myself seven thousand men who did not bow the knee to Baal" (11:4).[10]

Most interestingly, the Elijah narrative enables Paul to go beyond his preliminary answer to the question in 11:1b by constructing from the story a theological analogy between Elijah's time and Paul's own. But what is the nature of this "analogy"? Paul has already been presenting himself in prophetic terms in Rom 9–11.[11] In 10:16, Paul says, "But not all have obeyed the gospel. For Isaiah says, 'Lord, who has believed our message?'" Isaiah's message becomes fused with, or perhaps, is viewed in typological anticipation of, Paul's own message in the proclamation of the gospel. So also here, the divine answer to Elijah's complaint assures the apostle of the existence of a remnant ἐν τῷ νῦν καιρῷ (11:5; cf. 3:26), an eschatologically determined concept. Thus, the ὑπόλειμμα of which Isaiah spoke in Rom 9:27–29 is taken up again in the λεῖμμα of Elijah's time and now in Paul's own time. Paul infers that this remnant is "according to the election of grace" (κατ' ἐκλογὴν χάριτος) in an apparent interpretation of God's preserving for himself (κατέλιπον ἐμαυτῷ) the seven thousand.[12] In this way, by interpreting Israel's history as the foreshadowing work of divine providence, Paul also constructs a theological understanding of his present as typologically predetermined, and so well within the over-arching purposes of God.[13]

---

7. κύριε, τοὺς προφήτας σου ἀπέκτειναν, τὰ θυσιαστήριά σου κατέσκαψαν, κἀγὼ ὑπελείφθην μόνος καὶ ζητοῦσιν τὴν ψυχήν μου.

8. Cf. Rudolf Hoppe, "Der Topos der Prophetenverfolgung bei Paulus," *NTS* 50 (2004): 535–49; cf. also Odil H. Steck, *Israel und das gewaltsame Geschick der Propheten: Untersuchungen zur Überlieferung des deuteronomistischen Geschichtsbildes im Alten Testament, Spätjudentum und Urchristentum*, WMANT 23 (Neukirchen-Vluyn: Neukirchener Verlag, 1967); and James M. Scott, "Paul's Use of Deuteronomistic Tradition," *JBL* 112 (1993): 645–65.

9. So Koch, *Die Schrift als Zeuge des Evangeliums*, 104.

10. κατέλιπον ἐμαυτῷ ἑπτακισχιλίους ἄνδρας, οἵτινες οὐκ ἔκαμψαν γόνυ τῇ Βάαλ.

11. Rightly, Hoppe, "Prophetenverfolgung," 547–48; cf. also J. Ross Wagner, *Heralds of the Good News: Isaiah and Paul in Concert in the Letter to the Romans*, NovTSup 101 (Leiden: Brill, 2002).

12. So rightly C. E. B. Cranfield, *The Epistle to the Romans*, ICC (Edinburgh: T&T Clark, 1979), 547.

13. This is seen most clearly by E. Käsemann: "The point of comparison to the apostle is rather that he seemed to be alone among his people and had to bewail the unbelief of Israel as Paul does in 9:30–10:3. This is what gives the typology its special significance. It does not

Elijah in Romans 11 and Justin's Dialogue with Trypho

But this remnant theology must be understood in light of the argument that follows in 11:11–32. In returning to the metaphor of the race that previously animated 9:30–10:4, Paul asks, "Did [Israel] stumble in order to fall?" and answers this with his emphatic denial. The subsequent *a fortiori* arguments, buoyed by a reading of Deuteronomy's Song of Moses and expressed in the imagery of the olive tree, finally culminate in Paul's assertion of a mystery—all Israel will be saved. In light of this conclusion, Paul's remnant must be seen as a proleptic anticipation of the salvation of all Israel rather than a replacement for it. In this sense, for Paul the λεῖμμα ἐν τῷ νῦν καιρῷ functions with the logic of an ἀρραβών.

ELIJAH IN JUSTIN'S DIALOGUE WITH TRYPHO

If we turn, now, to examine Justin Martyr's *Dialogue with Trypho*, we find both interesting similarities and important differences from the portrayal in Rom 11. Elijah actually features in a number of different contexts in the *Dialogue*, some of which are clearly drawn from Synoptic tradition in portraying Elijah as the anointer of the Messiah, and so identified with John the Baptist.[14] For present purposes, however, we shall focus on Justin's use of 3 Kgdms 19.

---

just allow Paul to speak of the remnant. It integrates Paul's situation, prefigured in Elijah's history, into the salvation event. . . . Paul saw his mission as having salvation-historical character and he could thus see in himself the Elijah of the end-time" (*Commentary on Romans*, trans. G. W. Bromiley [Grand Rapids: Eerdmans, 1980], 301). So also Dunn, *Romans*, 638; contra, e.g., Markus Öhler, *Elia im Neuen Testament: Untersuchungen zur Bedeutung des alttestamentlichen Propheten im frühen Christentum*, BZNW 88 (Berlin: de Gruyter, 1997), 254–57.

14. *Dial.* 49.1–6 (cf. Matt 3:11–12; 17:10–13; Luke 3:16–17, 20); *Dial.* 51.3 (cf. Matt 3:2–3; 16:21; Luke 9:22); *Dial.* 87.4; cf. also 1 *Apol.* 46. Particularly intriguing is *Dial.* 8.3 [8.4 in some numerations], where Trypho says, "But if the Messiah has been born and exists anywhere, he is not known, nor is he conscious of his own existence, nor has he any power until Elijah comes to anoint him and to make him manifest to all." See Philippe Bobichon, *Justin Martyr*, Dialogue avec Tryphon: *Édition critique, traduction, commentaire*, Paradosis 47, 2 vols. (Fribourg: Academic Press, 2003), 1.85–86, who points also to the concept of a hidden Messiah in 4 Ezra 13.52; Midr. Ps 21:1; b. Sanh. 98a, etc. See also Bobichon, *Justin Martyr*, 1.85–86n37 for the anointing function of Elijah. He writes, "L'évocation d'Élie, dans les premiers chapitres du *Dialogue* paraît avoir pour principale fonction de préparer et d'annoncer les développements ultérieurs sur la transmission de l'Esprit, et le rôle de Jean-Baptiste." Cf. also L. W. Barnard, *Justin Martyr: His Life and Thought* (Cambridge: Cambridge University Press, 1967), 46–47; Peter Pilhofer, "Wer salbt den Messias? Zum Streit um die Christologie im ersten Jahrhundert des jüdisch-christlichen Dialogs," in *Begegnungen zwischen Christen-*

Chapter 9

Justin's use of 3 Kgdms 19 is in fact one of a series of instances in which the apologist has taken over Pauline scriptural citations for his own ends.[15] In Justin's *Dialogue with Trypho* we find amassed dozens of scriptural texts drawn in to serve the apologetic intention of that work. As table 2 indicates, drawing on the seminal work of Oskar Skarsaune, many of these scriptural texts have their parallels in the Pauline letters.

Table 2: Shared citations in Justin and Paul[16]

Scriptural Text	Justin	Paul
Isa 52:5	*Dial.* 17.2	Rom 2:24
Ps 14:1–3; 5:9; 140:3; 10:7; Isa 59:7–8; Ps 36:1	*Dial.* 27.3 (= esp. Rom 3:12–17)	Rom 3:10–18
Gen 15:6	*Dial.* 11.5; 23.4; 92.3; 119.5–6	Rom 4:3, 9
Ps 32:1–2	*Dial.* 141.2	Rom 4:7–8
Gen 17:5	*Dial.* 11.5; 119.4	Rom 4:17
Isa 1:9	*1 Apol.* 53.7; *Dial.* 140.3; cf. *Dial.* 32.2; 55.3	Rom 9:29
Isa 53:1	*Dial.* 42.2; 114.2	Rom 10:16
Ps 19:5	*Dial.* 42.1	Rom 10:18
Deut 32:21	*Dial.* 119.2 (includes Deut 32:16–23)	Rom 10:19
Isa 65:1–2	*Dial.* 119.4	Rom 10:20–21
1 Kgs 19:10, 14, 18	*Dial.* 39.1	Rom 11:3–4
Deut 32:43	*Dial.* 130.1, 4	Rom 15:10

---

tum und Judentum in Antike und Mittelalter: Festschrift für Heinz Schreckenberg, ed. D.-A. Koch and H. Lichtenberger, SIJD 1 (Göttingen: Vandenhoeck & Ruprecht, 1993), 335–45; and Jorg Christian Salzmann, "Jüdische Messiasvorstellungen in Justins Dialog mit Trypho und im Johannesevangelium," *ZNW* 100 (2009): 247–68, esp. 254, 266. In this essay the Greek text follows the editions by Bobichon and that by Miroslav Marcovich, ed., *Iustini Martyris Dialogus cum Tryphone*, PTS 47 (Berlin: de Gruyter, 1997), while translations generally follow Thomas B. Falls, *St. Justin Martyr:* Dialogue with Trypho, rev. ed. by Thomas P. Halton (Washington, DC: Catholic University of America Press, 2003).

15. This fact has been examined in R. Werline, "The Transformation of Pauline Arguments in Justin Martyr's *Dialogue with Trypho*," *HTR* 92 (1999): 79–93, who briefly mentions Elijah in Rom 11 (92).

16. Adapted from the tables in Oskar Skarsaune, *The Proof from Prophecy: A Study in Justin Martyr's Proof-Text Tradition; Text-Type, Provenance, Theological Profile*, NovTSup 56 (Leiden: Brill, 1987), 93–100.

Elijah in Romans 11 and Justin's Dialogue with Trypho

Scriptural Text	Justin	Paul
Isa 52:15	*Dial.* 118.4 (Isa 52:15–53:1)	Rom 15:21
Isa 29:14	*Dial.* 78.11 (Isa 29:13–14); *Dial.* 32.5; 123.4 (Isa 29:14)	1 Cor 1:19
Exod 32:6	*Dial.* 20.1	1 Cor 10:7
Ps 24:1	*Dial.* 36.3–4	1 Cor 10:26
Deut 27:26	*Dial.* 95.1	Gal 3:10
Deut 21:23	*Dial.* 96.1	Gal 3:13
Isa 54:1	*1 Apol.* 53.5	Gal 4:27
Ps 68:18	*Dial.* 39.4; 87.6	Eph 4:8

From a detailed investigation of the textual character of these quotations, Skarsaune concludes that "Justin seems in most cases to be directly drawing on Romans when he has OT quotations in common with Romans."[17] He goes on to note that Galatians also provides key texts for Justin, while the evidence from 1 Corinthians is less conclusive.[18] One particularly striking example of Justin's reliance on Paul's scriptural work is found in *Dial.* 95–96. There, without citing or mentioning Paul, Justin brings together the two Deuteronomy citations that form the centerpiece of Pauline argument in Gal 3:10-13, almost certainly indicating his dependence on the unmentioned Pauline letter.[19] But in so doing, Justin has inevitably transformed Paul's argument for his own context. He has, as Rodney Werline notes, "transformed Paul's argument that Jesus' death removes the curse of Torah, nullifies it, and unites Jew and Gentile in Christ, into a prophecy about the tensions between Jews and Christians in the second century CE."[20]

---

17. Skarsaune, *Proof from Prophecy*, 96; cf. 92–100.

18. Skarsaune, *Proof from Prophecy*, 99–100.

19. See, e.g., Charles H. Cosgrove, "Justin Martyr and the Emerging Christian Canon: Observations on the Purpose and Destination of the Dialogue with Trypho," *VC* 36 (1982): 209–32, here 225; and esp. Koch, *Die Schrift als Zeuge des Evangeliums*, 250–51; contra, e.g., Philipp Vielhauer, "Paulus und das Alte Testament," in *Studien zur Geschichte und Theologie der Reformation: Festschrift für Ernst Bizer*, ed. L. Abramowski and J. F. G. Goeters (Neukirchen-Vluyn: Neukirchener Verlag, 1969), 33–62, here 39n28. Note the discussion of options in Andreas Lindemann, *Paulus im ältesten Christentum*, BHT 58 (Tübingen: Mohr Siebeck, 1979), 353–55.

20. Werline, "The Transformation of Pauline Arguments," 91. Werline also provides a convincing argument that Justin has used and transformed Paul's picture of Abraham. See also the attention paid to the connections between Paul's arguments and Justin's in David Rokéah, *Justin Martyr and the Jews*, Jewish and Christian Perspectives 5 (Leiden: Brill, 2002),

Chapter 9

In the particular case of 3 Kgdms 19, cited most fully in *Dial.* 39.1, dependence on Romans seems likewise to be clear in light of the distinctive text attested there, probably due in part to Paul's own modifications of 3 Kgdms 19:10//19:14:

Rom 11:3: κύριε, τοὺς προφήτας σου ἀπέκτειναν, τὰ θυσιαστήριά σου κατέσκαψαν, κἀγὼ ὑπελείφθην μόνος καὶ ζητοῦσιν τὴν ψυχήν μου.

Dial. 39.1: Κύριε, τοὺς προφήτας σου ἀπέκτειναν καὶ τὰ θυσιαστήριά σου κατέσκαψαν· κἀγὼ ὑπελείφθην μόνος, καὶ ζητοῦσι τὴν ψυχήν μου.

LXX: τὰ θυσιαστήριά σου κατέσκαψαν καὶ τοὺς προφήτας σου ἀπέκτειναν ἐν ῥομφαίᾳ, καὶ ὑπολέλειμμαι ἐγὼ μονώτατος, καὶ ζητοῦσι τὴν ψυχήν μου λαβεῖν αὐτήν.

LXX[L]: τὰ θυσιαστήριά σου κατέσκαψαν καὶ τοὺς προφήτας σου ἀπέκτειναν ἐν ῥομφαίᾳ, καὶ ὑπελείφθην ἐγὼ μονώτατος, καὶ ζητοῦσι τὴν ψυχήν μου λαβεῖν αὐτήν.

It is clear especially from the vocative κύριε, the transposition of the clauses, the use of μόνος rather than μονώτατος, and the abbreviation of the sentence to exclude λαβεῖν αὐτήν, that Justin has followed Paul's adaptations. Though he nowhere cites Paul explicitly, that Justin has taken over important scriptural citations from Paul invites investigation as to whether Justin employs them in the same way as Paul or has recast them to express a different perspective.

In the midst of the ongoing discussion with his Jewish interlocutor Trypho,[21] Justin expresses frustration in his attempts to convince Trypho and his Jewish friends that Jesus, with all of his suffering lowliness, was in fact the expected Messiah of Israel's Scripture. In reacting to the resistance his

---

43–80, 130–32 (although Rokéah seems to me, at least partially, to misunderstand Paul and to overstate the hostility of both Justin and Paul to Jewish tradition).

21. That Trypho has been literarily crafted is clear, though opinions vary as to whether and to what degree historical events may lie behind the *Dialogue*. For a survey of opinions about Trypho, see Timothy J. Horner, *Listening to Trypho: Justin Martyr's* Dialogue *Reconsidered*, CBET 28 (Leuven: Peeters, 2001), 15–32 (though his quest for an original "Trypho text" is fraught with difficulties). For the argument that Justin derives his understanding of Jewish exegesis from firsthand contact with Jewish teachers (or from Jewish-Christians who had such firsthand contact), see Philippe Bobichon, "Comment Justin a-t-il acquis sa connaissance exceptionnelle des exégèses juives?," *RTP* 139 (2007): 101–26.

Elijah in Romans 11 and Justin's Dialogue with Trypho

christological proposals meet with, Justin invokes Elijah as an antecedent in *Dial.* 39.1-2:

> "It is small wonder," I continued, "that you Jews hate us Christians who have grasped the meaning of these truths, and take you to task for your stubborn prejudice. Indeed, Elijah, when interceding for you before God, spoke thus: *Lord, they have slain your prophets, and have destroyed your altars; and I am left alone, and they seek my life.* And God answered: [39.2] *I still have seven thousand men, whose knees have not been bowed before Baal.*[22] Therefore, just as God did not show his anger on account of those seven thousand men, so now he has not yet exacted judgment of you, because he knows that every day some of you are forsaking your erroneous ways to become disciples in the name of Christ, and this same name of Christ enlightens you to receive all the graces and gifts according to your merits."

Here it appears that Justin appeals to the Elijah episode in order to derive a remnant of Christ-believing Jews, on whose behalf God delays executing judgment on the Jews as a whole.[23] More negatively, a few chapters later in the *Dialogue*, Justin adduces the Elijah episode again, this time to stress the idolatrous tendency of Israel: "Notwithstanding this reminder [i.e., the *tefillin* and the *zizith*], you still continued to practice idolatry. In the times of Elijah, when God was enumerating those who had not genuflected to Baal, he could count only seven thousand. And in Isaiah he scolds you for having sacrificed your children to idols" (46.6). Similarly, later in the *Dialogue*, Justin again makes passing mention of the "slaughter of the prophets" as an indictment of Israel (*Dial.* 73.6: τοῦ αὐτοὺς τοὺς προφήτας ἀνῃρηκέναι).

Reflected in these instances, and especially in *Dial.* 39.2, we see operative a concept of the remnant: Jews chosen by God to believe in Christ.[24] The specific manner in which Justin sees this remnant to be operative may be observed from a few of his statements elsewhere. So, in *Dial.* 32.2, he writes, "Now, I shall derive all my proofs from all the words I adduce from your sacred and prophetic Scriptures, in the hope that someone may be found among you to

22. Ἔτι εἰσί μοι ἑπτακισχίλιοι ἄνδρες, οἳ οὐκ ἔκαμψαν γόνυ τῇ Βάαλ.

23. Note Bobichon, *Justin Martyr*, 2.686, who points to *1 Apol.* 28.2; 45.1; *2 Apol.* 7.1-2 for similar reasoning about the delay of the parousia.

24. On the remnant in Justin, note Theodore Stylianopoulos, *Justin Martyr and the Mosaic Law*, SBLDS 20 (Missoula, MT: Scholars Press, 1975), 39-44; Craig D. Allert, *Revelation, Truth, Canon and Interpretation: Studies in Justin Martyr's* Dialogue with Trypho, VCSup 64 (Leiden: Brill, 2002), 59-60, 239n87.

165

Chapter 9

be of that seed which, by the grace of the Lord of Sabaoth, is reserved for everlasting salvation." And in 55.3, citing explicitly the same text from Isa 1:9 that Paul adduces in Rom 9:29, Justin says, "Hence, we readily understand why, on account of your iniquity, God has hidden from you the power of discerning the wisdom of his words, with the exception of those few to whom, in his infinite mercy, 'he has left a seed' for salvation (to use the words of Isaiah), lest your race perish completely, 'as did the people of Sodom and Gomorrah.'"[25] As in Paul, the theological concept of the remnant functions positively to protect God's fidelity, but here we also observe a negative side: there is *only* a remnant, and this explains why Jews have been so unwilling to believe that Jesus is the Messiah. In this sense, Justin finds Paul's logic in Rom 9–11 helpful in explaining the continued resistance that the Christian message has met with from the Jewish interlocutors that, from Justin's perspective, failed to understand the plain sense of their own Scripture.

In an important respect, however, Justin stops short of endorsing the full breadth of Paul's argument in Rom 11. Justin can use the concept of the remnant from 3 Kgdms 19 and elsewhere to understand the small number of Jews who believe that Jesus is the Messiah, but he fails to take over the way in which Paul invests the remnant with significance as a token of God's continuing fidelity to Israel that will culminate in the final salvation of all Israel. It may be that in *Dial.* 39.2, in Justin's statement that, "so now he has not yet exacted judgment of you, because he knows that every day some of you are forsaking your erroneous ways to become disciples in the name of Christ," we can gain an indication of how the apologist might have made sense of Rom 11:25–26: as the gradual conversion of a few individual Jews through time, such that the complete remnant comes to take the place of "all Israel," that is, true Israel. Of course, we have no indication that Justin is actually interpreting the substance of Paul's conception in Rom 11, so the suggestion is inevitably speculative, though not unreasonable.

What is not speculative, however, is the fate Justin sees awaiting those Jews who do not believe in Christ.[26] So, in *Dial.* 44.1–2, he writes,

> And you are sadly mistaken if you imagine that, just because you are descendants of Abraham according to the flesh, you will share in the legacy of

---

25. Note also *Dial.* 64.3: "Had you given your full attention to the passages of Scripture which I have quoted, you would have already understood that those Jews who attain salvation are saved through him and are his partisans. Had you understood this, you certainly would not have questioned me in this regard."

26. Cf. Stylianopoulos, *Justin Martyr and the Mosaic Law,* 42n77.

Elijah in Romans 11 and Justin's Dialogue with Trypho

benefits which God promised would be distributed by Christ. No one can participate in any of these gifts, except those who in their mind have been conformed to the faith of Abraham, and who approve of all the mysteries.

Or again, in *Dial.* 47.4 we find the following statement:

Those persons, however, who had once believed and publicly acknowledged Jesus to be the Christ, and then later, for one reason or another, turned to the observance of the Mosaic Law, and denied that Jesus is the Christ, cannot be saved unless they repent before their death. The same can be said of those descendants of Abraham who follow the Law and refuse to believe in Christ to their very last breath. Especially excluded from eternal salvation are they who in their synagogues have cursed and still do curse those who believe in that very Christ in order that they may attain salvation and escape the avenging fire.

Clearly missing is any sense of a future unilateral action of God on behalf of the people of Israel, the apocalyptic hope that finally buoyed the apostle Paul in his tortuous argument in Rom 9–11.[27]

27. Note, however, the indications for at least some hope for Jews in Justin's eschatology, highlighted in Wolfram Kinzig, "Philosemitismus angesichts des Endes? Bemerkungen zu einem vergessenen Kapitel jüdisch-christlicher Beziehungen in der Alten Kirche," in *Kaum zu glauben: Von der Häresie und dem Umgang mit ihr*, ed. A. Lexutt and V. von Bülow, Arbeiten zur Theologiegeschichte 5 (Rheinbach: CMZ, 1998), 59–95, esp. 73–77. On the question of "Justin Martyr and the Jews," see further, e.g., Demetrios Trakatellis, "Justin Martyr's Trypho," *HTR* 79 (1986): 287–97; William Horbury, "Jewish-Christian Relations in Barnabas and Justin Martyr," in *Jews and Christians: The Parting of the Ways A.D. 70 to 135*, ed. J. D. G. Dunn, WUNT 66 (Tübingen: Mohr Siebeck, 1992), 315–45; Michael Mach, "Justin Martyr's *Dialogus cum Tryphone Iudaeo* and the Development of Christian Anti-Judaism," in *Contra Iudaeos: Ancient and Medieval Polemics between Christians and Jews*, ed. O. Limor and G. G. Stroumsa, Texts and Studies in Medieval and Early Modern Judaism 10 (Tübingen: Mohr Siebeck, 1996), 27–47; Daniel Boyarin, "Justin Martyr Invents Judaism," *Church History* 70 (2001): 427–61, much of which also appears in Daniel Boyarin, *Border Lines: The Partition of Judaeo-Christianity*, Divinations: Rereading Late Ancient Religion (Philadelphia: University of Pennsylvania Press, 2004), 37–73, 238–64.

Chapter 9

CONCLUSION

In conclusion, viewing Paul and Justin side by side on the question of their use of 3 Kgdms 19 in formation of a view of the remnant illuminates each. Paul's theological interpretation of Israel's history, oriented to the present as it was, provided a resource that continued to live on in the early church. The circumstances, however, in which the church addressed problems that were similar, though not identical to those faced by the apostle, led to an inevitable shift in emphasis. Paul uses the remnant motif to bridge the two major elements of his response to the question he wrestles with in Rom 9–11: has God's word to Israel fallen, thus also jeopardizing his future reliability as well? That God has always elected some in Israel and not others on the one hand, and that God had reserved a future salvation for all Israel on the other hand, were not concepts that seemed naturally to go together. But by portraying them as in temporal succession to one another, Paul sought to account for the present unbelief in his gospel on the part of many Jews while also holding out hope for an ultimate consummation. Indeed, Rom 11 itself has a widening crescendo as the focus moves from Paul himself as a representative of Israel to a remnant according to election, finally to the "all Israel" that will be saved.

To judge from Justin's reproduction of Paul's scriptural citations in his *Dialogue with Trypho*, Paul's letters apparently served as heuristic guides to the text of Scripture. In this case, we see that the *Dialogue* preserves what may be the earliest recoverable reception of Paul's remnant concept. But we also see the beginning of a fact that will recur in later centuries: the generations after Paul found it difficult to hold together aspects of Paul's argument in Rom 9–11 that stood in a tensive relationship to begin with. Reading Justin's *Dialogue*, and its alternately genuinely interested and vehemently negative response to Trypho the Jew, one is led to ask: has Justin taken over Paul's remnant theology without the apocalyptic consummation? What appears in Paul as an instance of prophetic critique from within now seems in Justin to be an instance of supersessionist critique from without.

10

Learning Scripture
in the School of Paul

From Ephesians to Justin

One of the striking features of early Christianity is the role played by the Scriptures of Israel, soon known as the Old Testament, in the theological argumentations and deliberations of its first theologians. Among the greatest of these early theologians and most creative readers of Scripture stands, of course, the apostle Paul. The sheer amount of recent scholarly attention to his engagement with Scripture is testament to the complexity and curious power of his forays into his ancestral "Bible." Indeed, the fascination with Paul had begun already in the first century, and resulted in an early influence, attested in the existence (or at least the presumed existence) of an eponymous school. In what follows I will examine in turn documents from the late first to mid-second century that stand under varying degrees of influence from Paul. If it would be impossible to class all of the authors that follow as members of a so-called *Paulusschule* (whose existence has necessarily been hypothetical anyway), I proceed with the more modest goal of showing that they treated Paul himself as teacher, and so may be said to have learned Scripture in the school comprised by Paul's epistolary remains.

These are not, of course, wholly uncharted waters. In the late nineteenth and early twentieth centuries, some scholars noticed the phenomenon of shared scriptural citations in various corpora and concluded that the early church relied on books of *testimonia*, culled and collected from the corners of Scripture to aid in early polemical encounters with Jewish contemporaries or to convince their hearers of the divine fore-ordination of the recent events in Palestine. The investigation of these *testimonia* achieved an early zenith in the two volumes by J. Rendel Harris, *Testimonies*—even if these volumes also functioned, in light of Harris's overly intrepid reconstructions, as a sort of *reductio ad absurdum* for the theory as well.[1] The enterprise of ascribing the majority of early Christian engagement with the Scriptures of Israel to such *testimonia* collections has

---

1. J. Rendel Harris, with Vacher Burch, *Testimonies*, 2 vols. (Cambridge: Cambridge University Press, 1916–1920).

Chapter 10

been often critiqued, though that some such collections did exist should not be doubted. Above I have offered a more thorough discussion of the *testimonia* hypothesis,[2] but here I simply want to make the *zeitgeistliche* observation that the *testimonia* hypothesis came to maturity at just the time that form criticism was flourishing in the study of the Gospels. Given that both share a common emphasis on an anonymous collective responsible for selecting and preserving authoritative traditions, it may not be coincidence that they arose at roughly the same time. Since much of the work once allocated to anonymous collectives has now been outsourced to creative individual authors, it may be worth examining the evidence again.

One of the greatest rivals to the *testimonia* hypothesis was put forth by C. H. Dodd. In his book *According to the Scriptures*, Dodd contended that, rather than individual citations cloistered away in notebooks of *testimonia*, the early church operated with its own selective "Bible," which consisted essentially of chapter-long "text-plots," many of which might be traced back to the formative influence of Jesus himself on his early disciples.[3] The suggestion of this investigation can be seen as offering a refinement of Dodd's theory in one particular direction: rather than positing a primitive "Bible of the early Church"—a suggestion which had, no doubt, certain structural similarities with Dodd's view of the primitive apostolic preaching—I suggest that early authors sometimes accessed the Jewish Scriptures by the sign-posts Paul provides, examining sections that Paul's letters have drawn to their attention, but sometimes evincing hermeneutical innovations of their own.

Needless to say, certain methodological difficulties should be kept in mind. Any attempt to chart the influence of Paul on other early Christian authors is problematized by questions of accessibility and how one defines such "influence." In this case, the authors whom I examine have been supposed to be influenced by Paul on mostly other grounds than the use of common scriptural *loci*—though it may be that noticing common scriptural engagement has some reciprocal effect in confirming Pauline influence in a necessarily circular way.[4] There are further difficulties involved: the fluid state of the scriptural text in this period, our lack of knowledge of intermediate sources that might have

2. See chapter 2.

3. C. H. Dodd, *According to the Scriptures: The Sub-Structure of New Testament Theology* (London: Nisbet, 1952).

4. On the difficulties of tracing "influence" in this period, see Andrew Gregory and Christopher M. Tuckett, "Reflections on Method: What Constitutes the Use of the Writings That Later Formed the New Testament in the Apostolic Fathers?," in *The Reception of the New Testament in the Apostolic Fathers*, ed. A. Gregory and C. M. Tuckett (Oxford: Oxford University Press, 2005), 61–82.

Learning Scripture in the School of Paul

suggested the scriptural texts in question, our ignorance of the compositional methods of these early Christian authors, and so forth. In what follows, I will attempt to be circumspect about the level of certainty attached to the conclusions I draw, and no doubt conviction will vary in individual cases, but I do hope to construct a cumulative case for the larger structural suggestion that Paul's reading of Scripture has influenced the selection of scriptural *loci* in these authors. By no means do I intend to suggest that the use of a similar scriptural text in a later author is *in every case* dependent upon Paul, but the purpose of this investigation is to make the patterns of usage clear. In order to do this, it may be necessary, to borrow Martin Heidegger's term, to "over-illuminate" the phenomenon of later reuse of Pauline citations. This, in turn, may yield some insight into the early perceptions of the Pauline corpus itself.

Now that the aim of the study has been roughly situated, we turn to the individual texts themselves. I will first examine Ephesians, Hebrews, and 1 Timothy before turning to some later writings that show Pauline influence, generally thought to be written by the mid-second century CE. To examine such a breadth of texts necessarily precludes making all but the briefest remarks on each, but to sketch a broad distribution of the phenomenon under consideration in the hundred years or so after Paul is key to this study's success.

Ephesians

Assuming for the sake of this investigation that Ephesians is a relatively early post-Pauline creation of a disciple of Paul, we may draw a few observations about the use of Scripture in the letter. If Ephesians is seen to be created by a disciple of Paul using Colossians as a base template, then one can see a certain scripturalization of the epistle—Colossians being famously devoid of explicit scriptural engagements. If, however, as seems less likely to me, both letters share a literary debt to another now lost, such a conclusion cannot be drawn. In any case, without solving the literary problem of Ephesians, one might note the following tendencies of its use of Scripture: with the exception of the curious and much-discussed citations of Ps 68:18 in Eph 4:8 and Isa 26:19 in 5:14, the scriptural citations and major allusions that are not paralleled in the undisputed Paulines all have a certain gnomic or aphoristic quality: "let each one of you speak truth to his neighbor"; "be angry and do not sin"; "do not get drunk with wine." The hortatory use of Scripture in this way perhaps adds even more authority to the apostolic ethical injunctions. In this light, it is striking to note that Eph 6:2–3 cites one of the ten commandments that is *not* cited elsewhere in Paul's letters, perhaps doing its best to fill in a perceived gap and

Chapter 10

to foreclose on any young, ethically intrepid interpreters taking advantage of the lacuna to dishonor their parents.

The way this has just been phrased, however, may be problematic: are we to think of the author of this letter as composing Ephesians with actual Pauline letters in front of him or simply with a knowledge of Pauline tradition, perhaps obtained by hearing the apostle himself? Of course, certainty is impossible, but given that the most substantial verbal parallels are with Colossians rather than the *Hauptbriefe*, the latter may be more likely. But it is worth noting that, as one can see from tables 3–4, six out of the eleven major allusions or citations here identified have parallels in either Romans or 1 Corinthians. Certainly to demonstrate a parallel is not yet to demonstrate dependence, and at this point the evidence is merely suggestive rather than decisive. Given that Ephesians is composed by someone wanting to further the Pauline legacy, to include citations and allusions known to have been used by Paul would be entirely in line with that purpose, though decisive proof is precluded by the nature of the evidence.

Table 3: Citations in Ephesians

Scriptural Text	Ephesians	Undisputed Paul
Ps 68:18	Eph 4:8	No parallel
Zech 8:16	Eph 4:25	No parallel
Ps 4:4	Eph 4:26	No parallel
Isa 26:19(?)	Eph 5:14	No parallel
Gen 2:24	Eph 5:31	1 Cor 6:16
Exod 20/Deut 5	Eph 6:2–3 (Exod 20:12/ Deut 5:16)	Rom 7:7 (Deut 5:21); 13:9–10 (Deut 5:17–19, 21)

Table 4: Major allusions in Ephesians

Scriptural Text	Ephesians	Undisputed Paul
Ps 8:7	Eph 1:22	1 Cor 15:25–27
Isa 57:19 + 52:7	Eph 2:17	Rom 10:15 (Isa 52:7)
Isa 28:16	Eph 2:20–21 (Isa 28:16)	Rom 9:33; cf. also Isa 28:11–12 in 1 Cor 14:21
Prov 23:31	Eph 5:18	No parallel
Isa 11:4–5; 59:17 + 52:7	Eph 6:14–17	1 Thess 5:8 (Isa 59:17); Rom 10:15 (Isa 52:7)

Learning Scripture in the School of Paul

HEBREWS

For the Epistle to the Hebrews, however, the overlap is even more striking. In her book arguing that Hebrews was deliberately composed as a Pauline pseudepigraphon, Clare Rothschild undertakes a comparison of Hebrews's use of Scripture with Paul's use in the undisputed letters.[5] As one can see from tables 5–6, the results are striking. As she summarizes her findings, "of roughly twenty-nine occasions on which Hebrews cites the Jewish scriptures seventeen are also cited by Paul. More than half the time, the identical passage is used. Most of these identical citations are found in the NT in Paul and Hebrews alone. The cumulative effect of so many allusions to the same passages makes dependence upon Paul the most likely explanation."[6]

That Hebrews might rely on Paul for some of its scriptural citations, however, is not a novel idea. Independently of Rothschild, I have traced the idea back at least as far as the 1829 work of Johann Christian Carl Döpke.[7] Rothschild's broader thesis that Hebrews intends to masquerade as a Pauline letter is susceptible to further interrogation, but this point is logically separable from that contention. In contrast to the overlap in citations with Ephesians, those with Hebrews attest some distinctive Pauline emphases: one thinks especially of the Song of Moses from Deut 32 and the repeated citation of Hab 2:4.

In one of these instances in particular, the citation of Deut 32:35 in Heb 10:30a and its parallel in Rom 12:19, we see a shared text that is peculiar: a proto-Symmachian reading elsewhere only preserved in the Syriac tradition.[8] It is certainly possible that both had independent recourse to the variant reading, but given that we have other grounds to suspect Pauline influence

5. Clare Rothschild, *Hebrews as Pseudepigraphon: The History and Significance of the Pauline Attribution of Hebrews*, WUNT 235 (Tübingen: Mohr Siebeck, 2009), 89–106.

6. Rothschild, *Hebrews as Pseudepigraphon*, 93.

7. "Das 32. Cap. des Deut. gebraucht Paulus ebenfalls mehrere Male und mann könnte also wohl vermuthen, dass der Verf. des Briefs an die Hebräer diesen Spruch aus dem Munde Pauli, dessen Schüler er, wie einige glauben, war, aufgenommen hätte." See Johann Christian Carl Döpke, *Hermeneutik der neutestamentlichen Schriftsteller* (Leipzig: Friedrich Christian Wilhelm Vogel, 1829), 267, though in part basing his judgment on the textually doubtful presence of λέγει κύριος in the citation.

8. This instance probably reflects Paul's reliance on a Greek text of Deuteronomy that has been revised toward the Hebrew. A marginal reading in a Syriac MS published by W. Baars (*New Syrohexaplaric Texts* [Leiden: Brill, 1968], 148; cf. Natalio Fernández Marcos, *The Septuagint in Context: Introduction to the Greek Versions of the Bible*, trans. Wilfred G. E. Watson [Leiden: Brill, 2000], 138), provides a reading from Symmachus that approximates the text seen in Rom 12:19 (and Heb 10:30 etc.). A similar reading is also seen in Tg. Onq.

Chapter 10

(especially the postscript in 13:20–25), the agreement is intriguing. Naturally the *Auctor ad Hebraeos* has his or her own hermeneutical program, and one might reasonably expect an author who has been alerted to an authoritative scriptural text by another author's use of that text to be free to employ that new discovery for his or her own interpretative ends.

Table 5: Exclusive agreements between Hebrews and Paul within the NT

Scriptural Text	Hebrews	Paul
Gen 15:5	Heb 11:12	Rom 4:18
Gen 21:12	Heb 11:18	Rom 9:7
Deut 32:35	Heb 10:30a	Rom 12:19
Deut 32:43	Heb 1:6	Rom 15:10
2 Sam 7:14	Heb 1:5	2 Cor 6:18
Jer 31:33–34	Heb 8:8–12; cf. 10:16–17	Rom 11:27 (cf. Isa 59:21)
Hab 2:4	Heb 10:37–38	Rom 1:17; Gal 3:11

Table 6: Texts drawn from similar contexts or also shared with other NT authors

Scriptural Text	Hebrews	Paul
Gen 2	Heb 4:4 (Gen 2:2)	1 Cor 15:45 (Gen 2:7); 1 Cor 6:16 (Gen 2:24)
Gen 22	Heb 6:13–14 (Gen 22:16–17); Heb 11:12 (Gen 22:17)	Gal 3:8, 16 (Gen 22:18)
Deut 17	Heb 10:28 (Deut 17:6)	1 Cor 5:13 (Deut 17:7 par.)
Deut 29	Heb 12:15 (Deut 29:18)	Rom 11:8 (Deut 29:4)
Deut 32	Heb 10:30b (Deut 32:36)	1 Cor 10:20 (Deut 32:17); Rom 10:19; 1 Cor 10:22 (Deut 32:21)
Ps 8:6	Heb 2:6–8 (Ps 8:4–6)	1 Cor 15:27 (Ps 8:6)
Ps 110:1	Heb 1:3, 13; 8:1; 10:12–13; 12:2	1 Cor 15:25
Prov 3	Heb 12:5–6 (Prov 3:11–12)	2 Cor 8:21 (Prov 3:4)
Isa 8	Heb 2:13 (Isa 8:17–18)	Rom 9:33 (Isa 8:14)
Isa 53	Heb 9:28 (Isa 53:12)	Rom 10:16 (Isa 53:1)

---

and Frg. Tg., as well as in the Latin tradition. For more detail, see D. Lincicum, *Paul and the Early Jewish Encounter with Deuteronomy* (Grand Rapids: Baker, 2013), 135–36.

Learning Scripture in the School of Paul

PASTORAL EPISTLES

In the Pastoral Epistles, we find an interesting phenomenon: as table 7 indicates, there are no substantial allusions to Jewish Scripture in Titus, 1 Timothy reproduces, almost woodenly in places, *loci* drawn from the undisputed Paulines, while 2 Timothy is apparently independent in its employment of Scripture. Might this lend some support to those who have argued that the Pastorals should not simply be treated as a homogeneous group? The question would take us beyond the remit of the present investigation but is at least intriguing.

In 1 Timothy, we find that two of Paul's references to Deuteronomic precepts elsewhere are translated into straightforward regulations for church practice. As I have argued above, 1 Tim 5:18a marks a routinization of Paul's surprising interpretation of Deut 25:4 in 1 Cor 9:9-10, while 5:19 appeals to Deuteronomy's "law of witnesses," cited by Paul in 2 Cor 13:1.[9] It would not be difficult to argue for something roughly similar in the case of Gen 1-3. In these cases, the prominence of the scriptural texts in Paul has served to draw them to the Pastor's attention, but not necessarily precluded further interpretative developments to address the needs of the Pastor's community.

Table 7: Citations and major allusions in 1-2 Timothy

Scriptural Text	Pastorals	Undisputed Paul
Gen 1-3	1 Tim 2:13-15 (esp. Gen 1:27; 2:7, 22; 3:6, 13)	1 Cor 11:7 (Gen 1:27); 1 Cor 15:45, 47 (Gen 2:7); 1 Cor 11:8-9 (Gen 2:18, 21-23); 1 Cor 6:16 (Gen 2:24); 2 Cor 11:3 (Gen 3:13)
Deut 25:4	1 Tim 5:18	1 Cor 9:9
Deut 19:15	1 Tim 5:19	2 Cor 13:1
Isa 52:5	1 Tim 6:1	Rom 2:24
Num 16:5 + 16:26(?)	2 Tim 2:19	No parallel
Exod 7:11-22	2 Tim 3:8-9	No parallel

9. See chapter 7, "Presentifying the Past: Actualization in the Pauline Tradition," in this volume.

Chapter 10

1 Clement

Turning now to early Christian literature outside the New Testament—some of which, it is possible, predates the composition of the Pastoral Epistles—we come to 1 Clement. This long letter treatise is written from the church at Rome to the church in Corinth in response to a division there concerning church leadership. Its author certainly knows of Peter and Paul, "upright pillars" and "good apostles," and Paul's suffering and missionary travels are briefly retold as an example to the Corinthians (5.4–7). Much later, 1 Clement makes reference to "the epistle of that blessed apostle, Paul," apparently referring to 1 Corinthians (47.1–3).[10] Therefore, in a letter-treatise written from Rome by someone who esteems Paul as an apostle and knows his epistolary communication with the Corinthian church, we have some *a priori* grounds for investigating connections between 1 Clement and Paul's letters to the Romans and Corinthians.[11]

Table 8: Shared citations in 1 Clement and Paul

Scriptural Text	1 Clement	Paul
Gen 15:5–6	1 Clem. 10.4–6	Rom 4:3
Gen 15:5	1 Clem. 32.2	Rom 4:18
Jer 9:22–23	1 Clem. 13.1	1 Cor 1:31
Isa 64:3(?)	1 Clem. 34.8	1 Cor 2:9
Ps 32:1–2	1 Clem. 50.6	Rom 4:7–9
Ps 24:1	1 Clem. 54.3	1 Cor 10:26

10. Andrew Gregory, "*1 Clement* and the Writings That Later Formed the New Testament," in Gregory and Tuckett, *The Reception of the New Testament in the Apostolic Fathers*, 129–57, here 144–45; see also Andreas Lindemann, "Paul in the Writings of the Apostolic Fathers," in *Paul and the Legacies of Paul*, ed. W. S. Babcock (Dallas: Southern Methodist University Press, 1990), 25–45; Andreas Lindemann, "Paul's Influence on 'Clement' and Ignatius," in *Trajectories through the New Testament and the Apostolic Fathers*, ed. A. Gregory and C. M. Tuckett (Oxford: Oxford University Press, 2005), 9–24, here 9–16.

11. Cf. also Rom 1:32 and 1 Clem. 35.6 ("For those who do these things are hateful to God—and not only those who do them, but also those who approve of them"; cf. Gregory, "*1 Clement* and the Writings That Later Formed the New Testament," 149). Or 1 Clem. 46.6: "Do we not have one God, and one Christ, and one gracious Spirit that has been poured out upon us, and one calling in Christ?" with Eph 4:4–6: "There is one body and one Spirit—just as you were called to the one hope that belongs to your call—one Lord, one faith, one baptism, one God and Father of all, who is over all and through all and in all." But on both of these, see the cautious assessment of Gregory, "*1 Clement* and the Writings That Later Formed the New Testament." Note Clare K. Rothschild, "Reception of First Corinthians in First Clement," in *New Essays on the Apostolic Fathers*, WUNT 375 (Tübingen: Mohr Siebeck, 2017), 35–60.

Learning Scripture in the School of Paul

Table 8 shows, in fact, that the overlaps in citation come from precisely these letters. This might be less surprising given the density of Paul's engagement with Scripture in those epistles, but there are also some shared textual traditions between Paul and 1 Clement that suggest the relationship may be one of dependence.[12] For example, 1 Clement cites a longer version of Jer 9:22–23 than Paul does but to a similar end. Most apparently, both have a distinctive form of the command not to boast except in the Lord. As Donald Hagner writes, "It is possible that both Paul and Clement derived the words from a different version of Jeremiah (or 1 Reigns), but more probably Clement has derived the words from 1 Corinthians, an epistle with which he was certainly acquainted."[13] Perhaps more striking is 1 Clement's reproduction of the citation found in 1 Cor 2:9—Paul may originally have been citing from Isa 64:3, but the form of the quotation is so variant that interpreters since Origen have wondered if he was citing a source now lost (Origen attributed the citation to the Apocalypse of Elijah). The citation is further taken up by the Martyrdom of Polycarp (2.3b) and by 2 Clement in slightly varying forms. Without solving the long-standing debates about the origins of the text, that 1 Clement reproduces a near verbatim citation of the same text leads me to agree with Andreas Lindemann and Donald Hagner that 1 Clement here depends on Paul. The slight variation that does occur, a substitution of τοῖς ὑπομένουσιν for Paul's τοῖς ἀγαπῶσιν, may be explicable due to the influence of the LXX of Isaiah and 1 Clement's own stress on ὑπομονή.[14]

Five of the six shared citations are marked by strong citation formulas in Paul (Ps 24:1 being the exception, though a γάρ is used). Elsewhere 1 Clement reproduces other scriptural citations that appear in the New Testament,[15] and

---

12. Note Gen 15:5–6 in 1 Clem. 10.4–6 and Rom 4:3, for which see Donald A. Hagner, *The Use of the Old and New Testaments in Clement of Rome*, NovTSup 34 (Leiden: Brill, 1973), 51, for shared variants; cf. also Ps 32:1–2 in 1 Clem. 50.6 and Rom 4:7–9 (Hagner, *Use*, 47).

13. Hagner, *Use*, 60; cf. 59–60 more broadly for textual connections.

14. Cf. Hagner, *Use*, 75–76: "Since it is certain that Clement was familiar with 1 Corinthians, it is natural to assume that he has borrowed the quotation from the latter. It is, of course, not impossible that Clement and Paul may be dependent upon a common source (which would then have to be non-canonical)." Note also Andreas Lindemann, *Paulus im ältesten Christentum*, BHT 58 (Tübingen: Mohr Siebeck, 1979), 187–88.

15. See Isa 29:13 in 15.2 (cf. Mark 7:6; Matt 15:8; see Hagner, *Use*, 53–54, for proximity to the Synoptics); Num 12:7 in 17.5 (cf. Heb 3:2); Prov 3:34 in 30.2 (cf. Jas 4:6; 1 Pet 5:5); Heb 1 and 1 Clem. 36, where Ps 104:4 (as in Heb 1:7), Ps 2:7–8 (as in Heb 1:5), and Ps 110:1 (as in Heb 1:13) are found in quick succession (cf. Gregory, "*1 Clement* and the Writings That Later Formed the New Testament," 152–53); and Prov 3:12 in 56.3–4 (cf. Heb 12:6). Note also Gregory's conclusion: "There are a number of points where Clement includes citations from the Jewish Scriptures that are included also in the synoptic gospels" (139).

177

Chapter 10

it appears that this strategy of cribbing scriptural references was not confined to Paul. He also, moreover, cites certain texts in close proximity with those Paul makes use of. For example, 1 Clement adduces Deut 32:15 in 3.1 ("My loved one ate and drank, and became large and grew fat and kicked out with his heels"),[16] concluding from this citation that "jealousy (ζῆλος) and envy" came about; might Paul's extensive use of the Song of Moses in Rom 10–11 have contributed to a reading of the chapter in terms of ζῆλος? This can, of course, remain no more than speculation, but the correspondence is at least worth noting.[17]

IGNATIUS OF ANTIOCH

An examination of the letters of Ignatius of Antioch yields slightly different results. In general, Ignatius's letters have few allusions to and citations of Scripture, no doubt due in part to the conditions under which they were composed on his way to martyrdom in Rome.[18] Ignatius clearly knows Paul and makes explicit reference to his letters: He writes to the Ephesians, "you are fellow initiates with Paul, the holy one who received a testimony and proved worthy of all fortune. When I attain to God, may I be found in his footsteps, this one who mentions you in every epistle (ἐν πάσῃ ἐπιστολῇ) in Christ Jesus" (Ign. *Eph.* 12.2). From an examination of allusions to Paul in the letters of Ignatius, Paul Foster has tentatively suggested that this curious means of expression may reflect Ignatius's knowledge of only those letters that mention Ephesus or the Ephesians: 1 Corinthians, Ephesians, and 1 and 2 Timothy.[19] While this is a somewhat uncertain and tentative suggestion,[20] it would be consistent with the lack of scriptural citation that could result from ignorance of Paul's letter

16. Translation from Bart Ehrman, *The Apostolic Fathers*, 2 vols., LCL 24 (Cambridge, MA: Harvard University Press, 2003), 1.39. See further Hagner, *Use*, 64–65; and Lindemann, "Paul's Influence on 'Clement' and Ignatius," 10.

17. For other correspondences, note Ps 19:1–3 (LXX 18:1–3) in 27.7 (cf. Ps 19:4 in Rom 10:18); and Isa 53:1 in 16.3 (cf. Rom 10:16, although 1 Clement goes on to cite all of Isa 53).

18. This assumes the traditional acceptance of the middle recension of the Ignatian corpus, which cannot be defended here. Note the rough correspondence to Isa 52:5, a text that was widely used in early Christianity, in Ign. *Trall.* 8.2 (cf. 2 Clem. 13.2; Pol. *Phil.* 10.2–3; cf. Rom 2:24); Prov 3:34 in Ign. *Eph.* 5.3 (cf. Jas 4:6; 1 Pet 5:5); and Prov 18:17 in Ign. *Magn.* 12.

19. Paul Foster, "The Epistles of Ignatius of Antioch and the Writings That Later Formed the New Testament," in Gregory and Tuckett, *The Reception of the New Testament in the Apostolic Fathers*, 159–86, here 164–72.

20. Contrast the explanation of Lindemann, "Paul's Influence on 'Clement' and Ignatius," 18. And see n. 39 below for possible indications of an early collection of the *corpus Paulinum*, which might threaten the interpretation that Foster here suggests.

Learning Scripture in the School of Paul

to the Romans, heavily indebted to Scripture as it is. But this is a point that should not be pressed.[21]

POLYCARP OF SMYRNA

In Polycarp's *To the Philippians* we find a similar dearth of scriptural citations. Polycarp clearly knows Paul and his letter-writing activity. He writes:

> For neither I nor anyone like me is able to replicate the wisdom of the blessed and glorious Paul. When he was with you he accurately and reliably taught the word of truth to those who were there at the time. And when he was absent he wrote you letters. If you carefully peer into them, you will be able to be built up in the faith that was given you (Pol. *Phil.* 3.2).[22]

The one place, however, where Polycarp does make an explicit appeal to Scripture may provide a telling confirmation of the suggestion I am advancing in this chapter. Near the end of his letter, Polycarp writes, "I am confident that you are well trained in the sacred Scriptures (*sacris literis*) and that nothing is hidden from you; but to me this has not been granted. Only, as it is written in these Scriptures (*his scripturis*), 'Be angry and do not sin, and do not let the sun go down on your anger'" (Pol. *Phil.* 12.1). Here Polycarp cites Ps 4:5 ("Be angry and do not sin") but also cites the material that immediately follows this where it is cited in Eph 4:26, thus indicating, perhaps inadvertently, the source of this citation. Does Polycarp intend to refer to Ephesians as Scrip-

---

21. From his explicit statements, we might gather that Ignatius was especially concerned with the prophetic predictions he found in Scripture: "And we should also love the prophets, because their proclamation anticipated the gospel and they hoped in him and awaited him. And they were saved by believing in him, because they stood in the unity of Jesus Christ, saints who were worthy of love and admiration, who were testified to by Jesus Christ and counted as belonging to the gospel of our mutual hope" (Ign. *Phld.* 5.2). "They have become convinced neither by the words of the prophets nor the Law of Moses, nor, until now, by the gospel nor by the suffering each of us has experienced" (Ign. *Smyrn.* 5.1); cf. also Ign. *Smyrn.* 7. But he is clear that he privileges Christ over Scripture: "For I heard some saying, 'If I do not find it in the ancient records, I do not believe in the gospel.' And when I said to them, 'It is written,' they replied to me, 'That is just the question.' But for me, Jesus Christ is the ancient records; the sacred ancient records are his cross and death, and his resurrection, and the faith that comes through him—by which things I long to be made righteous by your prayer" (Ign. *Phld.* 8.2).

22. He also refers to "the apostles who proclaimed the gospel to us and the prophets who preached, in advance, the coming of our Lord" (Pol. *Phil.* 6.3).

179

Chapter 10

ture *tout simple*? This is certainly possible, but it would be a surprisingly early explicit reference to Ephesians as Scripture. Might it not rather be the case, however, that Polycarp, not having been granted a thorough training in the sacred Scriptures by his own admission, perceives the presence of an authoritative scriptural tradition in Ephesians but erroneously believes the entirety of Eph 4:26 to be from Scripture? If so, then he may unwittingly betray his reliance on Ephesians when he has simply intended to cite Scripture, and we have caught Polycarp red-handed in this procedure.[23]

2 CLEMENT

Turning now to that curious homily conventionally referred to as 2 Clement, we find a use of Scripture marked by certain idiosyncrasies. The author has apparently had little independent recourse to Scripture itself. The homily ostensibly takes as its base text Isa 54:1 (2 Clem. 2.1–3), the same text that Paul adduces in Gal 4:27, though here put to a different end. Andrew Gregory suggests that the parallel between 2 Clem. 2.1 and Gal 4:27 "may be explained by each author's independent use of Isa. 54.1,"[24] citing Justin's similar use in *1 Apol.* 53.5 and *Dial.* 13.8. The parallel is striking, but it is equally possible, given Justin's proclivity for Pauline citations, to find here an independent recourse to Paul, rather than to the LXX or to dependence on a "testimony" book in the strict sense.[25] The relationship between 2 Clement and Justin is complicated,[26] but especially given the fact that almost all of 2 Clement's other citations are also cited in the New Testament (as table 10 shows) and that 2 Clement elsewhere *may* evince some knowledge of Paul's letters (though not all are convinced this is the case),[27] to posit independent access to the

23. For other ways of understanding this, see Michael Holmes, "Polycarp's *Letter to the Philippians* and the Writings That Later Formed the New Testament," in Gregory and Tuckett, *The Reception of the New Testament in the Apostolic Fathers*, 187–227, here 210n99; and Lindemann, "Paul in the Writings of the Apostolic Fathers," 36, 42.

24. Andrew Gregory and C. M. Tuckett, "*2 Clement* and the Writings That Later Formed the New Testament," in Gregory and Tuckett, *The Reception of the New Testament in the Apostolic Fathers*, 251–92, here 286.

25. Note also the argument of Karl Paul Donfried, *The Setting of Second Clement in Early Christianity*, NovTSup 38 (Leiden: Brill, 1974), 192–200.

26. Cf. Oskar Skarsaune, *The Proof from Prophecy: A Study in Justin Martyr's Proof-Text Tradition; Text-Type, Provenance, Theological Profile*, NovTSup 56 (Leiden: Brill, 1987), 110.

27. Cf., e.g., 2 Clem. 7 and 1 Cor 9:24–27 (the image of the athlete) or 2 Clem. 8 and Rom 9:19–24 (the image of the potter and clay, perhaps also with the influence of Jer 7);

Learning Scripture in the School of Paul

LXX requires argumentation. It may further be noted that all three citations are marked by a strong introductory formula in Paul (γέγραπται), and the two other citations of Isaiah recur broadly in early Christian literature. Second Clement is a traditionalist and lacks an innovative reading of Scripture, and it makes sense to see the homily as passing on a tradition of reading Scripture, common by the mid-second century, that has been nurtured on Paul's own citation choices. Whether 2 Clement has gained any of this knowledge from direct recourse to the apostle's writings is difficult to ascertain decisively,[28] but the suggestion merits further consideration.

Table 9: Shared citations in 2 Clement and Paul

Scriptural Text	2 Clement	Paul
Isa 54:1	2 Clem. 2.1–3	Gal 4:27
Isa 64:3(?)	2 Clem. 11.7 and 14.5	1 Cor 2:9
Isa 52:5	2 Clem. 13.2	Rom 2:24

Table 10: Non-Pauline scriptural citations in 2 Clement

Isa 29:13 in 2 Clem. 3.5	Cf. Matt 15:8; Mark 7:6; 1 Clem. 15.2
Isa 66:24 in 2 Clem. 7.6	Cf. Mark 9:44, 46, 48, etc.
Jer 7:11 in 2 Clem. 14.1	Cf. Matt 21:13; Mark 11:17; Luke 19:46
Gen 1:27 in 2 Clem. 14.2	Cf. Matt 19:4; Mark 10:6, etc.
Ezek 14:14, 20 in 2 Clem. 6.8	Note Justin, *Dial.* 45.3; 140.3
Isa 58:9 in 2 Clem. 15.3	
Isa 66:18 in 2 Clem. 17.4	

JUSTIN MARTYR

Finally, now, we come to Justin Martyr. In Justin we find fully flowering the branches of the tree whose roots are sunk in the soil of the early post-Pauline community itself. In Justin's *Dialogue with Trypho* we find amassed dozens

---

cf. Ehrman, *Apostolic Fathers*, 1.156. Note also, e.g., 1.8 with Rom 4:17. Cf. also 15.1 ("And whoever takes my advice will have no regrets, but will instead save both himself and me, the one who has given the advice") with 1 Tim 4:16 ("Keep a close watch on yourself and on the teaching. Persist in this, for by doing so you will save both yourself and your hearers"). Cf. also 19.2 with Eph 4:18.

28. Cf. Lindemann, "Paul in the Writings of the Apostolic Fathers," 27, though he may state the case too decisively.

Chapter 10

of texts drawn in to serve the apologetic intention of that work. As table 11 indicates, drawing on the seminal work of Oskar Skarsaune, many of these scriptural texts have their parallels in the Pauline letters. From a detailed investigation of the textual character of these quotations, Skarsaune concludes that "Justin seems in most cases to be directly drawing on Romans when he has OT quotations in common with Romans."[29] He goes on to note that Galatians also provides key texts for Justin, while the evidence from 1 Corinthians is less conclusive.[30] But in drawing on Paul's scriptural citations, Justin has inevitably transformed Paul's argument for his own context. Paul's letters seem to provide an entryway for Justin to read more broadly in Scripture. Justin has certainly done his own scouring of Scripture for any help it might lend to his apologetic cause, but this does not therefore exclude Pauline influence on his choice of texts. Paul's letters serve, in some instances at least, as heuristic guides to the text, but even then, so often the texts to which Paul appeals are transposed into a framework of anti-Jewish polemic that seems to be supersessionist in intent.[31] But this change in interpretation cannot be used as an argument against Pauline derivation—and this is a result that should be kept in mind when examining the earlier literature as well.

Table 11: Shared citations in Justin and Paul[32]

Scriptural Text	Justin	Paul
Isa 52:5	*Dial.* 17.2	Rom 2:24
Ps 14:1–3; 5:9; 140:3; 10:7; Isa 59:7–8; Ps 36:1	*Dial.* 27.3 (= esp. Rom 3:12–17)	Rom 3:10–18
Gen 15:6	*Dial.* 11.5; 23.4; 92.3; 119.5–6	Rom 4:3, 9
Ps 32:1–2	*Dial.* 141.2	Rom 4:7–8
Gen 17:5	*Dial.* 11.5; 119.4	Rom 4:17
Isa 1:9	*1 Apol.* 53.7; *Dial.* 140.3; cf. *Dial.* 32.2; 55.3	Rom 9:29
Isa 53:1	*Dial.* 42.2; 114.2	Rom 10:16
Ps 19:5	*Dial.* 42.1	Rom 10:18
Deut 32:21	*Dial.* 119.2 (includes Deut 32:16–23)	Rom 10:19
Isa 65:1–2	*Dial.* 119.4	Rom 10:20–21

29. Skarsaune, *The Proof from Prophecy*, 96.

30. Skarsaune, *The Proof from Prophecy*, 99–100.

31. But see Oskar Skarsaune, "Does the Letter to the Hebrews Articulate a Supersessionist Theology? A Response to Richard Hays," in *The Epistle to the Hebrews and Christian Theology*, ed. R. Bauckham et al. (Grand Rapids: Eerdmans, 2009), 174–82, here 178–79.

32. Adapted from Skarsaune's tables (*The Proof from Prophecy*, 93–100).

Learning Scripture in the School of Paul

Scriptural Text	Justin	Paul
1 Kings 19:10, 14, 18	*Dial.* 39.1	Rom 11:3–4
Deut 32:43	*Dial.* 130.1, 4	Rom 15:10
Isa 52:15	*Dial.* 118.4 (Isa 52:15–53:1)	Rom 15:21
Isa 29:14	*Dial.* 78.11 (Isa 29:13–14); *Dial.* 32.5; 123.4 (Isa 29:14)	1 Cor 1:19
Exod 32:6	*Dial.* 20.1	1 Cor 10:7
Ps 24:1	*Dial.* 36.3–4	1 Cor 10:26
Deut 27:26	*Dial.* 95.1	Gal 3:10
Deut 21:23	*Dial.* 96.1	Gal 3:13
Isa 54:1	*1 Apol.* 53.5	Gal 4:27
Ps 68:18	*Dial.* 39.4; 87.6	Eph 4:8

Negative Examples

It is possible for us to be blinded by the sheer facts of history to the reality that things might have been otherwise than they now are. We must not be beguiled into granting the inevitability that the use of such texts would suggest to us. In order to show that the prevalence of Pauline scriptural citations in other early Christian literature is in fact indicative of Pauline influence rather than inevitable Christian interpretation of these texts, let us now briefly consider two negative examples: the Didache and the Epistle of Barnabas.[33] These two texts do not show a broad Pauline influence, and their scriptural citations differ widely from those in the *corpus Paulinum*. The Didache is most closely associated with Matthean traditions. And while the citation of Scripture is not integral to its aims, one looks in vain for overlap with Pauline citations.[34]

In particular, the collocation of the command to love God (Deut 6:5) and to love neighbor (Lev 19:18) in Did. 1.2 is also found in Matt 22:37, 39 (cf. Mark 12:30–31) and Luke 10:27. The unknown text cited at Did. 1.6 shows some affinities to Sir 12:1–7. The order of the Decalogue reflected at Did. 2.2–4 (murder, adultery, theft, covetousness, false witness) follows the order of the Hebrew text (and some Greek manuscripts) of Exod 20:13–17, rather than Paul's preference for the order of Greek Deuteronomy (adultery, murder, theft) seen in Rom 13:9a. The Didache's order of the commandments corresponds closely to Matt 19:18–19, although the command against covetousness has been interposed in a manner that contradicts the order seen in both Matthew and

33. A similar case might further be argued for the Shepherd of Hermas.

34. There is one possible citation in common, though arguably this should rather be ascribed to common Jesus tradition (Zech 14:5 in Did. 16.7 and 1 Thess 3:13).

Chapter 10

Exodus. Didache 4.7 recalls either Ps 36:11 LXX or Matt 5:5, which echoes the psalm in its own right. The citation of Mal 1:11, 14 in Did. 14.3 similarly does not correspond with any of Paul's scriptural quotations.

With certain allowances, something similar might be claimed for the so-called Epistle of Barnabas. This author may have had some knowledge of Pauline traditions, for example, those concerning Abraham as the father of the uncircumcised (cf. Barn. 13.7 and Rom 4:11–12).[35] But Barnabas's theological solar system is not centered on a Pauline sun, and out of all of that epistle's numerous scriptural citations one might mention only Isa 65:2, which occurs in Barn. 12.4 and Rom 10:21 as a significant shared tradition.[36] Even here, however, the textual tradition is not exact, and while Pauline influence cannot be ruled out, it is by no means inevitable. What certainly is clear is that the overall distribution and weight of citations in Barnabas differs significantly from Paul and texts influenced by Paul, in both selection and the hermeneutical use to which the texts are put. This may suggest, conversely, that those texts that do in fact display the influence of the Pauline letters may be similarly indebted to Paul for their knowledge of at least some scriptural texts.

In the case of the Epistle of Barnabas, it is sufficient simply to note the quotations and major allusions from the epistle to demonstrate a lack of coincidence with Paul's own citations, as table 12 demonstrates.

Table 12: Scriptural citations in the Epistle of Barnabas and NT parallel citations

Epistle of Barnabas	Scriptural Citation	NT Parallel Citation
Barn. 2.5	Isa 1:11–13	
Barn. 2.7	Jer 7:22–23	
Barn. 2.8	Zech 8:17	
Barn. 2.10	Ps 51:17 (50:19 LXX)	

35. See James Carleton Paget, "The *Epistle of Barnabas* and the Writings That Later Formed the New Testament," in Gregory and Tuckett, *The Reception of the New Testament in the Apostolic Fathers*, 229–49, here 240–41, who concludes, "At the very least knowledge of a tradition influenced by Paul is evidenced at this point." He goes on, "It is difficult to prove that the author of *Barnabas* had a direct knowledge of any of the letters of Paul. But there is, I think, sufficient evidence to show that he was in contact with traditions which were at least conversant with aspects of Paul's theology" (245).

36. One might mention Ps 110:1 in Barn. 12.10, but the use to which this is put most nearly approximates the Synoptic usage (e.g., Mark 12:35–37 par.). A connection to Hebrews, however, has often been advanced (and in this respect, note Ps 22:22 in Barn. 6.16 and Heb 2:12).

Learning Scripture in the School of Paul

Epistle of Barnabas	Scriptural Citation	NT Parallel Citation
Barn. 2.10	a possible citation from a nonextant *Apocalypse of Adam*(?)[37]	
Barn. 3.1–5	Isa 58:4–10	Luke 4:18 (for Isa 58:6)
Barn. 4.3	Enoch	
Barn. 4.4	Dan 7:24	
Barn. 4.5	Dan 7:7–8	
Barn. 4.7	Exod 34:28 (cf. 31:18)	
Barn. 4.8	Exod 32:7	
Barn. 4.11	Isa 5:21	
Barn. 5.2	Isa 53:5, 7	1 Pet 2:24
Barn. 5.4	Prov 1:17	
Barn. 5.5	Gen 1:26	
Barn. 5.12	Zech 13:7	Matt 26:31; Mark 14:27
Barn. 5.13	Ps 22:20 (21:21 LXX)	
Barn. 5.13	Ps 119(118 LXX):120 with 22:16 (21:17 LXX)	
Barn. 5.14–6.2	Isa 50:6–9	
Barn. 6.2–3	Isa 28:16	Rom 9:33; 10:11; 1 Pet 2:6
Barn. 6.3	Isa 50:7	
Barn. 6.4	Ps 118(117 LXX):22, 24 LXX	Matt 21:42; Mark 12:10; Luke 20:17
Barn. 6.6	Ps 22:16 (21:17 LXX) and 118 (117 LXX):12 LXX	
Barn. 6.7	Isa 3:9–10	
Barn. 6.8 (cf. 6.13)	Exod 33:1, 3	
Barn. 6.12 (cf. 6.18)	Gen 1:26, 28	
Barn. 6.13	an unknown source	
Barn. 6.14	Ezek 11:19	
Barn. 6.16	Ps 42:2 (41:3 LXX) and 22:22 (21:23 LXX)	Heb 2:12 (Ps 22:22)
Barn. 7.3	Lev 23:29	Acts 3:23
Barn. 7.6–7 (cf. also 7.4)	Lev 16:7, 9, 8	
Barn. 7.8	an unknown source	
Barn. 9.1	Ps 18:44 (17:45 LXX)	
Barn. 9.1	Isa 33:13	

37. A marginal note in H (Codex Taphou 54) suggests this identification.

Chapter 10

Epistle of Barnabas	Scriptural Citation	NT Parallel Citation
Barn. 9.1	Jer 4:4	
Barn. 9.2	Jer 7:2–3	
Barn. 9.2	Ps 34:12 (33:13 LXX) (*inter alia*)	
Barn. 9.3	Isa 1:2, 10	
Barn. 9.3	Isa 40:3	Matt 3:3; Mark 1:3; John 1:23; Luke 3:4
Barn. 9.5	Jer 4:3–4	
Barn. 9.5	Deut 10:16	
Barn. 9.5	Jer 9:25 LXX	
Barn. 9.8	Gen 14:14; 17:23	
Barn. 10.1 (cf. 10.4–7)	Lev 11:7–15	
Barn. 10.2	Deut 4:10, 13	
Barn. 10.10	Ps 1:1	
Barn. 10.11	Lev 11:3	
Barn. 11.2	Jer 2:12–13	
Barn. 11.3	Isa 16:1–2	
Barn. 11.4	Isa 45:2–3	
Barn. 11.4–5	Isa 33:16–18	
Barn. 11.6–7	Ps 1:3–6	
Barn. 11.9	Zeph 3:19(?)	
Barn. 11.10	a possible allusion to Ezek 47:1–12?	
Barn. 12.1	a tradition in common with 4 Ezra 4:33; 5:5	
Barn. 12.2	an allusion to Exod 17:8–13	
Barn. 12.4	Isa 65:2	Rom 10:21
Barn. 12.6	Lev 26:21	
Barn. 12.7	Num 21:4–9	Cf. John 3:14
Barn. 12.9	Exod 17:14	
Barn. 12.10	Ps 110 (109 LXX):1	Matt 22:44; Mark 12:36; Luke 20:42; Acts 2:34; 1 Cor 15:25; Heb 3:13
Barn. 12.11	Isa 45:1	
Barn. 13.2	Gen 25:21–23	Rom 9:12 (Gen 25:23)
Barn. 13.4	Gen 48:11, 9	
Barn. 13.6	Gen 48:14, 18, 19	
Barn. 13.7	Gen 15:6	Rom 4:3; Gal 3:6; Jas 2:23
Barn. 14.2	Exod 24:18; 31:18	

186

Learning Scripture in the School of Paul

Epistle of Barnabas	Scriptural Citation	NT Parallel Citation
Barn. 14.3	Exod 32:7–8, 19	
Barn. 14.7	Isa 42:6–7	
Barn. 14.8	Isa 49:6–7	Acts 13:47 (for Isa 49:6)
Barn. 14.9	Isa 61:1–2	Luke 4:18–19
Barn. 15.1	Exod 20:8//Deut 5:12	
Barn. 15.2	Exod 31:13–17, etc.	
Barn. 15.3	Gen 2:2–3	Heb 4:4
Barn. 15.8	Isa 1:13	
Barn. 16.2	Isa 40:12; 66:1	Acts 7:49 (Isa 66:1)
Barn. 16.3, 5, 6	unknown sources	

Conclusion

In conclusion, we should take note of the social conditions that might go some way toward explaining this phenomenon. Some scholarship has suggested a notable degree of mobility in the early Christian movement, such that some texts spread quite quickly after their composition around the Roman Empire.[38] This travel is certainly reflected in the life of Paul himself, and we may have reason to suppose that those who came after the apostle would be interested in the literary remains of his travels. This has been repeatedly suggested by a number of studies that have argued that there may have been early collections of the *corpus Paulinum*—at the very least of the *Hauptbriefe* (where most of Paul's scriptural citations are found), with the other letters soon following.[39] While knowledge of Paul's letters and the use of them are logically separable, if we have reason to suspect knowledge of Paul's letters on other grounds it is worth asking about the more subtle as well as the more overt ways in which they were employed.

In this light, the evidence of this chapter's somewhat breathless investigation suggests that one of Paul's earliest literary influences was as a hermeneu-

---

38. Michael B. Thompson, "The Holy Internet: Communication between Churches in the First Christian Generation," in *The Gospels for all Christians*, ed. Richard J. Bauckham (Edinburgh: T&T Clark, 1998), 49–70.

39. So, e.g., David Trobisch, *Paul's Letter Collection: Tracing the Origins* (Minneapolis: Fortress, 1994); Harry Y. Gamble, *Books and Readers in the Early Church* (New Haven: Yale University Press, 1995), 58–66; Andreas Lindemann, "Die Sammlung der Paulusbriefe im 1. und 2. Jahrhundert," in *The Biblical Canons*, ed. J.-M. Auwers and H. J. de Jonge, BETL 153 (Leuven: Peeters, 2003), 321–51; and Stanley E. Porter, "When and How Was the Pauline Canon Compiled? An Assessment of Theories," in *The Pauline Canon*, ed. Stanley E. Porter, Pauline Studies 1 (Leiden and Boston: Brill, 2004), 95–127, etc.

Chapter 10

tical teacher: on his way to an ascending material authority himself, he was first sought for the entrance he provided to a greater authority: the Scriptures of Israel. It is one of the ironies of history that he himself should have come to eclipse in time the very authority upon which he drew. If the phenomenon that we observe so clearly in Justin's *Dialogue with Trypho*—dependence on Pauline scriptural citations without direct citation of Paul himself—can be legitimately discerned in the earlier authors here examined, this suggests that Paul's letters form a sort of virtual testimony book, sometimes directing its readers on to examine Scripture itself, at other times merely supplying the authoritative citation to be put to new use. This in turn suggests that, to adapt a phrase of Hans Hübner's, often with these authors we see a recourse not to the *Vetus Testamentum in se*, but to the *Vetus Testamentum in Paulo receptum*.[40]

The results of this investigation are naturally preliminary rather than definitive in nature. A further investigation might build on these results to see whether there are traces of Pauline interpretation in the redeployment of Pauline citations in the writings of other authors. Perhaps put more interestingly, how does the Pauline "interference" here suggested come to be transformed, actualized, resisted in the face of new authorial concerns and community demands? If it would be fair to characterize Paul's own hermeneutical ventures in, for example, the letter to the Galatians as exhibiting elements of intra-Jewish polemic, what happens to that polemic in later non-Jewish interpretative hands? Or again, if an apocalyptic forecast can buoy the apostle's hopes for Israel, what does the removal of that framework of hope do for the early understanding of his citations of Scripture in Rom 9–11? Yet again, as the river of Pauline hermeneutics becomes a mere tributary to the broader enterprise of early Christian biblical interpretation, is his narrative hermeneutic simply flattened by the prophecy-and-fulfillment scheme that soon rose to such prominence? Important as these questions are, they are questions for another investigation.

---

40. See Hans Hübner, "Vetus Testamentum und Vetus Testamentum in Novo Receptum: Die Frage nach dem Kanon des Alten Testaments aus neutestamentlicher Sicht," *Jahrbuch für biblische Theologie* 3 (1988): 147–62.

Afterword

Reading Scripture in the Messianic Community

The Macbride Sermon, which was the original context for these remarks, was named for Dr. John Macbride, Principal of Magdalen Hall, Oxford, and is preached in accordance with an anonymous bequest made to the University of Oxford in 1848. The rubric for the Macbride Sermon lays down that it is to be preached on "the application of the prophecies in Holy Scripture respecting the Messiah to our Lord and Saviour Jesus Christ."

To the casual observer, this may sound like an impossibly benign mandate, as though one were to ask a group of American grandmothers to extol the virtues of motherhood and apple pie. After all, to speak of how the Christian Bible refers to its own central figure—isn't this the sort of thing Christian preachers love to do?

In fact, however, more attentive observers will know that the task is complicated, much more so today than it might have been almost two centuries ago when the bequest was made. In mid-nineteenth-century Oxford, in the context of millenarian debates about the role and future of the Jewish people and in light of the overseas missionary movement,[1] to endow a perpetual demonstration of the evident fulfillment of Israel's expectations for the Messiah in the person of Jesus of Nazareth might have made good sense. The original terms did not simply require the positive demonstration of the application of messianic prophecies to Jesus, however, but also added a confrontational further clause: "with an especial view to confute the arguments of Jewish commentators and to promote the conversion to Christianity of the ancient People of God." This form of wording was officially dropped from the statutes in 1997, though it had long been qualified by individuals who offered the sermon before then.

The reasons for this change are not far to seek: since the mid-nineteenth century, we have come to have a much richer awareness of the common ground

---

1. For more on the context of the Macbride bequest, see S. Gillingham, "Messianic Prophecy and the Psalms," *Theology* 99 (1996): 114-24.

Afterword

Judaism and Christianity together share, and the horrific events of the twentieth century have exposed the catastrophic effects of anti-Semitism, to which some Christian theology had contributed in complex ways. And to suggest that interaction with another major faith should primarily have as its goal either conversion or confutation seems today shortsighted.[2] If in certain ways it might be true to say that Jews and Christians are two peoples divided by a common Bible, it is undeniable that there still exists a "special relationship" between us.

If we turn now to the positive task at hand, that of considering "the application of the prophecies of Holy Scripture respecting the Messiah to our Lord and Saviour Jesus Christ," we find ourselves confronted with the question of how messianic prophecy might be understood today. We might distinguish three basic options—the first two, I will suggest, are insufficient, while the third offers a promising way forward.

First, there is a long tradition of employing prophetic texts as proof of the identity of Jesus as the Messiah. Although one finds this line of approach in more or less sophisticated variations, its basic logic is straightforward: the Israelite prophets, inspired by God, foretold the coming of a Messiah. These predictions were manifold in form, ranging from detailed information about his place of birth to indications that he would suffer to offer a vicarious atonement for his people. After years of waiting and watching, Israel finally had the opportunity to welcome their expected Messiah in the person of Jesus, but, mistaking his identity, largely rejected him. His life and death possess such a striking correspondence to the prophetic predictions, however, that the truth of his identity can only be willfully denied. Impartial readers of the Hebrew Bible today should, therefore, be able to discern the nature of these correlations and, reasoning from prediction to fulfillment, judge the claim of Jesus's messiahship to be valid. So runs the argument.

This approach proceeds as though a reasonably attentive resident of Palestine in the early 30s CE might have been able to construct a long list of prophecies, marked as "to be fulfilled." Then, following Jesus from a safe distance, clipboard of prophecies in hand, she might have been able to tick with

---

2. Without denying the individuality of the Jewish and Christian traditions, nor downplaying the ongoing differences between the faiths, it is possible to see Judaism and Christianity as two sisters sharing both the closeness and the tensions associated with being siblings; cf., e.g., Alan F. Segal, *Rebecca's Children: Judaism and Christianity in the Roman World* (Cambridge, MA: Harvard University Press, 1986); Paul Joyce, "A Tale of Two Sisters: Judaism and Christianity," *Theology* 96 (1993): 384–90; and Martin Hengel, "The Beginning of Christianity as a Jewish-Messianic and Universalistic Movement," in *The Beginnings of Christianity*, ed. J. Pastor and M. Mor (Jerusalem: Yad Ben-Zvi Press, 2005), 85–100.

Reading Scripture in the Messianic Community

satisfaction each box as Jesus—by coincidence or providence—happened to do what the prophets foretold.

It must be admitted that this is a strategy employed in at least some early Christian literature, though it is not as widespread in the earliest texts as some imagine. But especially from the mid-second century, the "proof from prophecy" argument takes hold, with apologists like Justin Martyr amassing large numbers of fulfilled prophecies as indication of Jesus's identity.[3] Eventually these come to be used in formulaic fashion in the *adversus Judaeos* literature, polemical tractates written "against the Jews" that make ample use of prophecy in their attempt to dispossess or disinherit the Jews.[4] If a Google search on "messianic prophecy" is any indication, this approach is alive and well on the internet today.

Since the Enlightenment, however, and the concomitant historicization of European thought,[5] biblical scholarship has instructed us about the original social setting and function of Israelite prophecy. When the Hebrew Bible is treated first on its own terms, rather than as the Christian Old Testament, the referent of prophecy can often be found in the prophet's much more immediate context. So, to take but one well-known example in the Gospel of Matthew, Jesus and his family return from their exile in Egypt after the death of Herod, in order to fulfill what was written in Hos 11:1: "Out of Egypt have I called my son." When one turns to Hosea, however, one finds there not statements about the plight of an expected Messiah, but poetic reflections on the exodus of Israel directed to assuring Israel of divine election in the midst of the political turmoil of the eighth century BCE. In fact, it is not at all clear how this text could be straightforwardly considered to be predictive, and so in need of fulfillment.[6] Similar examples could be mustered.

---

3. On Justin, see Oskar Skarsaune, *The Proof from Prophecy: A Study in Justin Martyr's Proof-Text Tradition; Text-Type, Provenance, Theological Profile*, NovTSup 56 (Leiden: Brill, 1987).

4. See the classic treatments of this literature in A. Lukyn Williams, *Adversus Judaeos: A Bird's-Eye View of Christian Apologiae until the Renaissance* (Cambridge: Cambridge University Press, 1935); Marcel Simon, *Verus Israel: A Study of the Relations between Christians and Jews in the Roman Empire (AD 135–425)* (London: The Littman Library of Jewish Civilization, 1996 [French original, 1964]); and William Horbury, *Jews and Christians: In Contact and Controversy* (Edinburgh: T&T Clark, 1998).

5. On historicism, see Frederick C. Beiser, *The German Historicist Tradition* (Oxford: Oxford University Press, 2011).

6. In practice, of course, exegetes since antiquity have suggested a typological relationship between the exodus and Jesus's flight from Egypt, but the question of typology is another matter to the issue at hand.

Afterword

This realization that much of Israelite prophecy was directed not toward the coming of Jesus or another idealized figure in the far distance but rather toward problems on the prophets' more immediate horizons led some to reconsider the nature of the early Christian appeal to prophecy. So, second, we find an approach that, rather than emphasizing the proof from prophecy, suggests that early Christians may have simply invented or forged many of the correspondences. Rather than discovering history prophesied in advance, what we find in early Christianity is prophecy historicized, as the evangelists create events in the life of Jesus on the basis of scriptural texts in an *ex post facto* manner.[7]

One need not fully subscribe to a hermeneutics of suspicion to see the strength of this position. A number of the putative fulfillment texts seem quite clearly to betray early Christian scribal activity, and this realization significantly lessens their appeal as "proof," at least in any objective sense likely to convince anyone who was not already a believer. For some, such historicizing realizations have led to quite radical reassessments of the truth of Christian faith. One thinks of Thomas Hardy's memorable poem, "The Respectable Burgher on 'The Higher Criticism,'" in which the speaker, after considering the numerous unsettling discoveries of biblical criticism, finally resolves:

> Since thus they hint, nor turn a hair,
> All churchgoing will I forswear,
> And sit on Sundays in my chair,
> And read that moderate man Voltaire.[8]

But is there a middle ground, or perhaps better something beyond these two extremes of the evidentialist foundationalism of prophecy as proof on the one hand, and the searching skepticism of mere historicism on the other? To opt for the former seems to reduce the voice of the Old Testament to that of the New, while to choose the latter threatens to allow the Christian Bible to disintegrate into merely unrelated parts. Is there a way of thinking about messianic prophecy in the context of a community of Christian faith today that can do justice to this complexity? The task is too large to address appropriately in this afterword, but we can make a beginning.

---

7. A position perhaps most famously associated in recent times with John Dominic Crossan, but with long roots in the history of scholarship; see, e.g., Crossan, *Who Killed Jesus? Exposing the Roots of Anti-Semitism in the Gospel Story of the Death of Jesus* (San Francisco: HarperSanFrancisco, 1996).

8. In Samuel Hynes, ed., *The Complete Poetical Works of Thomas Hardy* (Oxford: Clarendon, 1982), 1.198–99.

Reading Scripture in the Messianic Community

Seeing the fulfillment of Scripture is a hermeneutical discipline of Christian faith, an appropriative reading strategy that follows from a self-involving stance toward Scripture that eventuates in action, rather than a mere neutral discovery that might be used to convince outsiders. This is a shared set of practices that find their place most naturally in the community of Christian belief. It is worth saying a bit more about this.

Reading a set of ancient texts as Scripture involves above all an act of appropriation. To read a text *as* Scripture means in some way to inhabit it, to find oneself addressed by it, to say, as Israel did when the law was read at Sinai: "we will hear and we will do it." There is in other words inherent in the act of confessing a text to be Scripture a self-involving claim to relate oneself to that Scripture in a posture of deference.

To describe the set of Israelite texts as "the Hebrew Bible" is to signal one's intention to read them neutrally, or at least in a publicly acceptable way in the religiously plural world. But as the Jewish New Testament scholar Amy-Jill Levine has argued, "Terms like *Hebrew Bible* and *Jewish Scriptures* serve ultimately either to erase Judaism (since 'Jews' are not 'Hebrews' and the synagogue reads not the 'Hebrew Bible' but the *Tanakh* . . .) or to deny Christians part of their own canon. . . . The so-called 'neutral' term is actually one of Protestant hegemony."[9] There is a legitimate place for such attempts at neutrality, but it is also true that to speak of the Hebrew Bible as it has been accepted by the Christian church is to speak of it as the Old Testament.

For those of us who are gentiles, to approach the Old Testament through the New Testament is precisely to find oneself generously included in the people of God to whom that word is addressed, by means of either the Pauline universalism that induces non-Jews to speak of "our ancestors in the wilderness," or alternatively by means the Matthean instruction of all nations, in which an attentiveness to the fullness of the law is communicated to nonethnic Jews.[10] In this sense, both Old and New Testament open into each other and together comprise a witness to the God of Israel's action in the world, culminating, for Christians, in their confession that God has sent his Messiah for the world's restoration.

---

9. Amy-Jill Levine, "Jewish-Christian Relations from the 'Other Side': A Response to Webb, Lodahl, and White," *Quarterly Review* 20 (2000): 297–304, here 298; cited to good effect in Richard B. Hays, "Can the Gospels Teach Us How to Read the Old Testament?," *Pro Ecclesia* 11 (2002): 402–18, here 404n5.

10. 1 Cor 10:1–13; Matt 28:18–20. Thus, the line between the Old and the New is not that between judgment and love, or national and personal. Neither is one absolutized over the other; cf. Brevard S. Childs, *Biblical Theology of the Old and New Testaments: Theological Reflection on the Christian Bible* (Philadelphia: Fortress, 1993).

Afterword

This is a stance we find reflected already in the New Testament itself, in which Scripture and gospel are mutually enlightening. Already for Jesus, these dialectics are at work. It is not as though Jesus stepped into a void, empty of expectation, and only afterward did people begin to ask how what he did aligned with what they already knew. Rather, he appeared on the scene in a period of competing ideas about Israel's current status and how God might redeem Israel (if she needed redemption), and he undertook to act intentionally to evoke some of those expectations. Rather than being a means of proving his identity, his enactment of prophecy suggests his vision of the kingdom of God and so invites his followers to join him in his task. So, for example, to ride into Jerusalem on a donkey seems to have been calculated to evoke Zech 9:9: "Behold, your king is coming to you; righteous and having salvation is he, humbled and mounted on a donkey, on a colt, the foal of a donkey." The evangelists—at least Matthew (21:1–11) and John (12:12–16)—recognize and exploit this fact, but the interpretation of the nature of his messiahship as involving humility seems to predate them and to be rooted in the actions of the historical Jesus himself. Which is to say that Jesus intended to enact prophecy and so initiated the novel interpretation of his life and ministry that his followers later continued. The author of the Fourth Gospel even hints as much, writing, "His disciples did not understand these things at first, but when Jesus was glorified, then they remembered that these things had been written about him and had been done to him" (12:16).

But it is also the case that Jesus did and suffered things that were not associated with messianic expectation. There is a theme in the Old Testament of the "righteous sufferer" (e.g., Pss 22, 37, 42, 43, 69, 140, etc.). But it is not, so far as our evidence allows us to discern, associated with specifically messianic expectation before the Christian period. It seems that the story of Jesus, who was both identified as the Messiah by some of his early followers and seen to have suffered in righteousness, had a kind of gravity that attracted multiple aspects of the scriptural vision, and so enabled a messianic reinterpretation of texts in a retrospective fashion from the standpoint of faith in him. Like a newly formed star that pulls the surrounding matter into its orbit, the life of Jesus became the focal point for the interpretation of prophecy.

This also means that asking after the application of messianic prophecy is a community-forming activity. Just as we observe in the ancient group at Qumran the formation of a community with a common strategy of reading the Hebrew Bible as directed toward their present day, reflected in some of the Dead Sea Scrolls, so also among the earliest Christ-believers we find a group activity of seeking to understand the meaning of the surprising life of the

Reading Scripture in the Messianic Community

one they confessed to be the Messiah, by searching the Scriptures for correspondences and new insights, precisely on the basis of their preexisting faith in and experience of Jesus as God's anointed one. Theirs was a faith seeking messianic understanding. We are the heirs to those searching activities, and the task of understanding the Christian Bible as in some sense testifying to the God of Israel's action in Jesus as Messiah is an ongoing one. The Christian Bible, consisting of both Old and New Testaments, therefore, comes to the Christian church not as a set of answers or proofs, but as a set of possibilities and tasks.

Followers of a crucified Messiah have no business indulging in narratives of triumph, over Jews or anybody else. If the apparent progress of human society once made it palatable to believe that history itself was progressing teleologically toward some immanent eschaton, achievable perhaps by human cooperation, gradually, from below, those hopes are now shattered. We have marked more than a century since the First World War, only one of the most eloquent displays of the human need for redemption from beyond ourselves. Among the prophecies in the Old Testament that one might consider messianic, at least in a broad sense, we find a substantial number that envisage not simply the coming of an individual, but the coming of a new age, an era of peace among nations, of human flourishing, and of the very presence of God.[11] As Christians we confess to have seen a glimpse of that new age in the coming of Jesus, whom we call the Christ, but we share with our Jewish friends an expectation that the full coming of the messianic age is yet to arrive, and so we live together in expectation of the restoration of all things.

And so we live, stretched between past and future. We are ever reaching backward, attempting to make sense of our shared confession that Jesus is the Messiah of Israel by listening attentively to the witness of Scripture. And we are ever reaching ahead, seeking in community to anticipate the full messianic coming in some small measure, to enact the eschatological peace and justice and harmony in some minor way here and now, as a shadow of its coming, as an outpost of what will be, as a *sacramentum futuri*. And as we stand, arms stretched out on either side, to the past and to the future, we live in the present experiencing the crucifixion of the Messiah in the tension between the ages.

The application of messianic prophecies, then, must be a set of embodied practices—neither the mere argumentative proof from prophecy that all too easily remains formalistic and unengaged, nor the detachment of critical judgment that keeps the question at arm's length, but an existential commitment

11. E.g., Isa 2:4; 11:6–9; 65:17–25; Jer 33:15–16; Mic 4:3–4, etc.

Afterword

that causes us as a community to look forward as much as back, to think about what is unfulfilled as much as what has been fulfilled. We face the future not with an optimism based on a hunch about human progress, but rather inspired by hope in the God who has promised to be with us in the crucified one. Paul knew something of that process of negotiating meaning, and the commentarial impulse in the Pauline tradition functions in part to generate hope in the tension between the ages. And in this time when so much is darkness, in the long vale of tears, we recall with Paul that "we are heirs of God and fellow heirs with the Messiah, provided we suffer with him in order that we may also be glorified with him" (Rom 8:17).

Acknowledgments

"Introduction: The Commentarial Impulse." Previously unpublished.

"How Does Paul Read Scripture?" Pages 225–38 in *The New Cambridge Companion to the Apostle Paul*. Edited by Bruce Longenecker. Cambridge: Cambridge University Press, 2020.

"Paul and the *Testimonia*: Quo Vadamus?" *Journal of the Evangelical Theological Society* 51 (2008): 297–308.

"Intertextuality, Effective History and Memory: Conceptualizing Paul's Use of Scripture." Pages 9–21 in *Paulinische Schriftrezeption: Grundlagen—Ausprägungen—Wirkungen—Wertungen*. FRLANT 268. Edited by Florian Wilk and Markus Öhler. Göttingen: Vandenhoeck & Ruprecht, 2017.

"Genesis in Paul." Pages 99–116 in *Genesis in the New Testament*. The New Testament and the Scriptures of Israel. Edited by S. Moyise and M. Menken. London: T&T Clark, 2012. Used by permission of Bloomsbury Publishing Plc.

"Paul's Engagement with Deuteronomy: Snapshots and Signposts." *Currents in Biblical Research* 7.1 (2008): 37–67.

"Transforming Stories and Permeable Selves: Conferring Identity in Romans 6." Previously unpublished.

"Presentifying the Past: Actualization in the Pauline Tradition." Previously unpublished.

"Mirror-Reading a Pseudepigraphal Letter." *Novum Testamentum* 59 (2017): 171–93. A previously unpublished appendix ("Twelve Ways of Looking at a Pauline Author") is added.

Acknowledgments

"Elijah in Romans 11 and Justin's *Dialogue with Trypho*." Previously unpublished.

"Learning Scripture in the School of Paul: From Ephesians to Justin." Pages 148–70 in *The Early Reception of Paul and His Letters*. Edited by K. Liljeström. Publications of the Finnish Exegetical Society 99. Helsinki: The Finnish Exegetical Society, 2011.

Afterword: "The Macbride Sermon: Reading Scripture in the Messianic Community." *Expository Times* 126 (2015): 296–300.

BIBLIOGRAPHY

Abasciano, Brian J. "Diamonds in the Rough: A Reply to Christopher Stanley Concerning the Reader Competency of Paul's Original Audiences." *NovT* 49 (2007): 153–83.

Achtemeier, Paul J. "*Omne Verbum Sonat*: The New Testament and the Oral Environment of Late Western Antiquity." *JBL* 109 (1990): 3–27.

Albl, Martin C. *"And Scripture Cannot Be Broken": The Form and Function of the Early Christian Testimonia Collections.* NovTSup 96. Leiden: Brill, 1999.

Alexander, Loveday. "IPSE DIXIT: Citation of Authority in Paul and in the Jewish and Hellenistic Schools." Pages 103–27 in *Paul Beyond the Judaism/Hellenism Divide.* Edited by Troels Engberg-Pedersen. Louisville: Westminster John Knox, 2001.

Alkier, Stefan. "Intertextuality and the Semiotics of Biblical Texts." Pages 1–22 in *Reading the Bible Intertextually.* Edited by Stefan Alkier, Richard B. Hays, and Leroy A. Huizenga. Waco: Baylor University Press, 2009.

Allegro, John M. "Fragments of a Qumran Scroll of Eschatological Midrashim." *JBL* 77 (1958): 350–54.

———. "Further Messianic References in Qumran Literature." *JBL* 75 (1956): 174–87.

———. *Qumrân Cave 4: I (4Q158–4Q186).* DJD 5. Oxford: Clarendon, 1968.

Allert, Craig D. *Revelation, Truth, Canon and Interpretation: Studies in Justin Martyr's Dialogue with Trypho.* VCSup 64. Leiden: Brill, 2002.

Althusser, Louis. "On Ideology." Pages 171–207 in *On the Reproduction of Capitalism.* London: Verso, 2014.

Amling, Ernst. "Eine Konjektur im Philemonbrief." *ZNW* 10 (1909): 261–62.

Arnold, Clinton E. *The Colossian Syncretism: The Interface between Christianity and Folk Belief at Colossae.* WUNT 77. Tübingen: Mohr Siebeck, 1995.

Ásta. *Categories We Live By: The Construction of Sex, Gender, Race, and Other Social Categories.* Oxford: Oxford University Press, 2018.

Attridge, Harold W. *Essays on John and Hebrews.* WUNT 264. Tübingen: Mohr Siebeck, 2010.

Bibliography

Austin, J. L. *How to Do Things with Words*. 2nd ed. Cambridge, MA: Harvard University Press, 1962.

Baars, W. *New Syrohexaplaric Texts*. Leiden: Brill, 1968.

Backhaus, K. "Der Hebräerbrief und die Paulus-Schule." *BZ* 37 (1993): 183–208. Reprinted as pages 21–48 in *Der sprechende Gott: Gesammelte Studien zum Hebräerbrief*. WUNT 240. Tübingen: Mohr Siebeck, 2009.

Balabanski, Vicky. "Where Is Philemon? The Case for a Logical Fallacy in the Correlation of the Data in Philemon and Colossians 1.1–2; 4.7–18." *JSNT* 38 (2015): 131–50.

Baltussen, Han. "From Polemic to Exegesis: The Ancient Philosophical Commentary." *Poetics Today* 28.2 (2007): 247–81.

Barclay, John M. G. *Colossians and Philemon*. Sheffield: Sheffield Academic, 1997.

———. "Mirror-Reading a Polemical Letter: Galatians as a Test Case." *JSNT* 31 (1987): 73–93.

Barnard, L. W. *Justin Martyr: His Life and Thought*. Cambridge: Cambridge University Press, 1967.

Barnes, A., and J. Barnes. "Time Out of Joint: Some Reflections on Anachronism." *The Journal of Aesthetics and Art Criticism* 47 (1989): 253–61.

Barr, James. "Paul and the LXX: A Note on Some Recent Work." *JTS*, n.s. 45 (1994): 593–601.

Barrett, C. K. "The Allegory of Abraham, Sarah, and Hagar in the Argument of Galatians." Pages 1–16 in *Rechtfertigung: Festschrift Ernst Käsemann*. Edited by Johannes Friedrich, Wolfgang Pohlmann, and Peter Stuhlmacher. Tübingen: Mohr Siebeck, 1976.

Barthélemy, Dominique. *Devanciers d'Aquila: Première publication intégrale du texte des fragments du Dodécaprophéton*. VTSup 10. Leiden: Brill, 1963.

Barton, John. "Déjà Lu: Intertextuality, Method or Theory?" Pages 1–16 in *Reading Job Intertextually*. Edited by Katharine Dell and Will Kynes. LHBOTS 574. London: Bloomsbury, 2013.

Bates, Matthew W. "Beyond Hays's *Echoes of Scripture in the Letters of Paul*: A Proposed Diachronic Intertextuality with Romans 10:16 as a Test Case." Pages 263–92 in *Paul and Scripture: Extending the Conversation*. Edited Christopher D. Stanley. Atlanta: Society of Biblical Literature, 2012.

Bauckham, Richard. *Jesus and the Eyewitnesses: The Gospels as Eyewitness Testimony*. Grand Rapids: Eerdmans, 2006.

———. "Pseudo-Apostolic Letters." *JBL* 107 (1988): 469–94. Reprinted as pages 123–49 in *The Jewish World around the New Testament: Collected Essays I*. WUNT 233. Tübingen: Mohr Siebeck, 2008.

Bauer, Thomas J. *Paulus und die kaiserzeitliche Epistolographie: Kontextualisierung*

Bibliography

und Analyse der Briefe an Philemon und an die Galater. WUNT 276. Tübingen: Mohr Siebeck, 2011.

Baum, Armin. *Pseudepigraphie und literarische Fälschung im frühen Christentum.* WUNT 2/138. Tübingen: Mohr Siebeck, 2001.

Baur, Ferdinand Christian. *Die sogenannten Pastoralbriefe des Apostel Paulus aufs neue kritisch untersucht.* Stuttgart: Cotta, 1835.

Beale, G. K., ed. *The Right Doctrine from the Wrong Texts? Essays on the Use of the Old Testament in the New.* Grand Rapids: Baker, 1994.

Beale, G. K., and D. A. Carson, eds. *Commentary on the New Testament Use of the Old Testament.* Grand Rapids: Baker Academic, 2007.

Beiser, Frederick C. *The German Historicist Tradition.* Oxford: Oxford University Press, 2011.

Bell, Richard H. *Provoked to Jealousy: The Origin and Purpose of the Jealousy Motif in Romans 9–11.* WUNT 2/63. Tübingen: Mohr Siebeck, 1994.

Bennett, Andrew. *The Author.* The New Critical Idiom. London: Routledge, 2005.

Berkley, Timothy W. *From a Broken Covenant to Circumcision of the Heart: Pauline Intertextual Exegesis in Romans 2:17–29.* SBLDS 175. Atlanta: Society of Biblical Literature, 2000.

Berthelot, Katell, Thierry Legrand, and André Paul, eds. *La Bibliothèque de Qumrân, 1: Torah—Genèse.* Paris: Editions du Cerf, 2008.

Betz, Hans Dieter. "Paul's 'Second Presence' in Colossians." Pages 507–18 in *Texts and Contexts: Biblical Texts in Their Textual and Situational Contexts; Essays in Honor of Lars Hartman.* Edited by Tord Fornberg and David Hellholm. Oslo: Scandinavian University Press, 1995.

Bindley, T. Herbert. Review of *Testimonies: Part II,* by J. Rendel Harris, with Vacher Burch. *JTS* 22 (1921): 279–82.

Blackman, Edwin Cyril. *Marcion and His Influence.* London: SPCK, 1948.

Blanc, C. *Origène: Commentaire sur Saint Jean.* 5 vols. SC 120, 157, 222, 290, 385. Paris: Cerf, 1966–1992.

Bloch, Renée. "Midrash." *DBSup* 5:1263–81. Reprint, pages 29–50 in *Approaches to Ancient Judaism: Theory and Practice.* Edited by W. S. Green. Missoula, MT: Scholars Press, 1978.

Bobichon, Philippe. "Comment Justin a-t-il acquis sa connaissance exceptionnelle des exégèses juives?" *RTP* 139 (2007): 101–26.

———. *Justin Martyr,* Dialogue avec Tryphon: *Édition critique, traduction, commentaire.* Paradosis 47. 2 vols. Fribourg: Academic Press, 2003.

Bockmuehl, Markus. "A Commentator's Approach to the 'Effective History' of Philippians." *JSNT* 60 (1995): 57–88.

———. "The Dead Sea Scrolls and the Origins of Biblical Commentary." Pages 3–29

Bibliography

in *Text, Thought, and Practice in Qumran and Early Christianity*. Edited by Ruth Clements and Daniel R. Schwartz. STDJ 84. Leiden: Brill, 2009.

———. *Jewish Law in Gentile Churches: Halakhah and the Beginning of Christian Public Ethics*. London: T&T Clark, 2000.

———. Review of *Jesus Remembered*, by James D. G. Dunn. *JTS* n.s. 56 (2005): 140–49.

Böhl, Eduard. *Die alttestamentlichen Citate im Neuen Testament*. Vienna: Braumüller, 1878.

———. *Forschungen nach einer Volksbibel zur Zeit Jesu und deren Zusammenhang mit der Septuaginta-Übersetzung*. Vienna: Braumüller, 1873.

Boismard, Marie-Émile. *La lettre de Saint Paul aux Laodicéens*. CahRB 42. Paris: Gabalda, 1999.

———. *L'énigme de la letter aux Éphésiens*. EBib 39. Paris: Gabalda, 1999.

———. "Paul's Letter to the Laodiceans." Pages 45–57 in *The Pauline Canon*. Edited by Stanley E. Porter. Leiden: Brill, 2004.

Bonsirven, Joseph. *Exégèse rabbinique et exégèse paulinienne*. Paris: Beauchesne et ses Fils, 1939.

Boomershine, Thomas E. "Jesus of Nazareth and the Watershed of Ancient Orality and Literacy." *Sem* 65 (1994): 7–36.

Bowman, Alan K. "Literacy in the Roman Empire: Mass and Mode." Pages 119–31 in *Literacy in the Roman World*. Edited by J. H. Humphrey. Journal of Roman Archaeology Supplementary Series. Ann Arbor: University of Michigan, 1991.

Boyarin, Daniel. *Border Lines: The Partition of Judaeo-Christianity*. Divinations: Rereading Late Ancient Religion. Philadelphia: University of Pennsylvania Press, 2004.

———. "Justin Martyr Invents Judaism." *Church History* 70 (2001): 427–61.

———. *A Radical Jew: Paul and the Politics of Identity*. Berkeley: University of California Press, 1994.

Boyd, Brian. *On the Origin of Stories: Evolution, Cognition, and Fiction*. Cambridge, MA: Belknap, 2009.

Brodie, Thomas L. "The Systematic Use of the Pentateuch in 1 Corinthians." Pages 441–57 in *The Corinthian Correspondence*. Edited by Reimund Bieringer. BETL 125. Leuven: Leuven University Press, 1996.

Brooke, A. E. *The Fragments of Heracleon*. Cambridge: Cambridge University Press, 1891.

Brooke, George J. "'The Canon within the Canon' at Qumran and in the New Testament." Pages 242–66 in *The Scrolls and the Scriptures: Qumran Fifty Years After*. Edited by Stanley E. Porter and Craig A. Evans. JSPSup 26. Sheffield: Sheffield Academic, 1997.

Bibliography

———. *Exegesis at Qumran: 4QFlorilegium in Its Jewish Context.* JSOTSup 29. Sheffield: JSOT Press, 1985.

Brox, Norbert, ed. *Pseudepigraphie in der heidnischen und jüdischchristlichen Antike.* Darmstadt: Wissenschaftliche Buchgesellschaft, 1977.

Bruce, F. F. "The Colossian Heresy." *BSac* 141 (1984): 195–208.

Bujard, Walter. *Stilanalytische Untersuchungen zum Kolosserbrief als Beitrag zur Methodik von Sprachvergleichen.* Göttingen: Vandenhoeck & Ruprecht, 1973.

Bultmann, Rudolf. Review of *Paulus und seine Bibel,* by Otto Michel. *TLZ* 9 (1933): 157–59.

Burkitt, F. C. *The Gospel History and Its Transmission.* Edinburgh: T&T Clark, 1906.

Burnett, Gary W. *Paul and the Salvation of the Individual.* BibInt 57. Leiden: Brill, 2001.

Byrskog, Samuel. "Co-Senders, Co-Authors and Paul's Use of the First Person Plural." *ZNW* 87 (1996): 230–50.

———. *Story as History—History as Story: The Gospel Tradition in the Context of Ancient Oral History.* WUNT 123. Tübingen: Mohr Siebeck, 2000.

Cadwallader, Alan H. "Refuting an Axiom of Scholarship on Colossae: Fresh Insights from New and Old Inscriptions." Pages 151–79 in *Colossae in Space and Time: Linking to an Ancient City.* Edited by Alan H. Cadwallader and Michael Trainor. Göttingen: Vandenhoeck & Ruprecht, 2011.

Calhoun, Craig. "Pierre Bourdieu." Pages 274–309 in *The Blackwell Companion to Major Contemporary Social Theorists.* Edited by George Ritzer. Oxford: Blackwell, 2003.

Campbell, Douglas A. "An Evangelical Paul: A Response to Francis Watson's *Paul and the Hermeneutics of Faith.*" *JSNT* 28 (2006): 337–51.

Campbell, Warren. *The Pauline History of Hebrews.* Oxford: Oxford University Press, 2025.

Campbell, William S. *Paul and the Creation of Christian Identity.* London: T&T Clark, 2006.

Cancik, Hubert. *Brill's New Pauly: Encyclopaedia of the Ancient World.* 22 vols. Leiden: Brill, 2002–2011.

Cappellus, Louis. *Critica Sacra, sive de variis quae in sacris veteris testamenti libris occurrunt lectionibus: Libri Sex.* Paris: Cramoisy, 1650.

Carleton Paget, James. "The *Epistle of Barnabas* and the Writings That Later Formed the New Testament." Pages 229–49 in *The Reception of the New Testament in the Apostolic Fathers.* Edited by A. Gregory and C. M. Tuckett. Oxford: Oxford University Press, 2005.

Carpzov, Johann Gottlob. *A Defence of the Hebrew Bible in Answer to the Charge of Corruption Brought against it by Mr. Whiston, in his* Essay towards restoring the true Text of the Old Testament, &c. *Wherein Mr. Whiston's Pretences are*

Bibliography

particularly Examined and Confuted. Translated by Moses Marcus. London: Bernard Lintot, 1729.

Carr, David M. *The Formation of the Hebrew Bible: A New Reconstruction.* Oxford: Oxford University Press, 2011.

Chadwick, Henry. "Florilegium." *RAC* 7:1131–60.

Childs, Brevard S. *Biblical Theology of the Old and New Testaments: Theological Reflection on the Christian Bible.* Philadelphia: Fortress, 1993.

———. *The Church's Guide to Reading Paul: The Canonical Shaping of the Pauline Corpus.* Grand Rapids: Eerdmans, 2008.

Clark, Elizabeth. *History, Theory, Text: Historians and the Linguistic Turn.* Cambridge, MA: Harvard University Press, 2004.

Clemen, August. *Der Gebrauch des Alten Testamentes in den Neutestamentlichen Schriften.* Gütersloh: Bertelsmann, 1895.

Collins, Anthony. *A Discourse on the Grounds and Reasons of the Christian Religion.* London: s.n., 1724.

———. *The Scheme of Literal Prophecy Considered: In a view of the Controversy, occasion'd by a late Book, Intitled,* A Discourse on the Grounds and Reasons of the Christian Religion. 2 vols. London: London and Westminster, 1726.

Cone, James H. "The Story Context of Black Theology." *ThTo* 32.2 (1975): 144–50.

Cook, Johann. "The Septuagint of Genesis: Text and/or Interpretation?" Pages 315–30 in *Studies in the Book of Genesis: Literature, Redaction and History.* Edited by André Wénin. Leuven: Peeters, 2001.

Cook, John Granger. "1 Cor 15:33: The *Status Quaestionis.*" *NovT* 62 (2020): 375–91.

Cosgrove, Charles H. "Justin Martyr and the Emerging Christian Canon: Observations on the Purpose and Destination of the Dialogue with Trypho." *VC* 36 (1982): 209–32.

Cranfield, C. E. B. *The Epistle to the Romans.* ICC. Edinburgh: T&T Clark, 1979.

Crawford, Sidnie White. "4QDtn: Biblical Manuscript or Excerpted Text?" Pages 13–20 in *Of Scribes and Scrolls: Studies on the Hebrew Bible, Intertestamental Judaism, and Christian Origins Presented to John Strugnell on the Occasion of His Sixtieth Birthday.* Edited by H. W. Attridge, John J. Collins, and Thomas H. Tobin. College Theology Society Resources in Religion 5. Lanham: University Press of America, 1990.

———. "Reading Deuteronomy in the Second Temple Period." Pages 127–40 in *Reading the Present in the Qumran Library: The Perception of the Contemporary by Means of Scriptural Interpretations.* Edited by Kristin de Troyer and Armin Lange. SBLSymS 30. Atlanta: Society of Biblical Literature, 2005.

Crossan, John Dominic. *Who Killed Jesus? Exposing the Roots of Anti-Semitism in the Gospel Story of the Death of Jesus.* San Francisco: HarperSanFrancisco, 1996.

Bibliography

Culler, Jonathan. *The Pursuit of Signs: Semiotics, Literature, Deconstruction.* London: Routledge, 1981.

D'Amico, Robert. "Historicism." Pages 243–52 in *A Companion to the Philosophy of History and Historiography.* Edited by Aviezer Tucker. Oxford: Wiley-Blackwell, 2009.

Daniélou, Jean. *Études d'exégèse judéo-chrétienne (Les Testimonia).* ThH 5. Paris: Beauschesne, 1966.

Davidson, Samuel. *Sacred Hermeneutics: Developed and Applied.* Edinburgh: Thomas Clark, 1843.

DeMaris, R. E. *The Colossian Controversy: Wisdom in Dispute at Colossae.* JSNTSup 96. Sheffield: Sheffield Academic, 1994.

Derrenbacker, R. A., Jr. *Ancient Compositional Practices and the Synoptic Problem.* BETL 186. Leuven: Leuven University Press, 2005.

Dettwiler, Andreas. "La lettre aux Colossiens: Une théologie de la mémoire." *NTS* 59 (2013): 109–28.

Devreesse, Robert. "Chaines exégétiques grecques." *DBSup* 1:1084–1233.

Dinter, Paul E. "Paul and the Prophet Isaiah." *BTB* 13 (1983): 48–52.

Dittmar, Wilhelm. *Vetus Testamentum in Novo: Die alttestamentlichen Parallelen des Neuen Testaments im Wortlaut der Urtexte und der Septuaginta zusammengestellt.* 2 vols. Göttingen: Vandenhoeck & Ruprecht, 1899–1903.

Dodd, C. H. *According to the Scriptures: The Sub-Structure of New Testament Theology.* London: Nisbet, 1952.

———. *The Old Testament in the New.* Philadelphia: Fortress, 1963.

Doering, Lutz. "Excerpted Texts in Second Temple Judaism: A Survey of the Evidence." Pages 1–38 in *Selecta colligere, II: Beiträge zur Technik des Sammelns und Kompilierens griechischer Texte von der Antike bis zum Humanismus.* Edited by Rosa Maria Piccione and Matthias Perkams. Alessandria: Edizioni dell-Orso, 2005.

Donelson, L. *Pseudepigraphy and Ethical Argument in the Pastoral Epistles.* HUT 22. Tübingen: Mohr Siebeck, 1986.

Donfried, Karl Paul. *Paul, Thessalonica, and Early Christianity.* Grand Rapids: Eerdmans, 2002.

———. *The Setting of Second Clement in Early Christianity.* NovTSup 38. Leiden: Brill, 1974.

Döpke, Johann Christian Carl. *Hermeneutik der neutestamentlichen Schriftsteller.* Leipzig: Friedrich Christian Wilhelm Vogel, 1829.

Driver, D. *Brevard Childs, Biblical Theologian.* Grand Rapids: Baker Academic, 2012.

Drusius, Johannes. *Parallela Sacra: Hoc est, Locorum veteris Testamenti cum ijs,*

Bibliography

quae in novo citantur coniuncta commemoratio, Ebraice et Graece. Franeker: Aegidius Radaeud, 1588.

Duff, Jeremy. "A Reconsideration of Pseudepigraphy in Early Christianity." DPhil thesis, University of Oxford, 1998.

Duncan, Julie A. "Deuteronomy, Book of." *EDSS* 1:198–202.

———. "Excerpted Texts of Deuteronomy at Qumran." *RevQ* 18/69 (1997): 43–62.

Dunn, James D. G. *Christianity in the Making.* Volume 1, *Jesus Remembered.* Grand Rapids: Eerdmans, 2003.

———. *The Epistles to the Colossians and to Philemon: A Commentary on the Greek Text.* NIGTC. Grand Rapids: Eerdmans, 1996.

———. *Neither Jew nor Greek: A Contested Identity.* Vol. 3 of *Christianity in the Making.* Grand Rapids: Eerdmans, 2015.

———. Review of *Holy Scripture in the Qumran Commentaries and Pauline Letters,* by Timothy H. Lim. *JR* 79 (1999): 284–85.

———. *Romans 9–16.* WBC 38B. Dallas: Word Books, 1988.

———. *The Theology of Paul's Letter to the Galatians.* Cambridge: Cambridge University Press, 1993.

———. *The Theology of Paul the Apostle.* Grand Rapids: Eerdmans, 1998.

Eastman, Susan Grove. *Paul and the Person: Reframing Paul's Anthropology.* Grand Rapids: Eerdmans, 2017.

———. Review of *Paul and the Hermeneutics of Faith,* by Francis Watson. *JBL* 125 (2006): 610–14.

Eco, Umberto. *Six Walks in the Fictional Woods.* Cambridge, MA: Harvard University Press, 1994.

Edsall, Benjamin A. "*Kerygma,* Catechesis and Other Things We Used to Find: Twentieth-Century Research on Early Christian Teaching since Alfred Seeberg (1903)." *CurBR* 10 (2012): 410–41.

———. "Paul's Rhetoric of Knowledge: The ΟΥΚ ΟΙΔΑΤΕ Question in 1 Corinthians." *NovT* 55 (2013): 252–71.

Edsall, Benjamin, and Jennifer Strawbridge. "The Songs We Used to Sing: Hymn 'Traditions' and Reception in Pauline Letters." *JSNT* 37 (2015): 290–311.

Ehrman, Bart. *The Apostolic Fathers.* 2 vols. LCL 24. Cambridge, MA: Harvard University Press, 2003.

———. *Forgery and Counterforgery: The Use of Literary Deceit in Early Christian Polemics.* Oxford: Oxford University Press, 2012.

Eisele, Wilfried. "Chronos und Kairos: Zum soteriologischen Verhältnis von Zeit und Ewigkeit in den Pastoralbriefen." *Early Christianity* 3 (2012): 468–89.

Ellis, E. Earle. *The Making of the New Testament Documents.* Leiden: Brill, 1999.

———. "Midrash, Targum and New Testament Quotation." Pages 61–69 in *Neo-*

testamentica et Semitica: Studies in Honour of Matthew Black. Edited by E. Earle Ellis and Max Wilcox. Edinburgh: T&T Clark, 1969.

———. *The Old Testament in Early Christianity: Canon and Interpretation in the Light of Modern Research.* WUNT 54. Tübingen: Mohr Siebeck, 1991.

———. *Paul's Use of the Old Testament.* Edinburgh: Oliver and Boyd, 1957. Reprint, Eugene, OR: Wipf & Stock, 2003.

Engberg-Pedersen, Troels. "Once more a Lutheran Paul?" *SJT* 59 (2006): 439–60.

Evans, Craig A. "Jesus and the Continuing Exile of Israel." Pages 77–100 in *Jesus and the Restoration of Israel: A Critical Assessment of N. T. Wright's Jesus and the Victory of God.* Edited by Carey C. Newman. Downers Grove, IL: InterVarsity, 1999.

———. "Listening for Echoes of Interpreted Scripture." Pages 47–51 in Evans and Sanders, *Paul and the Scriptures of Israel.* JSNTSup 83. SSEJC 1. Sheffield: Sheffield Academic, 1993.

———. *To See and Not Perceive: Isaiah 6.9–10 in Early Jewish and Christian Interpretation.* JSOTSup 64. Sheffield: JSOT Press, 1989.

Evans, Craig A., and James A. Sanders, eds. *Paul and the Scriptures of Israel.* JSNTSup 83. SSEJC 1. Sheffield: Sheffield Academic, 1993.

Evans, Robert. *Reception History, Tradition and Biblical Interpretation: Gadamer and Jauss in Current Practice.* London: T&T Clark, 2014.

Evanson, Edward. *The Dissonance of the Four Generally Received Evangelists, and the Evidence of their Respective Authenticity Examined.* Ipswich: G. Jermyn, 1792.

Falcetta, Alessandro. "The Testimony Research of James Rendel Harris." *NovT* 45 (2003): 280–99.

Falls, Thomas B. *St. Justin Martyr:* Dialogue with Trypho. Revised edition by Thomas P. Halton. Washington, DC: Catholic University of America Press, 2003.

Fernández Marcos, Natalio. *The Septuagint in Context: Introduction to the Greek Versions of the Bible.* Translated by Wilfred G. E. Watson. Leiden: Brill, 2000.

Finley, Kate, and Joshua Seachris. "Narrative, Theology, and Philosophy of Religion." Pages 1688–94 in vol. 3 of *The Encyclopedia of Philosophy of Religion.* Edited by S. Goetz and C. Taliaferro. Hoboken, NJ: Wiley-Blackwell, 2022.

Finsterbusch, Karin. *Die Thora als Lebensweisung für Heidenchristen: Studien zur Bedeutung der Thora für die paulinische Ethik.* SUNT 20. Göttingen: Vandenhoeck & Ruprecht, 1996.

Fitzmyer, Joseph A. *First Corinthians: A New Translation with Introduction and Commentary.* AB 32. New Haven: Yale University Press, 2008.

———. "4QTestimonia and the New Testament." *TS* 18 (1957): 513–37. Reprinted in

Bibliography

Essays on the Semitic Background of the New Testament. London: Geoffrey Chapman, 1971.

Foerster, W. *Gnosis: A Selection of Gnostic Texts.* Translated by R. McL. Wilson. 2 vols. Oxford: Clarendon, 1972–1974.

Foster, Paul. "The Epistles of Ignatius of Antioch and the Writings That Later Formed the New Testament." Pages 159–86 in *The Reception of the New Testament in the Apostolic Fathers.* Edited by A. Gregory and C. M. Tuckett. Oxford: Oxford University Press, 2005.

Foucault, M. "Technologies of the Self." Pages 16–49 in *Technologies of the Self: A Seminar with Michel Foucault.* Edited by L. H. Martin, H. Gutman, and P. H. Hutton. Amherst: University of Massachusetts Press, 1988.

Fowl, Stephen. "Learning to Be a Gentile: Christ's Transformation and Redemption of Our Past." Pages 22–40 in *Christology and Scripture: Interdisciplinary Perspectives.* Edited by A. T. Lincoln and A. Paddison. London: T&T Clark, 2007.

Francis, F. O., and W. A. Meeks, eds. *Conflict at Colossae: A Problem in the Interpretation of Early Christianity Illustrated by Selected Modern Studies.* Revised edition. Missoula, MT: Scholars Press, 1975.

Frank, Nicole. *Der Kolosserbrief im Kontext des paulinischen Erbes: Eine intertextuelle Studie zur Auslegung und Fortschreibung der Paulustradition.* WUNT 2/271. Tübingen: Mohr Siebeck, 2009.

———. "Der Kolosserbrief und die 'Philosophia': Pseudepigraphie als Spiegel frühchristlicher Auseinandersetzungen um die Auslegung des paulinischen Erbes." Pages 411–32 in *Pseudepigraphie und Verfasserfiktion in frühchristlichen Briefen.* Edited by Jörg Frey, Jens Herzer, Martina Janssen, and Clare K. Rothschild. WUNT 246. Tübingen: Mohr Siebeck, 2009.

Fredriksen, Paula. "Paul and Augustine: Conversion Narratives, Orthodox Traditions, and the Retrospective Self." *JTS* 37.1 (1986): 3–34.

Frei, Hans W. *The Eclipse of Biblical Narrative: A Study in Eighteenth and Nineteenth Century Hermeneutics.* New Haven: Yale University Press, 1974.

———. *The Identity of Jesus Christ.* Philadelphia: Fortress, 1975.

Funk, R. W. "The Apostolic *Parousia*: Form and Significance." Pages 249–68 in *Christian History and Interpretation: Studies Presented to John Knox.* Edited by W. R. Farmer, C. F. D. Moule, and R. R. Niebuhr. Cambridge: Cambridge University Press, 1967.

Fuß, Barbara. *"Dies ist die Zeit, von der geschrieben ist . . ." Die expliziten Zitate aus dem Buch Hosea in den Handschriften von Qumran und im Neuen Testament.* NTAbh 37. Münster: Aschendorff, 2000.

Gadamer, Hans-Georg. "Classical and Philosophical Hermeneutics." *Theory, Culture and Society* 23 (2006): 29–56.

—————. *Truth and Method*. 2nd ed. Translated by Joel Weinsheimer and Donald G. Marshall. London: Continuum, 1989.

Gamble, Harry Y. *Books and Readers in the Early Church: A History of Early Christian Texts*. New Haven: Yale University Press, 1995.

—————. "Marcion and the 'Canon.'" Pages 195–213 in *Origins to Constantine*. Volume 1 of *The Cambridge History of Christianity*. Edited by Margaret M. Mitchell and Frances M. Young. Cambridge: Cambridge University Press, 2006.

Ganzevoort, R. Ruard, Maaike de Haardt, and Michael Scherer-Rath, eds. *Religious Stories We Live By: Narrative Approaches in Theology and Religious Studies*. Studies in Theology and Religion 19. Leiden: Brill, 2014.

Gerhardsson, Birger. *Memory and Manuscript: Oral Tradition and Written Transmission in Rabbinic Judaism and Early Christianity with Tradition and Transmission in Early Christianity*. Biblical Resource Series. Grand Rapids: Eerdmans, 1998.

Gillingham, S. "Messianic Prophecy and the Psalms." *Theology* 99 (1996): 114–24.

Gnilka, Joachim. "Zur Interpretation der Bibel: die Wirkungsgeschichte." Pages 1589–1601 in *The Interpretation of the Bible: The International Symposium in Slovenia*. Edited by Joze Krašovec. JSOTSup 289. Sheffield: Sheffield Academic, 1998.

Gombis, Timothy G. "The 'Transgressor' and the 'Curse of the Law': The Logic of Paul's Argument in Galatians 2–3." *NTS* 53 (2007): 81–93.

Gough, Henry. *The New Testament quotations, collated with the Scriptures of the Old Testament, in the original Hebrew and the version of the LXX; and with the other writings, Apocryphal, Talmudic, and classical, cited or alleged so to be, with notes, and a complete index*. London: Walton and Maberly, 1855.

Gowan, Donald E. "The Exile in Jewish Apocalyptic." Pages 205–23 in *Scripture in History and Theology: Essays in Honor of J. Coert Rylaarsdam*. Edited by Arthur L. Merrill and Thomas W. Overholt. PTMS 17. Pittsburgh: Pickwick, 1977.

Gray, Patrick. *Paul as a Problem in History and Culture: The Apostle and His Critics through the Centuries*. Grand Rapids: Baker Academic, 2016.

Greenspoon, Leonard. "By the Letter? Word for Word? Scriptural Citation in Paul." Pages 9–24 in *Paul and Scripture: Extending the Conversation*. Edited by Christopher D. Stanley. Atlanta: Society of Biblical Literature, 2012.

Gregory, Andrew. "*1 Clement* and the Writings That Later Formed the New Testament." Pages 129–57 in *The Reception of the New Testament in the Apostolic Fathers*. Edited by A. Gregory and C. M. Tuckett. Oxford: Oxford University Press, 2005.

Gregory, Andrew, and C. M. Tuckett. "Reflections on Method: What Constitutes

Bibliography

the Use of the Writings That Later Formed the New Testament in the Apostolic Fathers?" Pages 61–82 in *The Reception of the New Testament in the Apostolic Fathers*. Edited by A. Gregory and C. M. Tuckett. Oxford: Oxford University Press, 2005.

———. "*2 Clement* and the Writings That Later Formed the New Testament." Pages 251–92 in *The Reception of the New Testament in the Apostolic Fathers*. Edited by A. Gregory and C. M. Tuckett. Oxford: Oxford University Press, 2005.

Griffiths, Paul J. *Religious Reading: The Place of Reading in the Practice of Religion*. Oxford: Oxford University Press, 1999.

Grinfield, Edward William. *An Apology for the Septuagint, in which its claims to biblical and canonical authority are briefly stated and vindicated*. London: Pickering, 1850.

———. *Novum Testamentum Graecum, editio Hellenistica*. 2 vols. London: Pickering, 1843.

———. *Scholia Hellenistica in Novum Testamentum*. London: Pickering, 1848.

Groves, J. W. *Actualization and Interpretation in the Old Testament*. Atlanta: Scholars Press, 1987.

Guignebert, Charles. Review of *Testimonies*, by J. Rendel Harris with Vacher Burch. *RHR* 81 (1920): 58–69.

Gunther, J. J. *St. Paul's Opponents and Their Background: A Study of Apocalyptic and Jewish Sectarian Teachings*. NovTSup 35. Leiden: Brill, 1973.

Gupta, Nijay. "Mirror-Reading Moral Issues in Paul's Letters." *JSNT* 34 (2012): 361–81.

———. "What Is in a Name? The Hermeneutics of Authorship Analysis Concerning Colossians." *CurBR* 11 (2013): 196–217.

Hadot, Pierre. *Philosophy as a Way of Life: Spiritual Exercises from Socrates to Foucault*. Edited by Arnold I. Davidson. Translated by Michael Chase. Oxford: Blackwell, 1995.

Häfner, Gerd. *'Nützlich zur Belehrung' (2 Tim 3,16): Die Rolle der Schrift in den Pastoralbriefen im Rahmen der Paulusrezeption*. HBS 25. Freiburg: Herder, 2000.

Hagner, Donald A. *The Use of the Old and New Testaments in Clement of Rome*. NovTSup 34. Leiden: Brill, 1973.

Hardy, Thomas. "The Respectable Burgher on 'The Higher Criticism.'" Pages 198–99 in vol. 1 of *The Complete Poetical Works of Thomas Hardy*. Edited by Samuel Hynes. Oxford: Clarendon, 1982.

Harl, Marguerite. *La Genèse*. La Bible d'Alexandrie 1. Paris: Éditions du Cerf, 1986.

Harnack, Adolf von. *Marcion: Das Evangelium von fremden Gott; Eine Monographie zur Geschichte der Grundlegung der katholischen Kirche*. TU 45. Leipzig: J. C. Hinrichs, 1921.

Bibliography

———. "The Old Testament in the Pauline Letters and in the Pauline Churches." Pages 27–49 in *Understanding Paul's Ethics: Twentieth-Century Approaches.* Edited by Brian Rosner. Grand Rapids: Eerdmans, 1995. English translation of "Das Alte Testament in den paulinischen Briefen und in den paulinischen Gemeinden." *Sitzungsberichte der Preußischen Akademie der Wissenschaften* (1928): 124–41.

Harrington, D. J. "Christians and Jews in Colossians." Pages 153–61 in *Diaspora Jews and Judaism: Essays in Honor of and in Dialogue with A. T. Kraabel.* Edited by Andrew J. Overman and Robert S. MacLennan. SFSHJ 41. Atlanta: Scholars Press, 1992.

Harris, J. Rendel, with Vacher Burch. *Testimonies.* 2 vols. Cambridge: Cambridge University Press, 1916–1920.

Harris, Murray J. *The Second Epistle to the Corinthians: A Commentary on the Greek Text.* NIGTC. Grand Rapids: Eerdmans, 2005.

Harrison, P. N. *Paulines and Pastorals.* London: Villiers, 1964.

———. *The Problem of the Pastoral Epistles.* London: Oxford University Press, 1921.

Hartog, Pieter B. *Pesher and Hypomnema: A Comparison of Two Commentary Traditions from the Hellenistic-Roman Period.* STDJ 121. Leiden: Brill, 2017.

Hasel, G. F. *Old Testament Theology: Basic Issues in the Current Debate.* Revised edition. Grand Rapids: Eerdmans, 1972.

Hatch, Edwin. *Essays in Biblical Greek.* Oxford: Clarendon, 1889.

Hatina, Thomas R. "Intertextuality and Historical Criticism in New Testament Studies: Is There a Relationship?" *BibInt* 7 (1999): 28–43.

Hauerwas, Stanley, and L. Gregory Jones. *Why Narrative? Readings in Narrative Theology.* Grand Rapids: Eerdmans, 1989.

Hayes, Christine. "The Complicated Goy in Classical Rabbinic Sources." Pages 147–67 in *Perceiving the Other in Ancient Judaism and Early Christianity.* Edited by Michal Bar-Asher Siegal, Wolfgang Grünstaudl, and Matthew Thiessen. WUNT 394. Tübingen: Mohr Siebeck, 2017.

———. "The Goy: A Synchronic Proposal." *Ancient Jew Review*, 27 February 2019. https://www.ancientjewreview.com/read/2019/2/13/the-goy-a-synchronic -proposal.

Hays, Richard B. "Can the Gospels Teach Us How to Read the Old Testament?" *Pro Ecclesia* 11 (2002): 402–18.

———. *Echoes of Scripture in the Letters of Paul.* New Haven: Yale University Press, 1989.

———. *The Faith of Jesus Christ: The Narrative Substructure of Galatians 3:1–4:11.* 2nd ed. Grand Rapids: Eerdmans, 2002.

———. "On the Rebound: A Response to Critiques of *Echoes of Scripture in the*

Bibliography

Letters of Paul." Pages 163–89 in *The Conversion of the Imagination: Paul as Interpreter of Israel's Scripture.* Grand Rapids: Eerdmans, 2005.

———. "Paul's Hermeneutics and the Question of Truth." *ProEccl* 16 (2007): 126–33.

———. Review of *Die Schrift als Zeuge des Evangeliums*, by Dietrich-Alex Koch. *JBL* 107 (1988): 331–33.

———. "The Role of Scripture in Paul's Ethics." Pages in 30–47 in *Theology and Ethics in Paul and His Interpreters.* Edited by Eugene H. Lovering Jr. and Jerry L. Sumney. Nashville: Abingdon, 2017. Reprinted as pages 143–62 in Richard B. Hays, *The Conversion of the Imagination.* Grand Rapids: Eerdmans, 2005.

Heil, John P. *The Rhetorical Role of Scripture in 1 Corinthians.* Studies in Biblical Literature 14. Leiden: Brill, 2005.

Heilig, Christoph. *Paul the Storyteller: A Narratological Approach.* Grand Rapids: Eerdmans, 2024.

———. *Paulus als Erzähler? Eine narratologische Perspektive auf die Paulusbriefe.* BZNW 237. Berlin: de Gruyter, 2020.

Heilmann, Jan. "Ancient Literary Culture and Meals in the Greco-Roman World: The Role of Reading during Ancient Symposia and Its Relevance for the New Testament." *JTS* 73.1 (2022): 104–25.

———. *Lesen in Antike und frühem Christentum: Kulturgeschichtliche, philologische sowie kognitionswissenschaftliche Perspektiven und deren Bedeutung für die neutestamentliche Exegese.* TANZ 66. Tübingen: Francke, 2021.

Heine, Ronald. *Origen: Commentary on the Gospel according to John.* 2 vols. Washington, DC: Catholic University of America Press, 1989–1993.

Hengel, Martin. "The Beginning of Christianity as a Jewish-Messianic and Universalistic Movement." Pages 85–100 in *The Beginnings of Christianity.* Edited by J. Pastor and M. Mor. Jerusalem: Yad Ben-Zvi Press, 2005.

———. "Tasks of New Testament Scholarship." *BBR* 6 (1996): 67–86.

Hengel, Martin, with Roland Deines. *The Septuagint as Christian Scripture: Its Prehistory and the Problem of Its Canon.* Translated by Mark E. Biddle. Edinburgh: T&T Clark, 2002.

Henze, Matthias, and David Lincicum, eds. *Israel's Scriptures in Early Christian Writings: The Use of the Old Testament in the New.* Grand Rapids: Eerdmans, 2023.

Hezser, Catherine. *Jewish Literacy in Roman Palestine.* TSAJ 81. Tübingen: Mohr Siebeck, 2001.

Hibshman, Grace. "Narrative, Second-Person Experience, and Self-Perception: A Reason It Is Good to Conceive of One's Life Narratively." *Philosophical Quarterly* 73.3 (2022): 615–27.

Hickling, C. J. A. "Paul's Reading of Isaiah." Pages 215–23 in *Studia Biblica 1979: III.*

Papers on Paul and Other New Testament Authors. Edited by Elizabeth A. Livingstone. JSNTSup 3. Sheffield: JSOT Press, 1980.

Hinchman, Lewis P., and Sandra K. Hinchman, eds. *Memory, Identity, Community: The Idea of Narrative in the Human Sciences.* Albany: SUNY Press, 1997.

Hirsh, J. B., R. A. Mar, and J. B. Peterson. "Personal Narratives as the Highest Level of Cognitive Integration." *Behavioral and Brain Sciences* 36.3 (2013): 216–17.

Hodgson, Robert. "The Testimony Hypothesis." *JBL* 98 (1979): 361–78.

Hofius, Otfried. "The Adam-Christ Antithesis and the Law: Reflections on Romans 5:12–21." Pages 165–206 in *Paul and the Mosaic Law.* Edited by James D. G. Dunn. Grand Rapids: Eerdmans, 2001.

———. "Der Psalter als Zeuges des Evangeliums: Die Verwendung der Septuaginta-Psalmen in den ersten beiden Hauptteilen des Römerbriefes." Pages 38–57 in *Paulusstudien II.* WUNT 143. Tübingen: Mohr Siebeck, 2002.

Holladay, Carl R. *Fragments from Hellenistic Jewish Authors.* 4 vols. Chico, CA: Scholars Press, 1983.

Holmes, Michael. "Polycarp's *Letter to the Philippians* and the Writings That Later Formed the New Testament." Pages 187–227 in *The Reception of the New Testament in the Apostolic Fathers.* Edited by A. Gregory and C. M. Tuckett. Oxford: Oxford University Press, 2005.

Holtz, G. *Die Pastoralbriefe.* THKNT 13. Berlin: Evangelische Verlagsanstalt, 1965.

Holtz, Traugott. "Zur Frage der inhaltlichen Weisungen bei Paulus." *TLZ* 106 (1981): 385–400. Reprinted as "The Question of the Content of Paul's Instructions." In *Understanding Paul's Ethics: Twentieth-Century Approaches.* Edited by Brian Rosner. Grand Rapids: Eerdmans, 1995.

Hommes, N. J. *Het Testimoniaboek: Studiën over O.T. Citaten in het N.T. en bij de Patres, Met Critische Beschouwingen over de Theorieën van J. Rendel Harris en D. Plooy.* Amsterdam: Noord-Hollandsche Uitgevers-Maatschappij, 1935.

Hooker, Morna. "In His Own Image?" Pages 28–44 in *What about the New Testament? Essays in Honour of Christopher Evans.* Edited by Morna Hooker and Colin Hickling. London: SCM, 1975.

———. "Were There False Teachers in Colossae?" Pages 315–31 in *Christ and Spirit in the New Testament: Essays in Honour of C. F. D. Moule.* Edited by B. Lindars and S. S. Smalley. Cambridge: Cambridge University Press, 1973. Reprint, pages 121–36 in *From Adam to Christ: Essays on Paul.* Cambridge: Cambridge University Press, 1990.

Hoppe, Rudolf. "Der Topos der Prophetenverfolgung bei Paulus." *NTS* 50 (2004): 535–49.

Horbury, William. "Jewish-Christian Relations in Barnabas and Justin Martyr." Pages 315–45 in *Jews and Christians: The Parting of the Ways A.D. 70 to 135.* Edited by J. D. G. Dunn. WUNT 66. Tübingen: Mohr Siebeck, 1992.

Bibliography

———. *Jews and Christians: In Contact and Controversy.* Edinburgh: T&T Clark, 1998.

Horne, Thomas Hartwell. *An Introduction to the Criticism of the Old Testament and to Biblical Interpretation, with an Analysis of the Books of the Old Testament and Apocrypha.* Reviewed and edited by John Ayre. London: Longman, Green, Longman, and Roberts, 1860.

Horner, Timothy J. *Listening to Trypho: Justin Martyr's* Dialogue *Reconsidered.* CBET 28. Leuven: Peeters, 2001.

Horsfall, Nicholas. "Methods of Writing, Memorisation, and Research." *JRA* 11 (1998): 565–71.

Hübner, Hans. "Der Diskussion um die deuteropaulinischen Briefe seit 1970. I, Der Kolosserbrief." *TRu* 68 (2003): 263–85, 395–440.

———. "Intertextualität—die hermeneutische Strategie des Paulus: Zu einem neuen Versuch der theologischen Rezeption des Alten Testaments im Neuen." *TLZ* 116 (1991): cols. 881–98.

———. Review of *Die Schrift als Zeuge des Evangeliums*, by Dietrich-Alex Koch. *TLZ* 113 (1988): 349–52.

———. *Vetus Testamentum in Novo. Band 2: Corpus Paulinum.* Göttingen: Vandenhoeck & Ruprecht, 1997.

———. "Vetus Testamentum und Vetus Testamentum in Novo Receptum: Die Frage nach dem Kanon des Alten Testaments aus neutestamentlicher Sicht." *Jahrbuch für biblische Theologie* 3 (1988): 147–62.

Hughes, Aaron. "Presenting the Past: The Genre of Commentary in Theoretical Perspective." *Method and Theory in the Study of Religion* 15, no. 2 (2003): 148–68.

Hühn, Eugen. *Die alttestamentlichen Citate und Reminiscenzen im Neuen Testamente.* Tübingen: Mohr Siebeck, 1900.

Hull, D. L. "In Defense of Anti-Presentism." *Scientia Poetica* 8 (2004): 251–54.

———. "In Defense of Presentism." *History and Theory* 18 (1979): 1–15.

Hurtado, Larry, and Chris Keith. "Writing and Book Production in the Hellenistic and Roman Periods." Pages 63–80 in *The New Cambridge History of the Bible, Volume 1: From the Beginnings to 600.* Edited by James Carleton Paget and Joachim Schaper. Cambridge: Cambridge University Press, 2013.

Iggers, G. C. "Historicism: The History and Meaning of the Term." *Journal of the History of Ideas* 56 (1995): 129–52.

———. "The Intellectual Foundations of Nineteenth-Century 'Scientific' History: The German Model." Pages 41–58 in *1800–1945.* Volume 4 of *The Oxford History of Historical Writing.* Edited by Stuart Macintyre, Juan Maiguashca, Attila Pók. Oxford: Oxford University Press, 2011.

Bibliography

Irwin, William. "Against Intertextuality." *Philosophy and Literature* 28 (2004): 227–42.

Janko, Richard. "The Derveni Papyrus ('Diagoras of Melos, Apopyrgizontes Logoi?'): A New Translation." *Classical Philology* 96.1 (2001): 1–32.

Jannidis, Fotis, Gerhard Lauer, Mathias Martinez, and Simone Winko, eds. *Texte zur Theorie der Autorschaft.* Stuttgart: Reclam, 2000.

Janssen, Martina. *Unter falschem Namen: Eine kritische Forschungsbilanz frühchristlicher Pseudepigraphie.* Frankfurt: Lang, 2003.

Jervis, L. Ann. *Paul and Time: Life in the Temporality of Christ.* Grand Rapids: Baker Academic, 2023.

Jewett, Robert. *Romans: A Commentary.* Hermeneia. Minneapolis: Fortress, 2007.

Johnson, Franklin. *The Quotations of the New Testament from the Old Considered in the Light of General Literature.* Philadelphia: American Baptist Publication Society, 1896.

Johnson, William A. *Readers and Reading Culture in the High Roman Empire: A Study of Elite Communities.* Classical Culture and Society. Oxford: Oxford University Press, 2010.

Joyce, Paul. "A Tale of Two Sisters: Judaism and Christianity." *Theology* 96 (1993): 384–90.

Judge, Edwin A. "The Early Christians as a Scholastic Community." *JRH* 1.1 (1960): 4–15.

———. "The Early Christians as a Scholastic Community: Parts I and II." Pages 526–52 in *The First Christians in the Roman World: Augustan and New Testament Essays.* Edited by J. R. Harrison. WUNT 2/229. Tübingen: Mohr Siebeck, 2010.

———. "The Early Christians as a Scholastic Community: Part II." *JRH* 1.3 (1961): 125–37.

Junius, Franciscus. *Sacrorum Parallelorum libri tres.* London: G. Bishop, 1591.

Kamesar, Adam. *Jerome, Greek Scholarship, and the Hebrew Bible: A Study of the Quaestiones Hebraicae in Genesim.* Oxford: Clarendon, 1993.

Karris, R. J. "The Background and Significance of the Polemic of the Pastoral Epistles." *JBL* 92 (1973): 549–63.

Käsemann, E. *Commentary on Romans.* Translated by G. W. Bromiley. Grand Rapids: Eerdmans, 1980.

Kautzsch, Emil Friedrich. *De veteris testamenti locis a Paulo Apostolo allegatis.* Leipzig: Metzger & Wittig, 1869.

Kelhoffer, James A. *Persecution, Persuasion and Power: Readiness to Withstand Hardship as a Corroboration of Legitimacy in the New Testament.* WUNT 270. Tübingen: Mohr Siebeck, 2010.

Bibliography

Kelsey, David H. *Proving Doctrine: The Uses of Scripture in Modern Theology.* Harrisburg, PA: Trinity Press International, 1999.

Kiley, Mark. *Colossians as Pseudepigraphy.* Sheffield: JSOT Press, 1986.

Kinzig, Wolfram. "Philosemitismus angesichts des Endes? Bemerkungen zu einem vergessenen Kapitel jüdisch-christlicher Beziehungen in der Alten Kirche." Pages 59–95 in *Kaum zu glauben: Von der Häresie und dem Umgang mit ihr.* Edited by A. Lexutt and V. von Bülow. Arbeiten zur Theologiegeschichte 5. Rheinbach: CMZ, 1998.

Klauck, Hans-Josef. *Ancient Letters and the New Testament: A Guide to Context and Exegesis.* Translated and edited by D. P. Bailey. Waco, TX: Baylor University Press, 2006.

Klauser Theodor et al., eds. *Reallexikon für Antike und Christentum.* 31 vols. Stuttgart: Hiersemann, 1950–.

Knibb, Michael A. "Exile in the Damascus Document." *JSOT* 25 (1983): 99–117.

———. "The Exile in the Literature of the Intertestamental Period." *HeyJ* 17 (1976): 253–72.

———. *The Qumran Community.* Cambridge Commentaries on Writings of the Jewish and Christian World, 200 BC to AD 200 (2). Cambridge: Cambridge University Press, 1987.

Koch, Dietrich-Alex. *Die Schrift als Zeuge des Evangeliums: Untersuchungen zur Verwendung und zum Verständnis der Schrift bei Paulus.* BHT 69. Tübingen: Mohr Siebeck, 1986.

Kok, Kobus. "Die Irrglaube in Kolosse: Aanbidding van of met engele in Kolossense." *HvTSt* 66 (2010): 1–7.

Kouremenos, Theokritos, George M. Parássoglou, and Kyriakos Tsantsanoglou. *The Derveni Papyrus.* Studi e testi per il Corpus dei Papiri Filosofici Greci e Latini 13. Firenze: Leo S. Olschki, 2006.

Kraft, Robert A. *The Apostolic Fathers: A Translation and Commentary; vol. III: The Didache and Barnabas.* New York: Thomas Nelson & Sons, 1965.

———. "Barnabas' Isaiah-Text and the 'Testimony Book' Hypothesis." *JBL* 79 (1960): 336–50.

Kratz, Reinhard G. "Text and Commentary: The Pesharim of Qumran in the Context of Hellenistic Scholarship." Pages 212–29 in *The Bible and Hellenism: Greek Influence on Jewish and Early Christian Literature.* Edited by T. L. Thompson and P. Wajdenbaum. Durham: Acumen, 2014.

Kristeva, Julia. *The Kristeva Reader.* Edited by Toril Moi. Oxford: Basil Blackwell, 1986.

———. *La révolution du langage poétique.* Paris: Éditions du Seuil, 1974. Partial English translation, pages 57–62 in *Revolution in Poetic Language.* Translated by Margaret Waller. New York: Columbia University Press, 1984. Extracts, pages 90–136 in Moi, *Kristeva Reader*, 90–136.

———. "Le mot, le dialogue et le roman." Pages 143–73 in *Sēmeiōtikē: Recherches pour une Sémanalyse*. Paris: Éditions du Seuil, 1969. English translation, pages 64–91 in *Desire in Language: A Semiotic Approach to Literature and Art*. Edited by Leon S. Roudiez. Oxford: Basil Blackwell, 1980.

Kujanpää, Katja. "From Eloquence to Evading Responsibility: The Rhetorical Functions of Quotations in Paul's Argumentation." *JBL* 136 (2017): 185–202.

———. *The Rhetorical Functions of Scriptural Quotations in Romans*. NovTSup 172. Leiden: Brill, 2019.

Lagrange, M.-J. Review of *Testimonies: Part II*, by J. Rendel Harris with Vacher Burch. *RB* 30 (1921): 612–14.

Laks, André, and Glenn W. Most. *Early Greek Philosophy: Later Ionian and Athenian Thinkers, Part 1*. LCL 529. Cambridge, MA: Harvard University Press, 2016.

Lavabre, Marie-Claire. "Historiography and Memory." Pages 362–70 in *A Companion to the Philosophy of History and Historiography*. Edited by Aviezer Tucker. Malden, MA: Wiley-Blackwell, 2009.

Le Déaut, Roger. "A propos d'une définition du midrash." *Bib* 50 (1969): 395–413. English translation in *Int* 25 (1971): 259–82.

Leipziger, Jonas. *Lesepraktiken im antiken Judentum: Rezeptionsakte, Materialität und Schriftgebrauch*. Materiale Textkulturen 34. Berlin: de Gruyter, 2021.

Leppä, Outi. *The Making of Colossians: A Study on the Formation and Purpose of a Deutero-Pauline Letter*. Publications of the Finnish Exegetical Society 86. Helsinki: Finnish Exegetical Society, 2003.

Levine, Amy-Jill. "Jewish-Christian Relations from the 'Other Side': A Response to Webb, Lodahl, and White." *Quarterly Review* 20 (2000): 297–304.

Lewis, Naphtali. *Papyrus in Classical Antiquity*. Oxford: Clarendon, 1974.

———. *Papyrus in Classical Antiquity: A Supplement*. Papyrologica Bruxellensia 23. Bruxelles: Fondation Égyptologique Reine Élisabeth, 1989.

Lichtenberger, Hermann. *Das Ich Adams und das Ich der Menschheit: Studien zum Menschenbild in Römer 7*. WUNT 164. Tübingen: Mohr Siebeck, 2004.

Liddell, Henry George, Robert Scott, and Henry Stuart Jones. *A Greek-English Lexicon*. 9th ed. with revised supplement. Oxford: Claredon, 1996.

Lieu, Judith. *Christian Identity in the Jewish and Graeco-Roman World*. Oxford: Oxford University Press, 2004.

———. *Image and Reality: The Jews in the World of the Christians in the Second Century*. Edinburgh: T&T Clark, 1996.

———. *Neither Jew nor Greek? Constructing Early Christianity*. Edinburgh: T&T Clark, 2002.

Bibliography

Lim, Timothy H. *Holy Scripture in the Qumran Commentaries and Pauline Letters.* Oxford: Clarendon, 1997.

Lincicum, David. "Intertextuality, Effective History, and Memory: Conceptualizing Paul's Use of Scripture." Pages 9–22 in *Paulinische Schriftrezeption: Grundlagen—Ausprägungen—Wirkungen—Wertungen.* Edited by Florian Wilk and Markus Öhler. FRLANT 268. Göttingen: Vandenhoeck & Ruprecht, 2017.

———. *Paul and the Early Jewish Encounter with Deuteronomy.* WUNT 2/284. Tübingen: Mohr Siebeck, 2010. Reprinted Grand Rapids: Baker Academic, 2013.

———. "Paul's Engagement with Deuteronomy: Snapshots and Signposts." *Currents in Biblical Research* 7.1 (2008): 37–67.

Lindemann, Andreas. "Die Sammlung der Paulusbriefe im 1. und 2. Jahrhundert." Pages 321–51 in *The Biblical Canons.* Edited by J.-M. Auwers and H. J. de Jonge. BETL 153. Leuven: Peeters, 2003.

———. "Paul in the Writings of the Apostolic Fathers." Pages 25–45 in *Paul and the Legacies of Paul.* Edited by W. S. Babcock. Dallas: Southern Methodist University Press, 1990.

———. "Paul's Influence on 'Clement' and Ignatius." Pages 9–24 in *Trajectories through the New Testament and the Apostolic Fathers.* Edited by A. Gregory and C. M. Tuckett. Oxford: Oxford University Press, 2005.

———. *Paulus im ältesten Christentum.* BHT 58. Tübingen: Mohr Siebeck, 1979.

Lindemann, Hilde. *Holding and Letting Go: The Social Practice of Personal Identities.* Oxford: Oxford University Press, 2014.

Litwak, Kenneth D. "Echoes of Scripture? A Critical Survey of Recent Works on Paul's Use of the Old Testament." *CurBS* 6 (1998): 260–88.

Lohse, Eduard. *Colossians and Philemon.* Hermeneia. Philadelphia: Fortress, 1971.

Longenecker, Bruce W. "Different Answers to Different Issues: Israel, the Gentiles and Salvation History in Romans 9–11." *JSNT* 36 (1989): 95–123.

———, ed. *Narrative Dynamics in Paul: A Critical Assessment.* Louisville: Westminster John Knox, 2002.

Longenecker, Richard N. *Galatians.* WBC 41. Waco: Word Books, 1990.

Lüdemann, Gerd. *Opposition to Paul in Early Christianity.* Translated by E. Boring. Philadelphia: Fortress, 1989.

Luz, Ulrich. *Matthew in History: Interpretation, Influence, Effects.* Minneapolis: Fortress, 1994.

———. "Wirkungsgeschichtliche Exegese: Ein programmatischer Arbeitsbericht mit Beispielen aus der Bergpredigtexegese." *BTZ* 2 (1985): 18–32.

Lyons, George. *Pauline Autobiography: Toward a New Understanding.* Atlanta: Scholars Press, 1985.

Macaskill, Grant. "History, Providence and the Apocalyptic Paul." *SJT* 70.4 (2017): 409–26.

Bibliography

Mach, Michael. "Justin Martyr's *Dialogus cum Tryphone Iudaeo* and the Development of Christian Anti-Judaism." Pages 27–47 in *Contra Iudaeos: Ancient and Medieval Polemics between Christians and Jews*. Edited by O. Limor and G. G. Stroumsa. Texts and Studies in Medieval and Early Modern Judaism 10. Tübingen: Mohr Siebeck, 1996.

MacLachlan, Helen. *Notes on References and Quotations in the New Testament Scriptures from the Old Testament*. Edinburgh: William Blackwood and Sons, 1872.

Maier, Harry O. "Reading Colossians in the Ruins: Roman Imperial Iconography, Moral Transformation, and the Construction of Christian Identity in the Lycus Valley." Pages 212–31 in *Colossae in Space and Time: Linking to an Ancient City*. Edited by Alan H. Cadwallader and Michael Trainor. Göttingen: Vandenhoeck & Ruprecht, 2011.

Manson, T. W. "The Argument from Prophecy." *JTS* 46 (1945): 129–36.

Marcovich, Miroslav, ed. *Iustini Martyris* Dialogus cum Tryphone. PTS 47. Berlin: de Gruyter, 1997.

Marshall, I. Howard. "An Assessment of Recent Developments." Pages 1–21 in *It Is Written: Scripture Citing Scripture; Essays in Honour of Barnabas Lindars, SSF*. Edited by D. A. Carson and H. G. M. Williamson. Cambridge: Cambridge University Press, 1988.

Martens, Peter W. *Origen and Scripture: The Contours of the Exegetical Life*. OECS. Oxford: Oxford University Press, 2012.

Martin, Troy W. *By Philosophy and Empty Deceit: Colossians as Response to a Cynic Critique*. JSNTSup 118. Sheffield: Sheffield Academic, 1996.

Martyn, J. L. "Francis Watson, *Paul and the Hermeneutics of Faith*." *SJT* 59 (2006): 427–38.

———. *Galatians: A New Translation with Introduction and Commentary*. AB 33A. New Haven: Yale University Press, 1997.

———. *Theological Issues in the Letters of Paul*. Nashville: Abingdon, 1997.

Mayerhoff, Ernst T. *Der Brief an die Colosser, mit vornehmlicher Berücksichtigung der drei Pastoralbriefe*. Berlin: Hermann Schultze, 1838.

McAdams, Dan P. "The Psychology of Life Stories." *Review of General Psychology* 5.2 (2001): 100–22.

McAdams, Dan P., Ruthellen Josselson, and Amia Lieblich, eds. *Identity and Story: Creating Self in Narrative*. Washington, DC: American Psychological Association, 2006.

Meade, D. G. *Pseudonymity and Canon*. WUNT 39. Tübingen: Mohr Siebeck, 1986. Reprint, Grand Rapids: Eerdmans, 1987.

Meech, John L. *Paul in Israel's Story: Self and Community at the Cross*. Oxford: Oxford University Press, 2006.

Bibliography

Menken, Maarten J. J. *Old Testament Quotations in the Fourth Gospel: Studies in Textual Form*. CBET 15. Leuven: Peeters, 1996.

Merz, Annette. "The Fictitious Self-Exposition of Paul: How Might Intertextual Theory Suggest a Reformulation of the Hermeneutics of Pseudepigraphy?" Pages 113–32 in *The Intertextuality of the Epistles: Explorations of Theory and Practice*. Edited by Thomas L. Brodie, Dennis R. MacDonald, and Stanley E. Porter. Sheffield: Sheffield Phoenix, 2006.

Michel, Otto. *Paulus und seine Bibel*. Darmstadt: Wissenschaftliche Buchgesellschaft, 1972.

Milik, J. T. "II. Tefillin, Mezuzot et Targums (4Q128–4Q157)." Pages 33–89 in *Qumrân Grotte 4.II*. Edited by Roland de Vaux and J. T. Milik. DJD 6. Oxford: Clarendon, 1977.

Miller, James D. *The Pastoral Letters as Composite Documents*. SNTSMS 93. Cambridge: Cambridge University Press, 1997.

Miller, Merrill P. "Targum, Midrash and the Use of the Old Testament in the New Testament." *JSJ* 2 (1971): 29–82.

Mitchell, Margaret M. *Paul, the Corinthians and the Birth of Christian Hermeneutics*. Cambridge: Cambridge University Press, 2010.

Moore, Stephen D., and Yvonne Sherwood. *The Invention of the Biblical Scholar: A Critical Manifesto*. Minneapolis: Fortress, 2011.

Moritz, Thorsten. *A Profound Mystery: The Use of the Old Testament in Ephesians*. NovTSup 85. Leiden: Brill, 1996.

Moyise, Steve. "Intertextuality and Historical Approaches to the Use of Scripture in the New Testament." Pages 23–33 in *Reading the Bible Intertextually*. Edited by Stefan Alkier, Richard B. Hays, and Leroy A. Huizenga. Waco: Baylor University Press, 2009.

———. *Paul and Scripture: Studying the New Testament Use of the Old Testament*. Grand Rapids: Baker Academic, 2010.

Moyise, Steve, and Maarten J. J. Menken, eds. *Deuteronomy in the New Testament*. LNTS 358. London: T&T Clark, 2007.

———, eds. *Genesis in the New Testament*. LNTS 466. London: T&T Clark, 2012.

———, eds. *Isaiah in the New Testament*. NTSI. London: T&T Clark, 2005.

———, eds. *The Psalms in the New Testament*. London: T&T Clark, 2004.

Moyo, A. M. "The Colossian Heresy in the Light of Some Gnostic Documents from Nag Hammadi." *JTSA* 48 (1984): 30–44.

Muddiman, John. *The Epistle to the Ephesians*. BNTC. London: Continuum, 2001.

Müller, Peter. *Anfänge der Paulusschule: Dargestellt am zweiten Thessalonicherbrief und am Kolosserbrief*. Zürich: TVZ, 1988.

———. "Gegner im Kolosserbrief: Methodische Überlegungen zu einem schwierigen Kapitel." Pages 365–94 in *Beiträge zur urchristlichen Theologiege-schichte*. Edited by W. Kraus. Berlin: de Gruyter, 2009.

Munro, Winsome. *Authority in Paul and Peter: The Identification of a Pastoral Stratum in the Pauline Corpus and 1 Peter*. SNTSMS 45. Cambridge: Cambridge University Press, 1983.

———. "Interpolation in the Epistles: Weighing Probability." *NTS* 36 (1990): 431–43.

Murphy, Roland E. "Reflections on 'Actualization' of the Bible." *BTB* 26 (1996): 79–81.

Murphy-O'Connor, Jerome. "Co-Authorship in the Corinthian Correspondence." *RB* 100 (1993): 562–79.

———. *Paul: A Critical Life*. Oxford: Oxford University Press, 1996.

———. "2 Timothy Contrasted with 1 Timothy and Titus." *RB* 98 (1991): 403–18.

Nelson, Katherine. "Self and Social Functions: Individual Autobiographical Memory and Collective Narrative." *Memory* 11.2 (2003): 125–36.

Neuschäfer, Bernhard. *Origenes als Philologe*. Schweizerische Beiträge zur Altertumswissenschaft 18/1–18/2. Basel: Friedrich Reinhardt, 1987.

Neusner, Jacob. *What Is Midrash?* Philadelphia: Fortress, 1987.

Nicholls, Rachel. *Walking on Water: Reading Mt. 14:22–33 in the Light of Its Wirkungsgeschichte*. Leiden: Brill, 2008.

Nicolet-Anderson, Valérie. *Constructing the Self: Thinking with Paul and Michel Foucault*. WUNT 2/324. Tübingen: Mohr Siebeck, 2012.

Niebuhr, Karl-Wilhelm. *Gesetz und Paränese: Katechismusartige Weisungsreihen in der früjüdischen Literatur*. WUNT 28. Tübingen: Mohr Siebeck, 1987.

Niehoff, Maren R. *Jewish Exegesis and Homeric Scholarship in Alexandria*. Cambridge: Cambridge University Press, 2011.

Noth, Martin. "Die Vergegenwärtigung des Alten Testaments in der Verkündigung." *Evangelische Theologie* 12 (1952): 6–17.

———. "The 'Re-Presentation' of the Old Testament in Proclamation." Pages 76–88 in *Essays on Old Testament Interpretation*. Edited by C. Westermann. Translated by J. L. Mays. London: SCM, 1963.

O'Brien, Kelli S. "The Curse of the Law (Galatians 3.13): Crucifixion, Persecution, and Deuteronomy 21.22–23." *JSNT* 29 (2006): 55–76.

O'Neill, J. C. "Paul Wrote Some of All, but Not All of Any." Pages 169–88 in *The Pauline Canon*. Edited by Stanley E. Porter. Leiden: Brill, 2004.

Öhler, Markus. *Elia im Neuen Testament: Untersuchungen zur Bedeutung des alttestamentlichen Propheten im frühen Christentum*. BZNW 88. Berlin: de Gruyter, 1997.

Ophir, Adi, and Ishay Rosen-Zvi. *Goy: Israel's Multiple Others and the Birth of the Gentile*. Oxford: Oxford University Press, 2018.

Bibliography

Owen, Henry. *The Modes of Quotation Used by the Evangelical Writers Explained and Vindicated*. London: J. Nichols, 1789.

Pate, C. Marvin. *The Reverse of the Curse: Paul, Wisdom, and the Law*. WUNT 2/114. Tübingen: Mohr Siebeck, 2000.

Pearson, Birger A. "Basilides the Gnostic." Pages 1–31 in *A Companion to Second-Century Christian 'Heretics'*. Edited by Antti Marjanen and Petri Luomanen. Leiden: Brill, 2008.

Peppard, Michael. "'Poetry', 'Hymns' and 'Traditional Material' in New Testament Epistles or How to Do Things with Indentations." *JSNT* 30 (2008): 319–42.

Perona, Edwin. "The Presence and Function of Deuteronomy in the Paraenesis of Paul in 1 Corinthians 5:1–11:1." PhD diss., Trinity Evangelical Divinity School, 2006.

Petersen, Norman. *Rediscovering Paul: Philemon and the Sociology of Paul's Narrative World*. Minneapolis: Augsburg Fortress, 1985.

Pilhofer, Peter. "Wer salbt den Messias? Zum Streit um die Christologie im ersten Jahrhundert des jüdisch-christlichen Dialogs." Pages 335–45 in *Begegnungen zwischen Christentum und Judentum in Antike und Mittelalter: Festschrift für Heinz Schreckenberg*. Edited by D.-A. Koch and H. Lichtenberger. SIJD 1. Göttingen: Vandenhoeck & Ruprecht, 1993.

Plooij, Daniel. *Studies in the Testimony Book*. Verhandelingen der Koninklijke Akademie van Wetenschappen te Amsterdam, Afdeeling letterkunde 32/2. Amsterdam: Noord-Hollandsche Uitgevers-Maatschappij, 1932.

Porter, Stanley E. "Pauline Techniques of Interweaving Scripture into His Letters." Pages 23–55 in *Paulinische Schriftrezeption: Grundlagen—Ausprägungen—Wirkungen—Wertungen*. Edited by Florian Wilk and Markus Öhler. FRLANT 268. Göttingen: Vandenhoeck & Ruprecht, 2017.

———. "The Use of the Old Testament in the New: A Brief Comment on Method and Terminology." Pages 79–96 in *Early Christian Interpretation of the Scriptures of Israel: Investigations and Proposals*. Edited by Craig A. Evans and James A. Sanders. JSNTSup 148/5. Sheffield: Sheffield Academic, 1997.

———. "When and How Was the Pauline Canon Compiled? An Assessment of Theories." Pages 95–127 in *The Pauline Canon*. Edited by Stanley E. Porter. Pauline Studies 1. Leiden and Boston: Brill, 2004.

Prior, M. *Paul the Letter-Writer and the Second Letter to Timothy*. JSNTSup 23. Sheffield: Sheffield Academic, 1989.

Prussner, Frederick C. *Old Testament Theology: Its History and Development*. London: SCM, 1985.

Punt, Jeremy. "Identity, Memory and Scriptural Warrant: Arguing Paul's Case." Pages 25–53 in *Paul and Scripture: Extending the Conversation*. Edited by Christopher D. Stanley. Atlanta: Society of Biblical Literature, 2012.

Bibliography

Rabens, Volker. "'Schon jetzt' und 'noch mehr': Gegenwart und Zukunft des Heils bei Paulus und in seinen Gemeinden." *Jahrbuch für biblische Theologie* 28 (2013): 103–27.

Rad, Gerhard von. *Old Testament Theology.* Volume 2: *The Theology of Israel's Prophetic Traditions.* New York: Harper & Row, 1965.

Räisänen, Heikki. "The 'Effective History' of the Bible: A Challenge to Biblical Scholarship." *SJT* 45 (1992): 303–24.

Randolph, Thomas. *The Prophecies and Other Texts, Cited in the New Testament, Compared with the Hebrew Original, and with the Septuagint Version, to which are added Notes.* Oxford: J. and J. Fletcher, [1782?].

Rea, Michael. "Gender as a Self-Conferred Identity." *Feminist Philosophy Quarterly* 8.2 (2022). doi.org/10.5206/fpq/2022.2.13959.

———. "The Metaphysics of the Narrative Self." *Journal of the American Philosophical Association* 8.4 (2022): 586–603.

Reinmuth, Eckart. *Geist und Gesetz: Studien zu Voraussetzungen und Inhalt der paulinischen Paränese.* TA 44. Berlin: Evangelische Verlagsanstalt, 1985.

Rese, Martin. "Intertextualität: Ein Beispiel für Sinn und Unsinn 'neuer' Methoden." Pages 431–39 in *The Scriptures in the Gospels.* Edited by Christopher M. Tuckett. BETL 131. Leuven: Leuven University Press, 1997.

Reumann, John. *Philippians.* AB 33B. New Haven: Yale University Press, 2008.

Reuter, R. "Paul's Terminology Describing Time, Periods of Time and History." Pages 247–67 in *Lux Humana, Lux Aeterna: Essays on Biblical and Related Themes in Honour of Lars Aejmelaeus.* Edited by A. Mustakallio. Publications of the Finnish Exegetical Society 89. Göttingen: Vandenhoeck & Ruprecht, 2005.

Richard, Earl. "Early Pauline Thought: An Analysis of 1 Thessalonians." Pages 39–51 in *Pauline Theology, Volume 1: Thessalonians, Philippians, Galatians, Philemon.* Edited by Jouette M. Bassler. Minneapolis: Fortress, 1991.

———. *Jesus, One and Many: The Christological Concept of New Testament Authors.* Wilmington, DE: Glazier, 1988.

Richards, E. Randolph. *Paul and First-Century Letter Writing: Secretaries, Composition and Collection.* Downers Grove, IL: InterVarsity, 2004.

———. *The Secretary in the Letters of Paul.* WUNT 2/42. Tübingen: Mohr Siebeck, 1991.

Ricoeur, Paul. *Oneself as Another.* Translated by K. Blamey. Chicago: University of Chicago Press, 1992.

Röhser, Günter. "Der Schluss als Schlüssel: Zu den Epistolaria des Kolosserbriefes." Pages 129–50 in *Kolosser-Studien.* Edited by Peter Müller. Biblisch-Theologische Studien 103. Neukirchen-Vluyn: Neukirchener Verlag, 2009.

Rokéah, David. *Justin Martyr and the Jews.* Jewish and Christian Perspectives 5. Leiden: Brill, 2002.

Bibliography

Rosen-Zvi, Ishay, and Adi Ophir. "Paul and the Invention of the Gentiles." *JQR* 105.1 (2015): 1–41.

Rosner, Brian S. *Paul, Scripture, and Ethics: A Study of 1 Corinthians 5–7.* AGJU 22. Leiden: Brill, 1994. Repr., Grand Rapids: Baker, 1999.

———, ed. *Understanding Paul's Ethics: Twentieth-Century Approaches.* Grand Rapids: Eerdmans, 1995.

Rothschild, Clare K. *Hebrews as Pseudepigraphon: The History and Significance of the Pauline Attribution of Hebrews.* WUNT 235. Tübingen: Mohr Siebeck, 2009.

———. "Reception of First Corinthians in First Clement." Pages 35–60 in *New Essays on the Apostolic Fathers.* WUNT 375. Tübingen: Mohr Siebeck, 2017.

Rowland, Christopher. "Apocalyptic Visions and the Exaltation of Christ in the Letter to the Colossians." *JSNT* 19 (1983): 73–83.

Royalty, Robert M. "Dwelling on Visions: On the Nature of the So-Called 'Colossians Heresy.'" *Bib* 83 (2002): 329–57.

Ruiten, J. T. A. G. M. van. Review of *Paul and the Language of Scripture*, by Christopher D. Stanley. *JSJ* 25 (1994): 127.

Rutledge, Jonathan C. "Narrative and Atonement: The Ministry of Reconciliation in the Work of James H. Cone." *Religions* 13 (2022): 985.

Salzmann, Jorg Christian. "Jüdische Messiasvorstellungen in Justins Dialog mit Trypho und im Johannesevangelium." *ZNW* 100 (2009): 247–68.

Sanders, E. P. "Literary Dependence in Colossians." *JBL* 85 (1966): 28–45.

Sanders, James A. "Paul and Theological History." Pages 52–57 in Evans and Sanders, *Paul and the Scriptures of Israel.* JSNTSup 83. SSEJC 1. Sheffield: Sheffield Academic, 1993.

Sappington, Thomas J. *Revelation and Redemption at Colossae.* JSNTSup 53. Sheffield: Sheffield Academic, 1991.

Sauter, Gerhard, and John Barton, eds. *Revelation and Story: Narrative Theology and the Centrality of Story.* Aldershot: Ashgate, 2000.

Sawyer, John F. A. *The Fifth Gospel: Isaiah in the History of Christianity.* Cambridge: Cambridge University Press, 1996.

Schechtman, Marya. *The Constitution of Selves.* Ithaca, NY: Cornell University Press, 1996.

———. "The Narrative Self." Pages 394–416 in *The Oxford Handbook of the Self.* Edited by Shaun Gallagher. Oxford: Oxford University Press, 2011.

Schenk, Wolfgang. "Der Kolosserbrief in der neueren Forschung (1945–1985)." *ANRW* II.25.4 (1987): 3327–64.

Schironi, Francesca. *The Best of the Grammarians: Aristarchus of Samothrace on the* Iliad. Ann Arbor: University of Michigan Press, 2018.

Bibliography

———. "Greek Commentaries." *Dead Sea Discoveries* 19 (2012): 399–441.

Schmid, Hansjörg. "How to Read the First Epistle of John Non-Polemically." *Bib* 85 (2004): 24–41.

Schmid, Konrad, and Christoph Riedweg, eds. *Beyond Eden: The Biblical Story of Paradise (Genesis 2–3) and Its Reception History*. FAT 2/34. Tübingen: Mohr Siebeck, 2008.

Schmithals, Walter. "Der Hebräerbrief als Paulusbrief: Beobachtungen zur Kanonbildung." Pages 319–37 in *Die Weltlichkeit des Glaubens in der Alten Kirche: Festschrift für Ulrich Wilckert zum siebzigsten Geburtstag*. Edited by Dietmar Wyrwa. BZNW 85. Berlin: de Gruyter, 1997.

Schnelle, Udo. *Apostle Paul: His Life and Theology*. Translated by M. Eugene Boring. Grand Rapids: Baker Academic, 2005.

Scholtz, G. "The Notion of Historicism and 19th Century Theology." Pages 149–67 in *Biblical Studies and the Shifting of Paradigms, 1850–1914*. Edited by W. R. Farmer and H. G. Reventlow. JSOTSup 192. Sheffield: Sheffield Academic, 1995.

Schröter, Jens. "Die Funktion der Herrenmahlsüberlieferungen im 1. Korintherbrief: Zugleich ein Beitrag zur Rolle der 'Einsetzungsworte' in frühchristlichen Mahltexten." *ZNW* 100 (2009): 78–100.

Schweizer, E. *The Letter to the Colossians*. Translated by A. Chester. London: SPCK, 1982.

Scornaienchi, Lorenzo. *Sarx und Soma bei Paulus: Der Mensch zwischen Destruktivität und Konstruktivität*. NTOA/SUNT 67. Göttingen: Vandenhoeck & Ruprecht, 2008.

Scott, James M., ed. *Exile: Old Testament, Jewish, and Christian Conceptions*. JSJSup 56. Leiden: Brill, 1997.

———. "'For as Many as Are of Works of the Law Are under a Curse' (Galatians 3.10)." Pages 187–221 in Evans and Sanders, *Paul and the Scriptures of Israel*. JSNTSup 83. SSEJC 1. Sheffield: Sheffield Academic, 1993.

———. "Paul's Use of Deuteronomistic Tradition." *JBL* 112 (1993): 645–65.

———. "Restoration of Israel." Pages 796–805 in *Dictionary of Paul and His Letters*. Edited by Gerald F. Hawthorne and Ralph P. Martin. Downers Grove, IL: InterVarsity, 1993.

———. "The Use of Scripture in 2 Corinthians 6.16c–18 and Paul's Restoration Theology." *JSNT* 56 (1994): 73–99.

Segal, Alan F. *Rebecca's Children: Judaism and Christianity in the Roman World*. Cambridge, MA: Harvard University Press, 1986.

Shum, Shiu-Lun. *Paul's Use of Isaiah in Romans: A Comparative Study of Paul's Letter*

Bibliography

to the Romans and the Sibylline and Qumran Sectarian Texts. WUNT 2/156. Tübingen: Mohr Siebeck, 2002.

Silva, Moises. "The Greek Psalter in Paul's Letters: A Textual Study." Pages 277–88 in *The Old Greek Psalter: Studies in Honour of Albert Pietersma*. Edited by Robert J. V. Hiebert, Claude E. Cox, and Peter J. Gentry. JSOTSup 332. Sheffield: Sheffield Academic, 2001.

Simon, M. *Verus Israel: A Study of the Relations between Christians and Jews in the Roman Empire (AD 135–425)*. London: The Littman Library of Jewish Civilization, 1996.

Sirat, C. "Le livre hébreu dans les premiers siècles de notres ère: Le témoignage des textes." Pages 115–24 in *Les débuts du codex*. Edited by A. Blanchard. Bibliologia 9. Brepols: Turnhout, 1989.

Skarsaune, Oskar. "Does the Letter to the Hebrews Articulate a Supersessionist Theology? A Response to Richard Hays." Pages 174–82 in *The Epistle to the Hebrews and Christian Theology*. Edited by R. Bauckham et al. Grand Rapids: Eerdmans, 2009.

———. *The Proof from Prophecy: A Study in Justin Martyr's Proof-Text Tradition; Text-Type, Provenance, Theological Profile*. NovTSup 56. Leiden: Brill, 1987.

Skeat, T. C. "Was Papyrus Regarded as 'Cheap' or 'Expensive' in the Ancient World?" Pages 88–105 in *The Collected Biblical Writings of T. C. Skeat*. Edited by J. K. Elliott. NovTSup 113. Leiden: Brill, 2004.

Small, Jocelyn Penny. *Wax Tablets of the Mind: Cognitive Studies of Memory and Literacy in Classical Antiquity*. New York: Routledge, 1997.

Smith, Claire S. *Pauline Communities as 'Scholastic Communities': A Study of the Vocabulary of 'Teaching' in 1 Corinthians, 1 and 2 Timothy, and Titus*. WUNT 2/335. Tübingen: Mohr Siebeck, 2012.

Smith, D. Moody. "The Pauline Literature." Pages 265–91 in *It Is Written: Scripture Citing Scripture*. Edited by D. A. Carson and Hugh Godfrey Maturin Williamson. Cambridge: Cambridge University Press, 1988.

———. "The Use of the Old Testament in the New." Pages 3–65 in *The Use of the Old Testament in the New and Other Essays: Studies in Honor of William Franklin Stinespring*. Edited by James M. Efird. Durham, NC: Duke University Press, 1972.

Smith, Ian K. *Heavenly Perspective: A Study of the Apostle Paul's Response to a Jewish Mystical Movement at Colossae*. LNTS 326. London: T&T Clark, 2006.

Spoerhase, Carlos. "Presentism and Precursorship in Intellectual History." *Culture, Theory & Critique* 49 (2008): 49–72.

Sprinkle, Preston. *Law and Life: The Interpretation of Leviticus 18:5 in Early Judaism and Paul*. WUNT 2/241. Tübingen: Mohr Siebeck, 2008.

Standhartinger, Angela. "Colossians and the Pauline School." *NTS* 50 (2004): 571–93.

Bibliography

———. *Studien zur Entstehungsgeschichte und Intention des Kolosserbriefs*. NovT-Sup 94. Leiden: Brill, 1999.

Stanley, Christopher D. *Arguing with Scripture: The Rhetoric of Quotations in the Letters of Paul*. London: T&T Clark, 2004.

———. "A Decontextualized Paul? A Response to Francis Watson's *Paul and the Hermeneutics of Faith*." *JSNT* 28 (2006): 353–62.

———. "The Importance of 4QTanḥumim (4Q176)." *RevQ* 15 (1992): 569–82.

———. "Paul and Scripture: Charting the Course." Pages 3–12 in *As It Is Written: Studying Paul's Use of Scripture*. Edited by Stanley E. Porter and Christopher D. Stanley. SBLSymS 50. Atlanta: Society of Biblical Literature, 2008.

———. *Paul and the Language of Scripture: Citation Technique in the Pauline Epistles and Contemporary Literature*. SNTSMS 74. Cambridge: Cambridge University Press, 1992.

———. Review of *Holy Scripture in the Qumran Commentaries and Pauline Letters*, by Timothy H. Lim. *JTS* 49 (1998): 781–84.

———. "The Significance of Romans 11:3–4 for the Text History of the LXX Book of Kingdoms." *JBL* 112 (1993): 43–54.

———. "What We Learned—and What We Didn't." Pages 321–30 in *Paul and Scripture: Extending the Conversation*. Edited Christopher D. Stanley. Atlanta: Society of Biblical Literature, 2012.

Steck, Odil Hannes. "Das Problem theologischer Strömungen in nachexilischer Zeit." *EvT* 28 (1968): 445–58.

———. *Israel und das gewaltsame Geschick der Propheten: Untersuchungen zur Überlieferung des deuteronomistischen Geschichtsbildes im Alten Testament, Spätjudentum und Urchristentum*. WMANT 23. Neukirchen-Vluyn: Neukirchener Verlag, 1967.

Stendahl, Krister. *The School of St. Matthew and Its Use of the Old Testament*. 2nd ed. Lund: Gleerup, 1968.

Stettler, Christian. "The Opponents at Colossae." Pages 169–200 in *Paul and His Opponents*. Edited by S. E. Porter. Pauline Studies 2. Leiden: Brill, 2005.

Steudel, Annette. *Der Midrasch zur Eschatologie aus der Qumrangemeinde (4QMidr-Eschat^(a.b)): Materielle Rekonstruktion, Textbestand, Gattung und traditionsgeschichtliche Einordnung des durch 4Q174 („Florilegium") und 4Q177 („Catena A") repräsentierten Werkes aus den Qumranfunden*. STDJ 13. Leiden: Brill, 1994.

Stirewalt, M. Luther, Jr. *Paul the Letter Writer*. Grand Rapids: Eerdmans, 2003.

Stowers, Stanley. *Letter Writing in Greco-Roman Antiquity*. LEC. Philadelphia: Westminster, 1989.

———. *A Rereading of Romans: Justice, Jews, & Gentiles*. New Haven: Yale University Press, 1994.

Bibliography

Streett, Daniel R. *They Went Out from Us: The Identity of the Opponents in First John*. BZNW 177. Berlin: de Gruyter, 2011.

Strugnell, John. "Notes en marge du volume V des 'Discoveries in the Judaean Desert of Jordan.'" *RevQ* 7/26 (1970): 163–276.

Stylianopoulos, Theodore. *Justin Martyr and the Mosaic Law*. SBLDS 20. Missoula, MT: Scholars Press, 1975.

Sumney, Jerry L. "Studying Paul's Opponents: Advances and Challenges." Pages 7–58 in *Paul and His Opponents*. Edited by S. E. Porter. Pauline Studies 2. Leiden: Brill, 2005.

Sundberg, A. C. "On Testimonies." *NovT* 3 (1959): 268–81.

Surenhusius, Guilielmus. ספר המשוה *sive* ΒΙΒΛΟΣ ΚΑΤΑΛΛΑΓΗΣ *in quo secundum veterum theologorum Hebraeorum formulas allegandi, & modos interpretandi conciliantur loca ex V. in N. T. allegata*. Amsterdam: Johannes Boom, 1713.

Swanson, Dwight D. Review of *Holy Scripture in the Qumran Commentaries and Pauline Letters*, by Timothy H. Lim. *JSS* 47 (2002): 153–56.

Swete, Henry Barclay. *An Introduction to the Old Testament in Greek*. Revised by Richard Rusden Ottley. Edited by Henry St. John Thackeray. Cambridge: Cambridge University Press, 1914.

Talmon, Shemaryahu. "Oral Tradition and Written Transmission, Or the Heard and Seen Word in Judaism of the Second Temple Period." Pages 121–58 in *Jesus and the Oral Gospel Tradition*. Edited by Henry Wansbrough. JSNTSup 64. Sheffield: Sheffield Academic, 1991.

Thackeray, Henry St. John. *The Relation of St. Paul to Contemporary Jewish Thought*. New York: Macmillan, 1900.

Thielman, Frank. *From Plight to Solution: A Jewish Framework for Understanding Paul's View of the Law in Galatians and Romans*. NovTSup 6. Leiden: Brill, 1989.

———. *Paul and the Law: A Contextual Approach*. Downers Grove, IL: InterVarsity, 1994.

Tholuck, Friedrich August Gottreu. "Citations of the Old Testament in the New." *BSac* 11 (1854): 568–616.

———. "The Use Made of the Old Testament in the New, and Especially in the Epistle to the Hebrews." Pages 2:181–245 in *A Commentary on the Epistle to the Hebrews*. 2 vols. Translated by James Hamilton and J. E. Ryland. Edinburgh: Thomas Clark, 1842.

Thompson, Michael B. "The Holy Internet: Communication between Churches in the First Christian Generation." Pages 49–70 in *The Gospels for all Christians*. Edited by Richard J. Bauckham. Edinburgh: T&T Clark, 1998.

Bibliography

Thornton, Allison Krile. "Narrating Narrative." Draft paper presented to the Center for Philosophy of Religion. University of Notre Dame, 25 March 2022.

Thrall, M. *The Second Epistle to the Corinthians*. ICC. London: T&T Clark, 1994.

Tomson, Peter J. *Paul and the Jewish Law: Halakhah in the Letters of the Apostle to the Gentiles*. CRINT 3/1. Minneapolis: Fortress, 1990.

Tov, Emanuel. "Excerpted and Abbreviated Biblical Texts from Qumran." *RevQ* 16/64 (1995): 581–600.

———. "A Modern Textual Outlook Based on the Qumran Scrolls." *HUCA* 53 (1982): 11–27.

Tov, Emanuel, Martin G. Abegg Jr., Armin Lange, Ulrike Mittmann-Richert, Stephen J. Pfann, Eibert J. C. Tigchelaar, Eugene Ulrich, and Brian Webster. *The Texts from the Judaean Desert: Indices and an Introduction to the Discoveries in the Judaean Desert Series*. DJD 39. Oxford: Clarendon, 2002.

Tov, Emanuel, Robert A. Kraft, and P. J. Parsons. *The Greek Minor Prophets Scroll from Naḥal Ḥever (8ḤevXIIgr)*. DJD 8. Oxford: Clarendon, 1990.

Toy, Crawford Howell. *Quotations in the New Testament*. New York: Charles Scribner's Sons, 1884.

Trainor, Michael. "Excavating Epaphras of Colossae." Pages 232–46 in *Colossae in Space and Time: Linking to an Ancient City*. Edited by Alan H. Cadwallader and Michael Trainor. Göttingen: Vandenhoeck & Ruprecht, 2011.

Trakatellis, Demetrios. "Justin Martyr's Trypho." *HTR* 79 (1986): 287–97.

Trebilco, Paul. "Christians in the Lycus Valley: The View from Ephesus and from Western Asia Minor." Pages 180–211 in *Colossae in Space and Time: Linking to an Ancient City*. Edited by A. H. Cadwallader and M. Trainor. Göttingen: Vandenhoeck & Ruprecht, 2011.

Trobisch, David. *Paul's Letter Collection: Tracing the Origins*. Minneapolis: Fortress, 1994.

Tuckett, Christopher M. "Paul, Scripture and Ethics: Some Reflections." *NTS* 46 (2000): 403–24.

———. "Scripture and Q." Pages 3–26 in *The Scriptures in the Gospels*. Edited by Christopher M. Tuckett. BETL 131. Leuven: Leuven University Press, 1997.

———, ed. *The Scriptures in the Gospels*. BETL 131. Leuven: Leuven University Press, 1997.

Turner, Geoffrey. "The Righteousness of God in Psalms and Romans." *SJT* 63 (2010): 285–301.

Turpie, David McCalman. *The New Testament View of the Old: A Contribution to Biblical Introduction and Exegesis*. London: Hodder and Stoughton, 1872.

———. *The Old Testament in the New: A Contribution to Biblical Criticism and Interpretation*. London: Williams and Norgate, 1868.

Bibliography

Van Broekhoven, Harold. "The Social Profiles in the Colossian Debate." *JSNT* 66 (1997): 73–90.

Vegge, Tor. "Polemic in the Epistle to the Colossians." Pages 255–93 in *Polemik in der frühchristlichen Literatur: Texte und Kontexte*. Edited by Oda Wischmeyer and Lorenzo Scornaienchi. BZNW 170. Berlin: de Gruyter, 2010.

Venard, L. "Citations de l'Ancien Testament dans le Nouveau Testament." Pages 2:23–51 in *Supplément au Dictionnaire de la Bible*. Edited by Louis Pirot. Paris: Letouzey et Ané, 1934.

Via, Dan O. *Kerygma and Comedy in the New Testament: A Structuralist Approach to Hermeneutic*. Philadelphia: Fortress, 1975.

———. "A Structuralist Approach to Paul's Old Testament Hermeneutic." *Int* 28 (1974): 201–20.

Vielhauer, Philipp. "Paulus und das Alte Testament." Pages 33–62 in *Studien zur Geschichte und Theologie der Reformation: Festschrift für Ernst Bizer*. Edited by L. Abramowski and J. F. G. Goeters. Neukirchen-Vluyn: Neukirchener Verlag, 1969.

Vliet, H. van. *No Single Testimony: A Study in the Adoption of the Law of Deut 19:15 par. into the New Testament*. STRT 4. Utrecht: Kemink & Zoon, 1958.

Vollmer, Hans. *Die alttestamentlichen Citate bei Paulus textkritisch und biblisch-theologisch gewürdigt nebst einem Anhang Ueber das Verhältnis des Apostels zu Philo*. Leipzig: Mohr Siebeck, 1895.

Wagner, J. Ross. *Heralds of the Good News: Isaiah and Paul in Concert in the Letter to the Romans*. NovTSup 101. Leiden: Brill, 2002.

———. "Isaiah in Romans and Galatians." Pages 119–32 in *Isaiah in the New Testament*. Edited by Steve Moyise and Maarten J. J. Menken. NTSI. London: T&T Clark, 2005.

———. "Moses and Isaiah in Concert: Paul's Reading of Isaiah and Deuteronomy in the Letter to the Romans." Pages 87–105 in *"As Those Who Are Taught": The Interpretation of Isaiah from the LXX to the SBL*. Edited by Claire Matthews McGinnis and Patricia K. Tull. Atlanta: Society of Biblical Literature, 2006.

———. "Paul and Scripture." Pages 154–71 in *The Blackwell Companion to Paul*. Edited by Stephen Westerholm. Malden, MA: Blackwell, 2011.

———. Review of *Holy Scripture in the Qumran Commentaries and Pauline Letters*, by Timothy H. Lim. *JBL* 120 (2001): 175–78.

Walker, William O. *Interpolations in the Pauline Letters*. JSNTSup 213. Sheffield: Sheffield Academic, 2001.

Waters, Guy P. *The End of Deuteronomy in the Epistles of Paul*. WUNT 2/221. Tübingen: Mohr Siebeck, 2006.

Watson, Francis. *Paul and the Hermeneutics of Faith*. 2nd ed. London: T&T Clark, 2015.

Bibliography

———. "Paul and the Reader: An Authorial Apologia." *JSNT* 28 (2006): 363–73.

———. "A Response from Francis Watson." *SJT* 59 (2006): 461–68.

———. "Response to Richard Hays." *ProEccl* 16 (2007): 134–40.

Watt, J. van der, ed. *The Eschatology of the New Testament and Some Related Documents.* WUNT 2/315. Tübingen: Mohr Siebeck, 2011.

Werline, R. "The Transformation of Pauline Arguments in Justin Martyr's *Dialogue with Trypho.*" *HTR* 92 (1999): 79–93.

Wevers, John William. *Notes on the Greek Text of Genesis.* SCS 35. Atlanta: Scholars, 1993.

Whiston, William. *An Essay towards Restoring the True Text of the Old Testament and for Vindicating the Citations Made Thence in the New Testament.* London: Senex and Taylor, 1722.

Whitehead, Anne. *Memory.* The New Critical Idiom. London: Routledge, 2009.

Wilder, Terry L. *Pseudonymity, the New Testament, and Deception.* Lanham, MD: University Press of America, 2004.

Wilk, Florian. "Between Scripture and History: Technique and Hermeneutics of Interpreting Biblical Prophets in the Septuagint of Isaiah and the Letters of Paul." Pages in 189–209 *The Old Greek of Isaiah: Issues and Perspectives.* Edited Arie van der Kooij and Michaël N. van der Meer. CBET 55. Leuven: Peeters, 2010.

———. *Die Bedeutung des Jesajabuches für Paulus.* FRLANT 179. Göttingen: Vandenhoeck & Ruprecht, 1998.

———. "Isaiah in 1 and 2 Corinthians." Pages 133–58 in *Isaiah in the New Testament.* Edited by Steve Moyise and Maarten J. J. Menken. NTSI. London: T&T Clark, 2005.

———. "Paulus als Interpret der prophetischen Schriften." *KD* 45 (1999): 284–306.

Williams, A. Lukyn. *Adversus Judaeos: A Bird's-Eye View of Christian* Apologiae *until the Renaissance.* Cambridge: Cambridge University Press, 1935.

Williams, H. H. Drake, III. *The Wisdom of the Wise: The Presence and Function of Scripture within 1 Cor. 1:18–3:23.* AGJU 44. Leiden: Brill, 2001.

Wilson, Adrian, and T. G. Ashplant. "Whig History and Present-Centred History." *The Historical Journal* 31 (1988): 1–16.

Wilson, R. McL. *Colossians and Philemon.* ICC. London: T&T Clark, 2005.

Wilson, Todd A. *The Curse of the Law and the Crisis in Galatia: Reassessing the Purpose of Galatians.* WUNT 2/225. Tübingen: Mohr Siebeck, 2007.

Wisdom, Jeffrey R. *Blessing for the Nations and the Curse of the Law: Paul's Citations of Genesis and Deuteronomy in Gal 3:8–10.* WUNT 2/133. Tübingen: Mohr Siebeck, 2001.

Wisse, Frederik W. "Textual Limits to Redactional Theory in the Pauline Corpus." Pages 167–78 in *Gospel Origins & Christian Beginnings in Honor of James M.*

Bibliography

Robinson. Edited by James E. Goehring, Charles W. Hedrick, Jack T. Sanders, with Hans Dieter Betz. *ForFasc* 1. Sonoma, CA: Polebridge Press, 1990.

Woyke, Johannes. "'Einst' und 'Jetzt' in Röm 1–3? Zur Bedeutung von νυνὶ δέ in Röm 3,21." *ZNW* 92 (2011): 185–206.

Wright, Addison. "The Literary Genre Midrash." *CBQ* 28 (1966): 105–38, 417–57. Reprinted as *The Literary Genre Midrash*. Staten Island: Alba, 1967.

Wright, N. T. "Curse and Covenant: Galatians 3.10–14." Pages 137–56 in *The Climax of the Covenant: Christ and the Law in Pauline Theology*. Minneapolis: Fortress, 1993.

———. *The Epistles of Paul to the Colossians and to Philemon*. TNTC. Grand Rapids: Eerdmans, 1986.

———. *Jesus and the Victory of God*. Minneapolis: Fortress, 1996.

———. *The New Testament and the People of God*. Minneapolis: Fortress, 1992.

———. "Paul, Arabia, and Elijah (Galatians 1:17)." *JBL* 115 (1996): 683–92.

———. *Paul and the Faithfulness of God*. London: SPCK, 2013.

Wucherpfennig, Ansgar. *Heracleon Philologus: Gnostische Johannesexegese im zweiten Jahrhundert*. WUNT 142. Tübingen: Mohr Siebeck, 2002.

Yarbrough, Mark. *Paul's Utilization of Preformed Traditions in 1 Timothy: An Evaluation of Paul's Literary, Rhetorical, and Theological Tactics*. LNTS 417. London: Continuum, 2009.

Yates, Roy. "Colossians and Gnosis." *JSNT* 27 (1986): 49–68.

Zahn, Theodor. *Einleitung in das Neue Testament*. Volume 1. Leipzig: Deichert, 1906.

Zurawski, Jason M. "Separating the Devil from the *Diabolos*: A Fresh Reading of Wisdom of Solomon 2.24." *JSP* 21.4 (2012): 366–99.

Index of Modern Authors

Abasciano, Brian J., 36, 48
Achtemeier, Paul J., 36
Albl, Martin C., 23, 25, 28–29, 33
Alexander, Loveday, 49
Alkier, Stefan, 44
Allegro, John M., 27, 29
Allert, Craig D., 165
Allison, Dale, 41
Althusser, Louis, 106
Amling, Ernst, 143
Arnold, Clinton E., 133
Ashplant, T. G., 118
Assmann, Jan, 51
Ásta, 113
Attridge, Harold W., 5
Austin, J. L., 113

Baars, W., 173
Backhaus, K., 156
Bakhtin, Mikhail, 43
Balabanski, Vicky, 142
Baltussen, Han, 3
Barclay, John M. G., 61, 130, 132, 137
Barnard, L. W., 161
Barnes, A., 119
Barnes, J., 119
Barr, James, 78
Barrett, C. K., 63
Barthélemy, Dominique, 12

Barthes, Roland, 44, 80
Barton, John, 15, 44, 101
Bates, Matthew W., 45
Bauckham, Richard J., 36, 127–28, 145–46
Bauer, Thomas J., 138, 153
Baum, Armin, 138–39
Baur, Ferdinand Christian, 147
Beale, G. K., 27, 119
Beiser, Frederick C., 118–19, 191
Bell, Richard H., 85
Bennett, Andrew, 152
Berkley, Timothy W., 44
Berthelot, Katell, 52
Betz, Hans Dieter, 140
Bindley, T. Herbert, 25
Blackman, Edwin Cyril, 72
Blanc, C., 5
Bloch, Renée, 29
Bloom, Harold, 44, 81
Bobichon, Philippe, 161–62, 164–65
Bockmuehl, Markus, 4, 36, 45, 96
Böhl, Eduard, 72, 75–77
Boismard, Marie-Émile, 155
Bonsirven, Joseph, 37, 76–77, 96
Boomershine, Thomas E., 36
Börner-Klein, D., 1
Bourdieu, Pierre, 139–40
Bowman, Alan K., 36

233

Index of Modern Authors

Boyarin, Daniel, 101, 167
Boyd, Brian, 101
Brodie, Thomas L., 85
Brooke, A. E., 4
Brooke, George J., 11, 29
Brox, Norbert, 138
Bruce, F. F., 133
Bujard, Walter, 136
Bultmann, Rudolf, 76, 102
Burch, Vacher, 23–25, 169
Burkitt, F. C., 24
Burnett, Gary W., 102
Byrskog, Samuel, 36, 154

Cadwallader, Alan H., 145
Calhoun, Craig, 140
Campbell, Douglas A., 92
Campbell, Matthew, 110
Campbell, Warren, 156
Campbell, William S., 101
Cappellus, Louis, 73
Carleton Paget, James, 184
Carpzov, Johann Gottlob, 74
Carr, David M., 42
Carson, D. A., 119
Chadwick, Henry, 31
Childs, Brevard S., 128, 193
Clark, Elizabeth, 118
Clemen, August, 75
Collins, Anthony, 74
Cone, James H., 115
Cook, Johann, 59
Cook, John Granger, 10
Cosgrove, Charles H., 72, 163
Cranfield, C. E. B., 160
Crawford, Sidnie White, 30, 37
Crossan, John Dominic, 192
Culler, Jonathan, 44

D'Amico, Robert, 119
Daniélou, Jean, 27

Davidson, Samuel, 75
Deines, Roland, 74
DeMaris, Richard E., 131, 133
Derrenbacker, R. A., Jr., 36
Dettwiler, Andreas, 142
Devreesse, Robert, 31
Dinter, Paul E., 83
Dittmar, Wilhelm, 75
Dodd, C. H., 7, 24–27, 170
Doering, Lutz, 31
Donelson, L., 122
Donfried, Karl Paul, 155, 180
Döpke, Johann Christian Carl, 75–76, 173
Driver, D., 118
Drusius, Johannes, 73
Duff, Jeremy, 138–39
Duncan, Julie A., 30
Dunn, James D. G., 36, 64, 101, 117, 138, 141, 144, 155, 159, 161

Eastman, Susan Grove, 94, 102–3
Eco, Umberto, 115
Edsall, Benjamin A., 108, 153
Ehrman, Bart, 126, 131, 137, 148–49, 178, 181
Eisele, Wilfried, 116
Ellis, E. Earle, 26, 29, 32, 72–73, 78, 153
Engberg-Pedersen, Troels, 92
Evans, Craig A., 82–83, 87
Evans, Robert, 45
Evanson, Edward, 136

Falcetta, Alessandro, 24–25
Falls, Thomas B., 162
Fernández Marcos, Natalio, 12, 173
Finley, Kate, 101, 105
Finsterbusch, Karin, 96
Fitzmyer, Joseph A., 25, 29–30, 60
Fladerer, L., 1
Foerster, W., 4

Index of Modern Authors

Foster, Paul, 178
Foucault, M., 110
Fowl, Stephen, 106, 129
Francis, Fred O., 133
Frank, Nicole, 144, 149
Fredriksen, Paula, 107
Frei, Hans W., 102, 135
Funk, R. W., 125
Fuß, Barbara, 17

Gadamer, Hans-Georg, 45
Gamble, Harry Y., 11, 72, 187
Ganzevoort, R. Ruard, 101
Gärtner, Hans Armin, 3
Gerhardsson, Birger, 36
Gillingham, S., 189
Gnilka, Joachim, 45
Gombis, Timothy G., 92
Gough, Henry, 74
Gowan, Donald E., 86–87
Gray, Patrick, 112
Greenspoon, Leonard, 42
Gregory, Andrew, 170, 176–77, 178, 180
Griffiths, Paul J., 111
Grinfield, Edward William, 74
Groves, J. W., 117
Guignebert, Charles, 25
Gunther, J. J., 133
Gupta, Nijay, 131, 133

Haardt, Maaike de, 101
Hadot, Pierre, 110–11
Häfner, Gerd, 20
Hagner, Donald A., 177
Halbwachs, Maurice, 51
Halton, Thomas P., 162
Hardy, Thomas, 192
Harl, Marguerite, 53, 69
Harnack, Adolf von, 19, 72, 95–96
Harrington, D. J., 148
Harris, J. Rendel, 23–28, 169

Harris, Murray J., 57
Harrison, P. N., 155
Hartog, Pieter B., 4
Hasel, G. F., 117
Hatch, Edwin, 28
Hatina, Thomas R., 44, 81
Hauerwas, Stanley, 101
Hayes, Christine, 106
Hays, Richard B., 14–15, 35, 43–45, 78, 80–82, 84, 91–92, 94–96, 105, 193
Heidegger, Martin, 171
Heil, John Paul, 46, 48
Heilig, Christoph, 105
Heilmann, Jan, 111
Heine, Ronald, 5
Hengel, Martin, 74, 151, 190
Henze, Matthias, 14, 71
Hezser, Catherine, 35
Hibshman, Grace, 113
Hickling, C. J. A., 82
Hiebert, Robert J. V., 58
Hinchman, Lewis P., 101
Hinchman, Sandra K., 101
Hirsh, J. B., 101
Hodgson, Robert, 23
Hofius, Otfried, 40, 60
Holladay, Carl R., 3
Hollander, John, 14, 43, 81
Holmes, Michael, 180
Holtz, G., 122
Holtz, Traugott, 96
Hommes, N. J., 25
Hooker, Morna D., 134, 152
Hoppe, Rudolf, 160
Horbury, William, 167, 191
Horne, Thomas Hartwell, 75
Horner, Timothy J., 164
Horsfall, Nicholas, 36
Hübner, Hans, 75, 81, 133, 153, 188
Hughes, Aaron, 1

Index of Modern Authors

Hühn, Eugen, 75
Hull, D. L., 118
Hurtado, Larry, 11
Hynes, Samuel, 192

Iggers, G. C., 119
Irwin, William, 44, 81

Janko, Richard, 2
Jannidis, Fotis, 152
Janssen, Martina, 138
Jervis, L. Ann, 116
Jewett, Robert, 66
Johnson, Franklin, 75
Johnson, William A., 111
Jones, Henry Stuart, 64
Jones, L. Gregory, 101
Josselson, Ruthellen, 101
Joyce, Paul, 190
Judge, Edwin A., 49, 112
Junius, Franciscus, 73

Kamesar, Adam, 5
Karris, R. J., 132
Käsemann, E., 160
Kautzsch, Emil Friedrich, 76
Keith, Chris, 11, 41
Kelhoffer, James A., 139
Kelsey, David H., 102
Kiley, Mark, 137, 146
Kinzig, Wolfram, 167
Klauck, Hans-Josef, 153
Knibb, Michael A., 86
Koch, Dietrich-Alex, 13, 16, 27, 29, 31–33, 39, 42, 53–54, 62–63, 65, 68, 72, 78–79, 159–60, 163
Kok, Kobus, 134
Kouremenos, Theokritos, 2
Kraft, Robert A., 12, 27, 155
Kratz, Reinhard G., 4

Kristeva, Julia, 15, 43–44, 80
Kujanpää, Katja, 20

Lagrange, M.-J., 25
Laks, André, 2
Lavabre, Marie-Claire, 51
Le Déaut, Roger, 29, 41
Le Donne, Anthony, 41
Legrand, Thierry, 52
Leipziger, Jonas, 111
Leppä, Outi, 142
Levine, Amy-Jill, 193
Lewis, Naphtali, 34
Lichtenberger, Hermann, 60
Liddell, Henry George, 64
Lieblich, Amia, 101
Lieu, Judith, 101
Lightfoot, J. B., 144
Lim, Timothy H., 29, 32, 79–80
Lincicum, David, 14–15, 37, 40, 46, 53, 71, 120, 174
Lindemann, Andreas, 163, 176–78, 180–81, 187
Lindemann, Hilde, 114
Litwak, Kenneth D., 35, 73, 80
Lohse, Eduard, 136, 143
Longenecker, Bruce W., 17, 105, 158
Longenecker, Richard N., 62–63
Lüdemann, Gerd, 112
Luz, Ulrich, 45
Lyons, George, 126

Macaskill, Grant, 109
Mach, Michael, 167
MacLachlan, Helen, 75
Maier, Harry O., 141
Manson, T. W., 27
Mar, R. A., 101
Marcovich, Miroslav, 162
Marshall, I. Howard, 27

Index of Modern Authors

Martens, Peter W., 5
Martin, Troy W., 131, 133
Martyn, J. L., 61, 64, 92, 116
Mayerhoff, Ernst T., 136
McAdams, Dan P., 101, 104
Meade, David G., 138
Meech, John L., 105
Meeks, Wayne A., 133
Menken, Maarten J. J., 40–41, 85
Merz, Annette, 139
Michel, Otto, 11, 25, 28, 32, 72, 76, 96
Milik, J. T., 30
Miller, James D., 155
Miller, Merrill P., 26, 72
Mitchell, Margaret M., 154
Moore, Stephen D., 43
Moritz, Thorsten, 41
Most, Glenn W., 2
Moyise, Steve, 40, 44, 63, 85
Moyo, Ambrose M., 133
Muddiman, John, 155
Müller, Peter, 134, 155
Munro, Winsome, 154
Murphy, Roland E., 118
Murphy-O'Connor, Jerome, 154–55

Nelson, Katherine, 101
Neuschäfer, Bernhard, 5
Neusner, Jacob, 29
Nicholls, Rachel, 45
Nicolet-Anderson, Valérie, 105
Niebuhr, Karl-Wilhelm, 96
Niehoff, Maren R., 3
Nora, Pierre, 51
Noth, Martin, 118

O'Brien, Kelli S., 92
Öhler, Markus, 161
O'Neill, J. C., 154

Ophir, Adi, 106
Owen, Henry, 74

Parássoglou, George M., 2
Parsons, P. J., 12
Pate, C. Marvin, 85
Paul, André, 52
Pearson, Birger A., 5
Peppard, Michael, 153
Perona, Edwin G., 97–98
Petersen, Norman, 135
Peterson, J. B., 101
Pilhofer, Peter, 161
Plooij, Daniel, 25, 27
Porter, Stanley E., 13, 38, 187
Prior, Michael, 155
Prussner, Frederick C., 117
Punt, Jeremy, 49

Rabens, Volker, 116
Rad, Gerhard von, 117
Räisänen, Heikki, 45, 93
Ramsay, William, 144
Randolph, Thomas, 74
Rea, Michael, 103–5, 113
Reinmuth, Eckart, 96
Rese, Martin, 44, 81
Reumann, John, 154
Reuter, R., 116
Richard, Earl, 154
Richards, E. Randolph, 153
Ricoeur, Paul, 51, 99, 115
Rodriguez, Rafael, 41
Röhser, Günter, 143–44
Rokéah, David, 163
Rösel, Martin, 59
Rosen-Zvi, Ishay, 106
Rosner, Brian S., 22, 96–98
Rothschild, Clare K., 67, 155, 173, 176
Rowland, Christopher, 133

Index of Modern Authors

Royalty, Robert M., 133, 142
Ruiten, J. T. A. G. M. van, 31
Rutledge, Jonathan C., 115

Salzmann, Jorg Christian, 162
Sanders, E. P., 143
Sanders, James A., 82
Sappington, Thomas J., 133
Sauter, Gerhard, 101
Sawyer, John F. A., 83
Schechtman, Marya, 103–4
Schenk, Wolfgang, 134, 144
Scherer-Rath, Michael, 101
Schironi, Francesca, 2–3
Schmid, Hansjörg, 150
Schmid, Konrad, 58–59
Schmithals, Walter, 156
Schnelle, Udo, 117
Scholtz, G., 119
Schröter, Jens, 41, 123
Schweizer, Eduard, 133
Scornaienchi, Lorenzo, 102
Scott, James M., 82, 85–89, 91, 98, 160
Scott, Robert, 64
Seachris, Joshua, 101, 105
Segal, Alan F., 190
Sherwood, Yvonne, 43
Shum, Shiu-Lun, 17, 83
Silva, Moises, 40
Simon, Marcel, 191
Sirat, C., 35
Skarsaune, Oskar, 162–63, 180, 182, 191
Skeat, T. C., 34
Small, Jocelyn Penny, 36, 42
Smith, Claire S., 49, 112
Smith, D. Moody, 72–73
Smith, Ian K., 134, 150
Spoerhase, Carlos, 118
Sprinkle, Preston, 19

Standhartinger, Angela, 143–44, 149
Stanley, Christopher D., 13, 20, 30–36, 38–39, 41–42, 47–49, 54–55, 57, 59, 62–63, 68, 73, 79–80, 91–92, 95, 158–59
Steck, Odil Hannes, 85–86, 88–89, 91
Stendahl, Krister, 26, 28
Stettler, Christian, 134, 148
Steudel, Annette, 29
Stirewalt, M. Luther, Jr., 153
Stowers, Stanley K., 107, 137, 153
Strawbridge, Jennifer, 153
Streett, Daniel R., 150
Strugnell, John, 27
Stylianopoulos, Theodore, 165–66
Sumney, Jerry L., 133
Sundberg, A. C., 27
Surenhusius, Guilielmus, 73, 76
Swanson, Dwight D., 80
Swete, Henry Barclay, 75

Talmon, Shemaryahu, 36
Thackeray, Henry St. John, 28, 75–76
Thatcher, Tom, 41
Thielman, Frank, 85, 87
Tholuck, Friedrich August Gottreu, 72, 75
Thompson, Michael B., 187
Thornton, Allison Krile, 104
Thrall, M., 121
Tomson, Peter J., 22, 96
Tov, Emanuel, 12, 30, 52, 79
Toy, Crawford Howell, 72, 75
Trainor, Michael, 142
Trakatellis, Demetrios, 167
Trebilco, Paul, 142
Trobisch, David, 156, 187
Tsantsanoglou, Kyriakos, 2

Index of Modern Authors

Tuckett, Christopher M., 22, 44, 81, 96, 170, 180
Turner, Geoffrey, 41
Turpie, David McCalman, 75

Van Broekhoven, Harold, 148
Vegge, Tor, 146
Venard, L., 72
Via, Dan O., 85
Vielhauer, Philipp, 72, 163
Vliet, H. van, 122
Vollmer, Hans, 28, 76

Wagner, J. Ross, 17, 33–34, 37–38, 40, 45, 65, 67, 80, 82–84, 87, 90, 121, 160
Walker, William O., 154
Waters, Guy P., 40, 89–91, 98
Watson, Francis, 17, 46–47, 66, 70, 82, 91–95
Watt, J. van der, 117
Werline, Rodney, 162–63
Wevers, John William, 53, 62, 65

Whiston, William, 73–74
Whitehead, Anne, 51
Wilder, Terence L., 138–39
Wilk, Florian, 17, 40, 83
Williams, A. Lukyn, 27, 191
Williams, H. H. Drake, III, 83
Wilson, Adrian, 118
Wilson, R. McL., 133
Wilson, Todd A., 92
Wisdom, Jeffrey R., 62, 87–88, 91
Wisse, Frederik W., 154
Woyke, Johannes, 117
Wright, Addison G., 29
Wright, N. T., 46–47, 87, 134, 157
Wucherpfennig, Ansgar, 5

Yarbrough, Mark, 153
Yates, Roy, 133

Zahn, Theodor, 143
Zurawski, Jason M., 58

Index of Subjects

Abraham, 21, 47, 52, 54, 60–66, 70, 119, 184
actualization, 117–20, 122, 124–25, 127–28
Adam, 54–60, 70, 109, 116
adversus Judaeos, 191
Ahab, 158
Alexandrian interpretation, 2, 4, 76
allegory, 3, 21, 60, 65, 74
amanuensis, 137, 139, 153–54
Aquila, 12, 57, 76
Aramaic Bible, 75
Archippus, 142–43
Augustine, 74

baptism, 108–9, 112, 122–24
Barnabas, Epistle of, 183–87
Basilides, 5
biography, 104, 109, 112, 115; autobiography, 104, 109, 113, 128

canon, 11, 26, 76, 150
circumcision, 61–62, 65–66, 88
Clement, First Epistle of, 176–78
Clement, Second Epistle of, 180–81
Colossae, 141–42, 144–45, 148
Colossians, Epistle to the, 19, 130–51, 171–72; Colossian error, 133–34, 146–50

commentary, 1–8, 16; commentarial impulse, 2, 4–5, 8, 196; commentators, 131, 133–34, 148; grammatical, 2; philological, 2; philosophical, 3
Corinthian church, 176
Corinthians, First Epistle to the, 60, 176–77
Corinthians, Second Epistle to the, 154
Corinthians, Third Epistle to the, 126
creation, 55–58, 70
crucifixion, 88, 100, 107–9, 116, 195
Cynic philosophy, 131

Dead Sea Scrolls. *See* Qumran
Deuteronomistic History, 86, 93
Deuteronomy, book of, 71–98, 120–21
Didache, 183–84

effective history, 38, 45–46, 50
Elijah, 52, 157–61, 165
Epaphras, 135, 143, 147
Ephesians, Epistle to the, 19, 171–72, 179–80
Esau, 18, 69
Eve, 55, 57
exile, 85–87, 89
Ezra, Fourth Book of, 93

fiction, 115, 138–39
forgery, 137–38, 148, 151

240

Index of Subjects

Galatians, Epistle to the, 6–66, 90, 92, 132, 136, 188
Genesis, book of, 52–70
Gnosticism, 147

Hagar, 21, 54, 60, 63–65, 68
halakah, 94
Hebrew Bible, 11, 41–42, 190–91, 193–94
Hebrews, Epistle to the, 173–74
Heracleon, 4
Hippolytus, 5
historiography, 118–19, 129
history. *See* effective history

Ignatius of Antioch, 178–79
imitatio Christi, 125
intertextuality, 13–15, 43–46, 50, 80–81
Isaac, 18, 21, 54, 65, 68–70
Isaiah, book of, 18, 82–84, 95, 121, 160
Ishmael, 18, 21, 65, 68–69

Jacob, 18, 69
Jerome, 74
Jerusalem, 11, 64, 66
Jezebel, 158
Job, book of, 76
John (disciple), 100
John the Baptist, 161
Josephus, 52, 120
Justin Martyr, 72, 161–68, 180, 181–83, 188, 191

Kingdoms, book of, 157

Laodiceans, Epistle to the, 126
law, 16, 60–64, 66, 87–88, 94; curse of the, 86, 88, 92–93, 95, 98
literacy, 49
liturgy, 37, 46, 51, 53, 56, 112, 124
Lord's Supper, 122–23

Lot, 61
Lycus Valley, 142, 144

Marcion, 72
martyrdom, 140
Mary, mother of Jesus, 100
Matthew, Gospel of, 7, 191
Melchizedek, 61
memory, 13, 35–37, 38, 40–42, 51, 111
midrash, 29
mirror-reading, 132–35, 148, 150
Moses, 60, 64. *See also* Song of Moses

narrative, 46–48
narrative selves, 103–5
narrative world, 135–36, 147

Onesimus, 135
Origen, 4–5, 99–100, 115, 177

Pastoral Epistles, 19, 122, 139, 175
Paul: analogy, 160; audience of, 8, 48–49, 54, 106–7, 128, 114, 147; *corpus Paulinum*, 17, 102, 118, 128, 151, 183, 187; death of, 140, 142; doctrine of justification, 66–67, 93; echoes of / allusions to Scripture, 13–15, 19–20, 43–46, 80–81; education of, 11, 36–37, 39; election, 18, 20, 67, 158, 191; eschatology, 22, 70, 78, 90–91, 105, 116–17, 120, 122, 137, 141, 160; ethics / ethical teaching, 22, 70, 94, 95–98, 171; gentile mission, 17–19, 84, 159; *Hauptbriefe*, 53, 96, 172, 187; history of Israel, 16–18, 47, 59, 67, 69, 85, 89, 93, 116, 158–60, 168; letters, deutero-Pauline, 19, 53, 117, 125, 127–29; letters, function of, 9, 125; letters, nature of, 20, 112; quotations of Scripture, 11–13, 19–21, 25, 30–33,

241

Index of Subjects

55, 67–69, 73–75; remnant theology, 18, 157, 160–61, 165–66, 168; salvation history, 109, 113; school of, 169; soteriology, 116, 124, 139; suffering of, 125, 139–40, 176; typology, 91, 160; *Vorlage*, 19, 22, 39, 40–41, 43, 50, 75, 77–79, 98

Pentateuch, 11–12, 18, 47, 52, 62, 92–95

Philemon, Epistle to, 135, 142–44

Philippians, Epistle to the, 154

Philo, 4, 52, 82, 110, 120

Polycarp of Smyrna, 179–80

prophecy, 188, 189–92, 194–95

pseudepigraphy, 126–28, 130–31, 135–41, 144, 173

Qumran, 11, 27–31, 52, 77–79, 82, 120, 194

rabbinic literature / exegesis, 73, 76–77

reading, 15, 30–31, 110–12, 193. *See also* mirror-reading.

reality effect, 130, 140–41, 150

Rebekah, 69

reception history. *See* effective history

referential world, 115, 135–36, 148

resurrection, 56, 58–59, 70, 108–9, 116, 124

rewritten Scripture, 52, 120

rhetorical composition, 131

rhetorical effects, 48–50

Romans, Epistle to the, 15, 24–25, 83, 89–91, 105–10, 113–15, 157, 182

Sarah, 54, 60, 63–65, 67–69

Scripture, material form of, 32, 83. *See also* rewritten Scripture

selfhood, 101–4; technology of the self, 110

Septuagint, 11–12, 39, 53, 57, 72–76, 78–80, 177, 180–81

Seth, 59

Sinai, 17, 21, 60, 64, 95, 193

Song of Moses, 18, 93, 161, 173, 178

speech act, 113

Stoicism, 111

Symmachus, 12, 76

synagogue, 32, 37, 51, 53

testimonia, 23, 30, 32–33, 35, 37, 169–70, 181, 188; *excerpta*, 28–31, 34–35; *Testimony Book*, 24–27; testimony hypothesis, 27–28, 32, 90, 170

text plots, 7, 170

Theodotion, 12, 57, 76

Thessalonians, First Epistle to the, 154

Torah, 37, 60–61, 65, 82, 93–95, 121

Index of Ancient Sources

Hebrew Bible/Old Testament

Genesis

1	56	2:22	175	16:15	60, 65
1–2	58	2:22–23	55	17:4–14	61
1–3	59, 175	2:24	53, 55, 172, 174–75	17:5	62, 67, 162, 182
1:3–4	57	3	57	17:8	63
1:11	56	3:6	175	17:10–11	66
1:11–12	56	3:13	60, 175	17:16	60, 65
1:12	56	3:16	56–57	17:17	65
1:20–27	56	3:17–19	57–58	17:23	186
1:21	56	5:3	59	18:1	69
1:24	56	6:1–4	56, 58	18:10	68
1:25	56	8:17	56	18:13	69
1:26	56, 185	8:21	54	18:14	68
1:26–27	56	12–22	61	18:18	60–62, 66
1:27	56, 59, 175, 181	12:1–3	54, 66, 88	21:2	60, 65
1:28	185	12:2	67	21:9	60, 65
2	55–56, 174	12:3	7, 60–62	21:10	60, 65
2–3	58, 60	12:7	63	21:12	67–68, 174
2:2	174	13:14–17	54	22	70, 174
2:2–3	187	13:15	60, 63	22:12	69–70
2:7	56, 58–59, 174–75	14	61	22:16	69–70
2:16	56	14:14	186	22:16–17	174
2:17	58, 60	15:1–6	54	22:17	67, 174
2:18	55, 175	15:5	67, 174, 176	22:17–18	66
2:18–24	56	15:5–6	176–77	22:18	7, 62, 174
2:21–23	175	15:6	53, 60–62, 66, 94, 162, 182, 186	24:7	63
		15:16	54	25:21–23	186
		16–21	63–64	25:23	69, 186
		16:10	65	25:24	69
				26:4	67

243

Index of Ancient Sources

32:31	54	**Numbers**		30:12–14	121
48:9	186	12:7	177	31	89–90
48:11	186	16:5	175	31:29 LXX	90
48:14	186	16:26	175	32	7, 14, 33, 82, 89–91,
48:18	186	19:18	183		93, 173–74
48:19	186	21:4–9	186	32:4–5	14
				32:15	178
Exodus		**Deuteronomy**		32:16–23	162, 182
6:18	95	4:7–8	121	32:17	174
7:11–22	175	4:10	186	32:21	18, 162, 174, 182
17:8–13	186	4:13	186	32:35	173–74
17:14	186	5	172	32:36	174
20	172	5:12	187	32:43	86, 162, 174, 183
20:8	187	5:16	172		
20:12	172	5:17–19	172	**1 Kingdoms**	
20:13–17	183	5:17–21	33	2:10	157
24:18	186	5:21	172	12:22	157, 159
25:9	64	6:5	183		
25:40	64	10:16	186	**2 Kingdoms / 2 Samuel**	
31:13–17	187	13:5	21	7:14	174
31:18	185–86	17	174	22:50	157
32:6	163, 183	17:6	174		
32:7	185	17:7	21, 174	**3 Kingdoms / 1 Kings**	
32:7–8	187	18	26	19	157, 159, 161–62,
32:19	187	18:15	7		164, 166, 168
33:1	185	18:19	7	19:10	159, 162, 164, 183
33:3	185	19:15	33, 175	19:14	159, 162, 164, 183
34:28	185	19:19	21	19:18	160, 162, 183
		21:23	72, 163, 183		
		25:4	16, 122, 175	**2 Chronicles**	
Leviticus		27–30	88–91, 93	20:7	68
11:3	186	27–32	85–86, 89–90		
11:7–15	186	27:26	72, 163, 183	**Ezra**	
16:7	185	29	90, 174	9	86
16:8	185	29–32	84		
16:9	185	29:4	174	**Nehemiah**	
18:5	19, 47	29:18	174	9	86
23:29	185	30	90–91, 121	9:7	62
26:21	186	30:11–14	19, 120		

Index of Ancient Sources

Psalms

1:1	186
1:3–6	186
2	7, 26
2:7–8	177
4:4	172
4:5	179
5:9	162, 182
7	7
8	26
8:4–6	174
8:6	174
8:7	172
10:7	162, 183
14:1–3	162, 182
17:50	157
18:44	185
19:1–3	178
19:4	178
19:5	162, 182
22	7, 194
22:16	185
22:20	185
22:22	184–85
24:1	163, 176–77, 183
31	7
32:1–2	162, 176–77, 182
34	7
34:12	186
36:1	162, 182
36:11 LXX	184
37	194
38	7
41	7
42	194
42–43	7
42:2	185
43	194
51:17	184

68:18	163, 171–72, 183
68:23–24	108
69	7, 194
78	7
93:14 LXX	157, 159
104:4	177
104:6	68
110	7, 26
110:1	174, 177, 184, 186
112:9	95
118	7
118:12	185
118:22	24, 185
118:24	185
119	185
120	185
130	7
140	194
140:3	162, 182
142:2 LXX	54

Proverbs

1:17	185
3	174
3:4	174
3:11–12	174
3:12	177
3:34	177–78
18:17	178
23:31	172
25:21–22	95

Isaiah

1–11	83
1:2	186
1:9	162, 166, 182
1:10	186
1:11–13	184
1:13	187

2:4	195
3:9–10	185
5:21	185
6:1–9:7	7
8	174
8:14	24, 33, 174
8:17–18	174
11:1–10	7
11:4–5	172
11:6–9	195
16:1–2	186
25:8	12
26:19	171–72
28–29	83
28:11–12	172
28:16	7, 24, 33, 172, 185
29:13	177, 181
29:13–14	163, 183
29:14	163, 183
33:13	185
33:16–18	186
40–51	83
40:1–11	7
40:3	186
40:12	187
41:8	68
42:1–44:5	7
42:6–7	187
45:1	186
45:2–3	186
49:1–13	7
49:6	187
49:6–7	187
49:8	121
50:4–11	7
50:6–9	185
50:7	185
52–54	83

245

Index of Ancient Sources

52:5	162, 175, 178, 181–82	7:11	181	9:9	194
		7:22–23	184	13:7	185
52:7	172	9:22–23	157, 176–77	14:5	183
52:13–53:12	7	9:25 LXX	186		
52:15	163, 183	31:10–34	7	**Malachi**	
52:15–53:1	163, 183	31:33–34	174	1:2–3	69
53	121, 174, 178	33:15–16	195	1:11	184
53:1	121, 162, 174, 178, 182			1:14	184
		Ezekiel			
53:5	185	11:19	185	**Deuterocanonical**	
53:7	185	14:14	181	**Books**	
53:12	174	14:20	181		
54:1	65, 163, 180–81, 183	47:1–12	186	**Wisdom of Solomon**	
				2:23–24	58
57:19	172	**Daniel**		2:24	58
58:4–10	185	7:7–8	185		
58:6	185	7:24	185	**Sirach**	
58:9	181	9	86	12:1–7	183
59:7–8	162, 182			25:24	57
59:17	172	**Hosea**		36:1–17	86
59:21	174	1–2	95		
61	7	11:1	191	**Baruch**	
61:1–2	187			1:15–3:8	86
64:3	176–77, 181	**Joel**		13:1–6	69
65:1–2	162, 182	2–3	7		
65:2	184, 186			**2 Esdras**	
65:17–25	195	**Micah**		19:7	62
66:1	187	4:3–4	195		
66:18	181			**Pseudepigrapha**	
66:22–23	57	**Habakkuk**			
66:24	181	2:4	47, 93, 173–74	**Apocalypse of Abraham**	
				1–8	61
		Zephaniah			
Jeremiah		3:19	186	**4 Ezra**	
2:12–13	186			3:7	58
4:3–4	186	**Zechariah**		4:33	186
4:4	186	8:16	172	5:5	186
7	180	8:17	184	7:118–119	58
7:2–3	186	9–14	7	13:52	161

Index of Ancient Sources

Jubilees

12:1–24	66

Letter of Aristeas

187–194	4

Psalms of Solomon

9:9	68
18:3	68

Testaments of the Twelve Patriarchs

Testament of Levi

13:2	53

DEAD SEA SCROLLS

1QS (Community Rule)

6:6–8	53

4Q175 (4QTestimonia)

21–30	30

4Q251

1:5	53

4Q266 (Damascus Documentª)

5 ii:1–3	53

4Q267

5 iii:3–5	53

ANCIENT JEWISH WRITERS

Aristobulus

Frag. 2	3

Demetrius

Frag. 2	3

Josephus

Antiquitates judaicae

1.27–2.200	52
16.43–45	53

Contra Apionem

2.175–178	53

Philo

De opificio mundi

134–135	59

De vita Mosis

2.38	53

Hypothetica

7.12–13	53

Legum allegoriae

1.105–107	58
3.18	111

Quis rerum divinarum heres sit

253	110–11

NEW TESTAMENT

Matthew

3:2–3	161
3:3	186
3:11–12	161
5:5	184
15:8	177, 181
16:21	161
17:10–13	161
18:16	122
19:4	181
19:5	55
19:18–19	183
21:1–11	194
21:13	181
21:42	185
22:37	183
22:39	183
22:44	186
26:31	185
28:18–20	193

Mark

1:3	186
7:6	177, 181
9:44	181
9:46	181
9:48	181
10:6	181
10:7	55
10:27	183
11:17	181
12:10	185
12:30–31	183
12:35–37	184
12:36	186
13:37	123
14:27	185

Luke

3:4	186
3:16–17	161
3:20	161
4:16–20	53
4:18	185
4:18–19	187
9:22	161
19:46	181
20:17	185

247

Index of Ancient Sources

20:42	186	3:12–17	162, 182	6:8	125
		3:14	42	6:11	110
John		3:15	42	6:12	107
1:23	186	3:18	42	6:13	107
3:14	186	3:20	54	6:19	107, 110
12:12–16	194	3:21	16	6:21	107
12:16	194	3:25	158	6:22	117
14:26	123	3:26	117, 160	7	60
15:26	123	4	47, 66–67, 158	7:7	22, 172
16:13–15	123	4:1–22	158	7:7–11	60
		4:3	66, 162, 176–77, 182, 186	7:11	60
Acts				8:1–4	94
2:34	186	4:7–8	162, 182	8:17	125, 196
3:23	185	4:7–9	176–77	8:20	57
7:49	187	4:8	42	8:22	125
13:15	53	4:9	66, 162, 182	8:32	69–70
13:47	187	4:10	66	9	47, 52, 95, 159
15:21	53	4:11–12	66, 184	9–11	17, 19, 86, 158, 160, 166–68, 188
17:28	10	4:13	62		
		4:13–15	66	9:1–5	17, 158
Romans		4:16–25	67	9:4–17	158
1	107	4:17	67, 162, 181–82	9:6	18, 67, 158
1:3	158	4:18	67, 174, 176	9:6–13	67
1:5	106	4:19	67	9:6–29	18, 158
1:6	120	4:22–23	66	9:7	67–68, 174
1:17	42, 47, 174	4:23–24	16	9:8	69
1:18	107	5	95	9:9	42, 68
1:18–32	107	5:12–21	57, 59–60, 158	9:10	69
1:21	108	5:13–14	60	9:12	69, 186
1:24	107	5:14	59	9:13	42
1:29	107	6	100, 106–7, 109, 112, 114–15	9:15	42
1:32	176			9:17	16, 42
2:19	108	6:1–4	108	9:19–24	180
2:24	42, 162, 175, 178, 181–82	6:1–11	124	9:23–24	137
		6:1–23	107	9:24	158
3:4	42	6:2	107	9:25	42
3:10	42	6:4	107–8, 125	9:25–29	158
3:10–18	162, 182	6:5	108	9:27	42
3:11	42	6:6	107, 125	9:27–29	160

Index of Ancient Sources

9:28	42
9:29	162, 166, 182
9:30–10:3	160
9:30–10:4	158, 161
9:30–10:21	18
9:32–33	24
9:33	33, 42, 172, 174, 185
10–11	178
10:5	42, 47
10:5–9	5–6
10:5–21	158
10:6–7	42
10:6–8	42, 120
10:7	42
10:11	42, 185
10:15	42, 172
10:16	121, 160, 162, 174, 178, 182
10:16–21	158
10:18	18, 162, 178, 182
10:18–21	159
10:19	42, 162, 174, 182
10:19–21	121
10:20–21	162, 182
10:21	42, 184, 186
11	9, 47, 52, 157–58, 161, 166, 168
11:1	18, 159
11:1–4	158
11:1–6	158
11:2	157, 159
11:3	42, 160, 164
11:3–4	157, 159, 162, 183
11:4	42, 160
11:5	160
11:8	42, 174
11:10	108
11:11–32	159, 161

11:13	10, 106
11:20	19
11:25–26	166
11:26	42
11:27	174
11:30	117
12:19	22, 33, 42, 173–74
12:20	95
13:8–10	22, 33
13:9	42, 183
13:9–10	33, 172
13:12	108
14:11	42
15:3	42
15:4	16, 120
15:9	42, 157
15:10	33, 86, 162, 174, 183
15:11	42
15:12	42
15:21	42, 163, 183
16:22	137, 153
16:25–26	137
16:25–27	154
16:26	120

1 Corinthians

1:19	42, 163, 183
1:31	42, 157, 176
2:7	137
2:9	176–77, 181
3:20	42
4:17	125–26
5	21
5–7	97
5–11	98
5:13	21, 174
6:16	55, 172, 174–75
7	55

7:10–12	123
7:25	123
8:4–6	121
9:9	175
9:9–10	16, 122, 175
9:13	158
9:24–27	180
10	47, 52, 119
10:1–4	122
10:1–10	158
10:1–13	193
10:7	163, 183
10:11	16, 109, 116, 120
10:20	174
10:20–22	91
10:22	174
10:26	163, 176, 183
11:1	126
11:2–12	55
11:3	56
11:7	55, 175
11:7–9	56
11:8	55
11:8–9	55, 175
11:9	55
11:17–34	123
11:23	124, 126
11:23–26	33, 123, 124
12:26	125
13:12	54
14:21	42, 172
14:33–35	57
14:33–36	154
14:34	57
15	56, 58, 95
15:3–4	16
15:3–5	33
15:20	117
15:21	58

249

Index of Ancient Sources

15:21–22	57–59	**Galatians**		4:23	54, 60, 64
15:22	58–59	1–2	126	4:24	64
15:25	174, 186	1:13–14	128	4:25	64
15:25–27	172	1:14	10	4:26	64
15:27	42, 174	2:15–21	62	4:27	163, 180–81, 183
15:33	10	2:19	125	4:28	54, 64
15:38	56	2:20	100	4:29	54, 60, 64–65
15:39	56	3	47, 65–66, 86, 119	4:30	21, 42, 54, 60, 65
15:45	42, 58–59, 174–75	3:1	63, 65	5:1	61
15:45–49	57–58, 158	3:1–29	61	6	66
15:47	59, 175	3:2	61	6:11	137, 153
15:49	59	3:6	42, 54, 60–61, 186	6:11–18	140
15:54	12	3:6–9	61, 158	6:15	57
15:55	42	3:6–14	61		
16:21	137, 153	3:6–29	60	**Ephesians**	
16:21–24	140	3:8	16, 42, 54, 60, 62, 174	1:22	172
				2:3	128
2 Corinthians		3:9	54, 62	2:6	125
3:7–18	158	3:10	42, 87, 163, 183	2:13	117
4:6	57	3:10–13	72, 163	2:17	172
4:10–11	125	3:10–14	89	2:20–21	172
5:16	117	3:11	47, 174	4:4–6	176
5:17	57	3:12	42, 47	4:8	163, 171–72
6:2	121	3:13	42, 88, 163, 183	4:18	181
6:16	42	3:14	90	4:25	172
6:16–18	95	3:15–18	61–62	4:26	172, 179–80
6:17	42	3:16	6, 54, 60, 62, 174	5:14	171–72
6:18	42, 174	3:16–18	158	5:18	172
7:3	125	3:18	54	5:31	53, 55, 172
8:15	42, 95	3:20	133	6:2–3	171–72
8:21	174	3:23–29	87	6:14–17	172
9:9	95	3:28	56		
10:11	125	3:29	54, 61	**Philippians**	
10:17	42, 157	4	21	2:5–11	153
11–12	126	4:8	183	2:14–15	14
11:3	57, 158, 175	4:21	63	2:15	91
11:22	68	4:21–31	6, 21, 60, 63, 68, 158	3:5	10
13:1	33, 122, 175	4:22	60, 64–65	4:18	54

250

Index of Ancient Sources

Colossians

1:1	139
1:2	135, 141–42, 144
1:7	135
1:8	135
1:15–20	150, 153
1:21	135
1:22	117, 144
1:23–25	139
1:24	125, 140
1:26	117
1:26–27	137
1:27	135
1:29	139
2	149
2:1	127, 135, 139–40, 142
2:4–23	149
2:5	125, 127, 135, 139–40
2:6	133
2:6–23	146
2:8	146
2:12	125
2:16–19	146
2:16–23	149
2:18	133, 149
3:1	125
3:7	135
3:8	117
4:3–4	139
4:7–8	139
4:7–18	138
4:10	143
4:11	143
4:12–13	135, 143
4:13	142, 144
4:14	143
4:15	142, 144
4:16	126, 142, 144
4:17	143
4:18	137–40, 153

1 Thessalonians

1:1–2:12	154
2:9–12	126
2:13–4:2	154
2:14–16	154
2:15–16	86
2:16	54
3:13	183
4:1–2	126
4:3–5:28	154
5:8	172

2 Thessalonians

2:5	127
3:17	137, 153
3:17–18	140

1 Timothy

1:8–11	122
1:12–16	128
2:12	57
2:13–15	53, 175
2:14	57
3:14–15	127
3:16	153
4:1–5	128
4:6	128
4:11	128
4:16	181
5:18	122, 175
5:19	175
6:1	175
6:2	128

2 Timothy

1:10	117
2:2	128
2:11	125
2:14	128
2:19	175
3:1	128
3:8–9	175
3:16	20
4:3–4	128
4:13	13

Titus

1:12	10
2:2	128
2:6	128
2:9	128
2:15	128
3:1	128

Philemon

2	143
19	137, 140, 153
23	143
24	143

Hebrews

1	177
1:3	174
1:5	174, 177
1:6	174
1:7	177
1:13	174, 177
2:6–8	174
2:12	184–85
2:13	174
3:2	177
3:7–4:11	6
3:13	186

Index of Ancient Sources

4:4	174, 187
6:13–14	174
8:1	174
8:8–12	174
9:28	174
10:12–13	174
10:16–17	174
10:30	173–74
10:37–38	174
11:12	174
11:18	174
12:2	174
12:5–6	174
12:6	177
13:20–25	174

James

2:23	186
4:6	177–78

1 Peter

2:6	185
2:6–8	24
2:24	185
5:5	177–78

2 Peter

3:15–16	126

RABBINIC WORKS AND TARGUMS

b. Sanhedrin

98a	161

Midrash Ps 21:1	161

Targum Neofiti

Gen 15:1	66

Targum Pseudo-Jonathan

Gen 15:1	66

y. Nedarim

5:5–6	35
39a	35

EARLY CHRISTIAN WRITINGS

Augustine

De civitate Dei

18.42–44	74

Barnabas

2.5	184
2.7	184
2.8	184
2.10	184–85
3.1–5	185
4.3	185
4.4	185
4.5	185
4.7	185
4.8	185
4.11	185
5.2	185
5.4	185
5.5	185
5.12	185
5.13	185
5.14–6.2	185
6.2–3	185
6.3	185
6.4	185
6.6	185
6.7	185
6.8	185

6.12	185
6.13	185
6.14	185
6.16	184
6.18	185
7.3	185
7.4	185
7.6–7	185
7.8	185
9.1	185–86
9.2	186
9.3	186
9.5	186
9.8	186
10.1	186
10.2	186
10.4–7	186
10.10	186
10.11	186
11.2	186
11.3	186
11.4	186
11.4–5	186
11.6–7	186
11.9	186
11.10	186
12.1	186
12.2	186
12.4	184, 186
12.6	186
12.7	186
12.9	186
12.10	184, 186
12.11	186
13.2	186
13.4	186
13.6	186
13.7	184, 186
14.2	186

Index of Ancient Sources

14.3	187
14.7	187
14.8	187
14.9	187
15.1	187
15.2	187
15.3	187
15.8	187
16.2	187
16.3	187
16.5	187
16.6	187

1 Clement

3.1	178
5.4–7	176
10.4–6	176–77
13.1	176
15.2	177, 181
16.3	178
17.5	177
27.7	178
30.2	177
32.2	176
34.8	176
35.6	176
36	177
46.6	176
47.1–3	126, 176
50.6	176–77
54.3	176
56.3–4	177

2 Clement

1.8	181
2.1	180
2.1–3	180–81
3.5	181
6.8	181
7	180
7.6	181
8	180
11.7	181
13.2	178, 181
14.1	181
14.2	181
14.5	181
15.1	181
15.3	181
17.4	181
19.2	181

Clement of Alexandria

Stromata

6.14	3

Cyprian

Testimonia

2.16	24

Didache

1.2	183
1.6	183
2.2–4	183
4.7	184
14.3	184
16.7	183

Eusebius

Praeparatio evangelica

8.7.12–13	53

Ignatius of Antioch

To the Ephesians

5.3	178
12.2	126, 178

To the Magnesians

12	178

To the Philadelphians

5.2	179
8.2	179

To the Smyrnaeans

5.1	179
7	179

To the Trallians

8.2	178

Justin Martyr

1 Apology

28.2	165
46	161
53.5	163, 180, 183
53.7	162, 182

2 Apology

7.1–2	165

Dialogue with Trypho

8.3	161
11.5	162, 182
13.8	180
17.2	162, 182
20.1	163, 183
23.4	162, 182
27.3	162, 182
32.2	162, 165, 182
32.5	163, 183
36.3–4	163, 183
39.1	162, 164, 183
39.1–2	165
39.2	165–66
39.4	163, 183
42.1	162, 182
42.2	162, 182

253

Index of Ancient Sources

44.1–2	166
45.3	181
46.6	165
47.4	167
49.1–6	161
51.3	161
55.3	162, 166, 182
64.3	166
73.6	165
78.11	163, 183
87.4	161
87.6	163, 183
92.3	162, 182
95	72
95–96	163
95.1	163, 183
96	72
96.1	163, 183
114.2	162, 182
118.4	163, 183
119.2	162, 182
119.4	162, 182
119.5–6	162, 182
123.4	163, 183
130.1	162, 183
130.4	162, 183
140.3	162, 181–82
141.2	162, 182

Martyrdom of Polycarp

2.3b	177

Origen

Commentarii in evangelium Joannis

1.23	99

De principiis (Peri archōn)

4.4.2	100

Polycarp

Epistle to the Philippians

3.2	126, 179
6.3	179
10.2–3	178
12.1	179

GRECO-ROMAN LITERATURE

Aristotle

Ethica nicomachea

1146b 7f	3

Politica

30.19.5	3

Topica

1.14	31
163b 1	3

Athenaeus

Deipnosophistae

8.336d	31

Aulus Gellius

Noctus atticae

17.21.1	31

Cicero

De inventione rhetorica

2.4	31

Epictetus

Diatribai

4.4.14–18	111

Plato

Apologia

24b	3

Phaedo

67e	110

Theaetetus

202d	3

Pliny the Younger

Epistulae

3.5	31
6.20.5	31

Plutarch

Moralia

464F	31

Xenophon

Memorabilia

1.6.14	31